CW01271253

THE REAL AGRICULTURAL REVOLUTION

Boydell Studies in Rural History

Series Editor
Professor Richard W. Hoyle

This series aims to provide a forum for the best and most influential work in agricultural and rural history, and on the cultural history of the countryside. Whilst it is anchored in the rural history of Britain and Ireland, it also includes within its remit Europe and the colonial empires of European nations (both during and after colonisation). All approaches and methodologies are welcome, including the use of oral history.

Proposals or enquiries are welcomed. They may be sent directly to the editor or the publisher at the e-mail addresses given below.

Richard.Hoyle@reading.ac.uk
Editorial@boydell.co.uk

The Real Agricultural Revolution
The Transformation of English Farming
1939–1985

Paul Brassley, David Harvey,
Matt Lobley and Michael Winter

THE BOYDELL PRESS

© Paul Brassley, David Harvey, Matt Lobley and Michael Winter 2021

All Rights Reserved. Except as permitted under current legislation no part of this work may be photocopied, stored in a retrieval system, published, performed in public, adapted, broadcast, transmitted, recorded or reproduced in any form or by any means, without the prior permission of the copyright owner

The right of Paul Brassley, David Harvey, Matt Lobley and Michael Winter to be identified as the authors of this work has been asserted in accordance with sections 77 and 78 of the Copyright, Designs and Patents Act 1988

First published 2021
The Boydell Press, Woodbridge

ISBN 978 1 78327 635 6

The Boydell Press is an imprint of Boydell & Brewer Ltd
PO Box 9, Woodbridge, Suffolk IP12 3DF, UK
and of Boydell & Brewer Inc.
668 Mt Hope Avenue, Rochester, NY 14620–2731, USA
website: www.boydellandbrewer.com

A CIP catalogue record for this book is available
from the British Library

The publisher has no responsibility for the continued existence or accuracy of URLs for external or third-party internet websites referred to in this book, and does not guarantee that any content on such websites is, or will remain, accurate or appropriate

This publication is printed on acid-free paper

Printed and bound in Great Britain by TJ Books Limited, Padstow, Cornwall

CONTENTS

Figures and Tables	vii
Preface and Acknowledgements	ix
Abbreviations	xi
1. Introduction: Exploring Agricultural Change	1
2. The Organisation of Agricultural Science, 1935–85	24
3. Knowledge Networks in UK Farming, 1935–85	46
4. Agricultural Policy, 1939–85	88
5. Dairy Farming	111
6. Land and Capital	163
7. Labour and Machinery	183
8. Specialisation and Expansion	199
9. The Declining Enterprises: Pigs and Poultry	216
10. Conclusions	244
Bibliography	264
Index	283

FIGURES AND TABLES

Figures

1.1.	Timeline for farm 3/1	19
5.1.	Nitrogen fertiliser use on FMS farms	129
5.2.	Nitrogen fertiliser use on FMS dairy and non-dairy farms	130
5.3.	Nitrogen fertiliser use on FMS farms of different tenure types	131
6.1.	Changes in tenure types on FMS farms	170
7.1.	Labour requirements on FMS farms	192
7.2.	Labour requirements (estimated FTEs) on dairy and non-dairy farms	193
7.3.	Output per £100 of labour cost on FMS farms	193
8.1.	Changes in the level of specialisation on FMS farms	211
8.2.	Changes in enterprises on FMS farms	212
8.3.	Contributions to total output of individual enterprises on FMS farms	213

Tables

1.1.	Farm-related questions for farm 3/1	20
2.1.	ARC research institutes	28
2.2.	ARC Research Units	32
2.3.	Numbers of university academics engaged in agricultural research	34
2.4.	Estimated public and private agricultural research expenditure	44
3.1.	Number of agriculture, forestry, and veterinary students in the UK	58
3.2.	Numbers of officers employed by the NAAS	64
3.3.	Stages in the transformation of farming practices	86
5.1.	Changes in dairy farming in England and Wales	114
5.2.	Changes in dairy farming in south-west England	115
5.3.	The changing popularity of cattle breeds in England and Wales	118
5.4.	National dairy herd breed distribution (percentages)	119

Figures and Tables

5.5.	Forage crop acreages in Cornwall, Devon, and Dorset ('000 acres)	138
5.6.	Hay and silage production (million tons)	140
5.7.	Number of forage harvesters in England and Wales	145
5.8.	Milking systems in England and Wales	151
5.9.	Bulk milk collection in England and Wales	153
6.1.	Changes in the area of agricultural land in England and the three south-western counties, 1939–79 ('000 acres)	166
6.2.	The proportion of the agricultural area and of holdings held by owner-occupiers in England and Wales, 1914–83	168
6.3.	The proportion of holdings and of the agricultural area held under different tenure types, England and Wales, 1960–83	169
6.4.	The balance sheet of UK agriculture, 1953–85 (£ million)	173
6.5.	Land prices (£ per hectare)	174
6.6.	Gross Fixed Capital Formation in UK agriculture	175
6.7.	Capital grants available for UK farmers	180
7.1.	Numbers of agricultural workers (excluding farmers, partners, and directors) in England and the three south-western counties (Cornwall, Devon, and Dorset), 1939–78	185
7.2.	The full-time labour force on farms in 1974	187
7.3.	Holdings and farmers in England and the three south-western counties, 1939–78	190
7.4.	Labour requirements for crops and livestock in 1945 and 1981	191
8.1.	Percentages of farms in different size groups, 1950–74	200
8.2.	Distribution of holdings and SMDs among size groups in England and Wales in 1965	201
9.1.	Boar breeds in Great Britain	220
9.2.	Percentage of FMS farms with pigs	222
9.3.	Poultry numbers and production in Great Britain, 1939–60	225
9.4.	The size structure of egg-producing flocks in England and Wales, 1948–65	227
9.5.	Laying hens in different housing systems as a percentage of the laying population in England and Wales, 1948–59	228
9.6.	Egg production in south-west (SW) England (Cornwall, Devon, Dorset, and Somerset) and the UK	237
9.7.	Pig numbers in Devon, Cornwall, and Dorset, 1953–83	240
9.8.	Number of holdings in England and Wales by size of total pig herd	241
9.9.	Pig performance data on farms in south-west England, 1953–84	242

PREFACE AND ACKNOWLEDGEMENTS

The intellectual origins of this book are explained in chapter 1, but, as with many books, there is a parallel story about its conception. It began in 2007, when three of the authors (MW, ML and PB) examined the Farm Management Survey archive at Exeter and rapidly concluded that it was potentially of great historical value. Since we had all been interested, from different perspectives, in the changes that had been occurring in agriculture throughout our working lives, it is tempting to speculate on whether we would ever have co-operated on researching the topic together in the absence of the archive; what we know, however, is that the potential threat to its existence, brought about by the relocation of the Centre for Rural Policy Research from one Exeter University building to another, precipitated a joint decision to explore the archive further. We obtained a British Academy grant in 2007–8 to employ a research assistant, Dr Helen Blackman, who catalogued its contents. The following year, together with another colleague (DH), we obtained an ESRC grant to fund work on the field books, looking specifically at the evidence for technical change and the explanatory variables associated with it. The grant enabled one of us (PB) to devote most of his time to the project and also to employ Dr Allan Butler as a research fellow.

It is this decision to concentrate on what the archive, together with other sources, can reveal about technical change in agriculture that determines the range of dates in the title of the book. As we explain in the text, the period between the late 1930s and 1985 was one in which UK agricultural policy more or less consistently promoted increasing output. Before and after those dates, the policy message was less clear, so additional variables played a part in farmers' decision-making on investment and the adoption of new technology. There is an interesting book to be written about changes in UK agriculture after 1985, but it is not this book.

Inevitably, we have accumulated numerous debts of gratitude in the course of our research and writing. Without Helen Blackman's rapid and efficient cataloguing work, we would not have been successful in obtaining the ESRC grant, and she later went on, with Katie Garvey, to help with the analysis of the field books. Most of the work on that, however, was done by Allan Butler, without whose forensic expertise we would have had much less data to work with. Marilyn Stephen uncomplainingly

Preface and Acknowledgements

added us into her extensive existing administrative workload to make sure that we had the resources we needed and a congenial atmosphere in which to use them. We were fortunate in having the advice of veteran FBS Investigative Officers in the form of Barry Nixon, Keith Robbins and the late Martin Turner, and in expert commentary from Richard Soffe, Geoff Hearnden, Hilary Crowe, Alan Cooper and Mark Riley. We thank the Beaford Archive (www.beafordarchive.org) for allowing us to use the cover photograph by James Ravilious. We would also like to thank Richard Hoyle and Caroline Palmer, Elizabeth McDonald, and their colleagues at Boydell & Brewer for all their patience and expertise in the production of this book. Finally, and most importantly, we are immensely grateful to the farmers who interrupted their busy lives to share their experiences with us, and who remain, in the following pages, known only by the code numbers of their farms.

ABBREVIATIONS

ADAS	Agricultural Development and Advisory Service
Agric. Hist. Rev.	*Agricultural History Review*
AI	artificial insemination
AIC	Agricultural Improvement Council
AFRC	Agricultural and Food Research Council (formed from the ARC in 1983)
ARC	Agricultural Research Council
ATB	Agricultural Training Board
CAEC	County Agricultural Executive Committee
CAP	the Common Agricultural Policy of the EEC (later the EU)
CWAEC	County War Agricultural Executive Committee
DSIR	Department of Scientific and Industrial Research
EEC	European Economic Community
EHF	Experimental Husbandry Farm
EU	European Union
FMS	the Farm Management Survey (now known as the Farm Business Survey)
J. Agric. Econs.	*Journal of Agricultural Economics*
MAF	Ministry of Agriculture and Fisheries (amalgamated in 1955 with the Ministry of Food to form MAFF) But note that both MAF and MAFF archives in the National Archives have the code letters MAF.
MAFF	Ministry of Agriculture, Fisheries, and Food
MLC	Meat and Livestock Commission
MMB	Milk Marketing Board
NAAS	National Agricultural Advisory Service
NIAB	National Institute of Agricultural Botany
NFU	National Farmers' Union
TNA	The UK National Archives, Kew
YFC	Young Farmers' Club

1

Introduction: Exploring Agricultural Change

> I always found when I was young that the most obscure period of time was that which was too old to be news and too young to be history – the day before yesterday, as it were.[1]

What If ...

If, by some miracle, a farmer's son, killed at Waterloo in 1815, at the end of the Napoleonic Wars, had been resurrected and sent to work on a small farm in September 1939, just in time for the Second World War, he would have known what to do. The horses and their harness would have been familiar to him, and the plough that they pulled, although perhaps a little lighter and stronger than those with which he had been brought up, was essentially the same. He would have known how to stack sheaves of corn on a wagon, and how to make them into a rick in the farmyard before they were thrashed. If he had no personal experience of them, he would at least have heard about seed drills and machines that thrashed out the corn, and milking the cows by hand would be a familiar task.

But if he had been resurrected in time to take part in the Falklands War, in 1982, he would have been completely baffled. Where were the horses? How were the cows milked by some strange device attached to their udders? And how could they possibly produce so much milk? Why were there no pigs or chickens or geese wandering around the farmyard? No ricks of corn waiting to be thrashed? What were those noisy, smelly, metal things that appeared to move on their own, without any horses to pull them? And where was everybody? How could those enormous cereal crops that he could see in the fields be harvested when hardly anybody appeared to work on the farm?

---

[1] Rupert Hart-Davis, writing to George Lyttelton, 8 April 1956: R. Hart-Davis (ed.), *The Lyttelton Hart-Davis Letters*, vols. 1 and 2, *1955–1957* (London, 1985), p. 116.

Agricultural Change 1939–85

The second half of the twentieth century saw almost unimaginable change in English agriculture. By the middle of the 1980s, an acre of land could produce three times as much wheat as it had fifty years earlier, and a cow twice as much milk, with only one-fifth of the workforce that had been in the industry at the beginning of the Second World War. Machinery and chemicals now did much of the work, and agriculture was now highly technical, rather than the repository of comfortable tradition. This book is about the technical changes that transformed farming, and about the various ways in which farmers responded to them.

Most people know that agriculture changed enormously after the Second World War. The story is well known and has been covered by historians to some extent, by scientists, and by agricultural economists.[2] Certainly anybody with any interest in farming knows that much depended on technical change. But, as we shall see, there are problems with the standard story, which suggests that we don't know enough about the process of technical change at the level of the individual decision makers: the farmers and their workers. What we do know is that there were considerable variations between one farm and another, and between different technical changes. The story of the national farm is the sum of the stories of two hundred thousand or so individual farmers, but it is not the story of any individual one of them. In this book, we shall therefore examine some farms in detail and integrate their story with the national picture with which we are more familiar. First, though, let us add more detail to the statements made in this paragraph and the previous one.

After, and even during, the Second World War, agriculture changed, not only in Britain but across the world. Between 1950 and 1989, the world population increased from 2.5 billion to 5.2 billion. Since we do not import food from extra-terrestrial sources, neglecting the extent to which diets increased or diminished in quantity and quality, world

---

[2] B.A. Holderness, 'Apropos the Third Agricultural Revolution: How Productive Was British Agriculture in the Long Boom, 1954–1973?', in P. Mathias and J.A. Davis (eds), *Agriculture and Industrialization from the Eighteenth Century to the Present Day* (Oxford, 1996); J. Martin, *The Development of Modern Agriculture: British Farming since 1931* (Basingstoke, 2000); P. Brassley, 'Output and Technical Change in Twentieth-Century British Agriculture', *Agric. Hist. Rev.* 48 (2000), pp. 60–84; K. Blaxter and N. Robertson, *From Dearth to Plenty: The Modern Revolution in Food Production* (Cambridge, 1995); A. Bailey, K. Balcombe, C. Thirtle, and L. Jenkins, 'ME Estimation of Input and Output Biases of Technical and Policy Change in UK Agriculture, 1953–2000', *J. Agric. Econs.* 55 (2004), pp. 385–400; C. Thirtle, L. Lin, J. Holding, L. Jenkins, and J. Piesse, 'Explaining the Decline in UK Agricultural Productivity Growth', *J. Agric. Econs.* 55 (2004), pp. 343–66.

agricultural production must therefore have more or less doubled.³ Compared with its pre-war level, according to Professor Federico's calculations, it actually trebled. In western Europe as a whole, according to Federico, pre-war agricultural production was at only about 40 per cent of its 1984 level.⁴ Another estimate suggests that western European output roughly doubled in the same period.⁵ This was a phenomenon shared with other developed capitalist economies in North America, Australia and New Zealand.⁶ In Great Britain, the volume of output increased from just over £4 billion before the Second World War (1935–9) to an average of nearly £12 billion (both measured in 1986 prices) in 1981–5.⁷ These are gross figures, but the net production more than doubled.⁸ Between the 1750s and 1860s, often seen as a period of agricultural revolution, the rate of agricultural output growth never exceeded 1 per cent per annum, and between 1867 and 1934 British agriculture hardly grew at all, whereas between 1945 and 1965 the annual rate of increase in the volume of output was 2.8 per cent.⁹ Farmers' memoirs written in the 1930s, such as the classic works of Adrian Bell and A.G. Street, emphasise problems; in those written from the 1940s onwards, the emphasis is on progress and expansion.¹⁰

Explaining Agricultural Change

Previous studies of post-1930s agriculture have identified several explanations for this agricultural expansion.¹¹ One was the impact of the Second

3   R. Cameron, *A Concise Economic History of the World: From Palaeolithic Times to the Present* (London, 1993), p. 325.
4   G. Federico, *Feeding the World: An Economic History of Agriculture, 1800–2000* (Princeton, NJ, 2005), pp. 235–6.
5   M. Martín-Retortillo and V. Pinilla, 'Patterns and Causes of the Growth of European Agricultural Production, 1950 to 2005', *Agric. Hist. Rev.* 63 (2015), pp. 132–59.
6   D. Grigg, *The Transformation of Agriculture in the West* (Oxford, 1992); B.L. Gardner, *American Agriculture in the Twentieth Century: How It Flourished and What It Cost* (Cambridge, MA, 2002), p. 5; Federico, *Feeding the World*, p. 236.
7   Brassley, 'Output and Technical Change', p. 84.
8   Martín-Retortillo and Pinilla, 'Patterns and Causes', p. 135.
9   S. Broadberry, B.M.S. Campbell, A. Klein, M. Overton, and B. van Leeuwen, *British Economic Growth 1270–1870* (Cambridge, 2015), p. 115; Brassley, 'Output and Technical Change' p. 84.
10 A. Bell, *Corduroy* (London, 1930); A.G. Street, *Farmer's Glory* (London, 1932); G. Henderson, *The Farming Ladder* (London, 1944); R.J. Ruck, *Place of Stones* (London, 1961); R.J. Ruck, *Hill Farm Story* (London, 1966); J. Cherrington, *On the Smell of an Oily Rag* (London, 1979); T. Harman, *Seventy Summers: The Story of a Farm* (London, 1986); A. Court, *Seedtime to Harvest: A Farmer's Life* (Bradford on Avon, 1987).
11 Another term used, often by geographers and not without some challenges, to

World War, in which Britain, unlike many other European countries, managed to overcome the shortage of inputs and expand its agricultural output. In part, this was an unintended benefit of what farmers at the time saw as seventy years of neglect. From the 1870s onwards, the British market was open to imports of agricultural products from around the world. Cereals came from Australia, Canada, the USA, and Argentina, lamb and dairy products from New Zealand, dairy products and bacon from Denmark and the Netherlands, beef and wool from Australia and Argentina. Between 1870 and 1935, the volume of world agricultural trade quadrupled, with European countries accounting for the bulk of the imports, and of these Britain was the dominant importer for most products apart from fresh pork.[12] Successive UK governments were content to see this expansion of imports, which kept domestic food prices down and allowed poorer people access to more fats and protein than they had been able to afford for much of the nineteenth century. Even in the First World War, when imports were threatened by naval warfare and domestic agricultural policy did encourage British farmers to increase cereal production, food imports only fell by about 15 per cent in energy terms.[13] In the interwar period in particular, British farmers responded to the import competition by concentrating on the products that were naturally protected from foreign competition by transport costs: fresh meat and dairy products:

> The British farmer decided to lose money in the slowest and easiest fashion. In other words he laid his land down to grass ... to save himself from bankruptcy, but in so doing, quite unconsciously, he saved the whole nation when war broke out in 1939. For underneath the turf of his pastures his livestock had placed a huge store of fertility. This was then tapped by the plough to grow heavy crops of human food per acre in the shape of wheat and potatoes.[14]

---

characterise agriculture in the period between the Second World War and the late 1980s was 'productivist'. See B. Ilbery and I. Bowler, 'From Agricultural Productivism to Post-productivism', in B. Ilbery (ed.), *The Geography of Rural Change* (Harlow, 1998), pp. 57–84; N. Evans, C. Morris, and M. Winter, 'Conceptualizing Agriculture: A Critique of Post-productivism as the New Orthodoxy', *Progress in Human Geography* 26 (2002), pp. 313–32.

[12] G. Aparicio, V. Pinilla, and R. Serrano, 'Europe and the International Trade in Agricultural and Food Products, 1870–2000', in P. Lains and V. Pinilla (eds), *Agriculture and Economic Development in Europe since 1870* (Abingdon, 2009), pp. 52–75; P. Brassley, 'International Trade in Agricultural Products, 1935–1955', in P. Brassley, L. Van Molle, and Y. Segers (eds), *War, Agriculture and Food: Rural Europe from the 1930s to the 1950s* (New York, 2012), pp. 33–51.

[13] P. Dewey, *British Agriculture in the First World War* (London, 1989), p. 227.

[14] A.G. Street, *Farmer's Glory* (2nd edn with postscript, Harmondsworth, 1951), p. 223.

More recent work by agricultural historians[15] has demonstrated that the wartime increase in wheat and potato production was achieved at the cost of reduced outputs of meat and eggs, but nevertheless the Second World War can be held responsible for several important factors contributing to post-war expansion: changes in agricultural policy, backed up by the increased national influence of the National Farmers' Union (NFU) and local enforcement activities by the County War Agricultural Executive Committees (CWAECs); the development of more effective advisory services; and a change in the image of farming from an industry in terminal decline to the wartime saviour of the nation.[16]

Across Europe as a whole, the immediate post-war years were marked by a rapid recovery of agriculture from wartime damage and disruption.[17] The UK was no exception. Following the war, and initially in response to the post-war balance of payments crisis, agricultural expansion was actively encouraged by the government. Market forces alone were not considered capable of delivering agricultural change.[18] Instead, a succession of governments over fifty years found it necessary to finance, or otherwise encourage, a plethora of agricultural executive committees, advisory services, marketing boards, commodity commissions and authorities, research stations, experimental husbandry farms, and university departments of agriculture. The formation of the Milk Marketing Board (MMB) in 1933 was particularly important for milk producers in south-west England, not only for its scientific and advisory work but also because it paid all producers the same price (the pool price), irrespective of whether their milk went to the higher-priced liquid market or the lower-priced manufacturing (butter, cheese, etc.) market. Farmers in the south-west were far from most urban markets, and much of their milk went to manufacturing, so they benefitted from the pool price system.[19] Arthur Court, who farmed on the borders of Somerset and Wiltshire from the 1920s to the 1980s, described the establishment of the MMB as 'a watershed in farming history', creating 'stability in an industry which had been struggling with its marketing problems for half a century'.[20] In addition to government initiatives, many commercial

---

15 For example, B. Short, C. Watkins, and J. Martin (eds), *The Front Line of Freedom: British Farming in the Second World War* (Exeter, 2007).
16 C. Griffiths, 'Heroes of the Reconstruction? Images of British Farmers in War and Peace', in Brassley et al., *War, Agriculture and Food*, pp. 209–28.
17 C. Martiin, J. Pan-Montojo, and P. Brassley (eds), *Agriculture in Capitalist Europe, 1945–1960: From Food Shortages to Food Surpluses* (Abingdon, 2016).
18 P. Self and H. Storing, *The State and the Farmer* (London, 1962); M. Winter, *Rural Politics: Policies for Agriculture, Forestry and the Environment* (London, 1996), pp. 100–6.
19 B. Hill and D. Ray, *Economics for Agriculture: Food, Farming and the Rural Economy* (Basingstoke, 1987), p. 60.
20 Court, *Seedtime to Harvest*, p. 45.

firms in the fertiliser, pesticide, feedingstuffs, and seeds trades were carrying out or commissioning their own research and employing their own advisory representatives. Expansionist policies came to an end in the mid-1980s, which is why the period analysed in this book ends in 1985, but until then it is generally accepted that the combination of government agricultural policy and technical change was responsible for the dramatic expansion quantified above.[21]

The effects of technical change were analysed at the time by a succession of agricultural economists.[22] Again, it was generally accepted that they involved a decrease in farm labour and an increase in the use of capital, in the form of machinery, buildings, and equipment, so that despite product prices that decreased in real terms, agricultural output increased. Federico argues that in contrast to the nineteenth century, in which world agricultural output was increased by increasing inputs, the twentieth century saw an increase in total factor productivity (TFP), producing more output per unit of input, as the major cause of output increases, in which public investment in research, development, and extension, resulting in technical change, played a major role.[23] Although there were input increases in the twentieth century, especially of machinery, fertilisers, and pesticides from outside the agricultural industry itself, other studies support Federico's findings. For the UK, Thirtle and his co-workers report annual TFP growth of 1.68 per cent up to 1984, but only 0.26 per cent from 1985 to 2000. They also suggest, on the basis of a study of the eastern counties' arable area of the UK, that crop TFP increased more rapidly than that in animal enterprises.[24] Within this overall pattern of productivity growth, however, there were significant differences between partial productivities. It is clear that land productivity, measured in terms of agricultural output per acre or hectare, increased. Average cereal yields, for example, increased from a little over 1 ton per acre in 1950 to 2.5 tons per acre in 1990. Similarly, as farm labourers left the land, the output (in constant price terms) per head of labour nearly doubled between 1950 and 1987.[25] On the other hand, capital productivity, which is more difficult to measure, probably decreased. Similarly, if we include the management efforts of farmers and the associated provision of knowledge through scientific research

---

[21] Martin, *The Development of Modern Agriculture*.
[22] See, e.g., Hill and Ray, *Economics for Agriculture*.
[23] Federico, *Feeding the World*, p. 221.
[24] C. Thirtle, L. Lin, J. Holding, and J. Piesse, 'Explaining the Decline in UK Productivity Growth', pp. 343–66; J. Amadi, J. Piesse, and C. Thirtle, 'Crop Level Productivity in the Eastern Counties of England, 1970–97', *J. Agric. Econs.* 55 (2004), pp. 367–83.
[25] H. Marks and D.K. Britton, *A Hundred Years of British Food and Farming: A Statistical Survey* (London, 1989), pp. 138, 150, 164.

and advisory work by government bodies and the ancillary industries as inputs to the agricultural industry, we might also find that the partial productivity associated with these inputs also decreased, although again this is not easy to measure.

Farmers en masse appear to have responded logically to increased labour costs and capital grants from government by adopting new output-increasing or labour-saving technology. The Second World War years and the forty years after the war saw increased use and improved formulations of feedingstuffs and fertilisers, a dramatic expansion in the use of silage as a means of forage conservation, much greater numbers of milking machines, tractors and many other kinds of agricultural machinery, and the intensification of pig and poultry production. There were new crop varieties, herbicides, insecticides and fungicides, the emergence of oilseed rape as a major commercial crop from the 1960s onwards, the expansion of vining peas for freezing in the eastern counties, changes in livestock breeds, the development of artificial insemination (AI) and embryo transfer, and more effective veterinary medicines. These were the technical changes that lay behind the increased wheat and milk yields that would have astonished the resurrected Napoleonic warrior that we met at the beginning of this chapter, and this standard story is well known in the agricultural industry and among agricultural historians. But this top-down view will only take us so far in explaining what happened.

Problems with Current Explanations

Even the national scale data suggest that this simple story of technology becoming available, and evenly taken up, as a simple consequence of the sticks wielded by the Agricultural Executive Committees and the carrots proffered by guaranteed prices, is inadequate. The national agricultural statistics reveal the persistence of small farms long after economic data suggest they are financially unviable. If the state's reach and efficacy were sufficient to explain changes, then we would expect improvements in performance and efficiency to be manifest across all farms and to be relatively uniform. And yet one of the findings of the Farm Management Survey (FMS) data (which we discuss below), year after year and indeed up to the present day, is that there is a remarkably wide range of farm economic performance. In other words, we can hypothesise that there is a differential take up of incentives and/or responsiveness to regulation. Or we might hypothesise that for individual farms, take-up/responsiveness is a necessary but not a sufficient condition to guarantee increases in productivity and so forth. We need a different, micro-historical, detailed, and grounded research approach.

Of course, the uneven development of the agricultural industry has not escaped the notice either of historians and geographers, or contemporaneous policy makers and commentators. Indeed, the conundrum provided the justification for sustained investment by the state in publicly funded provision of research, development, and advisory services designed to encourage farmers to adopt new technologies and business practices, as examined in detail in this book in chapters 2 and 3. As indicated earlier, it tends to be assumed that technology is both a prerequisite for change and that, once available, its adoption is inevitable. While there is a long-established literature about the rate of technology adoption using a bell-shaped curve, the overwhelming focus of much of this work is to attempt to explain and characterise early adopters and laggards.[26] In the bell-curve model, the initial adopters are called 'innovators', who represent only a small proportion of the total population. They are succeeded by early adopters, and then, clustered around the average date of adoption, are the early and late majority. The last people to adopt the innovation are the laggards. From at least the 1960s, this was a widely used model of technology adoption in agriculture, and several investigators identified the personal characteristics, values, social relationships, and communications behaviours of members of the various groups. Innovators, for example, were found to be young, wealthy, well educated, with large, specialised farms, risk takers, and users of impersonal channels of information. Those in the late majority, in contrast, were likely to operate small, non-specialised farms, to need a high degree of pressure from their peers before adopting a new technology, and to make little use of mass media. Laggards were risk-avoiders and suspicious of change agents.[27] Leaving aside the value-laden nature of the terminology used in the model, it is clear that individuals might not fit neatly into these different categories. It was, after all, only a model, and useful as far as it explained what had happened and what might happen in future.[28] It did, however, serve to highlight the fact that individual farmers made decisions about technology according to their own individual circumstances and objectives, at least for most of the period with which we are concerned.[29]

[26] E.M. Rogers, *Diffusion of Innovations* (New York, 1962).
[27] Hill and Ray, *Economics for Agriculture*, pp. 292–3.
[28] Other models are available. See, for example, N. Oudshoorn and T. Pinch, *How Users Matter: The Co-construction of Users and Technologies* (Cambridge, MA, 2003); P. Brassley, 'Cutting across Nature? The History of Artificial Insemination in Pigs in the UK', *Studies in the History and Philosophy of Biological and Biomedical Science* 38 (2007), pp. 462–87.
[29] The exceptional period was between 1939 and 1958, when the CWAECs, and subsequently the County Agricultural Executive Committees, had the power to dispossess farmers whose management of their farms was considered inadequate. See B. Short, *The Battle of the Fields: Rural Community and Authority in Britain during the Second World War* (Woodbridge, 2014), p. 383.

Another difficulty is that the characteristic bell-curve account rarely tells us anything about how long a fully developed and commercially available technology or innovation might be available before even the early adopters arrive on the scene. Might those early adopters in fact be rather late given how long a technology has been available, and if so why? There is some evidence that this might be the case with some aspects of agricultural innovation. For example, silage as a means of conserving grass as a winter feed for livestock was well understood by the late nineteenth century but it was not until the 1960s, 1970s, and 1980s that production really took off.[30] Its superiority over hay, both in terms of nutritional quality and the reduced dependence on a sustained period of dry weather, makes its late adoption hard to explain, although Brassley does suggest some factors.[31] We explore this example in greater detail in chapter 5, but one immediate possible explanation for its late adoption serves to open up some pressing questions over the received wisdom about the driving forces behind agricultural change. Silage was heavily promoted during the Second World War, but its use, though it increased fourfold from a very low base, remained very low despite this being a period of maximum state intervention.[32] And yet, in other respects the war, with its panoply of incentives, compulsions, and persuasions, was remarkable for the changes it induced in agriculture. For example, the area of land devoted to arable production in the UK increased from 13,088,000 acres to 19,183,000 acres between 1939 and 1945; the plough-up campaign was a success.[33] These characteristics of unevenness, variability, and heterogeneity are the prime drivers of this book.

All this suggests that we do not know enough about the process of technical change at the level of the individual decision-makers, the farmers and their workers. As Hoyle has argued, 'we know very little about farmers as either a social group or as individuals', and they are

---

[30] P. Brassley, 'Silage in Britain 1880–1990: The Delayed Adoption of an Innovation', *Agric. Hist. Rev.* 44 (1996), pp. 46–62.

[31] Ironically, in a later phase of policy in the 1990s and 2000s by which time farmers were being encouraged to revert to hay making for environmental purposes, farmers showed themselves to be tenaciously committed to silage. See M. Riley, '"Ask the Fellows Who Cut the Hay": Farm Practices, Oral History and Nature Conservation', *Journal of the Oral History Society* 32 (2004), pp. 42–51.

[32] Brassley, 'Silage in Britain', estimates that silage production in Great Britain grew from 250,000 tons in 1940 to one million tons in 1944. By 1950, it was 1,832,000 tons. In 1981, it was 30,193,000 tons.

[33] P. Brassley, 'Wartime Productivity and Innovation, 1939–45', in Short et al., *The Front Line of Freedom*, p. 41. See also D.C. Harvey and M. Riley, '"Fighting from the Fields": Developing the British "National Farm" in the Second World War', *Journal of Historical Geography* 35 (2009), pp. 495–516.

often absent from agricultural history.³⁴ While the top-down approach to technical change in agriculture emphasises the way in which new technology was produced, we also need to know how it was received.

Some farmers may be active agents of change through early adoption and a spirit of innovation. Others may resist change, holding out against new technologies. Still others may be neutral, standing apart or observing and biding their time. In attempting to account for output changes in UK agriculture, Brassley suggests some possible explanations, such as cost and price changes, the increase in owner-occupation, and state promotion of research, development, and extension. He makes the point that in the period of most rapid output growth, it was the adoption of existing technology that had the biggest impact and argues that 'the obvious next stage of research should be on the reasons for adoption'. The complexity of these reasons is demonstrated in a subsequent article examining a specific technology pointing towards changing business objectives for farmers, a topic investigated for just one example by Brassley.³⁵ For most agricultural studies, however, the farm is what Rosenberg refers to as a 'black box' into which goes science and technology, and from which emerges new products, lower costs, or higher outputs.³⁶ Work on the history of technology in general, however, has been mostly concerned with what happens *inside* the black box, but this work seems to have had little impact on historians of recent agricultural change.³⁷ Indeed, despite a proliferation of sociologically informed perspectives on technical change, not one of sixty-five references in Pinch's review of studies based on a social construction of technology (SCOT) is specifically concerned with agricultural technology.³⁸

In addition to needing to know more about the production of technology and about its reception on individual farms, we also need to explore the links between the two. There are interesting parallels here between

---

34 R. Hoyle, 'Introduction: Recovering the Farmer', in R. Hoyle (ed.), *The Farmer in England, 1650–1980* (Farnham, 2013), p. 2.
35 Brassley, 'Output and Technical Change', p. 77; Brassley, 'Cutting across Nature?', pp. 442–61.
36 N. Rosenberg, *Inside the Black Box: Technology and Economics* (Cambridge, 1982). We discuss Rosenberg's ideas in more detail in chapter 10.
37 Honourable exceptions include P. Palladino, 'Wizards and Devotees: On the Mendelian Theory of Inheritance and the Professionalization of Agricultural Science in Great Britain and the United States 1880–1930', *History of Science* XXXII (1994), 409–44; S. Wilmot, 'From "Public Service" to Artificial Insemination: Animal Breeding Science and Reproductive Research in Early Twentieth-Century Britain', *Studies in the History and Philosophy of Biological and Biomedical Sciences* 38 (2007), pp. 411–41.
38 Oudshoorn and Pinch, *How Users Matter*; T. Pinch, 'The Social Construction of Technology: A Review', in R. Fox (ed.), *Technological Change: Methods and Themes in the History of Technology* (Amsterdam, 1996), pp. 17–35.

agriculture and medicine. In both, governments have funded research, and in both there is the perception that those using it (general practitioners and hospital clinicians in the case of medicine, farmers in agriculture) are too busy actually doing the job to think much about research. In medicine, this has led to the concept of 'translational research', tracing the progress of new explanations, diagnostic tools, or treatments 'from bench to bedside'. Perhaps not surprisingly, one of the conclusions that emerges from this is that the idea of linear progress from pure to applied science, and from applied science to practical application, is an over-simplification. Studies of medical research suggest that it is more effective to regard the translational process as one of 'continuous data exchange within and between various research and non-research practices' and that scientific knowledge may not produce tangible benefits if 'it does not fit with the intended users' characteristics, practices and, most importantly, values'.[39] The significance of similar ideas for agriculture is obvious, but in the agricultural context it has been more common to refer to the whole process as the analysis of knowledge networks, and that is the term we use in performing our analysis in chapters 2 and 3.

To summarise the argument so far, we know that the output increases and input changes that characterised UK farming (and developed country farming in general) in the middle to late twentieth century were profoundly influenced by technical change, but that the processes by which the new technology was produced and applied have hitherto been largely analysed from the top downwards, and we know too little about what happened at the farm level, although it seems clear that what happened varied considerably between farms and between different technologies. Beneath the smooth surface of the official statistics lies turbulence and complexity.

An Alternative Approach

The steady progression outlined in the national accounts of increases in production is perhaps not quite so steady or as predictable as some of the narratives would have us believe. Some of these accounts might be criticised for not confronting all the available data, particularly the data already alluded to on variable farm economic performance, but such a confrontation is without purpose with neither an adequate framing of the problem nor alternative sources of data with which to interrogate the issue of uneven performance. In contrast to many of our predecessors writing on this period, we frame or conceptualise our account as a

---

[39] A.L. van der Laan and M. Boenink, 'Beyond Bench and Bedside: Disentangling the Concept of Translational Research', *Health Care Analysis* 23 (2015), pp. 32–49. We are grateful to Sabina Leonelli and James Lowe for drawing this concept to our attention.

sociological one as much as it is an economic one. Differential levels of economic performance and technology adoption suggest that issues of behaviour or human agency are likely to be as powerful, or more so, as economic explanations. Once this is accepted as plausible, it is but a small step to consider sources of data that give more voice to the individual farmers, and to sources that allow for a finer disaggregation of macro datasets. In our case, this meant using the hitherto largely unexplored individual farm returns for the FMS, supplemented by oral history interviews with some of those farmers whose individual farm accounts from the 1940s, '50s, '60s, and '70s we examined.

The FMS and Its Origins

Since we shall be making extensive use of its products, it is worth a short digression to examine the origins of the FMS. As D'Onofrio has suggested in the case of Italy, the collection of farm income data from the 1930s onwards did not emerge, fully formed, from an intellectual vacuum.[40] Historians of science have pointed out that by the mid-nineteenth century scientists were searching for objective knowledge, 'knowledge unmarked by prejudice or skill, fantasy or judgment, wishing or striving'.[41] Before long, similar ideas began to emerge in the social sciences and in public life. As Porter argues: 'In public affairs, reliance on nothing more than seasoned judgement seems undemocratic ... Ideally, expertise should be mechanized and objectified', and the 'reverence of social scientists for statistics enshrined a vision of personal renunciation and impersonal authority in the name of higher truths and public values'.[42] The initial institutional result in Britain of this epistemic change was seen in the formation of the London Statistical Society in 1834 (it became the Royal Statistical Society in 1887).[43] It was concerned in the nineteenth century with the collection of useful information about society in the form of facts and figures more than with statistical theories and methods, and the same appears to be true of the International Statistical Institute, founded in 1885 to bring together government statisticians from various countries. Major Craigie's report to the Royal Statistical Society on the 1897 meeting of the

[40] F. D'Onofrio, *Observing Agriculture in Early Twentieth-Century Italy: Agricultural Economists and Statistics* (Abingdon, 2016), pp. 4–10.
[41] L. Daston and P. Galison, *Objectivity* (New York, 2007), p. 17.
[42] T.M. Porter, *Trust in Numbers: The Pursuit of Objectivity in Science and Public Life* (Princeton, NJ, 1995) p. 7; T.M. Porter, 'Statistics and Statistical Methods', in T.M. Porter and D. Ross (eds), *The Cambridge History of Science*, vol. VII, *The Modern Social Sciences* (Cambridge, 2003), p. 250.
[43] M. Shabas, 'British Economic Theory from Locke to Marshall', in Porter and Ross, *The Cambridge History of Science*, VII, p. 179; D.A. Mackenzie, *Statistics in Britain, 1865–1930: The Social Construction of Scientific Knowledge* (Edinburgh, 1981), p. 8.

Introduction: Exploring Agricultural Change

International Statistical Institute at St Petersburg listed the topics under discussion as agricultural statistics, including crop statistics and forecasts, annual data on crop areas and livestock numbers, the distribution of landed property, and rural enquiries, in addition to population, judicial, commercial, labour, and anthropometric statistics.[44] Theoretical mathematical work formed the minority of papers in the deliberations of British and international societies, although of course basic ideas of probability, estimation, variation, error, regression, and so on were being formulated in the nineteenth century by Laplace, Gauss, Quetelet, Poisson, and other pioneers of statistical theory. But basic ideas of social research using sampling methods appeared only from the end of the nineteenth century and were still being debated in the International Statistical Institute in the late 1920s.[45] Unemployment, welfare, and the cost of living became matters of state intervention and legislation in the first thirty years of the twentieth century and consequently became the concerns of government statistical bureaux.[46] Thus the environment within which policy makers and administrators in general worked in the early twentieth century was increasingly objectified and quantified.

This trend was also apparent in the agricultural field. The agricultural counterpart to the International Statistical Institute was the International Institute of Agriculture (IIA), which had been established in Rome in 1905.[47] After the First World War, it was associated with the League of Nations. By the 1930s, sixty countries were affiliated, it was producing a wide range of statistical, economic, and scientific publications, and in 1930–1 it conducted a world agricultural census.[48] However, despite the expansion of agricultural education from the 1890s and the increased availability of research funding from the Development Commission after 1910, Britain in this period was lagging behind continental Europe,

---

[44] Mackenzie, *Statistics in Britain*, p. 8; A. Desrosières, 'Managing the Economy', in Porter and Ross, *The Cambridge History of Science*, VII, p. 232; P.G. Craigie, 'Notes on the Subjects Discussed at the St. Petersburg Meeting of the International Statistical Institute', *Journal of the Royal Statistical Society* 60 (1897), pp. 735–88.

[45] Porter, 'Statistics and Statistical Methods', pp. 238–42; A. Desrosières, 'The Part in Relation to the Whole: How to Generalise? The Prehistory of Representative Sampling', in M. Bulmer, K. Bales, and K.K. Sklar (eds), *The Social Survey in Historical Perspective 1880–1940* (Cambridge, 1991), pp. 217–18.

[46] Desrosières, 'Managing the Economy', p. 559.

[47] N. Mignemi, 'Italian Agricultural Experts as Transnational Mediators: The Creation of the International Institute of Agriculture, 1905 to 1908', *Agric. Hist. Rev.* 65 (2017), pp. 254–76; F. D'Onofrio, 'Agricultural Numbers: The Statistics of the International Institute of Agriculture in the Interwar Period', *Agric. Hist. Rev.* 65 (2017), pp. 277–96.

[48] J.A. Venn, *The Foundations of Agricultural Economics* (Cambridge, 1933), pp. 443–4.

especially Germany and the Netherlands, and the USA.[49] This was certainly true as far as agricultural economics and farm management specifically were concerned. Although the UK had had an agricultural census – the June returns – since the 1860s, it only collected physical data and thus provided no information on incomes or any other financial measure.[50] Similarly, the 1908 estimates of the agricultural output of Great Britain were also produced entirely in terms of acres, tons, and gallons.[51] In contrast, the US Department of Agriculture began to collect data on the costs of growing wheat from the 1890s, and at about the same time simple cash expenditure and receipt systems were being applied to German farms. In Switzerland, Professor Ernst Laur, a leading figure in the Swiss Peasants' Union, published the first statement of Swiss farm accounts in 1901, and farm accounting societies were established in Denmark from 1910. The Cornell Agricultural Experiment Station surveyed farms in New York State in 1911 and developed the idea of 'efficiency factors' such as output per labour unit. The *Journal of Farm Economics*, first published in the USA in 1910, can be seen as a baseline for the profession of agricultural economics, and many of the British agricultural economists of the interwar period spent some of their student years at Cornell or Iowa State universities.[52]

Britain was about twenty years behind. Among the pioneers of agricultural data collection in the UK were Sir Daniel Hall, who acted as adviser to the Guinness brewery hop farm (and in 1904 devised a full-cost accounting system), James Wyllie (of the West of Scotland Agricultural College), James Mackintosh (of Reading University), and A.G. Ruston, who began to collect cost accounting data in Leeds University.[53] Hall later became the leading figure in the Development Commission, which funded the establishment of the Agricultural Economics Research Institute (AERI) at Oxford University. Its Director, C.S. Orwin, published *Farm Accounts* in 1914, and *The Determination of Farming Costs* in 1917. A revised edition of the latter work, under the title *Farming Costs*, followed in 1921, and it is interesting to note that many of the references cited in the bibliography were American or German.[54] Notwithstanding these hesitant

---

[49] P. Brassley, 'Agricultural Science and Education', in E.J.T. Collins (ed.), *The Agrarian History of England and Wales*, vol. VII, *1850–1914*, part 1 (Cambridge, 2000), pp. 613–22; J. Bieleman, *Five Centuries of Farming: A Short History of Dutch Agriculture 1500–2000* (Wageningen, 2010), p. 161.

[50] S. Foreman, *Loaves and Fishes: An Illustrated History of the Ministry of Agriculture, Fisheries and Food, 1889–1989* (London, 1989), p. 87.

[51] Board of Agriculture and Fisheries, *The Agricultural Output of Great Britain*, Cd.6277 (1912).

[52] E. Whetham, *Agricultural Economists in Britain, 1900–1940* (London, 1981), pp. 25–9.

[53] Whetham, *Agricultural Economists in Britain*, pp. 23–4.

[54] C.S. Orwin, *Farm Accounts* (Cambridge, 1914); C.S. Orwin, *The Determination*

beginnings of data collection, some problems appeared to be enduring. The full-cost accounting method, as John King, the advisory economist at the Midland Agricultural College at Sutton Bonington, pointed out in 1927, required some brave assumptions about the contribution of each enterprise to what we would now call fixed costs (e.g. items such as rent and labour). These complexities required considerable time, expertise, and effort to analyse just one farm, even assuming that the farm kept records in the necessary detail.[55] Thus the idea of collecting comparable data over the range of different farming types, enterprises, and regions to be found in the UK was impracticable, unless some alternative method could be found.

The only realistic alternative was the survey method, which involved the collection of a more straightforward set of financial and physical data from a wider range of farms, subsequently analysed by type of farming and size of farm. This practice had been pioneered in the USA by Dr G.F. Warren and his co-workers at Cornell in the first decade of the twentieth century, and as Sir Thomas Middleton, a former professor of agriculture, leading civil servant in the Ministry of Food, and at that time secretary to the Development Commission, who clearly had personal knowledge of the procedure, subsequently wrote, Warren

> was personally very familiar with the types of farming followed in the Eastern States. Being himself unable to visit the hundreds of farmers whose business methods he wished to study, he drew up a careful schedule of questions, of a kind he knew farmers could answer; he then selected post-graduate students and sent them to collect and write down answers to his questions. Interesting information was thus collected which he interpreted with great skill.[56]

By the 1920s, Warren's approach was known and practised in the UK. Despite Orwin's expertise in cost accounting methods, the AERI over which he presided conducted a series of surveys, including Orr's studies of Oxfordshire (1916) and Berkshire (1918) and the four volumes on rural industries published in 1926 and 1927.[57] There were also national land use and woodland surveys in the interwar period, but these were hardly Warren-type surveys.[58] Warren's influence was, however, reflected in

---

of Farming Costs (Oxford, 1917); C.S. Orwin, *Farming Costs* (Oxford, 1921).
[55] J. King, *Cost Accounting as Applied to Agriculture* (London, 1927).
[56] TNA T161/487 (Survey of Farm Management), Middleton to Barnes, 10 June 1931.
[57] These were all listed in AERI (Agricultural Economics Research Institute), *Agricultural Economics, 1913–1938: Being the Twenty-Fifth Annual Report of the Agricultural Economics Research Institute* (Oxford, 1938).
[58] B. Short, C. Watkins, W. Foot, and P. Kinsman, *The National Farm Survey 1941–1943: State Surveillance and the Countryside in England and Wales in the Second World War* (Wallingford, 2000), p. 22.

J. Pryse Howell's work on hill farming, which has been identified by Moore-Colyer as 'the first British example of a carefully-conducted farm management survey'.[59] John Maxton, who was on the staff of the AERI at the time, wrote a report on Warren's methodology (of which the Ministry of Agriculture was aware, to judge from its presence in their files) for the Empire Marketing Board, and Currie and Long had employed it for their survey of seventeen parishes around Dartington in south Devon.[60] In 1930, the Cambridge University Farm Economics Branch (one of whose members, R.McG. Carslaw, had studied farm management research in the USA) carried out a survey of Hertfordshire.[61] By this time, it seems that most UK agricultural economists were leaning towards the survey approach, believing that in order to understand farming, the only meaningful method was the large-scale survey of inputs/outputs, costs, and incomes.[62] Thus there was an intellectual context within the strict confines of agricultural economics and policy that encouraged the systematic collection of datasets, although it is worth noting that collection of farm account data in Britain was probably still lagging behind that in continental Europe. By the end of the 1930s, farm account data was being collected on a significant scale in Switzerland, Denmark, the Netherlands, Belgium, and Germany, where it was compulsory for larger farms (over about 250 acres) to keep accounts.[63] And in Britain, this coincided with the advent of large-scale data gathering exercises in other branches of social science in the interwar period, such as the work on land use by Dudley Stamp.[64]

Using the FMS

By 1936, the Ministry of Agriculture had obtained approval from the Treasury to begin the FMS.[65] It was operated by the Provincial Agricultural Economists, who were based in university agriculture departments and some of the agricultural colleges. For the farms to be

---

[59] J. Pryse Howell, *The Productivity of Hill Farming* (Oxford, 1922); R. Moore-Colyer, *Farming in Wales 1936–2011* (Talybont, 2011), p. 91.
[60] J. Maxton, *The Survey Method of Research in Farm Economics* (London, 1929); TNA, MAF38/198, FMS proposals 1928–1931; J.R. Currie and W. Harwood Long, *An Agricultural Survey in South Devon* (Newton Abbot and Totnes, 1929).
[61] University of Cambridge, Farm Economics Branch, *An Economic Survey of Hertfordshire Agriculture* (Report no. 18, Cambridge, 1931).
[62] Whetham, *Agricultural Economists in Britain*, pp. 58–61.
[63] P. Lamartine Yates, *Food Production in Western Europe: An Economic Survey of Agriculture in Six Countries* (London, 1940), pp. 82, 149, 212, 391, 467.
[64] L.D. Stamp, *The Land of Britain: Its Use and Misuse* (London, 1948).
[65] There is a more detailed account of the process in P. Brassley, D. Harvey, M. Lobley, and M. Winter, 'Accounting for Agriculture: The Origins of the Farm Management Survey', *Agric. Hist. Rev.* 61 (2013), pp. 135–53.

investigated in Devon, Cornwall, and Dorset, it was originally based at Seale-Hayne Agricultural College outside Newton Abbot, but the Investigation Officers based there subsequently came under the control of the University of Bristol, and later moved to the University of Exeter. The farms in these counties were initially selected on the basis of their involvement in dairy farming, whereas those in other regions had different specialisations. This did not mean that they were purely dairy farms, or that they always remained in dairying, but it did imply that at some point in their history they had had a dairy herd. As the FMS unit moved between its various sites, it took its archives with it. At Exeter, the staff of what became the Agricultural Economics Unit were housed in a Victorian building with a cellar, in which were deposited over sixty years of the individual FMS field books. As each field book comprises over twenty pages and around 240 to 300 farms were included in the Survey in the south-west each year, the volume of field books was, and is, enormous. The cellar also yielded a large collection of published, often with only a limited circulation, and unpublished reports from the Agricultural Economics Unit, many of which were based directly or indirectly on FMS data. In short, for the historian of twentieth-century agriculture it proved a veritable treasure trove, the more so when we discovered, rather surprisingly, that it was not matched by similar collections elsewhere.[66] As far as we could determine, the field books at other FMS units had either been lost or deliberately destroyed. This is not to say that all the information has been lost. In order to maintain the anonymity of the survey, the analysed data from the field books was transferred to anonymised summary sheets, which were then sent to the Ministry of Agriculture. With the demise of the Ministry, these were transferred to the Museum of English Rural Life at the University of Reading, where they may be consulted. However, being anonymised, they do not reveal the names or addresses of the farmers and farms involved, which the field books at Exeter still do.[67]

In theory, no farmer was supposed to remain in the FMS sample for more than fifteen years. The logic behind this decision was that over time farmers might learn from the analyses of their farm businesses and change the management of their farms accordingly. In consequence, they might no longer be typical of their farm size and type, which would be a serious shortcoming in a survey that was designed to produce reliable

---

[66] The archive is now stored in the Exeter University building occupied by the Centre for Rural Policy Research, the successor to the Agricultural Economics Unit.

[67] Research on this archive, which provides the basic material of this book, was grant-aided by ESRC grant RES-062-23-1831 (Processes of Technical Change in British Agriculture: Innovation in the Farming of South West England 1935–1985) between 2009 and 2013.

data on farm incomes. In practice, it was not always easy to recruit new farms to the survey, so although some farms only remained in it for a few years, others remained for much longer. Some that were initially recruited in the 1940s were still part of the Survey in the 1980s. While there may have been questions about their typicality from an economic viewpoint, these long-serving members were especially useful for historians, as they made it possible to trace the history of a farm and the technical changes that affected it over, in some cases, a forty-year period. In total, it proved possible to extract data from the field books for 168 different farms, with some data for up to 215 separate variables. For about thirty of these farms, there was a significant quantity of data over twenty-five years or more.

Furthermore, in twenty-five cases it proved possible to contact the farmers involved and to interview them. The oldest of these farmers were in their nineties by the time of the interview, and there were many in their seventies and eighties. On other farms, the farmer originally involved in the Survey had died, but it was possible to interview the son (it was always a son) who had taken over the farm. Detailed preparation was required before the interview was carried out, including obtaining approval for the interview methodology from the Exeter University Ethics Committee. One of the stipulations of this approval was that all interviewees were asked to sign forms consenting to the interview and to its subsequent use in research. Before the interview, using the FMS data spreadsheet prepared for the farm together with the original field books, a short outline farm history of about seven hundred to a thousand words was written, covering the major changes in outputs and inputs, usually by the interviewer. From this, a timeline showing the major changes in land and enterprises, labour, investments, and technical changes was produced and printed on to a sheet of A3 paper (see fig 1.1). The purpose of this was to provide a focus for the interview, in that the interviewer could use it initially to summarise its purpose, and later to ask about specific changes.

A further series of questions, again using the farm history, was written to guide the interviewer. The first part of these related specifically to the farm, and some idea of the kind of detail that it is possible to explore can be seen from table 1.1, which shows some of the questions asked of a dairy farmer in Dorset.

In addition to the questions relating specifically to the farm, interviewees were also asked questions about their personal characteristics and management activities in order to provide information about their attitudes to risk and other business activities, and the sources of information they used in the course of making decisions. These included questions about their education and training, use of advisory services, membership of farming organisations, and use of printed and broadcast media. The interviews generally took between one and two hours,

Farm 3/1

Land & Enterprises (1939 – 1984):
- 1946 – 110 acres dairy
- 1958 – all grass farm
- 1969 end of poultry
- 1984 – 184 acres dairy

Labour (1939 – 1984):
- 1946 – 3 workers + farmer
- 1950 – J becomes partner
- 1964 – 1 worker + son + farmer
- 1976 – H becomes partner

Investment (1939 – 1984):
- 1958/61 deep litter houses
- 1966 new parlour & dairy
- 1972-83 drainage
- 1973-8 more cubicles

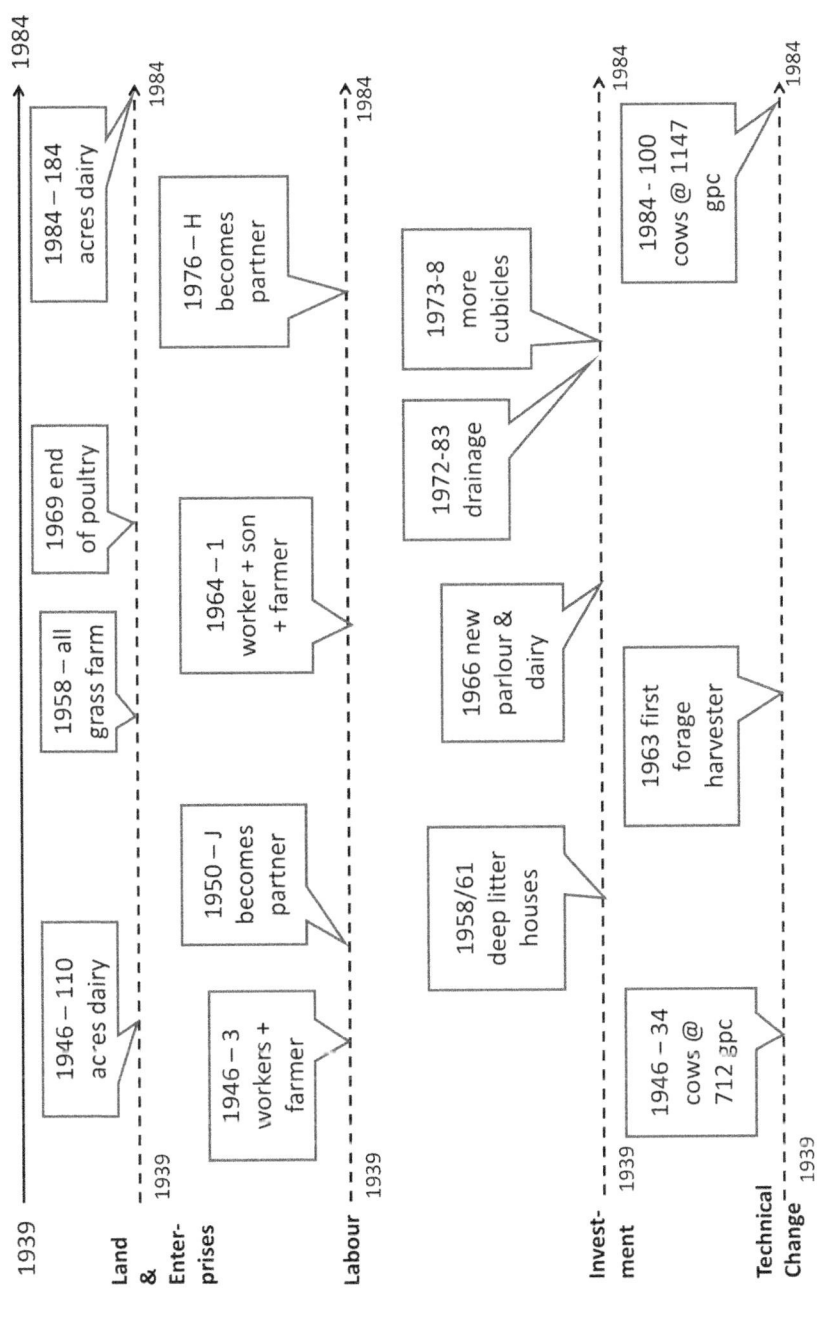

Technical Change (1939 – 1984):
- 1946 – 34 cows @ 712 gpc
- 1963 first forage harvester
- 1984 – 100 cows @ 1147 gpc

FIG. 1.1: Timeline for farm 3/1

TABLE 1.1. Farm-related questions for farm 3/1

Land and enterprises
Tenanted or owner-occupied?
How long has family farmed here?
Is this part of the Blackmore Vale dairy area?
Did the farm size expand by purchase or tenancy?
Poultry up to 650 hens on deep litter by 1964, but ended 1969 – why?
After 1958 an all-grass farm – why not grow cereals for concentrates?
Were the cattle always dairy followers – no beef?

Labour
Labour decreased by one from 1946 to 1964, when one worker + one son + farmer, and by 1984 was still one worker plus family. Was it never possible to dispense with employed labour?
Your father became a partner in 1950 – how much did grandfather still do?
You became partner in 1976 – how much did father still do?

Investment
Water mains laid 1968?
Always had mains electricity?
1972–83 drainage schemes – all with grant aid?
What happened to deep litter houses after poultry went?
Grandfather bought a milking machine for £140 in 1946 – was that the first?
First major investment was a new parlour and dairy in 1966 and cubicles for sixty-seven cows. Why was the investment made then?
Was that when you first went to a bulk tank (another bought in 1982)?
More cubicles in various stages between 1973 and 1978 – herd expansion?

Technical change
Milk production expanded by nearly five times over forty years, with more cows and more milk per cow. How could you keep more cows?
And how did you improve yields?
Breed changes?
You had three acres of maize for silage in 1946–7. The crop failed completely, but you were already producing grass silage – when did that start?
Were you aware of being an early silage adopter or was it common round here?
Moderate fertiliser use (125 units/ac 1984) and stocking rate?
Concentrates equivalent to 3.8lbs per gallon in 1978 – heavy concentrate use?
First forage harvester in 1963 – how did you make silage then?
New tractor for £303 in 1946 – was it the first?
1/3 share in sprayer after 1972 and buying sprays after that – what for?
Were the changes on this farm typical of those on Blackmore Vale dairy farms?

although some were longer, and when transcribed from the audio-recording were between five and ten thousand words.[68]

Of the twenty-five interviews, eleven were conducted with the farmer currently running the farm, speaking to one or two interviewers. He was usually the son of the farmer who had initially been recruited into the survey and had taken over the running of the farm part way through the survey period. In a further three cases, it was the farmer who had initially been recruited who was interviewed, again on his own. A further five sessions involved the farmer and his wife together, another two the farmer with his wife and son, and four with other combinations of family members: farmer and son, farmer and daughter (who by the time of the interview was herself running the farm), farmer, wife, son, and daughter, and farmer, father, mother, and sister. It goes almost without saying, but is worth emphasising nevertheless, that we are extremely grateful to these farming families who welcomed us into their homes, provided us with refreshment, readily revealed details of their lives, and gave us permission to use the richly detailed material that resulted. These interviews are extensively quoted throughout the book, the farmers concerned being identified by the FMS code numbers of their farms (e.g. farmer 466, or farmer 2/7).

No research has previously been undertaken that uses the FMS field books in this way. Not only do they comprise an un-tapped historical source but also one that is uniquely well suited to solving a long-standing problem in agricultural history. Work that uses an oral history approach has confirmed that farmers hold much data on agricultural and landscape change, especially connected with technological and farm developments, which can fill many of the gaps in official records.[69] Until now, this information has remained largely unexplored in academic terms because of its qualitative, discursive, and non-codified nature. The oral history element of this project is crucial in that it allows us to focus on local detail and the embedded experience of technology. Being both methodologically and theoretically innovative, the oral history approach provides a reservoir of 'soft data' to augment and add depth to the FMS and other data sources by forging a conceptualisation of local knowledge, as a distinctive way of knowing the world that is rooted in a particular *locale*, thus positioning the farmer as a 'contextual expert'.

---

[68] The transcriptions are available from the Essex University UK Data Archive, reference SN851111, Processes of Technical Change in British Agriculture: Innovation in the Farming of South West England, 1935–1985 (http://doi.org/10.5255/UKDA-SN-851111).

[69] Riley, '"Ask the Fellows Who Cut the Hay"'; Harvey and Riley, '"Fighting from the Fields"'; D.C. Harvey and M. Riley, 'Country Stories: The Use of Oral Histories of the Countryside to Challenge the Sciences of the Past and Future', *Interdisciplinary Science Reviews* 30 (2005), pp. 19–32.

Contents and Arguments

The structure of this book is determined by the arguments that we have outlined above. In other words, we accept that technical change in agriculture occurred in a context of off-farm research and development and expansionist agricultural policy and argue that the particular circumstances and characteristics of individual farms were instrumental in explaining the nature and rate of technical innovation and adoption. The book is therefore divided into two parts. In the remainder of part 1, we discuss the research and development and policy context. Although there have been previous surveys of agricultural science in the UK,[70] they have not attempted to explain why the resources devoted to research and development were expanded so significantly in the 1950s and '60s and subsequently reduced, and so this is our main focus in chapter 2. In chapter 3, we examine the various ways in which farmers became involved in this world of new technology, by trying to assess the development and impact of education and extension in UK agriculture. Then in chapter 4 we consider the agricultural policy context and trace the political changes behind the policy measures that encouraged farmers to increase production.

In the second part of the book, we change the focus to the farm and its technology. Since most of the farms that we investigated in detail were dairy farms, or at least began with a dairy herd, chapter 5 looks at dairy farming and the changes in breeding, feeding, housing, and disease control that transformed it. As we explain at the beginning of that chapter, we contend that there are good reasons why changes in dairy farming make it a good proxy for technical change in agriculture as a whole. What emerges from tracing the history of dairying is that the availability of capital and its investment were crucial factors in technical change, so in chapter 6 we look at credit and other sources of capital and discuss how they were influenced by changes in tenancy and the growth of owner-occupation in UK farming. The counterpart of increased capital investment was the decline in the farm labour force, so in chapter 7 we show how farmers and their families, assisted by increasing mechanisation, became the principal component of the labour force. One of the factors that facilitated this change was the increasing specialisation of farms as, usually, one main enterprise came to dominate the farming business, and we examine the history of this tendency in chapter 8, while in chapter 9 we look at the other side of this coin, asking why it was the pig and poultry enterprises that were the most usual casualties of specialisation on dairy farms. Finally, in chapter 10 we show how these

---

[70] E.J. Russell, *A History of Agricultural Science in Great Britain* (London, 1966); Blaxter and Robertson, *From Dearth to Plenty.*

Introduction: Exploring Agricultural Change

farm-level studies can reveal important conclusions about the process of technical change in UK agriculture as a whole.

First, though, we turn to the technical and political environment within which farmers in Britain had to work. Agricultural policy, as we shall see in chapter 4, changed radically in the ten years between 1937 and 1947, largely in response to forces external to agriculture. The farmers' technical environment changed too, partly because of the activities of firms in the agricultural supply industries, and partly in response to these agricultural policy changes, which led to associated changes in government spending on research and its transmission to the agricultural industry. This research and development story forms the subject of the following two chapters.

2

The Organisation of Agricultural Science, 1935–85

If the state requires an agricultural industry that produces more, and produces it more efficiently, and expects those output and efficiency gains to arise largely from scientific and technical changes, it should presumably, in a perfect world, invest in science to produce new technology and then ensure that farmers and their workers acquire familiarity with that new technology. This chapter is therefore concerned with investments in agricultural science, by both the state, on which there is much information, and by private firms, on which there is much less. It does not attempt to outline the work of agricultural scientists, their discoveries, and developments, or the resultant changes in technologies and practices in this period. There are two reasons for this: first, to do so would require another book of at least the length of the present one; secondly, two agricultural scientists, Sir Kenneth Blaxter and Noel Robertson, published almost exactly that book in 1995.[1] What they did not do was to explain at any length why governments chose to fund agricultural research, or how they administered it, or how its results were supposed to be passed on to farmers. This chapter concentrates on the first two of these questions, and the following chapter attempts to trace the problems encountered in moving from science to practice. As a shorthand term for this process, we shall refer to it as a knowledge network. Since the science and its onward transmission in knowledge networks are intimately linked, it is appropriate to begin with a brief survey of the literature that is relevant to both chapters.

There are numerous theoretical approaches to the analysis of knowledge networks, in which we include here the analysis of technical innovation, diffusion, and adoption, although it could be argued that a knowledge network is simply one part of that larger process. A crude division would be between economic and sociological models, and it is crude because many of the models analyse both economic and sociological variables, although some privilege an economic methodology while

---

[1] K. Blaxter and N. Robertson, *From Dearth to Plenty: The Modern Revolution in Food Production* (Cambridge, 1995).

others write from a sociological perspective. Thus Hayami and Ruttan with their induced innovation concept (essentially, that technical change is a response to factor price changes) would be among the more obviously economic in approach, although they emphasise the importance of land tenure and other rural institutions.[2] From a more sociological perspective, Oudshoorn and Pinch emphasise the role of users in constructing technical change, Clarke examines the 'social worlds' in which the various actors in the process of technical change interact, and Murdoch et al. attempt to identify the conventions operating in a market and how they change over time in response to technical change.[3] There are also other theoretical perspectives that are more difficult to slot neatly into the economic/sociological division. From the viewpoint of an industry such as agriculture, which has been extensively influenced by government policy in the last eighty years, one of the more interesting is the 'triple helix' concept, which examines university–industry–government relations and distinguishes between circumstances in which scientific peers assess quality and decide upon research priorities, or socio-economic problems determine the research agenda, and a triple helix in which groups from academia, industry, and government meet to address economic, institutional, and intellectual problems.[4] Another approach based on an agricultural study is the Authority–Discourse–Media model, which attempts to identify the ways in which new technologies achieve a dominant intellectual position and in so doing undergo changes in the discourses used to discuss them and the media in which the different discourses appear.[5] This could perhaps be seen as a similar approach, using different language, to the concept of 'travelling facts', analysed in an agricultural context by Howlett and Velkar.[6]

[2] Y. Hayami and V. Ruttan, *Agricultural Development: An International Perspective* (Baltimore, MD, 1985); see also B.M. Koppel, *Induced Innovation Theory and International Agricultural Development: A Reassessment* (Baltimore, MD, 1995); P. Geroski, 'Models of Technology Diffusion', *Research Policy* 29 (2000), pp. 603–25.

[3] N. Oudshoorn and T. Pinch (eds), *How Users Matter: The Co-construction of Users and Technologies* (Cambridge, MA, 2003); A.E. Clarke, *Disciplining Reproduction: Modernity, American Life Sciences, and 'the Problems of Sex'* (Berkeley, CA, 1998); J. Murdoch, T. Marsden, and J. Banks, 'Quality, Nature and Embeddedness: Some Theoretical Considerations in the Context of the Food Sector', *Economic Geography* 76 (2000), pp. 107–25.

[4] L. Leydesdorff, 'The Triple Helix: An Evolutionary Model of Innovations', *Research Policy* 29 (2000), pp. 243–55; T. Shinn, 'The Triple Helix and the New Production of Knowledge: Prepackaged Thinking on Science and Technology', *Social Studies of Science* 32 (2002), pp. 599–614.

[5] P. Brassley, 'Cutting across Nature? The History of Artificial Insemination in Pigs in the UK', *Studies in the History and Philosophy of Biological and Biomedical Sciences* 38 (2007), pp. 442–61.

[6] P. Howlett and A. Velkar, 'Technology Transfer and Travelling Facts: A

What emerges from this very brief and partial survey of the literature is that any analysis of a knowledge network should attempt to consider its whole history from the original commissioning of the relevant research, the principal concern of this chapter, to the established use of the resulting technologies, covered in the following chapter, in the context of agriculture in the United Kingdom.

Agricultural Science: Organisation and Administration

At the beginning of the Second World War, public agricultural science in the UK was funded by the Development Commission, working through the Agricultural Research Council (ARC), which had been established in 1931 and adopted a way of working that changed little until the late 1960s or early 1970s.[7] The basic pattern was that it funded a combination of research institutes and research units. For the latter, in particular, the policy was to match a problem with a research leader of proven ability, who would then be given the requisite staff, equipment, facilities, and funding and 'a free hand for the pursuit of the relevant research'. This emphasis on the pursuit of scientific knowledge was echoed in the ARC's attitude to research in the university schools of agriculture and veterinary medicine. Education was regarded as the primary function of such schools. Research was seen to be an essential part of their activities, but the Council felt that research programmes should be determined 'by the interests and capabilities of the members of the teaching staff ... and not by the general needs of practical agriculture'. These principles appear to have been discussed intensively in the Council meetings of November and December 1943 and appear to privilege a pure research approach, which is perhaps surprising given the state of the war at the time they were articulated.[8]

This question of the balance between fundamental and applied research also appeared in a confidential report on post-war agricultural research needs that the ARC sent to the Ministry in 1946.[9] The report was based on the findings of various specialist groups that had been meeting for the previous two years. While all of them discussed research in relation to the needs of the various branches of the agricultural industry – reclamation

---

Perspective from Indian Agriculture', in P. Howlett and M.S. Morgan (eds), *How Well Do Facts Travel? The Dissemination of Reliable Knowledge* (Cambridge, 2011), pp. 273–300.

[7] W. Henderson, 'British Agricultural Research and the Agricultural Research Council: A Personal Historical Account', in G.W. Cooke (ed.), *Agricultural Research 1931–1981: A History of the Agricultural Research Council and a Review of Developments in Agricultural Science during the Last Fifty Years* (London, 1981), pp. 3–113.

[8] Henderson, 'British Agricultural Research', pp. 33, 40.

[9] TNA, MAF 117/343, ARC, Post-War Programme, June 1946.

of peat soils, the effects of trace element deficiencies, drainage, and crop water requirements – they also emphasised the need for more basic science: in relation to animal physiology, for example, they argued for the establishment of an institute 'which, while pursuing fundamental research in the special physiology of farm animals (including animal nutrition), would also deal with applied aspects ...'[10] The general conclusions of the report re-emphasised this point. The Council felt that

> the essential requirement is for more fundamental knowledge, which would find practical applications in many directions. One possible instance of such an application is perhaps worth mention. It has been estimated that the capital needs for the modernisation of farm buildings amount to some £100 million, much of it in relation to milk production and the keeping of farm animals. The physiological needs of the animals are, however, not sufficiently known to ensure that such buildings are properly designed and the requisite information should clearly be obtained.[11]

An important corollary of this emphasis on the basic principles, the Council felt, was that research carried out in Britain would also be useful to the colonies, 'which tend to look to this country for fundamental research' even though their specific conditions might be different. The report identified several fields of research in which new institutes were needed, including vegetable production, fruit research in Scotland, grassland research, in which Stapledon's existing research station at Drayton in Warwickshire was thought 'too extreme in soil type to provide satisfactory conditions for research', plant pathology and entomology, animal breeding and poultry research. In other areas, the numbers of scientists and the provision of facilities in the existing institutions needed to be increased. The need to employ and extend the statistical expertise that Fisher and Yates had developed at Rothamsted for the benefit of all agricultural research workers was specifically mentioned.[12] In order to bring these changes about, the current expenditure of the ARC would have to nearly double, from £737,000 per year to £1,441,000, with an additional capital sum of £2,535,000. While this might appear to be a dramatic increase, the report argued, it in fact only represented an increase from a farthing to a halfpenny per pound sterling of agricultural output.

---

10   TNA MAF 117/343, p. 8.
11   TNA MAF 117/343, p. 13.
12   TNA MAF 117/343, pp.10–11; G. Parolini, '"Making Sense of Figures": Statistics, Computing and Information Technologies in Agriculture and Biology in Britain, 1920s–1960s' (unpublished Dottorato di Ricerca thesis, Università di Bologna, 2013), pp. 54–84.

The Agricultural Research Institutes and Units

The subsequent development of agricultural research institutions in Britain in the 1950s and 1960s suggests that the basic premises of this 1946 report, if not its fine detail, were accepted by succeeding governments. Several agricultural research stations had been financed by the Development Commission before the First World War, and the number increased between the wars, with their funding being brought under ARC control in 1931. As table 2.1 demonstrates, several new institutes were established in the immediate post-war years, and more in the 1950s and early 1960s, by which time there were nearly twice as many as there had been in 1939.

TABLE 2.1. ARC research institutes

Research institutes in existence by 1939	
Rothamsted Experimental Station, Harpenden, Herts	Soils, fertilisers, and crops
Long Ashton Research Station, Bristol	Fruit and cider
John Innes Institute, initially Merton, Surrey, finally Norwich	Botany and horticulture
National Institute for Research in Dairying, Shinfield, Reading	Dairying
Plant Breeding Institute, Cambridge	Crop breeding
Rowett Research Institute, Aberdeen	Animal nutrition
East Malling Research Station, Kent	Fruit
Experimental and Research Centre, Cheshunt, relocated to Littlehampton, Sussex, in 1953 as the Glasshouse Crops Research Institute	Horticulture
Welsh Plant Breeding Station, Aberystwyth	Crops and grass varieties
Animal Diseases Research Association, Moredun Institute, Edinburgh	Veterinary research
Scottish Plant Breeding Station, Edinburgh	Crop breeding
Foot and Mouth Disease Research Institute, Pirbright, later the Animal Virus Research Institute	Foot and Mouth Disease and other virus diseases
National Institute of Agricultural Engineering, Oxford, later at Silsoe	Farm machinery

Hannah Dairy Research Institute, Auchincruive, Ayrshire	Dairy farming
Macaulay Institute for Soil Research, Aberdeen	Soils
The Field Station, Compton, Berks, from 1963 the Institute for Research on Animal Diseases	Veterinary research
Research institutes established after 1939	
1940: Grassland Improvement Station, Drayton, Warwickshire, moved to Hurley, Berkshire, from 1950	Grassland management
1945: Animal Breeding Research Organisation, Edinburgh, formerly the Institute of Animal Genetics	Animal breeding
1947: The Poultry Research Centre, Edinburgh	Poultry farming, especially nutrition
1947: Wye College, Kent, Department of Hops Research	Hops
1948: Institute of Animal Physiology, Babraham, Cambridge	Physiology of farm livestock
1948: Houghton Poultry Research Station, Cambridge	Poultry disease
1948: The National Vegetable Research Station, Wellesbourne, Warwickshire	Vegetable crop improvement
1953: Hill Farming Research Organisation, Scotland	Ecology and animal nutrition on hill land
1953: Scottish Horticultural Research Institute, Invergowrie	Horticulture, especially soft fruit
1957: Radiobiological Laboratory, Letcombe, Wantage	Radioactivity in food
1960: Weed Research Organisation, Begbroke Hill, Oxford	Weeds and herbicides
1963: Meat Research Institute, Bristol	Carcase meat
1965: Food Research Institute, Norwich	Food storage

Source: W. Henderson, 'British Agricultural Research', pp. 17, 56–73, 351–7.

In addition to the organisations listed in table 2.1, there were others whose work was relevant to agriculture but were funded from non-ARC sources. They included the Central Veterinary Laboratory, Weybridge, the Agricultural Economics Research Institute in the University of Oxford, the Chipping Campden Station for Fruit and Vegetable Preservation, and the National Institute of Agricultural Botany, all of which had been established before 1939 and continued to operate after 1945.[13]

Other institutes, as table 2.1 demonstrates, changed their names and/or locations. What began as the Institute for Research in Agricultural Engineering in Oxford had re-located to Askham Bryan in Yorkshire as the National Institute for Agricultural Engineering (NIAE) by 1943 before eventually finding its permanent home at Silsoe in Bedfordshire. The Potato Virus Research Station at Cambridge became the Plant Virus Research Station, and the Scottish Plant Breeding Station, which had started life as the Scottish Society for Research in Plant Breeding in Edinburgh, moved to the Pentlandfield Research Station at Roslin, a few miles south of the city, by 1958 – hence the 'Pentland' prefix for the various potato varieties bred there. The NIAE Scottish Station also re-located from Howden in Midlothian to Penicuik, just down the road from Roslin, and the Hill Farming Research Organisation also started in Edinburgh although the bulk of its work was done on several research farms spread across Scotland. Other name changes included the Institute of Animal Genetics in Edinburgh, which had become the Animal Breeding Research Organisation by 1953; the Foot and Mouth Disease Research Institute, which became the Animal Virus Research Institute but remained at Pirbright in Surrey; the Field Experiment Station at Compton, which became the Institute for Research on Animal Diseases; and the Cambridge University Unit of Animal Physiology, which became the Institute of Animal Physiology at Babraham, south-east of the city. The Grassland Improvement Station, which began at Drayton near Stratford on Avon in 1940, under the direction of Sir George Stapledon, became the Grassland Research Institute in 1949 and moved to Hurley, near Maidenhead (Berks.). It is interesting to note that there were often English or Welsh and Scottish research institutes covering the same subject areas – Rothamsted and the Macaulay Institute both dealt with soils, the NIAE had a Scottish Station, and there were plant breeders in Cambridge, Aberystwyth, and Edinburgh. In part, obviously, this reflected the different strengths and requirements of different regions of the country. It would have made little sense to try to conduct Aberystwyth's grassland work in Cambridge or the Plant Breeding Institute's cereal breeding in Aberystwyth. But it may also have had something to do with the fact that English and Welsh research institutes were originally funded by the Ministry of Agriculture,

---

[13] Henderson, 'British Agricultural Research', p. 15.

The Organisation of Agricultural Science

whereas those in Scotland were funded by the Department of Agriculture and Fisheries for Scotland (DAFS), and this remained the case even after the ARC took over funding responsibility in England and Wales under the terms of the 1956 Agricultural Research Act.[14]

What emerges from this brief survey is that there was a significant institutional expansion in agricultural research after 1945. All of the institutes listed in table 2.1 continued in existence into the 1980s and often expanded their staffing and activities. In the decade after 1985, many were amalgamated, privatised, or closed down, but that story is beyond the remit of this book.[15]

In addition to supporting the work of these research stations and institutes, which were in some cases entirely independent bodies and in some cases affiliated to universities, the ARC also funded research units within research institutes and universities. In 1941, Lord Hankey's Committee recommended that more outstanding scientists should be attracted into agricultural research, and the ARC responded to this with the concept of the ARC Unit, in which a problem was matched with an able research leader who would be given staff, equipment, facilities, and funding, and 'a free hand for the pursuit of the relevant research'. The first two of these units were established in 1941: the Unit of Soil Enzyme Chemistry at Rothamsted under Dr J.H. Quastel, and the Unit of Animal Physiology at Cambridge under Sir Joseph Barcroft. Quastel's unit was disbanded when he moved to Canada in 1947, and Barcroft's unit developed into the Institute of Animal Physiology, but by then the model had become established.[16] Between 1947 and 1960, eighteen such units were established, as table 2.2 demonstrates. After 1960, the rate at which these research units were formed decreased, but another six emerged in the 1960s: on flower crop physiology at Reading, nitrogen fixation at Sussex, structural chemistry at University College London, muscle mechanisms and insect physiology at Oxford, invertebrate chemistry and physiology shared between Sussex and Cambridge, and developmental botany at Cambridge.[17]

---

[14] Henderson, 'British Agricultural Research', pp. 17, 21, 56–73, 351–7; R. Wilkins, S. Jarvis, and M. Blackwell (eds), *The Hurley and North Wyke Story: 60 Years of Grassland Research, 1949–2009* (Okehampton, 2009).

[15] Some of the story is told in C. Thirtle, P. Palladino, and J. Piesse, 'On the Organisation of Agricultural Research in the United Kingdom, 1945–1994: A Quantitative Description and Appraisal of Recent Reforms', *Research Policy* 26 (1997), pp. 557–76.

[16] Henderson, 'British Agricultural Research', p. 33.

[17] Henderson, 'British Agricultural Research', pp. 74–80.

TABLE 2.2. ARC Research Units

Unit name and location	Date established	Outcome
Virus research, Cambridge	1947	Absorbed into John Innes Institute, Norwich, 1967
Plant biochemistry, Cambridge	1947	Closed 1951
Animal reproduction, Cambridge	1949	Closed on Hammond's retirement in 1954
Experimental agronomy, Oxford	1950	Some staff founded the Weed Research Organisation, 1960; remainder continued until Blackman retired 1970
Biometrical genetics, Birmingham	1950	Closed 1967 after director moved to another university
Soil physics, Cambridge	1951	Disbanded 1978 and staff transferred to Rothamsted
Microbiology, Sheffield	1951	Moved to Norwich Food Research Institute 1965
Plant nutrition (micronutrients), Bristol	1952	Disbanded 1959 and staff transferred to Long Ashton
Cell physiology, Oxford	1953	Disbanded 1958
Plant growth substances and systemic fungicides, Wye	1953	Disbanded on Professor Ralph Wain's retirement in 1978
Embryology, Bangor	1953	Disbanded on Brambell's retirement in 1968
Statistics, Aberdeen	1954	Moved with Finney to Edinburgh in 1966
Reproductive physiology and biochemistry, Cambridge	1955	The continuation of Hammond's unit. Became part of the Institute of Animal Physiology in 1976
Animal genetics, Edinburgh	1957	Disbanded 1980
Farm buildings, NIAE Silsoe	1957	Integrated with NIAE 1966
Plant physiology, Imperial London	1959	Disbanded 1971
Plant morphogenesis and nutrition, Rothamsted	1959	Moved to Wye 1960. Disbanded 1964

Source: Henderson, 'British Agricultural Research', pp. 49–56.

The Organisation of Agricultural Science

As the titles of these units suggest, and as a reading of the Indexes of Research published by the ARC in 1954 and 1964 confirms, much of the research carried out in ARC institutes and units was basic investigation aimed at understanding processes rather than applied research on immediate practical farming problems, although this is not to say that such research had no practical impact. Blaxter's work on energy metabolism in ruminants at the Hannah Dairy Research Institute led to the formulation of new ruminant feeding standards to replace the old starch equivalent method; Lupton and Bingham's 'studies of selection techniques within hybrid populations' led to the breeding of important new winter wheat varieties, notably Maris Huntsman, at the Plant Breeding Institute (PBI); and Rowson and Polge at Cambridge pioneered techniques for semen preservation that improved the stock available to both pedigree breeders and commercial producers. On the other hand, Riley's work on 'cytogenetic structure and evolution of cereal species and their wild relatives' at the PBI, or Dawson's investigation of 'phospholipids in the epididymis' at the Cambridge Institute of Animal Physiology probably had longer-term objectives.[18]

The post-war increase in the number of research institutes was more than matched by the increase in their staff. The doubling of ARC expenditure recommended in the 1946 report (see above) was probably exceeded, to judge from the number of scientists employed. Immediately before the war, the research institutes in England and Wales had employed 144 'Graded Staff', equivalent to what was called the 'Scientific Officer' class after the war. In 1949, the number employed in this class in England and Wales had increased to 294, in 1953 to 366, and by 1955 to 438. In addition, there were in 1955 a further 161 Scientific Officers in the Scottish research institutes such as the Macaulay and the Rowett near Aberdeen and the Hannah Dairy Research Institute in Ayrshire, among others, and another 130 in the various ARC units, making a total of 729 Scientific Officer posts in the UK as a whole. By 1964, the number of scientists listed in the ARC's *Index of Agricultural Research* (and therefore probably employed in the Scientific Officer grade) reached 1,094. The work of these senior scientists was supported, in 1955 for example, by a further 567 Experimental Officers and scientific assistants. Clearly the twenty years after the war saw a major national investment in fundamental agricultural science.[19]

---

[18] ARC, *Index of Agricultural Research 1953-4* (London, 1954); ARC, *Index of Agricultural Research 1964* (London, 1965).
[19] TNA, MAF117/199, ARC, statements of staff employed on agricultural research; ARC, *Index of Agricultural Research 1964*, index.

Agricultural Research in the Universities

At the same time that the ARC-funded establishments were growing, the agriculture departments in the universities were also expanding, as table 2.3 demonstrates.

TABLE 2.3. Numbers of university academics engaged in agricultural research

	1950	1963	1975
Aberdeen	21	20	37
Belfast	32	48	53
Bristol	32	45	65
Cambridge	17 + some unnamed	24	18
Edinburgh	1 (list incomplete)	31	72
Exeter	Not listed	9	10
Leeds	21	24	9 (in animal physiology)
London Wye	40	53	71
Newcastle	22 (as King's Durham)	34	62
Nottingham	23	28	37
Oxford	35	14	26
Reading	40	109	120
Silsoe			5
Aberystwyth	35 + some unlisted economists	61	77
Bangor	7	17	8
TOTAL	326	517	670

Source:1950: British Council and Department of Scientific and Industrial Research, *Scientific Research in British Universities 1949–51* (London, 1950); 1963: DSIR and British Council, *Scientific Research in British Universities and Colleges, 1963–4* (London, 1964); 1975: British Library, *Scientific Research in British Universities and Colleges, 1974–5*, vol. II, *Biological Sciences* (London, 1975). The numbers include those listed under Animal Husbandry.

Table 2.3 cannot claim to be absolutely definitive. There is a possibility of overcounting because some researchers are listed twice, and of undercounting because some are listed under botany, zoology, and other applied sciences. It is also worth noting that the listings for the Cambridge Land Economy Department in vol. 3 (Social Sciences) of the 1975 edition are very different from those in vol. 2 (Biological Sciences) for the same year. But the overall trend is clear: to add to the thousand or more full-time agricultural researchers in the mid-1960s, there were another five hundred or so who carried out research in the universities in addition to their teaching and administrative activities, and expansion on a significant scale occurred in the quarter century between 1950 and 1975. The same trend is also revealed by another measure: the number of PhDs awarded in the largest faculty of agriculture, the one at Reading. It rose from an annual average of 1.4 in the 1930s, to 2.8 in the 1940s, 8.9 in the 1950s, 9.6 between 1960 and 1966, and 34.2 between 1988 and 1991.[20]

During the war, the Secretary of the ARC, Professor W.W.C. Topley, argued that the primary function of the universities and colleges was education, and that research, although essential, had to be 'adjusted' to that primary function. The choice of research topic, he suggested, should be determined by 'the interests and capabilities of the members of the teaching staff ... and not by the general needs of practical agriculture'.[21] Writing just after the war, Professor Comber of Leeds reiterated the primacy of the teaching function for the universities, and argued that it 'is much better for the student to have around him various teachers pursuing different lines of investigation and developing different ideas than to have teachers who are all working on the same problem and following one idea'.[22] The impact of these principles, insofar as they were widely accepted (and they do seem to have been) on the research activities of university staff, is not easy to gauge. The research topics listed in the annual guides to scientific research in British universities appear to be much the same as those listed for scientists in research institutions, which implies that the main thrust of the research effort was aimed at understanding principles rather than solving short-term problems. This interpretation seems to be supported by the departmental structure of the university schools of agriculture. In 1963, for example, only 117 academics out of a total of more than five hundred were listed as being in departments of agriculture, crop, animal or dairy husbandry, or agronomy, with the remaining four hundred being listed under specialist subjects such as agricultural botany or plant science, agricultural chemistry, agricultural zoology, or entomology or microbiology, soil science, agricultural engineering, and agricultural economics. Again, these are imperfect distinctions, because they rely on the way in which the universities chose to organise their staff and list them for the Department of Scientific and Industrial Research (DSIR). Professor Wain, at Wye, and his research team, were listed in the Chemistry Department, whereas

20 P. Harris, *The Silent Fields: One Hundred Years of Agricultural Education at Reading* (Reading, 1993), p. 114.
21 Henderson, 'British Agricultural Research', p. 40.
22 N.M. Comber, 'Discussion on the Organisation of Agricultural Research', *Agricultural Progress* 22 (1947), p. 20.

Professor Blackman at Oxford was returned under the Department of Agronomy, but both were carrying out similar work in the development of pesticides. And clearly the work of the specialists was not necessarily irrelevant to current farming concerns. In the Soil Science Department at Newcastle, for example, Professor Peter Arnold and his colleagues Peter Askew, Fred Hunter, and Joyce Pringle were listed as investigating restoration problems on open-cast coal sites, lime and fertiliser responses on hill swards, and soil–water relationships on moorland peats, all topics of direct relevance to the local farmers, as well as cation–anion relationships in soils and soil morphology.[23]

As the discussion above suggests, the major period of expansion of agricultural research came between the end of the war and 1960, when sixteen ARC units and ten research institutes were established. The Chairman of the ARC for much of this time (1948–58) was Lord Rothschild, an active and relatively young (thirty-seven at the time of his appointment) researcher on embryo fertilisation at Cambridge. He was soon joined by W.L. (later Sir William) Slater, who had also started his career as a practising scientist, in biochemistry with the nutritionist Sir Jack Drummond at University College London. In 1929, the Elmhirsts recruited him to establish the estate laboratory at Dartington, but he soon became involved in the management of the estate, developed a reputation as a competent administrator, and was seconded to the Ministry of Agriculture in 1942. Between 1944 and 1949, he was Secretary of the Agricultural Improvement Council (AIC) (see below), where he was closely involved in the establishment of the National Agricultural Advisory Service (NAAS).[24] It is tempting to attribute the steady expansion of the ARC in this period to the leadership of these two dynamic and well-connected figures at a time when policy requirements for agricultural expansion were reasonably clear and the administrative environment was generally stable, and there is some justification for such a view. Both were involved in the negotiations around the formulation of the 1956 Agricultural Research Act that resulted in the transfer of funding of the agricultural research institutes from the Ministry of Agriculture into direct ARC control, and the Trend Report on the organisation of civil science in 1963 suggested that no change was necessary in the administration of the ARC.[25] It is important to realise that the 1956 Agricultural Research Act did not arise from any government rethinking on the desirability of agricultural research, but simply because the Treasury 'want the ARC's funds removed from their Vote'.[26] It was not a controversial matter, or about how much research money there should be, but simply

[23] DSIR and British Council, *Scientific Research 1963–4*.
[24] Henderson, 'British Agricultural Research', pp. 64–5.
[25] *Committee of Enquiry into the Organisation of Civil Science*, Cmnd.2171, (1963–4).
[26] TNA, MAF117/409, Agricultural Research Bill 1956: papers.

about who should handle it. The only concern of civil servants at the Ministry of Agriculture, Fisheries, and Food (MAFF) at the time was that their Ministry should not lose its power to commission research if necessary. Nevertheless, the Trend Report was a sign of increasing questioning within central government of the organisation of research, in the light of increasing research expenditure and the breakdown of the pre-war distinction between pure research in the universities and applied research conducted by the research councils.[27] The Council for Scientific Policy, established in 1965, argued that the chances of securing research funding would be increased if there were some idea of the expected pay-offs, and in response the ARC Annual Report for 1965–6 contained an assessment of the value of agricultural research.[28]

The Trend Report had been commissioned by the outgoing Conservative government, and no further major questioning of scientific research spending appears to have taken place under the first Wilson government, but after the Conservatives returned to power in 1970 a Green Paper on research appeared that was to have radical implications for research in general and agricultural research in particular. This was the report by Lord Rothschild on the organisation and management of government research and development (R & D).[29] It is remembered for introducing the 'customer–contractor' principle into research funding, although it was a little more complex than that. It distinguished between basic or pure research, the simple pursuit of knowledge, for which, it argued, there is no real customer, and applied R & D. The objective of applied R & D, it argued, was to produce a product, a process, or a method of operation, and for this, it contended, scientists were not as well qualified to determine priorities as those responsible for ensuring that the needs of the nation were met. These – usually government departments – should be the customers, who decided upon a specific objective, normally with the advice of the Chief Scientist. In the case of the ARC, the customer department was clearly the Ministry of Agriculture, and Rothschild identified some £14.5 million out of the current ARC budget of £18.7 million that qualified as applied research.[30] Interestingly, Rothschild

[27] *Organisation of Civil Science*, Cmnd.2171, p. 23.
[28] Henderson, 'British Agricultural Research', p. 91.
[29] The Green Paper (Anon, *A Framework for Government Research and Development*, Cmnd.4814, 1971–2) contained two reports, one by Lord Rothschild (*The Organisation and Management of Government R & D*), and another by a working group of the Council for Scientific Policy chaired by Sir Frederick Dainton (F. Dainton, *The Future of the Research Council System*). It was followed a little later by a White Paper (Anon, *Framework for Government Research and Development*, Cmnd.5046, 1971–2), the title of which, confusingly, differed by only the initial indefinite article from the previous Green Paper. It accepted that document's major proposals.
[30] Rothschild, *Organisation and Management of Government R & D*, pp. 3–12.

had suggested something similar eighteen years earlier when, as ARC Chairman, he had spoken at the golden jubilee celebrations of the Long Ashton Research Station in 1953. He criticised the inadequate contact between farmers and researchers, the need to identify short-term problems and to prioritise work on them, and the inadequate organisation of agricultural research. Few farmers, he argued, knew much about the Agricultural Research Service or what it did.[31] The extent to which Rothschild carried these ideas with him is unknowable, but it is worth mentioning that Henderson's insider's comments on the Rothschild report are largely critical, complaining that it produced 'great resentment' throughout the Agricultural Research Service and was based on a misinterpretation by the Central Policy Review Staff of what they had been told about the likelihood of the practical application of ARC-funded work and thus how appropriate it was to customer–contractor relationships. In any case, the ARC argued, the real customers were the agricultural and ancillary industries, rather than the Ministry of Agriculture.[32] It is not surprising to find that the Ministry took a different view. Its Permanent Secretary at the time, Sir Basil Engholm, wrote a minute to the Minister, James Prior, arguing that 'if the customer is going to determine the programme and priorities for applied research, the organisation for doing this must be here since we are the customer, and not in the ARC since they are the contractor', and that 'four voices' – the scientific, that of the agricultural and food industries, the economists', and the policy voice – needed to make a contribution to the determination of research priorities.[33]

The Rothschild Report was the outward and visible sign of the change in the environment within which agricultural research was conducted. As we have seen, before the mid-1960s there was little overt questioning of the need for and conduct of research, except for Rothschild's 1953 speech, which does not appear to have had any immediate effect. In these circumstances, the pre-war domination of the research agenda by the scientists continued. But after Rothschild research in general was a political issue, and agricultural research was not isolated from the discussion. Within the ARC, a Joint Working Party, which subsequently evolved into the Joint

[31] Henderson, 'British Agricultural Research', pp. 64–5.
[32] Henderson, 'British Agricultural Research', p. 94.
[33] TNA, MAF117/544, Research and Development: proposed MAFF organisation consequent upon implementation of Rothschild Report recommendations, minute from Engholm to Prior, 30 November 1971. The Rothschild Report produced considerable discussion between the Ministry and the ARC on the necessary organisational changes. The records of these are found in a series of files from MAF 117/540 (1969–70) to MAF 117/147 (1972). However, they shed little light on the Ministry's attitudes to research in general; they are more concerned with ensuring that the administrative arrangements are in place to ensure that the Ministry's views are heard.

Consultative Organisation (JCO), was set up in 1972 involving representatives of the ARC, the agricultural departments (MAFF and DAFS), and the Department of Education and Science. The JCO operated through a structure of five Boards (Animals, Arable Crops and Forage, Horticulture, Engineering and Buildings, and Food Science and Technology), the first three of which were chaired by farmers and growers. Within these Boards were subsidiary committees, which were generally chaired by agricultural scientists. This became a large organisation, involving some three hundred people at one point, and in addition the Ministry of Agriculture also created an R & D Requirements Board of Deputy Secretaries and the Chief Economist, chaired by the Chief Scientist (a post created in 1972). This pattern appears to have been maintained until the ARC was reformed into the Agricultural and Food Research Council (AFRC) in 1983.[34] In 1984, the JCO was replaced by the Priorities Board for Research in Agriculture and Food, and in 1994 the functions of the AFRC were taken over by the Biotechnology and Biological Sciences Research Council (BBSRC).[35]

These developments in the administration and control of agricultural research follow the pattern that historians have observed in other subject areas. For example, Sabine Clarke has observed that the ARC was like the Medical Research Council in the 1950s and early 1960s, in that it was not subordinate to the authority of civil servants or politicians. Both councils claimed that this ensured free enquiry among research workers, which was the only way in which research could flourish.[36] Scientists, in other words, should decide upon what constituted knowledge and truth and what should be researched. The alternative, which was much closer to Rothschild's approach, was that social and economic problems should determine the research agenda. However, there is another school of thought that identifies a 'triple helix' of research in which 'specific groups inside academia, enterprise and the government meet in order to address new problems arising in a deeply changing economic, institutional and intellectual world'.[37] This would appear to be close to the concept of the AIC, the history of which is discussed further in chapter 3.

The evidence so far, therefore, on the motivations and attitudes of governments, scientists, advisers, farmers, and the ancillary industries on

---

[34] Henderson, 'British Agricultural Research', pp. 66, 101–2; P. Gummett, *Scientists in Whitehall* (Manchester, 1980), pp. 143–6.

[35] M. Winter, *Rural Politics: Policies for Agriculture, Forestry and the Environment* (London, 1996), pp. 250–3; Thirtle et al., 'On the Organisation of Agricultural Research', p. 559.

[36] S. Clarke, 'The Research Council System and the Politics of Medical and Agricultural Research for the British Colonial Empire, 1940–1952', *Medical History* 57 (2013), pp. 338–58.

[37] Shinn, 'The Triple Helix', p. 600.

agricultural R & D appears to indicate, as argued above, that it changed from generally uncritical enthusiasm for about twenty to twenty-five years from the beginning of the Second World War, to increasing questioning of the type and value of research in agriculture for the quarter century after 1965. A succession of governments before 1965 allowed agricultural scientists and the scientific establishment more generally to pursue a science-driven research agenda and appear to have accepted the argument that this was the most effective way of reacting to the then-current priority to respond to wartime food shortages and post-war foreign exchange shortages by increasing domestic agricultural production. Thereafter, various governments, but especially Conservative ones, questioned agricultural research spending and how it was administered. They also took the view that 'near market' research might be better done by the private sector, so the research contribution of commercial firms must now be examined.

Agricultural Research by Commercial Firms

Government-funded agricultural research is comparatively well documented in comparison with research by commercial firms, but it is important to recognise that these too carried out research, varying from the sort of straightforward plant breeding carried out by seed companies such as Nickersons, who developed their own breeding programme from 1959, to the chemical screening programmes of pesticide manufacturers and the husbandry research of the fertiliser companies.[38] It should almost go without saying that the scientists in the research establishments discussed earlier were operating in an international environment, in which papers in scientific journals and speakers at conferences might be drawn from anywhere in the world. Considerations of commercial confidentiality could mean that the same did not necessarily apply to the commercial world, but in practice international share ownership and licensing agreements usually meant that profitable products in one country soon found a market elsewhere, and some companies went to great lengths to ensure that their scientists remained involved in the professional, as opposed to commercial, world, and continued to publish in learned journals. May & Baker, for example, co-operated with the American firm Am Chem and Rhone-Poulenc in France, and with Professor Wain at Wye on the development of phenoxybutyrate herbicides, and ICI acquired Bayer Agriculture when they took over Plant Protection in the early 1950s. Commercial firms also had their own research stations. Fisons, for example, bought two farms at Levington near Ipswich in 1952 and established a fertiliser research operation

[38] D. Montague, *Farming, Food, and Politics: The Merchant's Tale* (Dublin, 2000), p. 291.

involving some four hundred acres of trials. Shortly afterwards, they acquired the Chesterford Park Research Station in Essex for pesticide research. The Shell oil company was heavily involved in the production and marketing of organochlorine insecticides and carried out field trials at their farm near Sittingbourne in Kent.[39]

The ICI research farm at Jealott's Hill, near Bracknell in Berkshire, was officially opened in 1929. ICI had acquired the German Haber-Bosch nitrogen-fixing technology as part of the post-First World War reparations and opened a fertiliser production plant at Billingham on Teesside, but they needed to persuade farmers to buy the product in much greater quantities than they had before the war. Accordingly, the original purpose of Jealott's Hill was to research and demonstrate the use of nitrogenous fertilisers on grass, but by the 1930s there was also a pest control operation there concerned with evaluating the biological effects of chemicals from the dyestuffs and general chemicals divisions of the company. Work on fertilisers, and associated products such as silage additives, continued in the post-war period, but it was probably the pesticide work that expanded most. It began during the war, with investigations of the herbicidal activity of MCPA (2-methyl-4chloro-phenoxyacetic acid), one of the first selective plant hormone weedkillers. It is important to note that it was not only the weedkiller itself that had to be developed but also the way in which it was applied to the crop. In contrast to previous herbicides such as sulphuric acid, the quantity of the active ingredient required was very small – less than five hundred grammes per acre – and the initial delivery system, which involved distributing it as a dust mixed with a large quantity of inactive filler, was unsatisfactory. It was therefore also necessary to develop a low-volume sprayer, and work on this too was carried out at Jealott's Hill in the late 1940s. The result was a liquid MCPA spray, marketed as 'Agroxone', which was on the market by 1949.[40] The other major herbicide programme in which scientists at Jealott's Hill were involved, from about 1955, was the development of paraquat (marketed as Gramoxone) and its use in direct drilling. They were also involved, again during the war, in the development of the insecticide gamma-BHC (benzene hexachloride, also known as HCH), and later in the 1960s in the development of the pyrimidine insecticides such as 'Pirimicarb' and fungicides such as 'Milstem'.[41]

This is not the place to give a detailed account of all the various pesticides that were developed at Jealott's Hill and similar commercial research

---

[39] Montague, *Farming, Food, and Politics*, pp. 351–7.
[40] W.G. Templeman, 'Low Volume Sprayers for Weed Control', *Agriculture* LV/10 (1949), pp. 441–3; G. Ordish, *The Constant Pest* (London, 1976), p. 197; F.C. Peacock (ed.), *Jealott's Hill: Fifty Years of Agricultural Research 1928–1978* (Bracknell, 1978), pp. 2–4, 36–7.
[41] Peacock, *Jealott's Hill*, p. 8.

establishments such as Levington. What needs to be emphasised here is the extent of the commercial research effort and the degree to which scientists employed by commercial firms co-operated with government and academic scientists. In the case of selective herbicides, for example, R.E. Slade of Jealott's Hill reported to the ARC that MCPA was effective in killing field poppy in cereal crops. This led to a meeting in December 1942 at the office of the Chief Scientist to the Ministry of Agriculture, Sir John Fryer, in which Lord Melchett, Slade, and William Templeman of ICI met scientists from Rothamsted who had been working on the related compound, 2,4-D (2,4-dichloro-phenoxyacetic acid), and Frank Rayns, Director of the Norfolk Agricultural Station, where field trials of the two products were subsequently established. Scientists from commercial firms also wrote for the Ministry of Agriculture's journal, *Agriculture*, and published in scientific journals. Sir William Gavin moved from being an ICI agricultural adviser to being Chief Agricultural Adviser at the Ministry of Agriculture, and S.W. Cheveley of ICI joined Gavin and Professor Stapledon of Aberystwyth on the Ministry's Technical Development Committee. Four of the scientists employed at one time or another at Jealott's Hill became Fellows of the Royal Society (Bartlett, Blackman, Boon, and Brian), and nine went on to university chairs.[42] By 1973, home sales of pesticides amounted to £40 million (exports were nearly as much again), which to put the figure in context, was roughly similar to the value of the sugar beet produced in the UK that year.[43] In the decade from 1963 to 1973, 85 per cent of the papers given to conferences of the British Crop Protection Council were on chemical control of pests, and these were very large conferences, with 1,600 delegates attending the 1974 meeting.[44] The evidence suggests, in other words, that commercial firms made a significant contribution to agricultural research. One way of measuring the input they made, although not the results of their work, is to assess their contribution to the funding of research, and to this the discussion now turns.

Expenditure on Agricultural Research

The complexity of agricultural research funding, and the various ways in which it changed over time, makes the construction of a consistent time series of expenditure difficult.[45] The ARC and its successor bodies, the MAFF and its companion bodies, DAFS and the Department of Agriculture for Northern Ireland (DANI), all funded research. University

---

[42] Peacock, *Jealott's Hill*, pp. 6, 145.
[43] Ordish, *Constant Pest*, p. 207; *Annual Review of Agriculture*, Cmnd.5977 (1975), p. 36.
[44] Ordish, *Constant Pest*, pp. 212–13.
[45] Thirtle et al., 'On the Organisation of Agricultural Research', pp. 557–76.

research was funded in part by general university funding and in part by specific awards, and in addition there was funding by private firms and by some organisations, such as MMB and the Meat and Livestock Commission (MLC), which might be seen as mid-way between private and public sources. Thirtle et al. provide an illustrative diagram of public spending increases from 1947 to 1993 but without any detailed discussion of their sources for the pre-1970 period, and Doyle and Ridout provide estimates for the years 1951 to 1981, but for public and private funding together, based on the assumption that private research funding roughly matched public expenditure.[46] Thirtle et al. reach the same conclusion for the years 1987–8.[47] At first sight, it appears that this assumption might overvalue the private contribution, but, as table 2.4 suggests, it was probably about right.

We can demonstrate this by constructing an estimate of public sector agricultural research spending based on ARC funding. There was little research expenditure at the beginning of the Second World War. One estimate put the total spending on research and education together at about £3 million in the later pre-war years.[48] By the end of the war, ARC spending was about £300,000, but the Ministry of Agriculture and its Scottish and Northern Irish equivalents – the Agriculture Departments – were spending twice as much again. From the 1950s to the 1970s, ARC spending increased relative to the research expenditure of the Agriculture Departments, so that the latter's spending was between 50 and 70 per cent of ARC spending each year.[49] It is therefore possible to obtain a rough estimate of total public spending by increasing ARC spending by an arbitrary figure in the middle of this range, say 60 per cent. Table 2.4 shows (column 2) how ARC spending increased in current price terms between the mid-1950s and the mid-1980s. After allowing for inflation (column 3), it is clear that in constant (1981) price terms this increase levelled out from the 1970s onwards. Column 4 in table 2.4 multiplies these ARC spending figures by 1.6 to estimate total public spending, and column 6 shows Doyle and Ridout's estimate of total public and private research expenditure, which is indeed very roughly double the estimated public expenditure.

---

[46] Thirtle et al., 'On the Organisation of Agricultural Research', p. 563; C.J. Doyle and M.S. Ridout, 'The Impact of Scientific Research on UK Agricultural Productivity', *Research Policy* 14 (1985), pp. 109–16.
[47] Thirtle et al., 'On the Organisation of Agricultural Research', pp. 569, 571.
[48] K.A.H. Murray, *Agriculture* (*History of the Second World War: UK Civil Series*) (London, 1955), p. 37.
[49] Trend, *Organisation of Civil Science*, Cmnd.2171, p. 11; Dainton, *The Future of the Research Council System*, Cmnd.4814, appendix A, p. 20; Rothschild, *Organisation and Management of Government R & D*, Cmnd.4814, pp. 8–9.

The Real Agricultural Revolution

TABLE 2.4. Estimated public and private agricultural research expenditure

ARC accounting year	ARC spending in current prices £million	ARC spending in constant (1981) prices £m	Estimated total public expenditure (1981 £million)	Total Research Expenditure (annual averages), constant (1981) prices, £million	
1	2	3	4	5	6
				1951–5	88.02
1956–7	3.845	24.218	38.749	1956–60	99.92
1963–4	7.063	37.864	60.583	1961–5	144.08
1969–70	14.726	61.197	97.915	1966–70	186.46
1973–4	23.148	67.576	108.122	1971–5	213.06
1979–80	56.111	67.831	108.529	1976–80	230.84
1984–5	83.048	67.453	107.925	1981	245.50

Source: column 2: TNA, MAF 200/134; 200/141; 200/146; 200/150; 200/156; 200/161. Annual reports of the ARC for the years stated; column 3 is calculated from column 2 using the formula (constant price = current price x retail price index for 1981/RPI for the year in question); column 6 calculated from Doyle and Ridout, 'The Impact of Scientific Research', p.110.

The figures in table 2.4 suggest that the expanding research effort in the 1960s was continued into the early 1970s, although perhaps at a slightly declining rate. After that, the static level of ARC spending was compensated to some degree by increased spending by the agricultural departments, as the figures in column 6 imply.[50] But there seems little doubt that the main period of expansion in agricultural research was the quarter-century after the war. This conclusion is supported by some of the closing words of Sir John Russell's history of agricultural science in Britain, written in 1965 from the perspective of a man who had played a leading role in agricultural science for over fifty years:

> Agricultural scientists ... have larger grants of public monies than most other scientific workers because in the past many of the results of their research work were so clearly marked in the field or the cattle stalls that its immense value for food production was obvious. The need for increasing this is constantly being emphasized by statesmen, medical men, social workers, politicians and others, and its achievement by a further development of agricultural science seems so obvious that requests for higher grants have been very favourably treated. Never before has there been anything approaching this generosity. Even more

[50] This is confirmed by Thirtle et al., 'On the Organisation of Agricultural Research', p. 563.

remarkable has been the complete absence of pressure on the research workers to produce results for the adornment of a Minister's speech. It would be affectation to pretend that this is due to any interest in agricultural science as such: it is certainly in the hope that agriculture itself will thereby become more efficient.[51]

Russell died not long after writing these words and so did not see the post-Rothschild changes. In any case, whether the hopes of a more efficient agriculture were to be realised was not simply a matter for agricultural scientists. It depended upon the extent to which their work was relevant to, communicated to, and understood by farmers. So too did the related question of whether the impact of agricultural research in terms of increased output or reduced costs was sufficient to justify the money invested in research. Therefore, it makes sense to delay coming to any conclusion about the value of agricultural research until the knowledge network that transmitted the research to the farmers and farm workers has been explored, in the following chapter.

---

[51] E.J. Russell, *A History of Agricultural Science in Great Britain* (London, 1966), p. 482.

3

Knowledge Networks in UK Farming, 1935–85

The previous chapter identified the principal developments in the administration and funding of agricultural science and the resultant activities of agricultural scientists. This chapter explores the links between research and the agricultural industry and considers the changes in agricultural education, extension, or advice, and other means, principally various forms of media, by which farmers became aware of technical developments. It then examines the varying experiences of individual farmers and their reactions to the knowledge available to them, before finally drawing conclusions from both this chapter and chapter 2 on the impact of research and its value to the farming industry.

The Agricultural Improvement Councils and Their Successors

Many agricultural scientists and university academics had close informal links with farmers through discussion groups, meetings, and the occasional necessity to carry out research or survey work on farms, but there were also official bodies designed to foster links between scientific research and practical agriculture. In 1941, the ARC was given the same status as the Medical Research Council and the Department of Scientific and Industrial Research, which meant that its role changed from an advisory one to a duty to undertake such research as it thought fit with the resources placed at its disposal. At the same time, two AICs, one for England and Wales and one for Scotland, were established. Sir Donald Fergusson, Chairman of the England and Wales AIC, identified the different roles to be played in a letter to Sir Thomas Middleton, then Chairman of the ARC: 'The ARC will concentrate their energies on strengthening the efficiency of the research organisation, but will not be concerned to get the results applied in practice. This will be the job of the AICs.'[1] Their functions were further defined in the 1942 report on

---

[1] W. Henderson, 'British Agricultural Research and the Agricultural Research Council: A Personal Historical Account', in G.W. Cooke (ed.), *Agricultural*

agricultural research in Great Britain as keeping in touch with scientific research, advising on testing promising results for incorporation into farming practice, and expediting this process, and also advising on farming problems in need of attention from researchers.[2] At this point in the war, there was also a Technical Development Committee, which had sub-committees in the counties, and which had apparently been established initially to solve urgent wartime problems. By 1942, it had become more interested in 'a more general examination of the technical aspects of agriculture', and so became a committee of the AIC.[3] The AICs initially operated through a system of committees examining specific problems. In 1944, for example, there were committees on hill sheep farming, AI, the supply of fruit plant stocks, seed potato production, and the deterioration of cereal varieties. When their work had been completed and action taken to implement their findings, they were automatically dissolved. The Technical Development Committee and the Committee for Liaison with the ARC were, however, permanent.[4]

By 1956, the AIC for England and Wales consisted of fourteen members meeting under the chairmanship of Sir Alan Hitchman, the Permanent Secretary of the Ministry. They included Sir James Turner, NFU President; the Duke of Northumberland; Harold Collison of the National Union of Agricultural Workers (NUAW) as it then was; Frank Rayns of the Norfolk Agricultural Experimental Station; Sir William Slater, Secretary of the ARC; and academics such as Professor Tom Wallace of Bristol; Sir James Scott Watson; and Sir Frank Engledow, professor of agriculture at Cambridge. When they met at the Ministry of Agriculture, Whitehall Place, at 11 am on 28 November of that year they agreed to a new committee structure in which the main Council would be supported by eight committees, for experimental husbandry, experimental horticulture, land management, poultry, horticulture, agriculture, taints ('to consider the question of taints and other harmful effects arising out of the use of plant protection chemicals'), and a joint committee of the AICs and the ARC, comprising two members each from the ARC, the England and Wales AIC, and the Scottish AIC. The other committees were composed of members from the AIC, the ARC, and the NAAS.[5] These committees could also generate

---

Research 1931–1981: A History of the Agricultural Research Council and a Review of Developments in Agricultural Science during the Last Fifty Years (London, 1981), pp. 33, 38.

2   Committee of the Privy Council for the Organisation and Development of Agricultural Research, *Agricultural Research in Great Britain*, Cmd.6421 (1943), pp. 9, 16.

3   Anon, 'Agricultural Improvement Council for England and Wales', *Agriculture* L (1944), pp. 464–8.

4   Anon, 'Agricultural Improvement Council', p. 466.

5   TNA, MAF 253/75, minutes of the 79th meeting of the AIC for England and Wales, 28 November 1956.

sub-committees. The experimental husbandry committee, for example, had an animal experiments sub-committee, which met between 1949 and 1954. Its records include detailed material on desirable experiments and the results of experiments carried out, and its members included Professor Hammond from Cambridge; Frank Rayns from Norfolk; Claude Culpin, the machinery expert from Silsoe and author of the standard work on farm machinery; and William Davies, the grassland expert.[6] This proliferation of committees and sub-committees produced a network of contacts between the universities, research institutes, experimental husbandry farms, advisory services, and the Ministry, which must have made it very difficult for those at the centre to remain in ignorance of any significant scientific work, and for the scientists to remain ignorant of the requirements of the farming industry and the Ministry.

These arrangements lasted until 1963 when the then Minister of Agriculture, Christopher Soames, replaced the AICs with the Agricultural Advisory Council (AAC) and the Horticultural Advisory Council, on the grounds that he wished his advisers to be independent of his Ministry, and he felt that the existing councils had become too large. Whether this was the real reason is something deserving of further research. What is interesting is that the press notice announcing this change gave biographical details of the members of the new Council, who exhibited a significant degree of continuity with the old AIC. The chairman was Mr J.D.F. Green, a former Controller of the Talks Division of the BBC, former BBC agricultural liaison officer, and former President of the National Pig Breeders' Association. There were three agricultural academics (Mac Cooper from Newcastle, Ian Lucas from Bangor, and Ford Sturrock from Cambridge), and perhaps a fourth if Dr H.G. Sanders, then the Ministry's Chief Scientific Adviser (Agriculture) and a future professor of agriculture at Reading, is included. Six of the members were farmers, landowners, or agents, all on a large scale: Nigel Strutt, Managing Director of Lord Rayleigh's Farms, with twenty thousand acres in East Anglia; G.F. Ross, manager of seven thousand acres of Northumberland for the Cooperative Wholesale Society (CWS); D.G. Pearce, Managing Director of a Cambridgeshire farming company with eight thousand acres; J.G. Jenkins, who farmed a thousand acres of Cambridgeshire as well as being a former President of the Scottish NFU; G.E. Limb, with seven hundred acres of Nottinghamshire, the chair of the NFU's Development and Education Committee; and F.A. Gray, the Treasurer of Christ Church, Oxford, and thus manager of the College's extensive estates. The remaining members were Harold Collison, General Secretary

---

[6] TNA, MAF 189/655, AIC experimental husbandry committee minutes. C. Culpin, *Farm Machinery* (London, 1938) was in its fourth edition by 1952 and still in print, in its twelfth edition, in the 1990s.

of the NUAW, and Dr E.G. Cox, the Secretary of the ARC.[7] Although it was a slimmed-down organisation, the basic function of the Council appears to have changed little from the previous AIC priority of getting new technology into practice. Like its predecessor, the AAC operated in part through technical sub-committees, now called 'panels', with, for example, one for sheep, another for irrigation, a third for plant introductions, and so on, but it also addressed more general issues. At its meetings in June and October 1963, for example, much discussion was devoted to the purpose and distribution of experimental husbandry farms, in response to a Ministry request for advice on the need for such farms and their desirable role, and it also approved the idea of an association for those engaged in producing agricultural television.[8] The AAC was still operating in 1973, but by 1975 it appears to have been transformed into the Advisory Council for Agriculture and Horticulture, which in 1979 was involved in a Quangos review, which it appears not to have survived.[9]

The Experimental Husbandry Farms

Not long after the establishment of the AICs, another link was forged between research and practical farming. Addressing the Agricultural Education Association in 1947, Sir John Fryer, the ARC Secretary, suggested that 'In pre-war days the criticism was sometimes made that agricultural research too seldom produced practical results. On the other hand, the research workers sometimes felt that the practical men made too little use of their discoveries.' These criticisms, Fryer felt, were 'not without a certain foundation', and the reason, he suggested, was that there was a gap between the two. The results from the experimental stations were not always ready for direct application, but there was no suitable place or institution in which they could be developed.[10] Two years earlier, in 1945, the Ministry of Agriculture's journal had announced that the ARC and the AIC for England and Wales were exploring the possibility of providing farms upon which this kind of development work could be done, and Fryer was announcing the establishment of what were to be called 'Experimental Husbandry Farms' (EHFs), working in connection

---

[7] TNA, MAF 132/40, press release 24 January 1963, A New Look at Research and Experiment.
[8] TNA, MAF 253/105, minutes and papers of AAC Council meetings June to October 1963.
[9] TNA, MAF 113/656, Agricultural Advisory Council: 43rd–48th meetings, 1972–3; TNA, MAF 113/659, Advisory Committee for Agriculture and Horticulture: bulls and public footpaths, 1975–6; TNA, MAF458, Review of Non-departmental Public Bodies, 1979–80.
[10] J. Fryer, 'The Organisation for Agricultural Research', *Agricultural Progress* 22 (1947), pp. 9–19.

with the NAAS at various locations in England and Wales.[11] On the advice of the AIC, the original intention was to buy eighteen farms scattered across England and Wales so as to represent various climates and soil types. By the end of 1952, nine had been acquired, and eventually there were twelve, two on the fens, three mixed farms on heavy land, three mainly arable farms on light land and three upland grass farms, covering altogether some six thousand acres, together with a three thousand-acre Welsh hill farm. They were managed by NAAS officers, and the Director of NAAS, writing in early 1953, outlined some of the work being carried out on them. It included comparisons of various rotations, post-harvest treatment of straw, the effect of different ploughing depths on optimum sowing dates, various fertiliser experiments, variety trials in conjunction with the National Institute of Agricultural Botany (NIAB), the effect of heifer nutrition on subsequent milk yields, and the value of feeding antibiotics to fattening pigs.[12] By 1963, their function and future was under discussion in the newly formed AAC because, as W. Emrys Jones, then Director of the NAAS, explained 'there had been pressure to reduce costs, and it was very difficult to obtain finance for new lines of experiment'.[13] The ARC and some individual members of the AAC wrote at some length on the functions of the EHFs and their desirability. While it was generally agreed that it was difficult to draw firm and clear lines between fundamental research and its application, it was clear that the EHFs had a role that was different from that of the research institutes. Sir Harold Sanders, a member of the AAC, considered that they had five functions: following up the work of ARC institutions, for example work on steaming up of dairy cows, building on initial work at the National Institute for Research in Dairying at Reading University; carrying out experiments on general questions, such as the management of continuous cereals; local problems identified by their own committees (e.g. the application of chalk on the Yorkshire Wolds); demonstrating up-to-date methods (the work on silage and cereals for cows at Bridgets near Winchester and leys versus permanent pasture at Great House in Lancashire); and, finally, acting as an 'inspiration' to NAAS. 'Snags arise', argued Sanders, 'when new ideas are put into practice, and it is still worthwhile for the NAAS to have experience to draw on when

---

[11] Anon, 'Agricultural Improvement Council for England and Wales: Second Note on Progress', *Agriculture* LI (1945), pp. 514–18.

[12] J.A. Macmillan, 'Experimental Farms and Stations of the NAAS, (1) Experimental Husbandry Farms', *Agriculture* LIX (1952), pp. 421–4; J.A. Macmillan, 'Experimental Husbandry Farms: Review of Progress', *Agriculture* LIX (1953), pp. 459–62; Anon, *Agriculture in Britain*, Central Office of Information Reference Pamphlet 43 (London, 1965), pp. 42–3.

[13] TNA, MAF 253/105, minutes and papers of AAC Council meetings, October 1963 minutes, p. 3.

advising those who are considering following the pioneering farmers.'[14] The EHFs remained in being until after 1985, although they have now been sold off to private farmers or farming companies. They were an officially funded link between researchers and farmers, but they were not the only one: education, extension, and the provision of information also had a role to play.

Agricultural Education

The pattern of formal agricultural education that lasted for most of the twentieth century was established before the First World War. It was composed of three parts: the university departments of agriculture, the colleges, and the farm institutes. The university departments, of which there were seven (Cambridge, King's College Durham (located in Newcastle upon Tyne), Leeds, Oxford, Reading, Aberystwyth, and Bangor), taught at first degree and postgraduate level, to small numbers of students. In the year before the war, there were 517 degree and postgraduate students in total in these departments, which means that the total output of agricultural graduates was less than 170 per year. Cambridge and Reading together accounted for nearly half of these, and at Bangor fewer than ten students per year graduated. The universities also often entered their undergraduate students for the National Diplomas in Agriculture or Dairying, in addition to having students (252 in total) studying only at diploma level. These National Diplomas were administered on a countrywide basis by the Royal Agricultural Society of England (and the Highland and Agricultural Society in Scotland), involved two years of study, and formed the main qualification for students at the national agricultural colleges, of which there were seven (The Royal at Cirencester, Swanley Horticultural College and Wye in Kent, the Midland Agricultural College at Sutton Bonington near Nottingham, Studley in Warwickshire, Harper Adams in Shropshire, and Seale-Hayne in Devon). Swanley and Studley were small colleges, exclusively for women, and the Royal Agricultural College and Wye were for men only. Again, the numbers involved were small. The biggest of them, Wye, had 187 students in total in 1938, and Seale-Hayne, Harper Adams, Studley, and Swanley all had fewer than eighty.[15] The fourteen farm institutes in England and four in Wales provided more practical training for a total

---

[14] TNA, MAF 253/105, minutes and papers of AAC Council meetings, October 1963 minutes.

[15] *Report of the Committee on Post-war Agricultural Education in England and Wales, 1943*, Cmd.6433 (1943), pp. 18–23; E.H. Whetham, *The Agrarian History of England and Wales*, vol. VIII, *1914–1939* (Cambridge, 1978), p. 204; P. Brassley, 'Agricultural Science and Education', in E.J.T. Collins (ed.), *The Agrarian History of England and Wales*, vol. VII, *1850–1914* (Cambridge, 2000), p. 632.

of 821 students, with most courses lasting for no more than one year, intended for farm workers or small farmers. There were also hundreds of day courses, evening classes, lectures, and demonstrations that probably involved far more people than the relatively small numbers enrolled in the full-time university, college, and farm institute courses. Nevertheless, total spending by the Ministry of Agriculture and the county councils together only amounted to £506,000 per year.[16]

The Second World War temporarily disrupted these arrangements, as many of the teaching staff were transferred to work for the CWAECs, and students were transferred to different locations. Wye College, in Kent, for example, was taken over by the Army, and the students were transferred to Reading University, which also accommodated students from the Royal Veterinary College who had been moved out of London.[17] Several colleges were turned over to the training of members of the Women's Land Army.[18] But the war clearly concentrated the official mind on the need for agricultural training and education, and three committees reported on the subject between 1943 and 1946. Luxmoore chaired the Committee concerned with post-war agricultural education in England and Wales, Alness with the same topic in Scotland, and Loveday with higher agricultural education in England and Wales.[19]

It is worth briefly considering these reports, for they suggest that official thinking was broadly satisfied that agricultural education could do what was required of it in the post-war world, given some easily achieved changes. The most significant criticisms made by the Luxmoore Report dealt with the farm institutes, the pre-war growth of which had been held up by restrictions on government spending and the fact that county councils were not legally obliged to establish them. It also disapproved of the tendency of some of them to 'usurp the function of an agricultural college' by providing higher level courses and felt that combining the role of County Agricultural Organiser with head of the farm institute meant that neither job was done properly. While essentially approving of those then in existence (although it found that some were too small, and the accommodation standards varied from the bleak to the 'unnecessarily extravagant'), the Committee felt that the number of farm institutes needed considerable expansion, to the point where each county

---

[16] *Post-war Agricultural Education*, Cmd.6433, p. 28.
[17] S. Richards, *Wye College and Its World: Centenary History* (Ashford, 1994), p. 137; the late Ivan Fincham, MRCVS, interview with P. Brassley, 12 July 2010.
[18] A. Humphries, *Seeds of Change: 100 Years' Contribution to Rural Economy, Society and the Environment* (Penrith, 1996), p. 73.
[19] *Post-war Agricultural Education*, Cmd.6433; *Report of the Committee on Agricultural Education in Scotland*, Cmd.6704 (1945); *Report of the Committee on Higher Agricultural Education in England and Wales*, Cmnd.6728 (1946).

had one, each catering for about seventy students.²⁰ Some of the seven agricultural colleges were also felt to be too small – two hundred students should be the minimum, the Committee suggested – their function was not always clear, there was little uniformity in their aims and methods, with too many of them having courses of no recognised standard, and their finances had been as problematic as the management of some of the college farms. Similarly, the Committee argued that the universities had too many diploma courses and insufficient emphasis on practical experience of farming, and the Ministry of Agriculture had little continuity in its education policy. Interestingly, it commended the activities of Young Farmers' Clubs (YFCs). But the solution to these difficulties, in the Luxmoore Committee's view, was to regularise the existing system rather than to embark on any radical rethinking. Thus it recommended more farm institutes with more students concentrating on basic courses, the same number of agricultural colleges, most of them with more students, concentrating on two-year diploma courses, and that the university agricultural departments should concentrate on degree-level work only. It suggested, though, that without a successful agricultural industry to create demand, any educational facilities would be 'but little used'.²¹

Whether or not there were sufficient agricultural students in higher (i.e. university and college level) education was the subject of detailed examination by the Loveday Committee. Their report went into great detail in assessing the need for graduates in agriculture and its associated sciences. As far as university graduates in agriculture were concerned, for example, it reported that the NAAS would require thirty-four graduates per year, with a further thirty as farm management advisers, eight would be needed to teach in farm institutes and five in universities, twenty-seven for the Colonial Agricultural Service, and a further six would satisfy the needs of the ancillary industries. Practical farming might require about 150. Altogether, the Committee identified a demand for 278 agricultural graduates per year, which, given three-year courses, meant that there should be 834 agricultural students at any one time. The existing university agriculture departments could cope with those numbers, and if they were to increase further there was a danger that 'the output of trained men will tend to exceed opportunities for employment'.²²

In comparing the supply of agricultural graduates with the demand for them, Loveday touched upon the principal question for post-war agricultural education: how much was needed. At the time the report was written, there were about six hundred thousand employed workers in British farming, and a further 250,000 or so farmers. By the time the graduates it enumerated retired, in the mid-1980s, there would be

20 *Post-war Agricultural Education*, Cmd.6433, pp. 37–8, 49.
21 *Post-war Agricultural Education*, Cmd.6433, pp. 46–50.
22 *Higher Agricultural Education*, Cmnd.6728, pp. 64–9.

roughly the same number of farmers but a little fewer than three hundred thousand employed workers.[23] If only the new entrants to the industry were to be trained, therefore, and each member of the labour force had a career lasting forty years, there would be a demand for between 21,250 training places (in the earlier years) and 13,750 forty years later. Clearly this is a purely theoretical calculation, for there were farmers who farmed for more than forty years, and workers who left the industry for better paid jobs in their mid-twenties, and in any case Loveday could not accurately predict the future size of the labour force. Nevertheless, it provides some kind of yardstick against which to measure the extent to which the farm labour force received some kind of technical training. And it is quite clear that agricultural education never reached anything like those numbers. The Loveday Report provides an interesting example of the thinking on the potential demand. As we have seen, they calculated that 150 agricultural graduates would be required. They arrived at this figure with reference to a random sample of two thousand farmers taken by the Wartime Social Survey in 1943/4, which revealed that 1 per cent of farmers had a university education. From this, they calculated a replacement rate of fifty graduates per year by taking 1 per cent of two hundred thousand farmers divided by the forty years they would spend in the industry. However, they felt that more highly educated farmers would be required in future, so they arbitrarily trebled the replacement rate to assess the future demand.[24] Even after expansion, therefore, the official view at the end of the war was that most farmers would not require graduate or diplomate level education, and that an expanded farm institute sector was where both they and their workers should receive their training.

The results of this policy emerged more than a decade later in the criticisms of the De La Warr Report on further education for agriculture. It found that agricultural education was now providing places for 1,700 university students, nearly twice the pre-war figure, and one thousand students in agricultural colleges, up by 30 per cent on the number in 1939. In line with Luxmoore's advice, it was the farm institutes that had undergone the greatest expansion, up from 774 students in sixteen farm institutes in 1939 to two thousand in thirty-seven institutes in 1957–8. The farm institutes and other centres were also catering for about five thousand day-release students, a fivefold increase from ten years earlier. These figures were still very small in comparison with other industries. De La Warr made the comparison with the building industry, in which there was also a proliferation of small firms: it had three times as many workers as agriculture, but more than eight times as many trainees. There

---

[23] H. Marks and D.K. Britton, *A Hundred Years of British Food and Farming: A Statistical Survey* (London, 1989), p. 138.
[24] *Higher Agricultural Education*, Cmnd.6728, p. 58.

were seven hundred thousand people in farming in 1957, forty thousand of whom were between fifteen and seventeen years old, but only 2,600 students with a full-time agricultural education in universities, colleges, and farm institutes entered the industry each year, a 'lamentably small' proportion. Only the numbers enrolled in evening and short courses — about twenty-two thousand, not all of whom were new entrants to the industry — were at all satisfactory. Agriculture needed 'a well organised and comprehensive system of technical education catering, not like the present arrangements, for only a minority of the working population, but for all'. All young entrants between the ages of fifteen and eighteen should attend part-time classes, and those with a suitable level of general education should then go on to farm institutes, the Committee recommended.[25] Shortly afterwards, the Bosanquet Committee's report on the demand for agricultural graduates supported De La Warr's findings on numbers without apparently endorsing their views on the need for expansion. Bosanquet produced some interesting data from the 1961 census, which found that there were then 10,180 people in Great Britain with a degree in agriculture or a similar subject, of whom 8,750 were in employment. Of these, 7,570 were employed in jobs that used their agricultural qualifications, 3,100 of whom were directly employed in farming or forestry. There were also 1,620 people with science or engineering degrees employed in agriculture. Of about four hundred students graduating annually in agriculture, only seventy or so went into practical farming, although the proportion of those with diplomas who did so was greater. Bosanquet concluded that there was no shortage of graduates in general agriculture, although there were shortages in the specialist disciplines such as agricultural economics.[26]

The Bosanquet Committee's views on the need for agricultural graduates were clearly informed by what actually happened in agriculture, rather than what might be desirable. Although a formally trained workforce might be thought desirable by those on the De La Warr Committee, it did not in practice exist. A survey of the East Anglian counties in 1974–5 found that only 15.8 per cent of farmers had a degree or diploma in agriculture, and 77.2 per cent had no formal agricultural qualifications of any sort. Of those who farmed a thousand acres or more, 45.1 per cent had a degree or diploma, but still 50 per cent had no formal qualification. These results were supported by an earlier (1972) survey of England and Wales suggesting that the proportion of farmers with agricultural qualifications increased with farm size. Only 6.1 per cent of those with farms of

---

[25] *Report of the Committee on Further Education for Agriculture Provided by Local Education Authorities*, Cmnd.614 (1958), pp. 1–13.
[26] *Report of the Interdepartmental Committee on the Demand for Agricultural Graduates*, Cmnd.2419 (1964), pp. 7–12, 34–5.

less than fifty acres had a qualification, in contrast to 24 per cent of those farming over five hundred acres.[27]

There was a long tradition of farmers learning from their fathers, and many young people entering agriculture felt like farmer 209: 'I wanted to leave school and get to work on the farm, despite my parents' suggestion that I went to Seale-Hayne.' As far as farmer 109 was concerned, 'colleges weren't about then'.[28] There is interview data about the agricultural education of twenty-five farmers, and of these fourteen had no full-time agricultural education at all. Farmer 162 went to Bicton for a fortnight's course while he was still at school, but he had no desire to go there for any longer course: 'I was never interested. I learned most from father, I suppose I must have admired what he did and I wanted to be like him, so to be home here was the natural thing to do.' And neither had his father been to college. Farmer 101, however, provided an interesting insight into this:

> I learned a lot at home from father, about what he did, and when I went to college [he went to Seale-Hayne] I learned *why* he did it. And when you learn why you did it, you learn to think about whether it can be done any other way to achieve results.

Farmer 466, who had a BSc in agriculture from Cambridge and an MA from Reading, made the same point: 'it's an attitude of mind. What the university education does is to introduce you to the upcoming technologies but also give you the ability to deal with them.' This farmer was the only one in the sample with a degree in agriculture, although farmer 929 had a geography degree from Exeter, farmer 826 a chemistry degree from Bristol, and farmer 2/9's father was an agricultural student at Reading in the 1920s, but he himself 'didn't like school, and when I had an opportunity to come back to the farm that's what I did', although the Reading contact was maintained when the university awarded him an honorary doctorate for the archaeological work he did later in life. Other farmers went to Seale-Hayne, the local agricultural college, or to the local farm institutes, Bicton in Devon, where farmer 193 did a one-year National Certificate in Agriculture (NCA) course, and Kingston Maurward in Dorset, where farmer 7/8 also did an NCA.

Of those with no formal full-time education, it is interesting to note that their children did later go to college. Farmer 535's daughter did

---

[27] H. Newby, C. Bell, D. Rose, and P. Saunders, *Property, Paternalism and Power: Class and Control in Rural England* (London, 1978), pp. 64–5; B. Hill and D. Ray, *Economics for Agriculture: Food, Farming and the Rural Economy* (Basingstoke, 1987), p. 179.

[28] These and subsequent quotations from individual farmers identified only by farm code number are taken from the transcripts of interviews conducted as part of the research on the FMS archive at Exeter University. See chapter 1, especially n. 68.

an agriculture degree at Oxford, farmer 844's son a Reading BSc, and farmer 209's son an OND (Ordinary National Diploma) at Bicton. Farmer 209 was one of several who, although they had no full-time agricultural education, did one or more part-time day release classes. He remembered that the 'first farming classes at Cornwall Technical College started in 1955, and I went in 1956 for the autumn and spring term, and then I did the advanced class the following year'. Farmer 576 remembered Cornwall Council starting local classes in 1960, 'that was at the back of the bakery over the bus depot in Liskeard, there were men who came up, the senior one was based at Truro, I did that for four years, they went on to City and Guilds stage 2, that was a day a week'. The City and Guilds qualifications, in several stages, were awarded for successful completion of day-release courses. Farmer 782 was anxious to succeed his father on a county council farm, against normal council policy, so he 'went to day release classes at Bicton, did City and Guilds stages 1, 2 and 3, which demonstrated that I was keen'.

In general, these courses appear to have been enjoyed and valued, but not always. Farmer 7/8, whose father had been at Seale-Hayne in the 1930s, and had done a cheesemaking course at the Somerset farm institute at Cannington, himself went to Kingston Maurward but felt that 'if you were a farmer's son you knew a lot of it before you went down there', although he also 'learned about the feeding of cows, how much cake they really wanted, and fertiliser use, and that sort of thing. It was useful.' Farmer 3/1 was more decided in his conclusions. Asked if his OND course at Seale-Hayne in the early 1970s had taught him anything, he replied 'Certainly in that era agricultural colleges were regarded as a finishing school by most farmers ... In terms of what I brought back to my own dairy farm, I would have to say probably "No". It was just too general. Ideally I would have been sent abroad ... I would personally send my son off to a big farm in New Zealand for two or three years', although he did admit that his sandwich year on a big dairy farm in Dorset 'showed me how *not* to farm'. What this interview evidence illustrates, therefore, is that the evidence of the numbers in agricultural education, and of the various post-war reports on the sector, show in general what was being experienced on individual farms. The range of educational experiences was very wide, and especially the numbers from higher education entering agriculture were very low in the 1950s and '60s, although they increased somewhat by the 1970s and 1980s, reflecting an expansion in post-school education in general and agricultural education too.

For post-school education, it is generally recognised that the Robbins Report on higher education, published in 1963, led to the remarkable expansion in student numbers in the following thirty years.[29] Although

---

29 *Higher Education: Report of the Committee Appointed by the Prime Minister*, Cmnd.2154 (1963).

Robbins did not in fact suggest any great expansion in numbers of agricultural students, his report had two major effects. One was that university agriculture departments, agricultural colleges, and farm institutes all grew in the general expansion, and the other was that his recommendations led to the breakdown of the former strict demarcation between universities awarding degrees and colleges preparing students for the National Diploma in Agriculture (NDA). Table 3.1 shows the only consistent statistical series of student numbers available over the whole period, and it needs to be taken only as a guide, because, as the source note explains, it does not reconcile exactly with estimates from other sources. On the other hand, it successfully captures the most important trends, namely the continuous expansion in student numbers up to the mid-1990s and the subsequent dramatic fall that led to the closure of courses and, in the case of Seale-Hayne and Wye, whole colleges.

TABLE 3.1. Number of agriculture, forestry, and veterinary students in the UK

1956–7	3,099
1961–2	3,406
1965–6	3,734
1974–5	4,741
1984–5	5,100
1990–1	6,100
1994–5	8,900
2001–2	2,900

Source: Central Statistical Office, *Annual Abstract of Statistics*, 1968, pp. 109, 112; 1976, p. 144; 1987, p. 97; 1988, p. 112; 2004, p. 73. There are several problems in interpreting these figures. First, they include veterinary students, who amounted to about one third of the total in the years (1955–66) in which they are noted separately, but whose numbers may not have increased as much as those of agricultural students. Secondly, the numbers probably included diploma students (National Diploma in Agriculture to 1973, and subsequently Higher National Diploma in Agriculture). Thirdly, they do not agree exactly, and sometimes even roughly, with other estimates. For 1962, for example, the *Annual Abstract* figure for agriculture and forestry students is 2,135. But Bosanquet (*Demand for Agricultural Graduates*, Cmnd.2419, p. 47) gives a total of 440 graduates in agricultural subjects in that year, suggesting a total student number in university agricultural departments of 1,200 to 1,500. Bosanquet gave no data for student numbers in the agricultural colleges, but Sir Keith Murray, chair of the University Grants Committee in 1962, quoted figures for that year of 1,735 degree and 1,359 diploma (i.e. college) students, making a total of 3,049 students in agricultural higher education (K.A.H. Murray, *Higher Agricultural Education in England and Wales* (the George Johnstone Lecture, Seale-Hayne College) (Newton Abbot, 1962), pp. 7–8).

The data for individual institutions reflects the national growth. Wye College, near Ashford in Kent, and part of London University, had a hundred students in 1946, but about three hundred in 1970 and nearly seven hundred in the early 1990s, about a quarter of whom were postgraduates, and 40 per cent of whom were women.[30] Before 1965 at Aberystwyth there were usually fewer than twenty graduates each year in Rural Sciences (which included agriculture, agricultural botany, agricultural chemistry, and agricultural economics); after 1968, the numbers were always over fifty.[31] Similarly, at Seale-Hayne College in Devon (from the author's personal recollection), numbers grew from seventy or so before the war to about 250 diploma students in the early 1970s and nearly one thousand at its peak in the late 1980s, by which time it was also teaching at degree and postgraduate level.[32] At the same time, the range of courses increased, and part of the change in agricultural student numbers can be attributed to the fact that university departments and colleges added agricultural economics, various forms of rural environmental studies, food technology, and tourism studies to the traditional mix of agriculture, agricultural sciences, and dairying. From 1969, the agricultural colleges also changed from the old two-year NDA courses to three-year Ordinary and Higher National Diploma courses, both of which involved a period of practical work on farms supervised by the college, the 'sandwich period'. Ten years later, at least two of the colleges – Harper Adams and Seale-Hayne – had also introduced degree courses, as did other colleges a few years later.[33] In the further education sector, the farm institutes saw a similar period of expansion from the 1960s. By the mid-1990s, they were more likely to be called agricultural colleges, they had an average of four hundred full-time enrolments with up to 1,800 additional part-time students, and in addition to agriculture they were teaching a vast range of courses. At Newton Rigg in Cumbria, they ranged from forestry to floristry and horse management to childcare.[34]

By the 1970s, and certainly by the 1980s, there was a greater chance that a farmer's son or daughter would go to some form of vocational education relating to a rural career than there had been thirty years earlier. The same applied to farm workers. Did this mean that farming had become increasingly professionalised? There are various ways of defining what is meant by professionalism, but, in relation to agricultural education, the existence of traits such as the exercise of uncommon

---

[30] Richards, *Wye College and Its World*, p. 318.
[31] R. Colyer, *Man's Proper Study: A History of Agricultural Education in Aberystwyth, 1878–1978* (Llandysul, 1982), appendix III.
[32] From the personal recollection of one of the authors (PB).
[33] H. Williams, *The Lure of the Land: A Century of Education at Harper Adams* (Newport, Shropshire, 2001), p. 219; C. Beale and G. Owen, *Writtle College: The First Hundred Years 1893–1993* (Chelmsford, 1993), p. 71.
[34] Humphries, *Seeds of Change*, pp. 2–4.

skills, entry only after an approved and regulated course of training, and exclusion of the unqualified from the profession are the ones worth considering. It is certainly the case that every day farmers and farm workers use skills and expertise that the average urban worker would be unlikely to possess, although they may acquire these by experience or demonstration by their peers as opposed to formal training courses. Similarly, it is possible to buy a farm and attempt to farm it with little or no previous training or experience, as long as one has the money to do so, although some kind of qualification was increasingly required by landlords looking for new tenants in the period we are concerned with. The most basic courses were developed to try to minimise the danger that participants presented to themselves and the public in general. Thus there were courses in tractor driving for young people, and schemes for ensuring that those who used chainsaws and pesticides did so safely, but for most of this period there was no compulsion to attend these or any other training courses before farming or working on a farm. Probably the last time the unqualified were excluded from farming was during the Second World War, when those listed as C grade farmers in the National Farm Survey of 1942 faced the possibility of having their farms managed by the CWAEC.[35] The people most likely to have had formal training were those employed as salaried farm managers, of whom there were about eight thousand in the UK over most of the post-war period (in comparison with two hundred thousand or more owner-occupiers and tenant farmers). A survey carried out in 1970 found that, of a sample of 276 managers, 88 per cent had formal agricultural qualifications, a quarter of whom had degrees, and they all felt that formal training was either essential or desirable for a manager. All but 3 per cent of them continued to update their training, and for 28.6 per cent that meant attending formal training courses. Interestingly, while 28.9 per cent were the children of farmers or farm managers, 62.7 per cent came from families with no farming connection, so clearly a farm manager's job was a way into farming for those with ability but no capital.[36] The calculations above on the number of new entrants into farming, compared with the number of training places available, suggest, however, that the agricultural labour force was not technically over-educated, although the extent to which they received a technical education clearly increased from the 1940s to the 1980s. And the dramatic decrease in numbers in education in the 1990s clearly proved the wisdom of the Luxmoore Committee's observation that without the demand created by a successful and profitable agricultural industry, agricultural education would be 'but little used'.[37] By 1958,

[35] P. Brassley, 'The Professionalisation of English Agriculture?', *Rural History* 16 (2005), pp. 235–51.
[36] A.K. Giles and F.D. Mills, *The Farm Managers* (Coventry, 1970), pp. 9–10.
[37] *Post-war Agricultural Education*, Cmd.6433, p. 46.

when only 10 per cent of the children of farmers in south-east England went to a farm institute or college, it appeared that even with a successful industry Luxmoore's gloomy predictions were accurate, and although the figures improved somewhat by the mid-1960s, when 15 per cent of those entering the industry had had at least a year's course, with a further 2.5 per cent having two or more years, it clearly took a long time for the agricultural labour force to acquire a reasonable level of formal training.[38]

Extension and Advice

Formal education and training shades imperceptibly into advice and on-the-job training and was only one of the sources of information and expertise available to the agricultural industry in the forty years after the war. Indeed, despite the space given to it above, it might be argued that it was the least important, for it was something that many farmers did not experience at all, and those that did have an agricultural education mostly went through it at the beginning of their careers, often before they had much input into the management of the farms on which they worked. Conversely, it came at a time when people were at their most receptive and impressionable, and perhaps most likely to challenge the views and practices of those managing their farms. In any case, even the most technically up to date agricultural graduate needed to be kept informed of developments once university, college, or farm institute had been left behind, and so did farmers and workers who had been doing the job for years.

To keep them informed was the task of a variety of extension and media organisations, together with the advertising and advisory departments of firms in the ancillary industries, and it is important to realise that although the following discussion, for the sake of simplicity, separates out these various bodies, in practice they overlapped in numerous ways. Thus the NAAS produced books and pamphlets, as did the publishing industry, and had a presence at agricultural shows, as did the commercial firms. Producers of farming radio and TV programmes took information from the Ministry of Agriculture and interviewed members of commercial firms, and those firms advertised in agricultural journals and made sure that both journalists and advisory officers were aware of their products. And of course those in agricultural education used all of these media in their teaching. Since the agricultural industry was one of small firms, individual farms did not have the advertising, marketing, training, and research departments that big firms in more concentrated industries had, and these functions were in effect provided by national and regional

---

[38] J. Martin, *The Development of Modern Agriculture: British Farming since 1931* (Basingstoke, 2000), p. 93; J.G.S. and F. Donaldson with D. Barber, *Farming in Britain Today* (Harmondsworth, 1972), p. 42.

organisations discussed below. The dividing line between the agricultural industry and those advising, selling to, and buying from it was not clearly defined, and many of those in education and advisory work in fact saw themselves as part of the industry. It should also be remembered that the numbers of people involved were not inconsiderable. At the end of this period, Craig et al. estimated that some forty thousand public sector employees worked in education and the civil service in areas related to agriculture, and they had their counterparts in the commercial firms too, so the following discussion concerns a significant number of people in relation to those working on farms.[39]

An inspection of the reference book *Farming and Mechanised Agriculture* gives some idea of the complexity of the system. The fourth edition was edited by Sir George Stapledon, at that point one of the most prominent agricultural scientists in the country, and published in 1950. It contained descriptions of the work of forty-one government and public bodies and forty-six private organisations, together with contact details of a further 247 organisations 'interested in farming and mechanised agriculture', from the Autosexing Breeds Association to the Wickham Market Fruit Station, and seventy breed societies. Details of the membership and terms of reference of fifty officially appointed committees, from the Agricultural Wages Board and the Advisory Committee on Schoolboy Harvest Camps to the British Agricultural Machinery Mission to Canada, took up twenty-five pages, and a book list 'intended for the practising farmer and countryman' occupied a further twenty-six pages of small print. The list of journals, from the mainstream *Farmer and Stockbreeder* and *Farmers Weekly*, both available for sixpence per week or an annual subscription of 34s 8d, to the *Dairy Goatkeeper* at one shilling per month, took up a further six pages. It included learned journals such as the *Journal of Agricultural Science* (annual subscription £2) and the *Journal of Soil Science* (seventeen shillings annually). Finally came a list of 291 films on agricultural subjects, most lasting between ten and thirty minutes, available for hire from thirty-eight distributors and film libraries.[40] The point of reciting this list is to emphasise not only the enormous amount of effort that was put into representing and informing the agricultural industry at the end of the war but also the fact that the following discussion of advisory work and the agricultural media inevitably picks out only some of the more significant organisations, agencies, and publications.

Before the Second World War, advisory work in England and Wales was partly financed by the Ministry of Agriculture but effectively under county council control. In 1939, there were fifty-five County Agricultural Organisers and 468 staff, charged with providing basic agricultural

---

[39] G.M. Craig, J.L. Jollans, and A. Korbey (eds), *The Case for Agriculture: An Independent Assessment*, CAS Report no. 10 (Reading, 1986), pp. 94–9.
[40] G. Stapledon, *Farming and Mechanised Agriculture* (4th edn, London, 1950).

education and acting as advisers to deal with the more basic questions that farmers might pose. More complex issues could be referred up to the Provincial Advisory Service, centred on university departments and colleges and employing specialists in agricultural chemistry, zoology, botany, plant pathology, economics, and so on.[41] The Luxmoore Committee felt that this system had been inadequate, in part at least because it was underfunded. Neither did the farmers escape their censure: 'The attitude of the farmers to the service cannot escape adverse comment. In many cases they have failed to recognise the value of scientific knowledge to agricultural practice', although they saw that this was now changing 'in the right direction' thanks to the work of the CWAECs. Nevertheless, there remained a lack of uniformity and a need for central control, and they proposed the establishment of a national service, combining the county and provincial advisory services into one unified organisation. At its base should be the District Officers, several in each county, in frequent contact with their farmers, and under the guidance of a County Officer, who in turn reported to a Provincial Director.[42] Luxmoore's proposals were accepted, and in the October 1946 edition of the Ministry of Agriculture's journal Professor J.A. Scott Watson, the Ministry's chief education and advisory officer, wrote an article introducing the NAAS.[43] As a leading advisory officer pointed out many years later, the Minister at the time of the Luxmoore Report, Robert Hudson, justified the continued provision of 'some assurance of stability to the industry' (i.e. farm subsidies) by the balancing 'guarantee of a measure of reasonable efficiency in the industry', and his junior minister (and successor) Tom Williams repeated this point and suggested that it was the job of the advisory services to produce it.[44]

By 1950, an official statement from NAAS claimed that 'about 1,950 officers with practical farming experience and academic training are required to staff the service', although as table 3.2 shows the numbers employed never reached that level. As the table shows, the service employed a range of specialists. In addition to the categories listed in table 3.2, there were those working in the NAAS HQ in London together with Regional Directors and their deputies, crop husbandry, grassland husbandry and farm machinery specialists, bacteriologists, soil chemists,

---

[41] *Post-war Agricultural Education*, Cmd.6433, p. 17; C.J. Holmes, 'Science and the Farmer: The Development of the Agricultural Advisory Service in England and Wales, 1900–1939', *Agric. Hist. Rev.* 36 (1988), pp. 77–86.
[42] *Post-war Agricultural Education*, Cmd.6433, pp. 41, 55.
[43] J.A. Scott Watson, 'The National Agricultural Advisory Service', *Agriculture* LIII (1946).
[44] R.J. Dancey, 'The Evolution of Agricultural Extension in England and Wales', *J. Agric. Econs.* 44 (1993), pp. 375–93.

nutrition chemists, entomologists, plant pathologists, and, from 1963, a farm management adviser in each region.[45]

TABLE 3.2. Numbers of officers employed by the NAAS

	1950	1954	1964	1970
Total officers employed	1,524	1,532	1,408	1,831
Of whom				
General agricultural advisers	466	455	455	
Livestock husbandry advisers	115	105	95	
Milk production advisers	222	231	23	
Poultry husbandry advisers	106	104	105	
Horticultural advisers	181	168	165	
Working on EHFs	15	47	112	

Source: the 1950–64 data is from TNA, MAF 114/807, NAAS and the Farmer: A Follow-Up Report to the First Eight Years of NAAS. The 1970 figure is from N. F. McCann, *The Story of the National Agricultural Advisory Service: A Mainspring of Agricultural Revival 1946–1971* (Ely, 1989). His data is arranged by pay grade and shows 866 officers in grade III, which he identifies as the main District Adviser (i.e. general agricultural adviser) grade.

But the District Advisory Officers were the general practitioners and the people that farmers contacted first. For farmer 3/1 in Dorset, they were

> our biggest single contributor to farm information, they were the first port of call for new technical information, and within ADAS [see below] it was the District Adviser. We only rarely went beyond him to the specialist advisers, we used the DA as a general practitioner, and they helped the industry a lot.

The annual reports of the County Agricultural Officers provide a useful survey of the activities of NAAS, and later the Agricultural Development and Advisory Service (ADAS), at a local level. Throughout the 1950s, '60s,

---

[45] TNA, MAF 114/807, NAAS and the Farmer: a follow-up report to the first eight years of NAAS, an unpublished report written in 1964 by Dr Coles and 'worth preserving as a historical record' according to the Director of the Service at the time.

and '70s, the basis of their work remained the individual advisory visits to farms, but in addition individual officers or county teams carried out their own research work – those in Devon worked, for example, on the use of wheat reed for thatching and control of fat hen in kale in 1962–3 – held advisory meetings, attended conferences and shows, co-operated with local authorities, bankers, and accountants, wrote articles for the press, and appeared on radio and television programmes. They also played a major part in organising emergency fodder supplies by airlift and road to over three hundred farms during the blizzards in the cold winter of 1962–3.[46] In his report for 1952–3, the County Officer for Devon emphasised the success of the informal discussion meetings that had been held in small village halls for an audience of thirty to forty people, which 'have brought in many farmers who would not go to the local market town, and would not rise to ask questions at a formal meeting'.[47] This question of the success with which advisory services were connecting with farmers remained central to the concerns of both county and national advisory officers. The county reports always quantified the number of advisory visits, and a national report on the first eight years of the service's operation included a statistical survey of the activities of NAAS officers for the year 1953–4, which included 375,223 advisory visits, equating to an average of roughly one per farmer per year in England and Wales. Of course, some farmers were visited much more often and others not at all. A six-month national study in the spring and summer of 1967 demonstrated that advisers had visited 25 per cent of fifty- to 150-acre farms but over 40 per cent of farms bigger than five hundred acres. In Cambridgeshire, between 1954 and 1961, advisers had visited nearly half of all holdings of less than fifty acres, two-thirds of ten- to 150-acre holdings, and four-fifths of all holdings larger than 150 acres.[48]

One of the concerns often voiced in NAAS reports was the possibility of conflicts between the advisory and statutory parts of the District Adviser's job: 'It remains the aim of the NAAS to gain and keep the confidence of the farmer, and this is more difficult to achieve if the advisory officer has enforcement duties.' At the beginning, when CWAECs were still in being, and had both statutory duties and responsibilities for the promotion of agricultural production policy, NAAS officers worked closely with them, and in addition the service had its own responsibilities for plant health, clean milk production, and livestock improvement (which in practice mostly meant bull and boar licensing). In reality, a

---

[46] TNA, MAF114/747, South Western Province, Advisory Services, HQ Administration, Devon County Report 1962–3.
[47] TNA, MAF 114/241, South Western Province, Advisory Services, HQ Administration, Devon County Report 1952–3.
[48] N.F. McCann, *The Story of the National Agricultural Advisory Service: A Mainspring of Agricultural Revival 1946–1971* (Ely, 1989), p. 73.

statutory visit often also resulted in conversations or discussions in which the District Officer advised the farmer, and whatever government policy, the view that NAAS took was that 'advisory officers have full freedom to give whatever technical advice they themselves consider appropriate'.[49] Among the specific benefits claimed to have been produced by NAAS officers were new hill land reclamation techniques associated with the Farm Improvement Scheme, co-operation with the National Institute for Research in Dairying to improve milking machine efficiency, involvement in the development of self-feed silage and forage harvesters, and the importation of Charolais cattle (although the opinion of at least one of the breeders was at variance with the last of these).[50]

NAAS also ran several EHFs (see above), in conjunction with the AIC, with the aim of carrying on work that 'cannot be taken further by the research stations, nor yet be recommended with confidence to commercial producers without further trial'.[51] As farmer 570 said of his local EHF at Liscombe: 'They were doing research, but it was such down to earth research.' In the mid-1960s, this had a big effect on the local uptake of silage for grass conservation:

> Everybody got into the idea by going to Liscombe ... you could look at the bullocks, and those had been fed silage, and those silage and meal, and ... you could see the difference between them, and you learned how to do it, and what improved grasses to put in.

Initially, NAAS advisers were mainly concerned with the technical changes required to produce output maximisation, but from the late 1950s it became clear that this was a less urgent requirement, and at the same time research workers such as Brian Camm, John Nix, and Chris Barnard developed the gross margin farm accounting system.[52] As a result, some NAAS advisers began to specialise in farm management advice, using gross margin analysis to show farmers how they could increase the profitability of their farms. McCann's history, written to celebrate twenty-five years of the existence of NAAS, claimed that between 1960 and 1963 the farms using NAAS farm management advice, of which there were 176, increased their net income by 141 per cent; one hundred similar farms costed by the FMS only increased incomes by 7.55 per cent.[53] NAAS

---

[49] TNA, MAF 114/332, Report on NAAS 1946–54, pp. 59–61.
[50] McCann, *The Story of the National Agricultural Advisory Service*, p. 75; T. Harman, *Seventy Summers* (London, 1986), pp. 226–32.
[51] J.A. Macmillan and C.E. Hudson, 'NAAS Experimental Husbandry Farms and Horticulture Stations', *Agriculture* LXIII/5 (1956).
[52] C.S. Barnard and J.S. Nix, *Farm Planning and Control* (Cambridge, 1973); J.S. Nix, 'Farm Management: The State of the Art (or Science)', *J. Agric. Econs.* 30 (1979), pp. 277–92.
[53] McCann, *The Story of the National Agricultural Advisory Service*, p. 77.

remained in being during the twenty post-war years when agricultural output increased most rapidly. It was changed in 1971 when NAAS was brought together with the Agricultural Land Service, the Land Drainage Department, and the Ministry's Veterinary Service to form the ADAS, but its services remained essentially free to farmers until about the mid-1980s, after which it was gradually commercialised and run down.[54] Farmers were less willing to use it once they had to pay. As farmer 2/21 said:

> I was quite an avid supporter of NAAS, I had good friends who were in it, ... and I always valued their advice, which was free at the point of need, like the Health Service. I resented having to pay for it, ... but we did make very good use of NAAS and their specialist services on agronomy, chemistry, but I think as with a lot of farmers the willingness to get involved fell away once charges were being made and there was less emphasis on increased production.

The national advisory services were not the only sources of advice available to farmers. The MMB, for example, ran a Low Cost Production (LCP) Service from 1962 that involved monthly visits by Consulting Officers to participating farms, of which there were 3,700 by 1973. It also had a scheme for an annual test of milking machines to which a further 7,500 producers subscribed.[55] Other organisations concerned with particular commodities such as the British Sugar Corporation, the Home-Grown Cereals Authority (HGCA), and the MLC also provided technical information, although it was not the purpose for which they were specifically established. The MLC emerged in 1967 and incorporated two previously existing organisations, the Pig Industry Development Authority (PIDA) and the Beef Recording Association, both of which had technical change as part of their remit, and employed fieldsmen to visit farms and give advice, and also to run courses on specific topics, such as on-farm artificial insemination of pigs.[56] In 1966, the government established the Agricultural Training Board (ATB), one of a number of industrial training boards, to provide training beyond that provided by the agricultural education system and the commodity organisations.[57] What they provided was essentially in-service training for farmers and their workers. As farmer 3/1 recalled of the ATB: 'I went on some courses,

---

54 S. Foreman, *Loaves and Fishes: An Illustrated History of the Ministry of Agriculture, Fisheries and Food 1889–1989* (London, 1989), p. 117.
55 S. Baker, *Milk to Market: Forty Years of Milk Marketing* (London, 1973), pp. 230–3.
56 P. Wormell, *Anatomy of Agriculture: A Study of Britain's Greatest Industry* (London, 1978), p. 505; P. Brassley, 'Cutting across Nature? The History of Artificial Insemination in Pigs in the UK', *Studies in the History and Philosophy of Biological and Biomedical Sciences* 38 (2007), pp. 442–61.
57 Foreman, *Loaves and Fishes*, p. 103.

foot trimming, for example, and they were good, they were held on farms, very specific, so you went to look at one thing, how to stop dermatitis or whatever, and they would be a one-day course, fitted in between milkings.'

The NIAB had been established before the Second World War to provide advice on varieties of all farm crops, for which it carried out trials all over the country, and subsequently published recommended lists of varieties and held numerous meetings to demonstrate new varieties to farmers and the seed trade. NIAB might be seen as an attempt to ensure the honesty of the seed trade, for it emerged from the realisation that many of the different varieties on sale at the end of the First World War were identical in all respects apart from the names given to them by the seed company that was selling them. This had not generally mattered much, as the differences in performance between varieties was not great, until potato wart disease became a problem. Some varieties were immune to it, and others were not, and it was important to know the difference, so wart testing stations were set up.[58] It was from this system that NIAB emerged, and by the 1950s, when testing methods became sophisticated enough to determine whether some varieties of all crops were better suited to some conditions than others, it was an increasingly important part of the knowledge network, issuing recommended lists of varieties for each crop with details of yield variations, disease resistance, suitability for different soils, and so on.[59] Any farmer could join NIAB and so receive these lists, as farmer 2/7 in Dorset did: 'I used to look forward every January to the NIAB leaflets coming out to see what was recommended for the spring planting.' In the Blackmore Vale dairy district of Dorset, however, farmer 3/1 felt that recommended lists were of more use to cereal farmers than grassland specialists, and instead 'you'd ask the seeds rep – often the cake rep, the same firm – and he'd say "I'll send you some bags of No.4."'

Agricultural Shows

Another, more traditional, source of information for farmers was the agricultural show. There was an enormous variety of these, from the local show to the county or regional shows such as the Royal Cornwall, the Devon, the Bath and West, the Great Yorkshire, and the national show, the Royal, which moved around the country until 1963 when it held the first Show at its permanent showground at Stoneleigh in Warwickshire. Although in their nineteenth-century origins most or all of these had as their objective the promotion of technical change – 'improvement' in the

---

[58] Brassley, 'Agricultural Science and Education', p. 528.
[59] D.J. Berry, 'Genetics, Statistics, and Regulation at the National Institute of Agricultural Botany, 1919–1969' (unpublished Ph.D. dissertation, University of Leeds, 2014), especially chapters 4 and 5.

language of the time – by the mid-twentieth century it was clear that the more local shows were essentially social events, where rural people met their friends and engaged in friendly competition showing all kinds of products from breeding animals to jam. The big regional and national shows were different. For traditional livestock breeders wishing to sell their animals at high prices, a presence and a good performance at such shows was essential, and for machinery manufacturers, seed firms, fertiliser, and pesticide companies they represented an opportunity to present their latest products to farmers who operated on a big enough scale to be able to take one or more days away from the farm and travel some distance. Banks and advisory services also had a permanent presence at such shows. Attendance at the Royal Show rose steadily to the mid-1970s, when there were around two hundred thousand visitors and exhibitors each year, and these numbers were maintained or even exceeded until the mid-1980s. While a proportion of those attending the Royal may have had little or no connection with agriculture and simply sought a day's entertainment, visitor surveys found that 36 per cent of all male visitors in 1975, and 43 per cent in 1983, were farmers, farm managers, or farm workers. Sixty per cent of the male visitors in 1972 were connected with agriculture in some way, and in that year over twenty-six thousand farmers and farm managers visited the show. Since they farmed a total of eleven million acres, which represents 423 acres each, it is clear that, as suggested above, they tended to be drawn from the ranks of those farming on a larger than average scale. And this minority of the farming population were there to do business: a 1986 survey found that two-thirds of the farmers, managers, and workers attending the show made a purchase related to what they had seen within seven months.[60]

The Agricultural Press

Agricultural shows, with the exception of the Smithfield livestock show in December, were held in the summer months, but throughout the year the print and broadcast media aimed their output at farmers. As with the shows, agricultural journals aimed at farmers had existed from at least the eighteenth century. The market leaders in the 1950s and '60s were *Farmer and Stockbreeder*, which had first been published in 1889, and *Farmers Weekly*, which began in 1934. The former was effectively taken over by the NFU in 1971 and became *British Farmer and Stockbreeder* before closing in 1984, leaving the latter as the principal weekly farming publication, although by no means the only one.[61] There was also *Farmers Guardian*,

[60] N. Goddard, *Harvests of Change: The Royal Agricultural Society of England 1838–1988* (London, 1988), pp. 264–7.
[61] N. Goddard, 'Agricultural Institutions: Societies, Associations and the Press', in E.J.T. Collins (ed.), *The Agrarian History of England and Wales*, vol. VII,

published in the north of England, and a range of specialist magazines, from those aimed at the ordinary producer such as *Dairy Farmer* and *Pig Farmer* to high-priced specialist newsletters such as *Agra Europe*, which emerged in 1963, was concerned with CAP policy making, and was probably read by more civil servants, ancillary industry managers, academics, and journalists than farmers. The Ministry of Agriculture had its own journal, *Agriculture*, published monthly (originally as *The Journal of the Board of Agriculture*) since 1894, until it was closed in 1972. Again, it was probably read more by advisers and academics than by farmers in general, as was the *NAAS Quarterly Review*, published from 1948.[62] It was claimed in 1978 that there were 126 farming magazines or other publications in existence, and in addition the serious national newspapers and some of the regional newspapers such as the *Western Morning News* all had full-time agricultural correspondents. At that time, *Farmers Weekly* had a circulation of 130,000, and the combined circulations of the *Farmers Guardian* and the specialist publications such as *Dairy Farmer, Power Farming, Arable Farmer, Big Farm Weekly, and Big Farm Management* amounted to as many again.[63] Even taking account of the fact that some farmers would read several of these publications each week, it would have been unusual, given these numbers, for a farmer *not* to have been exposed to some source of printed farming news each week. Certainly, most of the farmers interviewed mentioned reading, often the *Farmers Weekly*, as a major source of information. As farmer 2/7 said: 'The *Farmers Weekly* has been my compulsion every Saturday morning for fifty years.'

Commercial publishers also found it worthwhile to produce books on farming technique, many of which sold well beyond the student market. *Farming for Profits*, the first edition of which was published by Penguin, was written by Dr Keith Dexter and Derek (later Sir Derek) Barber, both of whom worked for NAAS at the time. It sold twenty-five thousand copies between 1961 and 1963.[64] In 1955, the Ministry of Agriculture published *The Farm as a Business*, giving advice on 'the principles underlying farm business analysis and planning', and from 1963 this was converted into eight booklets in an *Aids to Management* series, comprising a general introduction to management and individual booklets on beef, sheep, pigs, poultry, labour and machinery, arable crops, and dairying, each available at 2s 6d (which was roughly the cost of a Penguin paperback in 1963).[65] Standard textbooks must have sold well too, for there were four new editions of Fream's *Elements of Agriculture* between 1948 and 1983, and

---

1850–1914 (Cambridge, 2000), pp. 650–90; Wormell, *Anatomy of Agriculture*, pp. 541–50.

[62] Foreman, *Loaves and Fishes*, pp. 90–2.
[63] Wormell, *Anatomy of Agriculture*, pp. 541–50.
[64] K. Dexter and D. Barber, *Farming for Profits* (2nd edn, London, 1967).
[65] MAFF, *Aids to Management: Dairying* (London, 1967), pp. iv, 1.

four of Watson and More's *Agriculture* between 1945 and 1962.[66] As far as the press and the publishers were concerned, agriculture was clearly a market worth catering for.

Agricultural Radio and Television

Radio programmes on farming technology were broadcast from 1937 onwards, although they escaped notice in Briggs's history of the BBC, which restricts any mention of farming broadcasts to *The Archers*.[67] Godfrey Basely, its originator, argued that *The Archers* was indeed technically oriented. By the end of the war, radio broadcasts were central to public information and the formation of a national, as opposed to local or regional, culture, and the BBC was seen as having a propaganda role in post-war reconstruction. In 1948, a discussion between farmers and BBC staff in Birmingham on how best to transmit specialist information led to the suggestion of what would now be called a radio soap opera – a 'farming *Dick Barton*' in the language of the time – as a more effective way of getting technical points over to a farming audience than the dry academic discourse that had hitherto characterised farming talks. Baseley saw the technically conservative small Midland farmer as the audience he needed to reach and, using the *Dick Barton* scriptwriters, created a combination of instruction, information, and entertainment that became a fixture on BBC radio from 1951.[68]

Whether this was the only radio farming programme in the 1950s is unclear, but by 1958 BBC radio was broadcasting a *Market Report* for farmers in the early morning. In July 1962, the early morning market report was incorporated into a ten-minute *Farm Bulletin* of news items broadcast from 6:40 am each weekday. A minute in the MAFF's Broadcasting Advisory Committee file noted that

> The Ministry's technical services have contributed to this programme because they feel it is an excellent opportunity to impact on farmers about technical matters. All over the country we are receiving reports

---

[66] C.R.W. Spedding (ed.), *Fream's Agriculture* (16th edn, London, 1983); J.A.S. Watson and J.A. More, *Agriculture* (11th edn, Edinburgh, 1962).

[67] A. Briggs, *The BBC: The First Fifty Years* (Oxford, 1985) A search of the online *Radio Times* listings (https://www.bbcgenome.co.uk) reveals the existence of radio talks entitled *Farming Today* from 1937. We are grateful to Tom Hercock of the BBC Written Archives Centre, Caversham Park, Reading, for this information. The scripts of the wartime (and later) programmes were published as Anon, *Farming Today Broadcasts: A Series of Agricultural Education and Technical Development Broadcast Talks* (Worcester, 7 volumes published between 1942 and 1948).

[68] S. Laing, 'Images of the Rural in Popular Culture', in B. Short (ed.), *The English Rural Community: Image and Analysis* (Cambridge, 1992).

that farmers are listening to this programme ... Thus the programme is becoming a valuable adjunct to our advisory work.

In particular, it was felt that radio was the right medium for urgent news on pests, diseases, and control methods. Whether it was broadcast at the right time was a different question: 'The best farmers are working at 6:40am while those who could benefit are still abed.'[69] By 1965, the programme had become *Farming Today*, broadcast from Monday to Saturday between 6:35 and 6:50 am, still with market prices at the beginning, and continuing to attract favourable comments from the Ministry of Agriculture.[70] There was also a weekly radio programme, *Farm Fare*, which soon changed its title to *On Your Farm*. It was broadcast on Wednesday lunchtimes but later became a regular fixture on early Saturday mornings until the twenty-first century. At that time, the BBC Home Service divided at some points in the day to broadcast regional programmes, and for most regions these included a twenty-five-minute farming programme. On the West Home Service, it was called *The Farmer*, broadcast weekly at lunchtime. In January 1958, for example, it included comments on the week's farming news, together with a specific item: machinery sharing, dairy cattle breeding, calf rearing methods, self-feeding silage, rabbit problems, a visit to a hatchery, and generating electricity by waterpower were among the topics discussed that month. By the early 1960s, it had settled into a format involving a technical talk by an expert, a farm visit, and for the last three or four minutes 'something of a lighter nature' to appeal to an audience that would include womenfolk in the farmhouse, YFCs, farm workers, and others connected with farming but not actually farming on their own account.[71]

BBC Television farming programmes began on 3 October 1957. The programme was simply called *Farming* and usually consisted of three items, linked by a chairman, who was always a farmer with the kind of large farming business that allowed him to be absent from the farm for up to fifty days each year (according to one of them, John Cherrington).[72] By the autumn of 1960, it had settled into a Sunday lunchtime slot and had evolved to use much more film and outside broadcast material. Of the fourteen programmes televised between late September and the end of the year, six involved visits to farms, one to an Experimental Horticulture Station, and three to shows. The schedule for the spring of 1966 embraced controversy and farming abroad to a greater extent than before, with

[69] TNA, MAF 197/40, BBC Audience Research Report, 1961, later minuted by R.J. Searsby, 9 October 1962.
[70] TNA, MAF 197/44, minutes of the BBC Central Agricultural Advisory Committee, 21 January 1965.
[71] TNA, MAF 197/40, BBC Audience Research Report, 1961; TNA, MAF 197/44, minutes of the BBC Central Agricultural Advisory Committee.
[72] J. Cherrington, *On the Smell of an Oily Rag* (London, 1979), p. 145.

programmes on the export of beef to the Netherlands, the impact of the Irish Free Trade Agreement on dairy farming, the Agricultural Central Trading Company's role, and the agricultural policies of the three main political parties, although there were still four farm visits in thirteen programmes and an interview with the pioneering farmer Captain Bennett Evans.[73] Independent (commercial) television began in 1955, but farming programmes did not begin everywhere from that time. In the west of England, the regional company Westward Television began in 1961 and immediately introduced the half-hour *Farming News*. Like the BBC farming programmes, it was aimed at an agricultural audience with little attempt to relate to the wider population. Unlike the BBC, it included advertising, a significant amount of which was sold for products targeted at the agricultural audience, especially livestock health products. When Television South West (TSW) took over the franchise from Westward in 1981, the presenter changed (Peter Forde was replaced by Ron Bendell) but the farming programme continued.[74]

It is important to remember that when these developments in broadcasting were taking place, not all farms were connected to a mains electricity supply, a fact that apparently came as something of a surprise to some members of the BBC's Agricultural Broadcasting Advisory Committee.[75] A little over 80 per cent of farms had a mains supply by 1958.[76] This did not necessarily mean that they had no access to broadcasting, because radios could be powered by rechargeable batteries, and some farms without a mains supply nevertheless had an electrical generator. But television was 'better with the mains – less voltage surge and drop', according to farmer 162, and when farm 669 went on to a mains supply in 1964 a television and a washing machine were the first purchases. These connection problems were probably not the major factor affecting the response to agricultural broadcasting, although they would have been important to some farmers, but they do not entirely explain the relatively low proportion of farmers listening or watching. In 1961, the BBC commissioned an Audience Research Report on farming programmes, based on a sample of nearly three thousand farmers selected at random from NFU and Scottish NFU members. It revealed that only about a third of farmers were regular listeners (i.e. at least three or four times a week) to the early morning farming programme and

---

[73] TNA, MAF 197/40, BBC Audience Research Report, 1961; TNA, MAF 197/44, minutes of the BBC Central Agricultural Advisory Committee.
[74] J. Constable, South West Film and Television Archive, emails to PB, 13 February and 4 March 2013.
[75] TNA, MAF 197/40, ABAC minutes, 30 January 1958.
[76] P. Brassley, 'Electrifying Farms in England', in P. Brassley, J. Burchardt, and K. Sayer (eds), *Transforming the Countryside: The Electrification of Rural Britain* (Abingdon, 2017), p. 92.

concluded that about a quarter of farmers saw the BBC television farming programme regularly. The audience for the ITV farming programmes was even smaller.[77]

Inevitably, some programmes provoked discussion or even controversy. As ever, some members of the audience were unhappy about programme changes, as for example when the reporting of market information changed in 1971 to give regional average prices rather than prices and quantities in specific markets. Although the change was a reaction to the changing pattern of livestock and arable product marketing at the time, some farmers were annoyed enough to write to the Minister to demand a reversion to the old arrangements.[78] A member of the Ministry's farm safety branch was horrified to see television programmes in which someone dangled his coat within a few inches of an unguarded power take-off shaft, and children were shown riding on trailers behind tractors, and ensured that the BBC's agricultural liaison officer's attention was drawn to the problem.[79] In 1958, the head of the Ministry's Information Division, Mr C.H.A. Duke, provoked a discussion in the Agricultural Broadcasting Advisory Committee on the extent to which farming programmes should comply with national policy. The question arose from a programme in which a small farmer had been advised to expand his milking herd to increase his income at a time when, said Mr Duke, 'they all knew that there was more milk in the country than was needed'. Mr Phillips, a member of the BBC staff, responded by saying that the adviser

> had told the farmer what was best for his particular farm, and in his view it was the responsibility of the Milk Marketing Board and the Ministry to look after the flood of milk ... The aim of the programme had not been to produce more milk but to show small farmers that they must specialise.

Part of the problem, argued Mr Ferro of the Ministry, supporting his colleague and identifying one of the perennial problems of television, was that TV farming programmes tended to be superficial. In this case, for example, more information on costs and returns was needed. Professor Bywater of Leeds produced a neat summary of the issue:

> one of the important issues in agriculture was the reconciliation of the aims of the individual and of the industry and the nation as a whole. He had sympathy with Mr Duke's point of view, but thought it would be

---

[77] TNA, MAF197/40, BBC Audience Research Report, 1961.
[78] TNA, MAF 197/84, BBC: morning broadcasts; policy.
[79] TNA, MAF 197/40, minute from T.A. McDowell to C.F. Pennison, 7 April 1961.

a mistake not to underline the steps which ordinary farmers could take to increase profit and production.[80]

Even more heated was the discussion over a programme the BBC broadcast in 1964 on the 'feather bedding' of farming. Many of the points it made were unanswerable, but the Ministry's Press Branch went to the extent of issuing detailed comments and rebuttals on some of the points of fact in the programme.[81] In general, however, it seems clear from both the Advisory Committee minutes and the programme contents that agricultural broadcasting at this formative point in the late 1950s to the mid-1960s was much more concerned with promoting output and technical innovation in farming than with producing controversial programmes.

One reason for this technical focus in agricultural broadcasting was almost certainly the composition of the committees advising the programme makers. Both the BBC and ITV had advisory committees overseeing their agricultural output. Most of those on the BBC's Committee were farmers or landowners, but in 1958 there were also two Ministry of Agriculture civil servants, a publisher, and the Professor of Agriculture at Leeds University. The Committee was chaired in 1958 by Clyde Higgs, a prominent farmer who had also been involved in making radio programmes, and in 1965 by Tristram Beresford, a farmer and agricultural journalist.[82] The chair of the Agricultural Advisory Board for Westward TV from the 1960s until the end of its franchise in 1981 was R.G. Pomeroy, a North Devon farmer and a member of the MMB. There were also three farmers, one from each of the counties of Devon, Cornwall, and Dorset, representatives of the Ministry of Agriculture and the NFU, an independent agricultural adviser, and the Director of the Agricultural Economics Unit at Exeter University.[83] This farmer dominance was reinforced by other connections with government advisory bodies promoting technical change in farming. In June 1963, the Minister's AAC gave general approval to its chairman's proposal to form 'an association of those engaged in agricultural television'. The chairman, Mr J.D.F. Green, was himself a former BBC agricultural liaison officer, and his paper argued that while television was 'of great importance as a developing medium for the dissemination of agricultural knowledge', it currently lacked 'some of the authority or impact of agricultural journalism ... probably because techniques are uncertain

---

[80] TNA, MAF 197/40, ABAC minutes, 30 January 1958.
[81] TNA, MAF 197/44, ABAC minutes, 21 January 1965.
[82] TNA, MAF 197/40 and 197/44, minutes of the Agricultural Broadcasting Advisory Committee.
[83] J. Constable, South West Film and Television Archive, emails to PB, 13 February and 4 March 2013.

and reactions less easily gauged'. In contrast to the BBC monopoly of radio, he pointed out, there were several different television companies engaged in producing farming television, so the purpose of his proposed organisation would be to 'co-ordinate their efforts so that important questions of interest to farmers are not neglected'. A similar organisation in the USA had 'proved to be a powerful ally of the U.S. Department of Agriculture'.[84]

Whether or not the association was ever formed is unclear, but what is interesting as far as the transmission of technical change is concerned is that the discussion took place in the AAC. It shows how one of the official bodies most concerned with making agricultural research and development available to farmers was aware of the role and importance of the media. Technical change in 1960s agriculture was not just something that could be left to the vagaries of the market mechanism, but a process to be managed and promoted.

The Farmer and the Rep

The purpose of discussing these meetings in some detail is to emphasise the difficulties involved in getting official policy relating to output and technical change over to farmers, the importance attached by the Ministry to doing so, and the methods that they were willing and able to use.[85] The market mechanism, as manipulated by agricultural policy, sometimes needed a little lubrication from the oil of public relations. This is not to say that the market mechanism, as embodied in those firms in the agricultural supply industries, proved unwilling to promote technical change. One agricultural journalist estimated that in the 'heady days' of the 1960s and '70s there were 'at least 50,000 people' calling on farmers, advising them, and arranging technical events for them.[86] Farmer 2/7 in Dorset remembered having 'a chap called ..., he used to sell Boots products, Isocornox etc, and we used to rely on his advice, he was the technical rep', and then in the 1980s 'we went on to the independent adviser ... you would pay him about £3 an acre and he would do this farm and several others in the locality'. Farmers had often dealt with the same firm for years and trusted their judgement. As farmer 787 said, 'If you're interested in something you find out anyway, I ask people, I wanted some machinery for the corn, and I went and talked to a dealer.' Similarly, farmer 3/1 remembered that 'Everybody had a firm they dealt with. We had one at Bruton called Sheldon Jones, they were a compounder, but they expanded into dairy

---

[84] TNA, MAF 253/105, minutes of the third meeting of the Agricultural Advisory Council, 6 June 1963.
[85] There is further consideration of this topic in chapter 4.
[86] D. Montague, *Farming, Food, and Politics: The Merchant's Tale* (Dublin, 2000), p. 111.

seeds. It was all very friendly', and farmer 109's memories support this: 'We didn't avoid reps, we still know some. There were a lot of reps about in those days, but we always had the same one, from Wyatt and Bruce ... And there was Tuckers, we dealt with Tuckers as well, Mr [...], for seeds and feeds, and fertilisers.'

Fertiliser producers such as Fisons and ICI, and feed firms such as British Oil and Cake Mills (BOCM), might charter complete trains to take three thousand farmers at a time to demonstration farms or factories. Most farmers bought their feeds, seeds, and fertilisers from agricultural merchants rather than directly from the producers, but many of the bigger producers nevertheless employed their own teams of technical representatives who would visit farms to advise on the use of increasingly technically complex products. These men (and they were then, in contrast to later, almost all men) not only knew about their own products but would also have called on numerous other farms in the district, so they often had a well-informed picture of technical changes beyond their own immediate commercial interests. Talking over such things was a way to capture a potential customer's interest, and many of these representatives were trusted by farmers and seen as a free and reliable source of technical information. BOCM, one of the larger feed manufacturers, was one of those that did not sell direct to farmers, but nevertheless there are eighty-three people in a photograph of its technical sales team taken in the 1960s. Firms such as ICI and Fisons were one of the bigger recruiters of agricultural students from universities and colleges during this period, and when serious attempts were made to control agricultural output in the 1990s it was these firms in the ancillary industries that were among the first to feel the effects. At its peak, ICI had five thousand people in its fertiliser operation; by 1995, they were down to 350, of whom six were the sales force.[87] The impact on graduate recruitment was immediate and significant.

'Living in a Sea of Information'

If, as the above discussion suggests, the supply of information and training available to farmers increased dramatically in the forty post-war years, what happened to the demand for it? Having provided numerous wells of experience and fountains of knowledge, as it were, to what extent were the farm horses prepared to drink? To judge from the uptake of agricultural education, they were not especially thirsty, but the extent to which commercial firms were prepared to keep technical reps in the field in the 1960s and '70s suggests that they were providing something that many farmers were willing to consume. The problem is that the

---

[87] Montague, *Farming, Food and Politics*, pp. 110–11, 260–1.

relationship between farmers and technical training and information is not easy to measure because much of it is an informal process, and what evidence there is tends to be anecdotal. The evidence from the sample of farmers interviewed in the south-west is that, as in many other aspects of farming, there were considerable differences from one farmer to another. As with their experiences of education, discussed above, what worked for one farmer might be anathema to another.

Few farmers among those interviewed used no sources of advice or information whatsoever, and it is perhaps significant that those nearest to being complete non-users were no longer farming when they were interviewed. Farmer 692 belonged to the YFC, where he learned to shear sheep, but apart from that he 'didn't have much to do with ADAS or demonstration farms … didn't often read *Farmers Weekly* … I used to watch the farming programme on TV but I didn't get a lot of information from it … you gradually learn from each other.' Farmer 2/9 felt that his father 'wasn't quite the typical farmer … he was also a Methodist lay preacher, so when he wasn't farming he didn't tend to socialise in farming circles', and he himself was more interested in archaeology and wildlife than in farming. He had never joined the YFC or discussion groups, and although he received ADAS leaflets, he 'wouldn't say that they influenced me a great deal', although his father had used NAAS advice. Most of the farmers interviewed, however, were integrated to some degree into what might be called a knowledge network. Farmer 162, who had a 132-acre livestock farm on the edge of Exmoor, used to read the literature sent to him by the advisory services and the Ministry, but he 'never asked for any help', and although he was a keen member of the YFC it was 'more a social thing' than a source of information or training. On the other hand, he was always heavily involved in a sheep breed society, and farming newspapers and magazines were 'very important when I was leaving school, I used to read everything that was going'. His father used to listen to the early morning radio programme for the fatstock prices, and both his father and mother followed *The Archers*, but more for the story than for any technical information. The 'best guide of the lot', he felt, was the Exeter University FMS report, because it 'showed you where you were earning a pound'. Farmer 826 also felt that he received useful advice from the Investigation Officer who visited him regularly, and farmer 782 found that the FMS figures were 'very useful, they influenced my decisions to a certain extent'. Farmer 209 found that 'sometimes it wasn't good reading, because you weren't doing as well as you thought you were, but it told you what to stop doing'.

Farmer 162 also emphasised the importance of the informal knowledge network:

> Generally speaking the farmers round here got together and talked among themselves, what their plans were, and one of them would say

that he'd tried something, and the others would look over the hedge. [*Were they formal meetings?*] No, if they met on the road, or rent day, or harvest festival.

Farmer 243, with a small dairy farm in East Devon, made the same point:

> I got my information by asking people who I thought knew something about it, neighbours and so on ... I very rarely went to demonstrations. You used to pick up hints from the Young Farmers' Club, talking to people you met there. And for machinery we had Medland Sanders and Twose who had a base at Plymtree, and several of their workmen used to live round here, and you'd say 'Come and have a look at this', and they'd say 'You want this' or something, and they'd make it up for you. So it was an informal way of doing things.

As farmer 782 said, 'You pick up things talking to other farmers, chatting at market for example.' Farmer 2/7, who had a 680-acre farm in Dorset, emphasised the importance of 'meeting the other members of the family socially, who are all farming, that gave me a lot of my information', rather than any published sources:

> You learned by a process of osmosis, I suppose, when you were chatting to farmers, you learn on the shooting field, you say 'That's a good crop there, or what have you done about so and so, how did you plant that, why are you growing that?' You don't know you are learning or taking it in.

As farmer 535 put it: 'from journals, and YFC, and NFU, you get lectures, and you meet people – you are living in a sea of information and you pick out what you want ... and I would talk with my cousin, and my wife's brother – it was a network'.

At the opposite extreme from those farmers who emphasised the informal knowledge networks were those who seemed to use all possible sources of information and training. Farmer 209, who began with a thirty-four-acre rented farm in Cornwall in the 1940s and is now farming over seven hundred acres, was never a full-time agricultural student, although he did day release classes, and it is worth quoting his experience in some detail, as it shows very well the range of information available to a farmer:

> I read Kenneth Russell's *Dairy Farming* book, then there was the *Farmer and Stockbreeder*, and I went to Farmers' Union meetings with Dad, and then it was more like Grassland Society now, you had a talk by somebody after the business meeting, some of them were ADAS people, others were well-established farmers, with good sized farms, and there would be non-agricultural talks as well, the machinery dealers would give talks, it might be the owner, or the top salesman or manager. I wasn't involved in Young Farmers Club, there was another mistake ... And there was the Royal Cornwall Show, and I was involved

with the local show. There weren't as many demonstrations as there are now. We had quite a bit of ADAS advice back then, either at a meeting or somebody coming here. It was free then, it would be from the District Adviser, Truro office. Back in the '50s and '60s there were many more reps coming round to farms, feeding you information. I read *Dairy Farmer*, and *Farmer and Stockbreeder*, and then I went over to *Farmers Weekly*. Now there's more material than you've got time to read, back then you could keep pace with it. It's more difficult to know what direction to take now than it was fifty years ago. Government policy was clearer then, they had a clearer agenda back then.

He also mentioned the value of television farming programmes and professional advice from bank managers, vets, and consulting agronomists, whom he employed from the 1970s onwards, and concluded that 'your real detailed information comes from your agronomist and your vet and your machinery dealer ... the real detailed stuff you have to get for yourself. You have to make the decision in the end yourself.'

Farmer 466 had a very different educational background, with degrees in agriculture and agricultural economics, but he and his father also used a wide range of information sources:

> ICI used to have men out in the sticks, teaching farmers to use fertiliser and that sort of thing, there was one in this village who only died recently, from the days when my father and uncle were together in the early '30s, right up to the time they abolished them altogether, in the 1990s, and there was one after another, and they all happened to live in this village. They weren't called salesmen, but they were selling the ideas. They were technical reps. They ran things like grassland clubs, and we all trotted off to the Grassland Society, and it was very effective technical extension work, and later on we said we don't want to be in hock to those people, but as well as using ADAS we would use these people, because they would pay for us to go places and look at things. It was effective because new ideas were coming along quickly – one thinks of tractors, but it was much broader than that, fertilisers, weedkillers, new varieties of seed, and it was effective because these people would take a bunch of farmers to farmer so and so and it was very practical extension work at no cost to the farmer except his time. You could see it happening on the ground. With milking parlours, ADAS would have a demonstration if somebody had a new milking parlour.

Like other farmers, he also read the farming press, watched farming television programmes, and went to shows (the Royal for 'pioneering techniques' and local shows for social reasons). Unlike most, he had a Nuffield scholarship in the 1970s, which he used to study grassland management methods in the Netherlands and high-yielding dairy herds in Israel, and was a member of an elite Cornish farmers' club,

> a bunch of twenty or thirty, complete variety, it stopped me from becoming an in the rut cow farmer, because these were intelligent

farmers doing different things, so it was a useful network. That becomes extremely valuable as time goes on, because your education recedes into the background.

The question that emerges most clearly from these interviews is whether farmers 209 and 466, with their wide range of formal and informal information and training sources, are more typical of the average farmer than those quoted earlier, with their reliance on the informal knowledge networks. This immediately raises the question of whether the FMS sample is typical, which has been an issue ever since the FMS began, but since the Ministry was prepared to accept that it was reasonably typical, it seems justifiable to accept this interviewed subset as also typical. It certainly seems to cover the range of use and non-use of advice and information sources, and what is perhaps most remarkable is what an enormous number of sources there were. Those provided by official organisations have been described above, but what the interviews show is that there were all sorts of unofficial information sources too. As farmer 466 describes, there were farmer discussion groups, either self-organised or set up by an official or semi-official body. Farmer 744 in south Devon, for example, 'joined the Dartington Discussion Society, you got quite a bit of sound advice from them every so often, and then I joined the Devon Grassland Society, which was another source of information'. In east Cornwall, farmer 576 was a member of the MMB's LCP scheme but also had 'one or two very knowledgeable milk recorders, and they would say so and so has done this, and its going right'. Coupled with YFC and NFU meetings, NAAS/ADAS, ATB, and MMB advice, farming journals and magazines, television and radio programmes, and a steady flow of representatives of merchants and feed and fertiliser firms, not to mention the information exchange that was likely to occur whenever two farmers met, there was indeed, as farmer 535 said, a 'sea of information' from which farmers could take whatever they could use, according to their capital and abilities.

Conclusions: Research, Knowledge Networks, and the Adoption of Technology

The various theoretical approaches briefly surveyed at the beginning of chapter 2 usually contain some useful insights into the process by which original scientific research is transformed into farmyard practice. The diffusionist models probably provide a reasonable description of the timing of many technical changes, such as the adoption of tractors or milking machines (slow initially, followed by a more rapid phase, followed by a plateau – the S-shaped curve), but not much explanation of why they occurred. Social worlds theory highlights the importance of informal contacts between farmers and the difficulties of integrating the different social worlds of farmers and scientists.[88] User co-constructionist theories emphasise the role of farmers, as the users of new technologies, in taking, say, the work of scientists on silage making methods and converting them into everyday practice.[89] The 'triple helix' approach to research, in which different groups from academia, relevant enterprises, and appropriate government departments meet to identify and address evolving problems would appear to find a perfect example in the AICs.[90] Examining the development of AI for pigs, Brassley emphasised the way in which the people, professions, and organisations that were respected as being the authorities on the subject changed over time, with consequent changes in the types of language, or discourses, used to transmit the technology, and in the media used to do so.[91]

It is more difficult to make an overall judgement about the impact of the research. A classic study of cereal yields in the post-war period, for example, concluded that about half of the yield increase was the result of varietal changes, but that led to subsequent studies attempting to explain more detailed reasons for the observed increases.[92] If the detailed studies of specific technologies – silage and pig AI – already available show anything, it is that the process of technical change is complex and multifactorial, and that there is often a significant gap between the original science, where it exists, and the eventual technology.[93] Nevertheless, it is worthwhile to try to assess the linkages between research and technical change at the farm level. In their annual report for 1965–6, the ARC devoted four pages to an assessment of the value of the research they had funded. They highlighted the increase in plant and animal performance through the application of genetics, improved husbandry and animal feeding practices, better disease control in plants and animals, and pest and weed control in crops, and improved harvesting, handling, and storage methods. In each case, they related the change to the

---

[88] S. Wilmot, 'From "Public Service" to Artificial Insemination: Animal Breeding Science and Reproductive Research in Early-Twentieth-Century Britain', *Studies in the History and Philosophy of Biology and Biomedical Sciences* 38 (2007), pp. 411–41.

[89] P. Brassley, 'Silage in Britain, 1880–1990: The Delayed Adoption of an Innovation', *Agric. Hist. Rev.* 44 (1996), pp. 63–87.

[90] T. Shinn, 'The Triple Helix and the New Production of Knowledge: Prepackaged Thinking on Science and Technology', *Social Studies of Science* 32 (2002), pp. 599–614.

[91] Brassley, '"Cutting across Nature?"'.

[92] V. Silvey, 'The Contribution of New Varieties to Increasing Cereal Yield in England and Wales', *Journal of the National Institute of Agricultural Botany* 14 (1978), pp. 367–84. For details of some subsequent studies, see P. Brassley, 'Crop Varieties', in E.J.T. Collins (ed.), *The Agrarian History of England and Wales*, vol. VII, *1850–1914* (Cambridge, 2000), p. 529, n. 113.

[93] Brassley, 'Silage in Britain'; Brassley, '"Cutting across Nature?"'.

science that they had financed.[94] In the case of crop varieties, it is clear that the Plant Breeding Institute at Cambridge had a major impact on cereal varieties and the Scottish Plant Breeding Institute produced many important new potato varieties, although it is worth remembering that commercial breeders such as Nickersons also produced new varieties, and that some varieties were imported from foreign breeders. Pesticide research was carried out in ARC institutes such as Rothamsted, in university departments, especially at Wye College, and by commercial firms such as ICI, Fisons, and May & Baker, and again some products were developed abroad. With fertilisers, it is more difficult to identify any clear link between research and increased use. The identification of nitrogen, phosphorus, and potassium as the macro-nutrients dates back to before the First World War, and although fertiliser usage increased significantly after 1945 it was not because scientists suddenly demonstrated any important new scientific principles relating to fertiliser use. It is true that fertiliser companies did produce compounds that included all three nutrients in each individual particle, so that separation problems were overcome, and ammonium sulphate was superseded by the more concentrated ammonium nitrate, but these were not the reasons for increasing fertiliser applications. Indeed, as far as cereals were concerned, the reason for increased fertiliser use had little to do with the industry itself, and much to do with the development of dwarf varieties by the plant breeders.[95]

Probably the greatest single improvement in the effectiveness of tractors arose from the principle of weight transfer, originally incorporated into the post-war Ferguson tractor and later adopted by every other tractor manufacturer. This was clearly a product of the manufacturer rather than any research institute, but it is possible to find other mechanisation developments that can be traced back to work in the universities or research institutes. The original impetus for the most important of the new crops, oilseed rape and vining peas, came from the processors, United Oilseeds in the case of rape and the freezing companies, Birds Eye, Ross/Findus, and Salvesens in the case of peas. The initiative for the importation of the Charolais breed came from dairy and arable farmers, rather than beef producers,[96] but the techniques of AI and, later, embryo transplantation, that enabled new genes to be spread more rapidly through the national herds and flocks were largely developed at Cambridge University. Similarly, the expansion of silage after 1970 can be credited to a combination of farmers such as Richard Waltham, the Grassland Research Institute, and the work of commercial firms on

---

[94] TNA, MAF 200/142, Report of the ARC 1965–6.
[95] P. Brassley, 'Output and Technical Change in Twentieth-Century British Agriculture', *Agric. Hist. Rev.* 48 (2000), p. 72.
[96] Harman, *Seventy Summers*, pp. 221–35.

silage additives. New veterinary medicines seem to have been largely a product of the pharmaceutical industry. The design of the milking machine hardly changed at all between 1940, when it was a rarity, and 1960, when it was virtually ubiquitous. Similarly, there were no basic changes in the content of concentrated feedingstuffs, but there was a major change in the calculation of optimum rations with the introduction of the new feed calculations based on ARC research in the 1970s. And finally, the enormous changes in intensive livestock production can probably be traced to a combination of livestock breeding companies such as Thornbers (for poultry) and the Pig Improvement Company (PIC), and the processors and retailers who saw market opportunities as meat consumption increased.

There is an old joke in the advertising industry that states that half of all advertising expenditure is wasted, but one never knows which half. To judge from the previous paragraph, the same might be true of money, especially government money, spent on research. The ARC, in assessing the value of research in the mid-1960s, pointed out that the £8.5 million that they were then spending annually on agricultural research was still less than 1 per cent of the net agricultural product and 'confidently claimed that the economic returns of research have exceeded many times its cost'. Nevertheless, it is noticeable that some of the practical results of research that they mentioned were more potential than actual: '*If the results already produced by the Rothamsted Experimental Station were properly applied*, it is calculated that £4 million a year *could* be saved on manuring of cereals alone, without any loss of yield', and 'considerable increases in production *could* be achieved if the proportion of crossbred sows in the country were increased [our italics]'.[97]

Leaving potential responses aside, there have been various attempts to quantify the economic returns to agricultural research. Doyle and Ridout related research expenditure to changes in agricultural productivity and calculated that the average rate of return declined from between 20 and 30 per cent in 1966–70 to between 10 and 20 per cent in 1976–80.[98] Thirtle et al. quoted various studies that found wildly varying rates of return to research expenditure, from minus 38 per cent to plus 84 per cent, but concluded that the most reliable figure was 18 per cent, and that this applied to both the period 1953–72 and the years 1973–90, after entry into the Common Agricultural Policy (CAP).[99] Writing twenty years after the ARC report, the Economic Development Committee for Agriculture,

---

[97] TNA, MAF 200/142, Report of the ARC 1965–6, pp. 2, 4.
[98] C.J. Doyle and M.S. Ridout, 'The Impact of Scientific Research on UK Agricultural Productivity', *Research Policy* 14 (1985), pp. 109–16.
[99] C. Thirtle, P. Palladino, and J. Piesse, 'On the Organisation of Agricultural Research in the United Kingdom, 1945–1994: A Quantitative Description and Appraisal of Recent Reforms', *Research Policy* 26 (1997), pp. 557–76.

part of the government's National Economic Development Office, was less sanguine than its predecessor and provided an explanation for its scepticism. The value of research, it found, 'was too often judged on the publication of research papers with lack of regard for the practical value of the end product'.[100] Perhaps this was not surprising, for the Committee also argued that 'In public sector research, the motivation of staff is often directed towards an improvement in general scientific understanding rather than to dealing with the specific identified needs of users.' Perhaps as a consequence of this, scientists did not always communicate well with farmers. The report contained several case studies on the adoption of specific technical changes, which 'showed the continuing difficulty of presenting research findings to the industry in a meaningful way. They are often presented as scientific papers, written in the language of the researcher, and do not indicate how the research might be applied in farming systems.'[101] Nor were farmers exempt from criticism. Despite the industry's generally good record of technical adoption, not all farmers, the Committee felt, were technically competent, although 'the buoyant state of the industry and the availability of free advice has masked deficiencies among some farmers'.[102]

It is important to remember the state of the industry and of government policy at the time when these comments were produced. It was a time when agricultural surpluses and environmental problems were increasingly prominent politically. The public expenditure plan produced in January 1985 had called for a 10 per cent cut in R & D expenditure by the agriculture departments, and advisory services were also to be cut by 10 per cent. The AAC, which had succeeded the AIC, but was similarly responsible for co-ordinating agricultural science and practical farming, had been emasculated in 1975 and euthanised in 1979 (see above). The 1985 report was thus written in a different economic, administrative, and political climate from the ARC report of twenty years earlier. However, to know which of the two comes nearer to producing an accurate picture of the connections between agricultural science, knowledge transfer mechanisms, and farmers, requires more work. It may be that they were both accurate for the times in which they were written, and it is certainly the case that very few technical changes can be attributed uniquely to one institution or group of people. In the case of one of the few farmers who might be identified as a researcher, Brian Cadzow, the initiative to develop a new breed of sheep was certainly his, but he received much help from the nearby Animal Breeding Research Organisation at Edinburgh.[103]

[100] Agriculture EDC (Economic Development Committee), *The Adoption of Technology in Agriculture: Opportunities for Improvement* (London, 1985), p. 31.
[101] Agriculture EDC, *Adoption of Technology in Agriculture*, pp. 14, 18.
[102] Agriculture EDC, *Adoption of Technology in Agriculture*, p. 22.
[103] Acording to the recollection of one of the authors (PB), who worked for

The incentive to grow oilseed rape may have come from United Oilseeds, but other organisations were involved, from the plant breeders producing the right varieties to the mechanisation specialists in NAAS who worked on the problems of combining the crop. Technical change, to restate the point made earlier, rarely emerges fully formed from the laboratory, and individual laboratories are rarely entirely responsible for new developments. That there were more research institutes, ARC units, university research teams, and commercial laboratories, not to mention international contacts, probably meant that the chances of coming up with new ideas increased.

At the risk of producing yet another theoretical framework that confuses categorisation with analysis, it is tempting to identify four stages in the formation of new agricultural practices derived from scientific discoveries. These are summarised in table 3.3.

TABLE 3.3. Stages in the transformation of farming practices

Traditional practice	Acquired by practice and interpersonal transmission
	Employs traditional discourses
Agricultural science	Commissioned by government and industry
	Produced by scientists
	Acquired by scientists, advisers, and journalists
	Employs scientific discourses
Agricultural technology	Developed by scientists, advisers, and farmers
	Disseminated by advisers and journalists
	Acquired by farmers and farm workers
	Employs technical discourses
New practice	Validated by advisers, journalists, and farmers
	Disseminated by practice and interpersonal transmission
	Becomes a commonly used discourse

It is an interesting exercise to consider how the various stages in table 3.3 encapsulate the process of adopting new science into everyday farming practice. Scientists communicated with each other in a technical language using scientific periodicals and academic conferences that were not read or attended, or perhaps even understood, by farmers. Although from time to time they might write articles in the farming press, in general it was more likely that farmers would hear about new technologies through intermediaries in the knowledge network in the form of advisers, journalists, technical representatives, or even other farmers.[104] These

---

Cadzow in the autumn of 1965.

[104] For an example of a research scientist writing for the farming press, see C.

intermediaries might be seen as 'cultural amphibians', capable of relating to both elitist/scientific and popular cultures.[105] An alternative term is 'translators', defined as those who 'pass information between worlds by selecting information from one world [agricultural science] which is relevant to another [practical agriculture] and present it in a format that the second world will understand, so that eventually the science affects the practice'.[106]

The discussion in this chapter involves much detailed consideration of the officially inspired developments in research, advice, and education, but although these have generated much paper in the archives, what emerges most clearly from the evidence provided by individual farmers is the importance of informal non-institutional sources of information, the considerable variation in the rate at which different farmers adopted, or even became aware of, new technology, and the enormous variety of influences on different farmers. Clearly, what persuaded one farmer to adopt new technology might have no impact whatsoever on a neighbouring farm, but what was adopted on a neighbouring farm might be exactly what persuaded another farmer to follow the same technical path. As that wise old farmer A.G. Street observed, after his tour of farming England in late 1936,

> It isn't fair,
> It isn't wise,
> It isn't safe,
> To generalise.[107]

Polge, 'AI May Soon Help You to Breed Better Pigs', *Pig Farming* (November 1954), p. 27.

[105] The term 'cultural amphibians' is taken from M. Macdonald, 'The Secularization of Suicide in England', *Past and Present* 111 (1986), pp. 50–100.

[106] J. Marie, 'For Science, Love, and Money: The Social Worlds of Poultry and Rabbit Breeding in Britain, 1900–1940', *Social Studies of Science* 36 (2008), pp. 919–36.

[107] A.G. Street, *Farming England* (London, 1937), p. 111.

4

Agricultural Policy, 1939–85

The business environment within which farmers made decisions about whether or not to adopt new technologies was at least influenced, if not determined, by government agricultural policy, so any account of technical change should pay attention to policy developments. Income and price support measures, grants, and subsidies, as well as the provision of advice and ministerial encouragement, could all encourage farmers to invest and produce more; and at the end of this period the imposition of quotas and changes in support regimes provided signals to restrict production. These agricultural policies were formulated within historical, political, and economic contexts, which should therefore at least be outlined in charting their evolution. Consequently, this chapter examines the major changes in agricultural policy and attempts to put them in context. It distinguishes between policies aimed at influencing the payments received by farmers for their products, and other policies, but does not attempt, for reasons that will become obvious, to produce a detailed and comprehensive account of agricultural policy changes between 1939 and 1985.

The Pre-War Policy Context

Government policies affecting agriculture can be traced back as least as far as regulations affecting the wool trade in the medieval period. From the later seventeenth century, export bounties and import duties regulated international trade in cereals, and by 1750 there were numerous measures to encourage the cultivation of alternative crops such as hemp, flax, and madder, to promote land drainage, regulate enclosure, tithes, and markets, control animal disease, especially cattle plague, and prevent the import of Irish cattle.[1] In 1846, the regulations on cereal imports and exports – the Corn Laws – were repealed, and at the same time a wide range of duties on other food imports, such as dairy products, fruit,

---

[1] J. Thirsk, 'Agricultural Policy: Public Debate and Legislation', in J. Thirsk (ed.), *The Agrarian History of England and Wales*, vol. V (ii), *1640–1750* (Cambridge, 1985), pp. 298–388.

vegetables, and sugar, were also discontinued. At first sight, therefore, apart from a few years during and after the First World War, there was no agricultural policy between 1846 and the early 1930s. This is a misconception. Although there may have been no direct intervention in market prices, there were measures to protect animal health that led to intervention in agricultural trade from the 1870s onwards, to protect farmers from adulteration of fertilisers and feedingstuffs, and to promote smallholdings and rural industries as a means of retaining labour on the land.[2] Although the formation of the Board of Agriculture in 1889 was largely an administrative convenience to bring together the veterinary and statistics branches of the Privy Council with the Land Commission, the establishment of the Development Commission in 1909 provided central government funds for agricultural research and the encouragement of rural industries, forestry, rural transport, especially roads, and inland navigation.[3]

The outbreak of the First World War as the harvest of 1914 was being brought in led to no immediate change in agricultural policy. Food imports were maintained, although animal feed prices rose, and farmers responded to market price changes by producing more wheat and oats and less meat and milk. But by 1916 food prices were 60 per cent higher than they had been in 1914, there had been a poor potato harvest, and shipping losses were rising. Following the replacement of the Asquith government by Lloyd George's administration in December 1916, the Ministry of Food was established, and a Food Production Department was set up within the Board of Agriculture to encourage the expansion of domestic production. The 1917 Corn Production Act provided for guaranteed prices for wheat and oats for four years, although in 1917 these were less than the prevailing market prices. The Act also established an Agricultural Wages Board to determine the wages of agricultural workers, and CWAECs, the main function of which was to encourage the cultivation of land for cereal and potato production.[4]

The guaranteed prices were continued under the terms of the 1920 Agriculture Act but came to an end when the Act was controversially repealed in 1921.[5] Not that there was anything new about controversies

---

[2] J.R. Fisher, 'Agrarian Politics', in E.J.T. Collins (ed.), *The Agrarian History of England and Wales*, vol. VII, 1850–1914 (Cambridge, 2000), pp. 321–57.

[3] A. Rogers, *The Most Revolutionary Measure: A History of the Rural Development Commission, 1909–99* (Salisbury, 1999).

[4] E.H. Whetham, *The Agrarian History of England and Wales*, vol. VIII, 1914–1939 (Cambridge, 1978), pp. 89ff; P. Dewey, *British Agriculture in the First World War* (London, 1989).

[5] E.H. Whetham, 'The Agriculture Act, 1920, and Its Repeal: The "Great Betrayal"', *Agric. Hist. Rev.* 22 (1974), pp. 36–49; E.C. Penning-Rowsell, 'Who "Betrayed" Whom? Power and Politics in the 1920/1 Agricultural Crisis', *Agric. Hist. Rev.* 45 (1997), pp. 176–94.

over agricultural policy. Arguments about the desirability or otherwise of agricultural support had been going on since food imports began to increase at the end of the nineteenth century and became a major issue with Joseph Chamberlain's tariff reform campaign, launched in 1903.[6] In 1919, the year in which the Board of Agriculture was reconstituted as the Ministry of Agriculture and Fisheries (MAF), a Royal Commission on agriculture was evenly split, half arguing for continued price support, and the other half against. The latter group summarised their reasoning in what, from a late twentieth-century perspective, would appear to be prophetic accuracy:

> It could not, in our opinion, be other than detrimental to the best interests of agriculture were it obliged to conduct its operations on the uncertain basis provided by guaranteed prices. These guarantees can only be given by Act of Parliament, and no Parliament can bind its successors. Political opposition to guaranteed prices is certain. Electoral controversies will rage over the question of the continuance of the policy. A cleavage of interest between town and country is likely. The industry will be distracted by the necessity of interfering in politics. It will be tempted to support its claims by exaggerated estimates of the costs of production – a tendency only too noticeable in much of the evidence submitted to us. It will look to the taxpayer for its profit rather than to the development and improvement of its technique and business methods. In the event of the policy of the guarantees being continued by successive Parliaments, other industries will claim, with as much or as little reason, to be put on the same footing. This in turn will serve to divert the attention of the industry from its own legitimate sphere of action.[7]

This was the view that prevailed during the 1920s. In 1923, for example, the Conservative Prime Minister, Andrew Bonar Law, told a deputation of farmers and farm workers that 'agriculture must lie on an economic basis', and the 1926 White Paper on Agricultural Policy also emphasised the need to help farmers 'to organise themselves on an economic basis'.[8] Arguments about whether intervention in agricultural markets could be in the public interest continued into the 1930s, but the Ottawa Conference and the Wheat Act, both in 1932, signalled the beginnings of a more interventionist agricultural policy, continued in the establishment of the various marketing boards from 1932 onwards, the beef cattle subsidy in

---

[6] M. Winter, *Rural Politics: Policies for Agriculture, Forestry and the Environment* (London, 1996), pp. 72–6.
[7] *The Interim Report of the Royal Commission Appointed to Inquire into the Economic Prospects of the Agricultural Industry in Great Britain*, Cmd.473 (1919).
[8] A. Howkins, *The Death of Rural England: A Social History of the Countryside since 1900* (London, 2003), p. 50; J. Sheail, 'The White Paper, *Agricultural Policy*, of 1926: Its Context and Significance', *Agric. Hist. Rev.* 58 (2010), pp. 236–54.

1934, the establishment of the Food (Defence Plans) Department of the Board of Trade in 1936, the forerunner of the wartime Ministry of Food, and the 1937 Agriculture Act, with its price subsidies for oats and barley and fertiliser subsidies.[9]

By 1939, therefore, history, economics, and politics had already combined to produce a range of agricultural and food policies. Historically, there was by then a tradition more than sixty years old of free access to world markets with well-established trading links. In 1934–8, Britain produced less than 20 per cent of its flour, butter, and sugar consumption, and less than 40 per cent of its bacon and ham, and cheese. By the 1890s, it was importing live cattle from Argentina, and although this trade was soon stopped because these animals brought foot and mouth disease with them, refrigeration technology developed so that by 1900 it was possible to import Argentinian beef as chilled carcases. In the late 1930s, Britain only produced half of its meat supplies, with Australia, New Zealand, Argentina, Denmark, and Eire becoming the principal source of imports. Even a significant proportion of 'fresh' eggs were imported, principally from Denmark, Eire, the Netherlands, and Poland.[10] By the outbreak of the Second World War, Britain was the dominant importer on the world market, responsible for nearly half of the trade in wheat and feed grains and the majority of the beef, bacon, and butter imports.[11] The reasons for this are well established: the availability of cheap food on the world market and Britain's ability to pay for it, resulting initially from a surplus of industrial exports, but by the 1930s – in fact since before 1900 – dependent upon the income from overseas investments.[12] It was this combination of history and economics that accounted for the absence of farm price support up to the 1930s. The countervailing pressures thereafter were largely political, in the form of the increasing power of the NFU, and, latterly, fears of an approaching European war.[13] There was

---

[9] Whetham, *Agrarian History*, vol. VIII, p. 261; A. Wilt, *Food for War: Agriculture and Rearmament in Britain before the Second World War* (Oxford, 2001); C. Griffiths, 'Farming in the Public Interest: Constructing and Reconstructing Agriculture on the Political Left', in P. Brassley, J. Burchardt, and L. Thompson (eds), *The English Countryside between the Wars: Regeneration or Decline?* (Woodbridge, 2006), pp. 164–75.

[10] H.T. Williams (ed.), *Principles for British Agricultural Policy* (London, 1960), pp. 32–7; C.K. Harley, 'The World Food Economy and Pre-World War I Argentina', in S.N. Broadberry and N.F.R. Crafts (eds), *Britain in the International Economy* (Cambridge, 1992), pp. 244–68.

[11] P. Brassley, 'International Trade in Agricultural Products, 1935–1955', in P. Brassley, L. Van Molle, and Y. Segers (eds), *War, Agriculture and Food: Rural Europe from the 1930s to the 1950s* (New York, 2012), pp. 34–5.

[12] Williams, *Principles for British Agricultural Policy*, pp. 38–9.

[13] Winter, *Rural Politics*, pp. 94–9; A.F. Cooper, *British Agricultural Policy, 1912–36: A Study in Conservative Politics* (Manchester, 1989); Wilt, *Food for War*.

also an international dimension, centred on arguments about international trade, imperial preference, and nutrition, but, as we shall suggest later, these became more significant, as far as policies affecting British farmers were concerned, in the years at the end of and after the Second World War.

Agricultural Policy in the Second World War

The war changed the political and economic contexts of agricultural policy. As Dewey has argued in the context of the First World War, there were three ways of dealing with the food security problems presented by the war: the use of naval power to maintain seaborne imports, the use of rationing and other means of controlling domestic food consumption and supply, and the expansion of domestic agricultural production.[14] From November 1939, all these were under the overall control of a policy mechanism that saw them as part of domestic civil policy as a whole. At the operational level, the Ministry of Food was responsible for imports of food and animal feedingstuffs and the purchasing, sales, pricing, and distribution of food and agricultural products. As far as farmers were concerned, the Ministry of Food was the only buyer of their produce. The Ministry of Agriculture was responsible for translating food policy into detailed production plans, for which purpose it maintained increasingly close contacts at the national level with the NFU.[15] At a local level, implementation was the responsibility of the CWAECs, usually known to farmers as 'the War Ag'.

The mechanisms used to put wartime agricultural policy into effect included both product prices and measures to affect inputs. Although the Ministry of Food was the sole buyer of their output, and farmers had to take the prices offered, there was considerable negotiation between the Ministries of Food and Agriculture to determine what output was desirable and what price levels were necessary to achieve it. The NFU was increasingly also involved in these national-level negotiations.[16] The CWAECs were more directly involved at a local level with the policies that affected inputs. The most notable of these was the plough-up campaign. The Agricultural Development Act of 1939 had provided for a grant of £2 per acre for farmers to plough up permanent grassland, beginning before the war in May 1939. This was later extended to remain in effect throughout the war.[17] One of the main tasks for the CWAECs and their District Committees was to encourage farmers to take up this grant and

---

[14] Dewey, *British Agriculture in the First World War*, pp. 30–4.
[15] K.A.H. Murray, *Agriculture*, in K. Hancock (ed.), *History of the Second World War: United Kingdom Civil Series* (London, 1955), pp. 311–15.
[16] Murray, *Agriculture*, pp. 94, 129–32; Winter, *Rural Politics*, pp. 100–1.
[17] Wilt, *Food for War*, p. 113; Murray, *Agriculture*, pp. 57, 73.

then to persuade them to plant the resultant arable with the most needed crops. They were also responsible for ensuring adequate farm labour supplies, allocating farm machinery, administering the animal feedingstuffs rationing scheme, and providing technical advice.[18]

It is not part of the main purpose of this chapter to assess the success of these wartime policy measures. On the other hand, the extent to which they were felt to be successful at the time was important in the post-war policy debate. In 1945, the Ministry of Information published a well-illustrated book of about a hundred pages that proclaimed the successes of the agricultural industry, and Murray's official history, which came ten years later, although more nuanced, also concluded that wartime agriculture was a success story, 'successful far beyond the calculations and estimates of the pre-war planners'.[19] More recently, revisionist historians have pointed out that although British agriculture successfully changed its output mix away from meat and towards the cereals, potatoes, and dairy products that were more urgently needed during the war, the overall volume of output expanded by a relatively modest amount, perhaps as little as 8 per cent, and that this was only achieved by the use of significant quantities of labour and capital, so that British agriculture's total factor productivity probably declined during the war.[20] Moreover, although food imports in total were almost halved, prioritisation of human food in the mix, together with an effective domestic rationing programme, meant that total calorie consumption in 1943 was only about 5 per cent lower than its pre-war level.[21] What mattered at the time, however, according to Professor Griffiths, was that 'one of the major shifts promoted by agriculture's experience of war was towards a more favourable public image for farming, as a successful, modern industry', while at the same time the war 'diluted farmers' traditional individualism, making them more conscious of the potential benefits of closer dependence on government and the advantages of conceding some of their autonomy in favour of

---

[18] B. Short, *The Battle of the Fields: Rural Community and Authority in Britain during the Second World War* (Woodbridge, 2014), pp. 73–86.

[19] Ministry of Information, *Land at War: The Official Story of British Farming 1939–1944* (London, 1945). A facsimile edition was published in 2001; Murray, *Agriculture*, p. 340.

[20] J. Martin, *The Development of Modern Agriculture: British Farming since 1931* (Basingstoke, 2000), pp. 47–58; P. Brassley, 'Wartime Productivity and Innovation, 1939–45', in B. Short, C. Watkins, and J. Martin (eds), *The Front Line of Freedom: British Farming in the Second World War* (Exeter, 2007), pp. 36–54; and see other chapters in Short et al., *Front Line of Freedom*.

[21] P. Brassley, 'International Trade in Agricultural Products, 1935–1955', in P. Brassley, L. Van Molle, and Y. Segers (eds), *War, Agriculture and Food: Rural Europe from the 1930s to the 1950s* (New York, 2012), p. 42; L. Collingham, *The Taste of War: World War Two and the Battle for Food* (London, 2011).

greater economic certainty'.[22] However, in the harsh post-war world, there were other significant factors, such as food shortages and balance of payments problems, also affecting agricultural policy.

The 1947 Agriculture Act

The 1947 Agriculture Act is generally recognised as the most important single piece of legislation between the Second World War and Britain's entry into the European Economic Community (EEC) as far as farmers were concerned. At the beginning of the Committee stage of its passage through the House of Commons, Mr Anthony Hurd moved an amendment to insert the words 'and fully productive' after the word 'efficient' in the preamble to the Bill, which stated that its objective was to promote and maintain 'a stable and efficient agricultural industry capable of providing such part of the nation's food and other agricultural produce as in the national interest it is desirable to produce in the United Kingdom'. After discussing the amendment for two and a half hours, the Committee put it to the vote. They divided, mostly along party lines, and the 'noes' prevailed.[23] Nothing more was heard of the amendment, but the discussion had focused on the crucial feature of post-war UK agricultural policy: whether or not it would give farmers confidence to expand output.

Hurd had been the Conservative MP for Newbury since the 1945 election. Before the war, he had been an agricultural journalist and a member of the councils of both the Royal Agricultural Society of England and the NFU; during the war, he was Assistant Agricultural Adviser at the Ministry of Agriculture. Party loyalties aside, his background and affiliations suggest that he represented the agricultural industry. What worried him was the phrase 'such part of the nation's food'. Many commentators have quoted it as a masterpiece of parliamentary draughtsmanship, allowing subsequent governments to respond flexibly to changing circumstances. That was precisely what worried Hurd. He felt that it 'may mean much, or it may mean little'.[24] Therefore his purpose in inserting the phrase 'fully productive' into the Bill was to ensure the long-term survival of the guarantees of support it contained.

The discussion that followed revealed how both old and new circumstances were affecting the formation of agricultural policy. Memories of the repeal of the 1920 Agriculture Act clearly lay behind the remarks of Mr Victor Collins, the Labour MP for Taunton, when he asked 'To what end, then, if the national interest now calls for that expansion, should we

[22] C. Griffiths, 'Heroes of the Reconstruction? Images of British Farmers in War and Peace', in Brassley et al., *War Agriculture and Food*, p. 224.
[23] House of Commons, *Parliamentary Debates: Standing Committees*, Session 1946–7, vol. II, Agriculture Bill, 11 February–24 April 1947.
[24] House of Commons, Agriculture Bill, col. 4.

subsequently expand production if, subsequently, for some reason we cannot now foresee but can only suspect, that production should later be contracted?'[25] As Major Mott-Radclyffe, the Conservative MP for Windsor, argued, the national interest in 1947 lay in maximising home food production, otherwise 'we shall have to import food from overseas which will have to be paid for in foreign exchange which we are told we do not possess'.[26] The income from overseas investments that had financed pre-war food imports had been considerably diminished as those investments were liquidated to pay for the war. Addressing the Agricultural Economics Society in 1948, John Raeburn, who had spent the war as a Ministry of Food economist, concluded that 'we may be almost a debtor country on capital account'.[27] Manufacturing exports had decreased too. During the war itself, the problem was overcome by the US Lend-Lease programme, and by the generosity of Canada, which supplied a great deal of food as an outright gift.[28] In the changed post-war world, those sources were no longer available, and there was also uncertainty about what would happen in international agricultural markets.

In February 1947, when this meeting was being held, Britain was in the grip of a cold winter, and post-war food shortages, exacerbated by weather problems and shipping shortages, continued to affect the whole world. The only notable exception was in the export performance of the United States, which had returned to the world market, having ceased to be a major seller in the 1930s.[29] In these circumstances, it was not surprising that there was extensive international discussion of food supply problems. In fact, these can be traced back to the inter-war years, when international organisations such as the IIA, based in Rome, and the French-led Commission Internationale d'Agriculture (CIA) were operating in association with the League of Nations.[30] The League's work on health, from the early 1930s, had made it clear that health improvements were dependent upon improvements in living conditions, and that people living in rural areas were often the worst affected. In the late 1930s, preparations were being made for a European Conference on Rural Life to be held in July 1939, with an extensive agenda of topics to

---

25 House of Commons, Agriculture Bill, col. 11.
26 House of Commons, Agriculture Bill, col. 8.
27 J.R. Raeburn, 'The Food Economy of the UK in Relation to International Balance-of-Payment problems', *J. Agric. Econs.* 8 (1948), pp. 20–47; G.E. Dalton, 'In Memoriam: Professor John R. Raeburn CBE, FRSE (1912–2006)', *J. Agric. Econs.* 58 (2007), pp. 396–8.
28 Brassley, 'International Trade in Agricultural Products, 1935–1955', p. 40.
29 Brassley, 'International Trade in Agricultural Products, 1935–1955', p. 44.
30 J. Pan-Montojo, 'International Institutions and European Agriculture: From the IIA to the FAO', in C. Martiin, J. Pan-Montojo, and P. Brassley (eds), *Agriculture in Capitalist Europe, 1945–1960: From Food Shortages to Food Surpluses* (London, 2016), pp. 23–43.

be discussed, including demographic problems, land tenure systems, and technical improvements in agriculture.[31] It is clear from the Ministry of Agriculture files on the conference that neither Ministry civil servants, nor those in the Foreign Office who were also involved, thought that the conference would do more than duplicate the work of the IIA. As it turned out, the conference was postponed for three months in March 1939, and 'taking present circumstances into account', postponed 'until further notice' on 6 September 1939.[32] The impression that emerges is that the Ministry operated on the assumption that food was available on the world market and Britain could afford it. The war changed all that. In 1942, the Combined Food Board was established to manage the supply and shipping problems involved in getting agricultural products from the USA and Canada to Britain, and by 1944 it had expanded and involved many more countries to ensure food supplies across Europe. In 1946, it became the International Emergency Food Council. By then, a conference had been held at Hot Springs, in Virginia, bringing together nutritionists, agronomists, and economists to think about the problems of feeding the post-war world. It eventually led to the transformation of the IIA into the UN Food and Agriculture Organization and attempted to take the planning of post-war food supplies beyond the simple working of international markets.[33] In arguing for a 'fully productive' British agriculture, Mr Hurd was careful to point out that

> under the terms of the resolutions which we endorsed at the Hot Springs conference ... we are bound to use our land fully to feed our own people properly first of all before we start to call on world surpluses which might very well be used elsewhere to the better advantage of the world as a whole.[34]

Once more, therefore, changes in historical, political, and economic circumstances produced changes in agricultural policy. The reduction in the country's manufacturing export capacity and its overseas capital holdings led to a shortage of foreign exchange. Both this, and the obligation to produce food wherever it was possible to do so, agreed at Hot Springs, lent an impetus to expand an industry that had been one of the few in Europe to maintain and even increase its output during the war. That this was in part due to a successful planning scheme was no disadvantage in the eyes of a Labour government with a big majority and

---

[31] League of Nations, *European Conference on Rural Life: Report of the Preparatory Committee on the Work of Its First Session, April 4–7, 1938* (Geneva, 1938).
[32] TNA, MAF 38/38, League of Nations European Conference on Rural Life.
[33] Brassley, 'International Trade in Agricultural Products, 1935–1955', pp. 40, 45; Pan-Montojo, 'International Institutions and European Agriculture', pp. 29–30.
[34] House of Commons, Agriculture Bill, col. 4.

big problems to solve. The Bill became the 1947 Agriculture Act, and its essential provisions remained in effect for nearly thirty years until the UK entered the EEC in 1973. Within this period, it is generally agreed that there were three policy phases: the first, up to the early 1950s, when the emphasis was upon output expansion; the second, up to about 1960, when the emphasis changed from expansion to efficiency; and the third, after 1960 and leading up to EEC entry, when the emphasis returned to expansion.[35] The following discussion will deal with each of these in turn.

Post-War Agricultural Expansion

In the summer of 1947, the government had announced a five-year agricultural expansion plan with the aim of increasing output to 20 per cent above its existing level, or 50 per cent above the pre-war level, by 1952. The mechanisms to be used were those embodied in the Agricultural Act: price guarantees and input grants. Under the terms of the Act, there were guaranteed prices for twelve main products: the cereals, wheat barley, oats and rye, together with potatoes and sugar beet, cattle, sheep and pigs, and milk, eggs, and wool. These were the prices paid by the Ministry of Food, which until 1953 was the sole first buyer of farm produce. Other products, mainly horticultural, were protected by a variety of trade measures involving various tariffs. The levels of guaranteed prices were decided by discussions between ministers (not only the Minister of Agriculture but also ministers responsible for Scotland and Wales) and representatives of the farmers, led by the NFU. This was a process that had emerged during the war and had been described to the House of Commons in December 1944 by Mr Robert Hudson, the Minister of Agriculture at the time.[36] Much of the annual discussion, at the level of officials on both sides, was concerned with establishing and agreeing the current position on outputs, costs, and farm incomes. Once these figures were agreed, the more politically sensitive matters of what the government wanted from the industry and what farmers' representatives felt it could produce could begin.

Since the alternative source of supply to home production was imported produce, and it was the import price that determined the price paid by the domestic consumer, it was possible for a deficit to exist between what the Ministry of Food paid for domestic production and what it was sold for, in which case the shortfall was paid for by the Treasury, or, in other words, the taxpayer.[37] When world prices were high, as they were

---

35 J. Bowers, 'British Agricultural Policy since the Second World War', *Agric. Hist. Rev.* 33 (1985), pp. 66–76; Winter, *Rural Politics*, p. 106.
36 W.E. Heath, 'Price Fixing Policies in Agriculture', *J. Agric. Econs.* 8 (1948), pp. 4–19.
37 Bowers, 'British Agricultural Policy', pp. 66–7; Martin, *The Development of Modern Agriculture*, pp. 70–2; Winter, *Rural Politics*, p. 106.

immediately after the war, the Treasury's liability was small; as they subsequently fell, it grew. Discussing the Act at their annual conference in 1948, members of the Agricultural Economics Society foreshadowed many of the arguments that would subsequently emerge about the system. Professor Nash, who would later be one of its severest critics, pointed out that the food consumer and the taxpayer (not always the same people) had little say in the negotiations. Mr John Kirk, a Ministry of Agriculture economist at the time and later a professor at Wye College, said that he knew of only two people who understood part 1 of the 1947 Act, the part that Mr Hurd had questioned at the Committee stage. Several speakers identified the potential costs in the event of a world agricultural depression, and others wondered how effective the policy would be in producing further output expansion.[38]

In addition to these price measures, there were also several grants and subsidies available to farmers. The grant of £2 per acre for ploughing up permanent grassland, and the field drainage and ditching grants, all of which dated back to the war, were still available, and under the terms of the Agricultural Development (Ploughing Up of Land) Act, 1946, the ploughing up grant was extended to grassland that had only been established for three years, rather than the seven years of the previous regulations. In the same year, grants were instituted to promote the establishment of AI centres, and the Hill Farming Act made grants available to both landowners and farmers for improving hill land and keeping hill breeds of sheep and cattle. Many of these provisions were extended further down the hill under the terms of the 1951 Livestock Rearing Act.[39] The Agriculture (Miscellaneous Provisions) Act, 1949, brought in grants for grass and forage crop drying and subsidies for calf rearing. There were also control measures, such as the Animals Act, 1948, aimed at eradicating bovine tuberculosis, and the introduction of bull licensing in 1945, and boar licensing in the following year, both of which aimed at improving the standard of breeding stock. The 1947 Act also provided for what were in effect continuations of the War Ags, now known as the County Agricultural Executive Committees, but still with considerable powers to direct farmers and take measures against bad husbandry.[40]

The political and economic circumstances in which the 1947 Act were passed were more or less maintained until the early 1950s. Although world food production recovered remarkably rapidly after the war, so that by the early 1950s it was more or less back to its pre-war level, problems for the UK as the major world importer still remained.[41] The

[38] Heath, 'Price Fixing Policies in Agriculture', pp. 13–19.
[39] R.G. Stapledon, *Farming and Mechanised Agriculture* (4th edn, London, 1950), pp. 69–70; Martin, *The Development of Modern Agriculture*, p. 69.
[40] Stapledon, *Farming and Mechanised Agriculture*, p. 65.
[41] P. Brassley, C. Martiin, and J. Pan-Montojo, 'European Agriculture, 1945–1960:

devaluation of the pound sterling in 1949 increased the effective price of imports, and the outbreak of the Korean War (1950–3) in 1950 increased the unpredictability of world markets.[42] These factors alone, never mind the political benefits of ending food rationing, would have been enough to promote an expansionist policy. Some idea of the impact of the Korean War on official thinking emerges from the Ministry of Agriculture archive files on agricultural defence planning. In January 1951, for example, one of the Ministry's senior civil servants, A.N. Duckham, presented a preliminary note to his colleagues about the problems of maintaining agricultural production in the event of conventional and nuclear war.[43] A subsequent and more detailed report followed in the July of that year, making the point that 'Net [agricultural] output is markedly higher than that attained during the last war. But it would be idle to suppose that a spectacular increase in production could be achieved in a future war or even that the present high level of production could easily be maintained', due to shortages of labour, fuel, fertilisers, and machinery.[44] In April 1952, the British delegation took the same message to the Financial and Economic Board of NATO, which subsequently suggested that member states should stockpile both food and fertilisers.[45]

As Duckham observed, persuading farmers that a rapid increase in output was needed was not always easy in the post-war years. There were times when the Ministry of Agriculture felt the need to augment the effects of its agricultural policy with the direct exhortation of a publicity campaign. One of these, not surprisingly, was during the Korean War. The Ministry's files on public relations policy and the minutes of its Publicity Working Party at this time show some of the various methods it used to encourage farmers to produce more, and the problems encountered in doing so.

From early 1951, Duckham prepared a number of briefing and discussion documents on publicity and public relations, often in correspondence with Sir Richard Haddon, at that time editor of the *Farmer and Stockbreeder*, one of the two leading agricultural weeklies. These, together with subsequent discussion in the Publicity Working Party, provide some interesting corrective insights to the assumption that increased output

---

An Introduction', in C. Martiin et al., *Agriculture in Capitalist Europe*, p. 9.
[42] Martin, *The Development of Modern Agriculture*, p. 70.
[43] A.N. Duckham was familiarly known as Jim and had joined the Ministry in 1931. During the war, he was concerned with food rationing and from 1945 to 1950 was agricultural attaché in Washington. He left the Ministry in 1955 to take up the Chair of Agriculture at Reading University until his retirement in 1968; see P. Harris, *The Silent Fields: One Hundred Years of Agricultural Education at Reading* (Reading, 1993), pp. 75–7.
[44] TNA, MAF 250/154, Ministry of Agriculture and Fisheries, Departmental Defence Plans Committee, 1951–4.
[45] Pan-Montojo, 'International Institutions and European Agriculture', p. 32.

followed naturally from the policies introduced in the 1947 Agriculture Act. The impact of the cold war and shortages resulting from world stockpiling and rearmament increased the desirability of completing the expansion programme, Duckham asserted, while the 'controls and psychological aids we had in 1939–45' were no longer in being. Thus the objective of the public relations policy should be 'to capture or retain the farmers' confidence (the will to produce)', and it was as important to do this as it was to provide them with guaranteed prices, capital grants, or advisory services. Farmers, he argued, were 'less responsive than townspeople to the usual advertising techniques and emotional appeals' and were 'getting tired of open exhortation'. He then went on to assess the various options available to the Ministry to put its views across to farmers. The Ministry's relations with the technical farming press, he felt, were excellent, and should be further encouraged. The national and provincial daily newspapers were of little use for getting messages across to farmers, but the provincial and county press was more likely to be read by farmers and so more useful. Broadcasting appeared to be of little use, although he did not explain why, and he went on to examine the effectiveness of agricultural shows, demonstrations, discussion groups, films, Ministry publications, speeches, and the use of the direct mail that every farmer received each year from either the Ministry or the County Agricultural Executive Committee (CAEC). More controversially, he suggested that it should be part of the role of the County, District, and Sub-Committee members, and the Ministry's professional staff (who together amounted to about ten thousand people, one for every twenty-five farmers) to carry the public relations message. This produced an immediate response from senior figures in the NAAS, concerned by 'any mixture of propaganda with technical work ... Our first job as technical officers is to merit and to obtain the farmer's confidence ... We do not want to be involved too closely or openly with all forms of propaganda or exhortation.'[46]

By the following year, Duckham was preparing for a new expansion policy to be announced later in the year. He no longer expected assistance from NAAS but thought it important to secure the co-operation of the NFU, the Country Land and Business Association (CLA), possibly YFCs and workers' unions, and the press. He was a little more positive about the BBC ('BBC resent pressure from us, but generally co-operate if not pushed'), and saw an important role for the CAECs: 'Essential to impress upon CAECs that, despite any natural dislike of publicity, propaganda for production is their job, is not really so tainted as some of them think, and is, in effect, replacing cropping directions, etc. which are no longer necessary, or considered politically acceptable.' The title of the expansion programme, he suggested, should both summarise the

[46] TNA, MAF 114/275, Agricultural Public Relations: policy, 1951.

policy and carry a message: 'The war-time "Grow More" Campaign had more appeal than the 1947 "Agricultural Expansion Programme"', and he went on to suggest several possibilities (National Farm Well Campaign, Farm Well and Feed Well Campaign, Plough More, Feed More Campaign, etc.). There could also be associated slogans, catchphrases, and jingles, of which he suggested several, from the straightforward ('Plough More, Breed More, Graze More, Feed More; More Grass, More Grain, More Stock, More Gain') to 'putting new teeth in old saws', such as 'Up Horn and Up Corn', and 'The best manure is the farmer's mind', to the more whimsical ('There is no harm in / Higher Farmin').[47]

Duckham was clearly preparing for the meeting of the Ministry's Publicity Working Party that met in June 1952, with Sir Richard Haddon in the chair, and members drawn from the NFU and the agricultural merchanting trade, as well as Ministry officials. By this time, the Minister had announced a policy of increasing production by 60 per cent over the following four years, so none of Duckham's suggestions for its title were accepted; the Working Party decided on 'The 60 Plus Drive' and was split on the utility of slogans and catchphrases.[48] More significantly, the meeting spent some time discussing the reasons why farmers might be reluctant to expand. Sir Reginald Franklin, the Ministry's Deputy Secretary, had visited several CAECs and found 'a very mixed response to appeals to grow more food … Some farmers felt that expansion meant more effort, more risks, and higher taxation than they were willing to incur'. He was supported by Mr Swallow, an agricultural merchant from Grantham, who argued that 'Labour supply difficulties, in Lincolnshire particularly during the potato harvest, had meant a fall in production. The general feeling was that increased production meant more risks, a lot more work and little better return.' A further meeting of the Working Party, in February 1953, heard from Lord Carrington, Parliamentary Secretary (Lords) to the Ministry, who had visited the CAECs in about half the counties in the country in recent months. He reported that 'The three difficulties invariably mentioned as deterrents to the production drive were (i) shortage of capital; (ii) military call-up and general labour shortage; and (iii) use of land.'[49] The Devon County Agricultural Officer, writing his annual report in May 1953, noted that the 60 Plus Drive had not started well during the previous summer, largely due to ineffective discussions between the county Executive and District Committees,

---

[47] TNA, MAF 197/15, Public Relations: policy, 1949–52.
[48] TNA, MAF 197/15, Public Relations: policy, 1949–52; in the event, gross output increased by a little over 20 per cent between 1952 and 1956 – see H. Marks and D.K. Britton, *A Hundred Years of British Food and Farming: A Statistical Survey* (London, 1989), p. 149.
[49] TNA, MAF 197/18, Food Production Drive Publicity Working Party: minutes of meetings, 1952–3.

but that progress was made when the county branch of the NFU was involved and more farmers were involved in carrying out farm surveys of neighbouring farms and discussing the results with those surveyed.[50]

By November 1953, with the Korean War over (the armistice was signed on 27 July 1953), the objectives of the 60 Plus campaign had undergone a subtle change. The Publicity Working Party meeting on the twenty-sixth of that month held a lengthy discussion on the topic during which it emerged that some farmers had had difficulty in disposing of their grain after the 1953 harvest, with the result that farmers in general were beginning to be confused about the objectives of current agricultural policy. The Ministry officials present explained that in their view what was now most important was an improvement in productivity rather than simply in production. For pigs in particular, what was needed was higher quality not a simple increase in numbers. It was important, the Committee concluded, to explain what this change of policy meant to individual farmers; a discussion of the best means of doing so was placed on the agenda for the next meeting.[51]

In retrospect at least, Labour's agricultural policy, and its continuation under the Conservatives from 1951, was popular with farmers. One of the authors (PB) remembers a conversation in the 1960s with a farmer who had been in the industry since the 1920s and was a lifelong Conservative voter. Nevertheless, he described Tom Williams, who held the agriculture portfolio throughout the post-war Labour governments, as the best Minister of Agriculture that he could remember. Whether Labour's policy produced the desired results, or would have done if the party had continued in office after 1951, was a more complex question. Writing in 1955, when the relevant statistics were available, Edith Whetham found that the overall 20 per cent output increase target had been met, livestock output had risen, milk output had expanded so that some of it now had to be diverted into the lower-priced manufacturing market, and the increase in physical investment, in tractors and other machinery, new farm buildings, and breeding stock, was plain for all to see. On the other hand, the tillage area was down. It was as if twelve million acres of crops were 'as much worry and risk as farmers are willing (except in wartime) to undertake'.[52] Or was it, perhaps, that many of those taking the management and investment decisions on farms in the post-war decade were old enough to remember the decade after the previous war and were still not quite convinced that guaranteed prices would be available in the long run?

[50] TNA, MAF114/241, NAAS Devon County Agricultural Officer's Annual Report 1952–3, p. 1.
[51] TNA MAF197/18, Publicity Working Party minutes, 26 November 1953.
[52] E.H. Whetham, 'The Agricultural Expansion Programme, 1947–51', *J. Agric. Econs.* 11 (1955), pp. 313–19.

Agricultural Policy in the Later 1950s

The previous section dealt with the policy context and the development of policy mechanisms in some detail because the immediate post-war years set the pattern for the period up to the 1970s and entry into the EEC. The 1950s saw a continuation of the basic policy mechanisms of guaranteed prices and grants and subsidies, albeit with some changes in detail. New grant schemes, all of which had the expressed intention of improving the efficiency of agriculture, included the silo subsidy in 1956, providing for grants of 50 per cent of the cost of erecting silos for silage, the Farm Improvement Scheme in 1957, financing one-third of the capital cost of buildings and fixed equipment, and the Small Farmer Scheme for those entering into an agreed improvement plan from 1959.[53] As far as individual farmers were concerned, the most obvious change in the guaranteed price mechanism came in 1953, when direct purchasing by the Ministry of Food ceased and they sold to marketing boards, in the case of milk and potatoes, or agricultural merchants and meat traders for most other products. The new system, announced, in the case of cereals, in September 1953, involved a weekly assessment of the average market price for each supported commodity.[54] The difference between that and the guaranteed price negotiated between the government and the farmers' unions formed the deficiency payment. Thus marketing efficiency was promoted because farmers had an incentive to seek the best price they could in the market for their products, and they subsequently received a cheque from the Ministry of Agriculture for the deficiency payment. In other words, if they presented a better than average product, they would get more than the guaranteed price, and vice versa for inferior quality products.

The system was counter-inflationary, because consumers could buy food at market prices, which for most products were world prices, and progressive as far as income distribution was concerned because taxpayers, who tended to be the better-off members of society, bore the cost of the deficiency payments. It worked reasonably well in the 1950s when UK agriculture was producing about half of the country's temperate foodstuffs; as we shall see, it became too expensive in the 1970s when self-supply levels rose to around 70 per cent.[55] Even in the 1950s, the government set limits, known as 'standard quantities', on the level of production they were prepared to support. These were introduced in 1957 for milk and potatoes and in the 1960s for cereals.[56] By 1957,

---

[53] B. Hill and D. Ray, *Economics for Agriculture: Food, Farming, and the Rural Economy* (Basingstoke, 1987), p. 397.
[54] *Guarantees for Home Grown Cereals*, Cmd.8947 (1953).
[55] Hill and Ray, *Economics for Agriculture*, pp. 348–9.
[56] Winter, *Rural Politics*, p. 113.

lower world prices and consequent increased support costs were raising concerns among farmers that the whole system was unsustainable, and the older ones probably remembered the repeal of the Agriculture Act in 1921. The government responded to these concerns by introducing what it called 'Long Term Assurances' to the industry. These promised that the price for any individual commodity would be not less than 96 per cent of its value in the previous year, and that the overall value of guarantees would be not less than 97.5 per cent of the previous year's.[57]

The Third Phase: Agricultural Policy from the Early 1960s to the Early 1970s

From a political perspective, the 1950s and early 1960s might appear to be a period of stability. There was no change in the government party between 1951 and 1964, and the established procedure of the NFU conducting annual negotiations with the Ministry of Agriculture continued. Indeed, it has been identified as a period in which agricultural policy was made in a 'tight and closed policy community' that non-agricultural interests found difficult to penetrate.[58] Nevertheless, the late 1950s often saw years in which increases in guarantee payments did not cover cost increases, and standard quantities implied penalties for over-production. Then in December 1960 a rather curious White Paper was published giving an account of talks that had been held between the agricultural departments of the government and the farmers' unions.[59] Given that there were routine negotiations in the price review negotiations in February each year, it is surprising that further talks were needed, and the White Paper itself only justified them as covering 'a wide range of subjects in a way which is not possible in the timetable and circumstances of the Annual Review'.[60]

This bland façade fronted an important, and at times heated, series of discussions between the NFU, MAFF, and the Treasury. In April 1960, Harold Woolley, the NFU President, wrote to Harold Macmillan, the Prime Minister, about the concerns of farmers. Woolley subsequently met John Hare, then Minister of Agriculture, who formed the view that what farmers were really concerned about was output restriction. This led to a series of meetings between NFU and MAFF officials over the summer and autumn of 1960.[61] To begin with, there were technical arguments over the

---

[57] 285 *Long Term Assurances for Agriculture*, Cmnd.23 (1956).
[58] Winter, *Rural Politics*, p. 106.
[59] *Agriculture: Report on Talks between the Agriculture Departments and the Farmers' Unions, June–December 1960*, Cmnd.1249 (1960); see also Bowers, 'British Agricultural Policy', p. 70; Winter, *Rural Politics*, p. 113.
[60] *Agriculture: Report on Talks*, Cmnd.1249, paragraph 1.
[61] TNA, MAF 317/63, 1960, Government Talks with Farmers' Unions.

calculation of efficiency in agriculture and the extent to which efficiency increases should be set against the support bill, but by the beginning of November the Treasury were involved in the talks. By that time, it was clear that the NFU and MAFF were on one side of the argument, and the Treasury was on the other.[62] And the question at issue had changed. It was now about agriculture's contribution to the balance of payments. The Treasury copy of the minutes of the meeting on 1 November has a handwritten note at the top to the effect that it had been 'A battle Royal', and a note between two Treasury officials on 30 November clarifies the source of the disagreement: the importance farmers attach

> to what might seem, at first sight, to be a rather academic discussion. In fact they almost certainly hope to use our balance of payments difficulties as a weapon to further their main object, which is encouragement to expand output irrespective of its cost to the taxpayer or in national resources.[63]

The Treasury lost the argument, and when the White Paper giving an account of the talks was published three weeks later an editorial in the *Financial Times* called it 'a Christmas card for farmers'.[64]

At first sight, the White Paper does little beyond restating the obvious, that agriculture was an important industry that would continue to receive government support, but paragraph 1 contained a reference to the effects of future closer trading relations with Europe on agriculture, and paragraph 4 discussed agriculture's impact on the balance of payments. It was these two issues that provoked a decade of argument over agricultural policy.

The balance of payments crisis came first. In 1960, the Conservative government, which had looked so secure in winning the 1959 general election, began to suffer from the effects of its expansionist economic policy. Increased consumer demand generated a rapid rise in imports. The balance of payments deficit on visible trade rose from £117 million in 1959 to £406 million in 1960.[65] It was to remain a chronic problem throughout the 1960s.[66] Both exports and imports to and from Europe were increasing before the establishment of the EEC at the beginning of

---

[62] TNA, T224/342, 1960, discussions between MAFF and the NFUs on agricultural guarantee policy.
[63] TNA, T224/343, 1960, discussions between MAFF and the NFUs on agricultural guarantee policy.
[64] *Financial Times*, editorial, 20 December 1960.
[65] D. Porter, '"Never-Never Land": Britain under the Conservatives 1951–1964', in N. Tiratsoo (ed.), *From Blitz to Blair: A New History of Britain since 1939* (London, 1997), p. 126.
[66] K.O. Morgan, *The People's Peace: British History 1945–1990* (Oxford, 1992), p. 214.

1958, and in 1961 the Macmillan government reversed previous policy and applied for EEC membership. Although this initial application was rejected in 1963, the EEC, and the differences between its CAP and current UK policy, continued to have some influence even before renewed negotiations were successful in the early 1970s.[67] Both factors promoted the desirability of increasing the output of domestic agriculture.

The food import controls announced in the 1964 Annual Review were followed in 1965 by the new Labour government's National Plan, which not only called for increased agricultural output but also for agriculture to release labour to other industries. Although the Plan as a whole did not survive for long, the policy of agricultural expansion outlived it, assisted by a report entitled *Agriculture's Import-Saving Role*.[68] By the early 1970s, when it became clear that the negotiations for EEC entry were likely to be successful, there was an additional argument for expansion, in that the higher the level of domestic output the lower would be the required financial contribution to the CAP. In part, the incentive for farmers to increase output remained the support of the prices they received through the deficiency payments system, but in both current and constant price terms that peaked in the early 1960s. However, other forms of support continued to increase.[69] In 1968, when the Ministry produced a small (18 x 11 cm) booklet, *At the Farmer's Service*, it required eighty-one pages to summarise all the government activities in support of agriculture.[70] They included advisory and educational services; management assistance; safety and wages regulations; the agricultural chemicals approval scheme; various measures in support of crop production, such as seed certification, crop variety testing, and the registration of plant breeders' rights; assistance for livestock producers in the form of AI services, brucellosis accreditation, bull and boar licensing; and a veterinary products safety scheme, together with measures to promote pest control, such as grants to rabbit clearance societies and the provision of cartridges with which to shoot wood pigeons. It also listed twenty-four separate grant schemes, which included those already mentioned above, such as the Farm Improvement Scheme, as well as schemes to promote agricultural and horticultural co-operation, bracken eradication, the restoration of ironstone land, farm business recording, small farm business management, the improvement of farm structures, and hill land improvement. There were also subsidies for fertilisers, lime, beef cows, calves, hill cows, and hill sheep. Although the CAECs

---

[67] P. Clarke, *Hope and Glory: Britain 1900–1990* (London, 1996), p. 279.
[68] NEDO (National Economic Development Office), *Agriculture's Import Saving Role: A Report by the Economic Development Committee for the Agricultural Industry* (London, 1968).
[69] Bowers, 'British Agricultural Policy', pp. 67–8.
[70] MAFF, *At the Farmer's Service* (Pinner, 1968).

had lost their significance by the late 1960s, the picture that emerges of this time is one of deep and wide state involvement in the agricultural industry, concerned especially to promote technical change as a means of improving both output and efficiency.

British Agriculture in the CAP

The countries of western continental Europe that signed the Treaty of Rome in 1957 – France, Germany, and Italy, together with Belgium, the Netherlands, and Luxemburg – all emerged from the Second World War with similar problems as far as agriculture was concerned. The war had been fought over their countryside, resulting in considerable physical damage, and their capacity to produce industrial goods for export was similarly reduced. They had a pre-war tradition of maintaining a high level of domestic self-sufficiency in food, but in 1946 cereal output in France and Italy was about 20 per cent below its pre-war average, and in Germany it was about 40 per cent lower. The recovery, however, was rapid, and even in Germany farm output had recovered to pre-war levels by 1951.[71] The common feature of their various agricultural policies was a relatively free internal market operating within a ring of protection from the world market. During the negotiations leading up to the Treaty of Rome, it became clear that the exclusion of agriculture from the general common market would be undesirable: without free trade in farm products, national food price levels could differ, thus producing input cost differences that would undermine the common policies to be introduced for other industries. Although there was a general similarity between existing agricultural policies, there were numerous differences in detail, so the Treaty of Rome included the basis of agreement for a new CAP.[72]

Although the underlying principle of the CAP price mechanism was that producers should receive the market price for their output, it was a market price that was allowed to fluctuate only between predetermined upper and lower limits, so protecting the farmer against excessively low prices, and the consumer against very high prices. If market prices fell to a level known as the 'intervention price', the producer could sell to a CAP-funded intervention store. Foreign suppliers were dissuaded from attempting to sell to intervention stores by the imposition of an import levy. However, if domestic CAP prices rose above a level called the

---

[71] Brassley et al., 'European Agriculture, 1945–1960: An Introduction', p. 9.
[72] G. Thiemeyer, 'The Failure of the Green Pool and the Success of the CAP: Long Term Structures in European Agricultural Integration in the 1950s and 1960s', in K.K. Patel (ed.), *Fertile Ground for Europe? The History of European Integration and the Common Agricultural Policy since 1945* (Baden-Baden, 2009), pp. 47–51.

'target price', it would be worthwhile for foreign producers to sell into the European market even after paying the levy. Thus the upper and lower limits for the market prices to be received by European farmers were established, and the level at which target and intervention prices were set was proposed by the European Commission and decided by negotiation between the member states, a process in which the representatives of farmers could also make a significant contribution. In addition, the CAP also provided for several grant schemes to improve the structure of agriculture, mostly by providing incentives for small uneconomic firms to leave the industry, and to promote the modernisation of agriculture, mostly by providing capital grants.[73]

Georges Pompidou's accession to the Presidency of France in 1969, and the election of the Heath government in 1970, 'pushed Europe to the top of the agenda'.[74] The two heads of government met in May 1971, and with French support negotiations for UK membership of the EEC went ahead rapidly. Agricultural trade problems that had seemed difficult in the 1960s were resolved, partly because two of Britain's major trading partners, Denmark and Ireland, were applying for membership at the same time, and partly because the UK market was no longer so important to traditional trading partners such as New Zealand. All three applicants became members of the EEC on 1 January 1973. The major world importer, and two of its principal suppliers, therefore had to be integrated into an agricultural market that was based on domestic self-sufficiency. But in fact UK agricultural policy had already begun to change before 1973. The February 1971 Annual Review White Paper began by stating that 'Developments over the past two decades have made the time ripe for changes in our support system', and 'The Government's declared aim is to adapt the present system of agricultural support to one relying increasingly on import levy arrangements, under which the farmer will get his return increasingly from the market.'[75] The UK was signalling a move towards the CAP support system before the heads of government met, although not before officials had begun consultations.[76]

Coincidentally, the UK joined the EEC just at the time when primary product prices in general were increasing. The Organization of the Petroleum Exporting Countries (OPEC) increased oil prices in 1973, and between the first quarter of 1973 and the last of 1974 the United Nations index of primary product prices doubled. On world agricultural markets,

---

[73] P. Brassley, 'The Common Agricultural Policy of the European Economic Community', in R.J. Halley (ed.), *The Agricultural Notebook* (17th edn, London, 1982), pp. 575–84.
[74] Clarke, *Hope and Glory*, p. 342.
[75] *Agriculture Acts 1947 and 1957: Annual Review and Determination of Guarantees 1971*, Cmnd.4623 (1971), paragraph 1.
[76] Winter, *Rural Politics*, p. 119.

some major exporting countries had started to decrease stocks at the same time as consumption increased.[77] From being a high-price island in a low-price sea in the 1960s, the EEC countries found themselves in the reverse position, so that whereas it might have been predicted that access to the CAP would mean that the UK had to pay above world market prices for imported feed grains, in fact it had access to European cereals at less than world market prices. Nevertheless, the years after accession saw considerable price rises for farm products. Average returns for wheat, in current prices, more than doubled between 1970 and 1975, and by the end of the decade had tripled. Much of this was due to inflation, but even in constant price terms wheat returns increased by 25 per cent between 1970 and 1976. In the same period, returns to milk producers rose by about 12 per cent in real terms.[78] Inflationary effects notwithstanding, governments were content to see the output-stimulating effects of these price increases, because greater domestic output meant lower imports, and under CAP regulations imports from outside the EEC increased the levies payable to CAP central funds. As the 1971 White Paper had observed, not only was it important to increase agricultural efficiency, but in addition 'A rising trend in production is also of particular importance in connection with possible entry into the EEC.'[79] UK self-sufficiency in temperate food products rose from 67 per cent in 1970 to a peak of 82 per cent in 1984.[80] It was not simply a response to the CAP. UK government policy, expressed in two White Papers, took the view 'that a continuing expansion of food production in Britain will be in the national interest' in 1975, and in 1979 came to the 'settled conclusion that the continued expansion of agricultural net product over the medium-term is in the national interest'.[81] Even in 1981, one of the authors (PB) remembers Peter Walker, the Conservative Minister of Agriculture, quoting the 1979 White Paper's conclusions with approval.

The End of Expansion

Within five years, expansion came to an end. If it was a shock at the time, in hindsight the pressure had been gradually increasing. For several years, intervention stores had been filling faster than they could be emptied. Popular parlance referred to 'butter mountains' and 'wine lakes', and there was a joke about the 'Theogeophysical' theory of the

---

[77] S. Harris, *The World Commodity Scene and the Common Agricultural Policy* (Ashford, 1975), pp. 5–6, 36.
[78] Marks and Britton, *British Food and Farming*, pp. 171, 235.
[79] *Annual Review and Determination of Guarantees 1971*, Cmnd.4623, paragraph 5.
[80] Marks and Britton, *British Food and Farming*, p. 121.
[81] *Food from Our Own Resources*, Cmnd.6020 (1975), paragraph 4; *Farming and the Nation*, Cmnd.7458 (1979), paragraph 25.

CAP: that it was the greatest creator of lakes and mountains since God. By 1985, the European Community was more than self-sufficient in cereals, vegetables, butter, cheese, skimmed milk powder, beef and veal, and poultrymeat. The surpluses not only created a budget cost – 60 per cent of total EEC budget spending for most of the 1980s – but, since they were sold on the world market at less than their cost of production, they antagonised the traditional food exporting countries, which increasingly made their displeasure felt in international trade negotiations. In addition, agricultural expansion, and its concomitant increases in fertilisers and pesticides, had increasingly detrimental effects on wildlife habitats. If these might have been acceptable back in the 1940s, they were much less so at a time of food surpluses when more and more people were interested in wildlife and landscape for recreational purposes. On 31 March 1984, the EEC Council of Ministers introduced milk quotas with immediate effect. It was a decision that signalled the end of a policy of agricultural expansion that had lasted since before the outbreak of the Second World War in Britain.[82]

---

[82] P. Brassley, 'The Common Agricultural Policy of the European Union', in R.J. Soffe (ed.), *The Agricultural Notebook* (19th edn, Oxford, 1995), pp. 3–16; Winter, *Rural Politics*, pp. 129–41.

5

Dairy Farming

The previous chapters, dealing with research and development, education and advice, and agricultural policy, have been concerned with the context within which technical change took place in the agricultural industry in the UK. They have demonstrated that, at a national level, there was a more or less consistent policy over the fifty years between the mid-1930s and the mid-1980s to increase agricultural output, and that after about 1950 this was accompanied by a desire also to increase efficiency. Both of these objectives were supported by considerable investment, on the part of both the state and the ancillary industries, especially the feed, fertiliser, pesticide, and agricultural machinery industries, in research, development, education, and advice to farmers. The following chapters are concerned with the impact of these policies and investments. They deal with the impact of technical change at both the national and the farm level and examine in particular the processes involved in adopting new technologies.

If, as we argued in chapter 1, the adoption of technology is contingent upon individual circumstances, it follows that these need to be followed up in greater detail. Each of the following chapters will therefore begin by examining the national picture, then go on to narrow the focus to the three south-western counties of England for which we have more detailed data, and finally examine the experience of individual farmers. We begin by examining technical change in dairy farming. The reason for this is not only that it was a major farming type in the south-west, but also because it was the farm type upon which the south-western FMS, from which our individual farm data is drawn, concentrated its efforts. From this study of dairying, we shall see that changes in breeding, feeding, and housing were significant. More generally, and applying not only to dairying but also to farming in general, there were also changes in capital and land, labour and machinery, specialisation and expansion, and in the fact that some enterprises declined, and each of these aspects will be the subject of succeeding chapters.

Developments in Dairy Farming

From the late 1930s to the 1980s, dairy farming was one of the most important single enterprises in UK farming, always accounting for at least 20 per cent of total output, and sometimes over 25 per cent.[1] For Astor and Rowntree, it was 'the corner-stone of our agriculture'; in 1949, it was 'the most important product of British agriculture, both as regards the total income and the number of farms engaged in the enterprise'; and later the 'sheet anchor' and 'the backbone' of British agriculture.[2] By the end of the 1960s, a survey of agriculture found that 'More than half of the agricultural land of England and Wales is occupied by farms on which it is a major interest, while a majority of farmers depend on it for a living.'[3] It is not difficult to account for its pre-eminence. The formation of the MMB in 1933 overcame price negotiation problems and improved transport and handling systems. Producers had a dependable cash flow in the form of the monthly milk cheque. Wartime price regulation and welfare milk schemes maintained the market and increased the proportion sold for higher-priced liquid consumption. After the war, the MMB put a lot of effort into improving production techniques, especially through their efforts in breed improvement and AI. Most importantly, especially from the viewpoint of small- and medium-sized farms, cows produced a bigger gross margin per acre than any other land-using enterprise, often nearly twice as much as spring barley and almost three times as much as fat lamb production.[4]

Nobody pretended that it was an easy life: cows required 'as much attention (and in a remarkably similar way) as a six-months-old baby, with all that constant feeding, cleaning, bedding and nursing', but it kept many small- and medium-sized farms going.[5] Equally, it was not a system of farming that was anywhere near its possible peak of performance. Writing in the mid-1950s, Professor M. McG. Cooper of Newcastle University (but born and raised in New Zealand) produced a

---

[1] H. Marks and D.K. Britton, *A Hundred Years of British Food and Farming: A Statistical Survey* (London, 1989), pp. 149, 229.

[2] Viscount Astor and B.S. Rowntree, *British Agriculture: The Principles of Future Policy* (Harmondsworth, 1939), p. 186; E.J. Roberts, 'Production of Milk', in J.A. Hanley (ed.), *Progressive Farming: The Maintenance of High Production* (London, 1949), pp. 157–201; M.McG. Cooper, *Competitive Farming* (London, 1956), p. 117; K. Dexter and D. Barber, *Farming for Profits* (2nd edn, London, 1967), p. 133.

[3] J.G.S. and F. Donaldson, with D. Barber, *Farming in Britain Today* (Harmondsworth, 1972), p. 172.

[4] J. Nix, *Farm Management Pocketbook* (2nd edn, Ashford, 1968, 14th edn, 1984); Universities of Bristol and Exeter, *Farm Management Handbook* (Exeter, 1968); University of Exeter, *Farm Management Handbook* (Exeter, 1985).

[5] Dexter and Barber, *Farming for Profits*, p. 134.

trenchant criticism of UK dairy farming as he found it: poor management, the excessive use of dual-purpose breeds rather than specialist dairy breeds, little culling of low-yielding cows, poor feeding, with excessive concentrate use and poor-quality silage, too many small herds, insufficiently capitalised, and consequently excessive reliance on inappropriate buildings, with too much cowshed milking and not enough milking parlours. He admitted that there was a wide range in costs and cow output, but there were too many farms at the wrong end of the range.[6] To what extent were these problems overcome in the following thirty years?

The principal changes in dairy farming in England and Wales from the beginning of the war emerge clearly from table 5.1. Cow numbers rose a little after the war but thereafter remained fairly constant. The number of milk producers peaked in the late 1940s but fell thereafter, and the herd size increased correspondingly. Milk yield per cow increased steadily, whereas liquid milk sales were fairly flat, so the extra output had to go into lower-priced manufacturing milk. This was only one of the reasons why, after taking account of inflation, it can be seen that the prices received by milk producers fell to only about half of their wartime value by 1985.

In the high rainfall, grass growing, south-west of England, dairying was at least as important, and probably more so, as in the country as a whole. In 1938, there were between seventy-five and one hundred cows and heifers per one thousand acres in Devon, up to 150 in Cornwall, and between 150 and two hundred per thousand acres in Dorset and Somerset, according to the maps prepared for *A Century of Agricultural Statistics*. By 1966, the numbers had increased to 150 to two hundred for Devon, two hundred to 250 for Cornwall, and over 250 cows and heifers per thousand acres in Dorset and Somerset. Only the counties in the north-west of the country could show comparable figures.[7] A survey of Devon farming in 1952 found that dairying was especially concentrated to the east of Dartmoor and the River Exe, and attributed this to soil, climate, topography, and good rail transport to London for the liquid milk trade. There was also a concentration of dairy cattle around the urban market of Plymouth, and, to a lesser extent, Barnstaple and Bideford.[8] Table 5.2 shows how the variables identified in table 5.1 changed in the three south-western counties (Cornwall, Devon, and Dorset).

There are some interesting comparisons to be made between tables 5.1 and 5.2. The latter deals with south-west England in two ways. Several rows refer to 'Far Western' data, because the MMB divided counties into

---

[6] Cooper, *Competitive Farming*, pp. 117–30.
[7] MAFF, *A Century of Agricultural Statistics: Great Britain 1866–1966* (London, 1968).
[8] Devon Agriculture Study Group, *Devon Farming: A First Study* (no place of publication recorded, 1952), p. 19.

TABLE 5.1. Changes in dairy farming in England and Wales

	1939	1945	1955	1965	1975	1985
Dairy cow numbers ('000)	[1,998]*	[2,292]*	2,415	2,650	2,701	2,580
Producer numbers	136,519	158,011	142,792	100,449	60,279	37,815
Average dairy herd size	15**	15**	17	26	46	67
Total milk sales (million litres)	5,086	5,397	7,516	9,044	11,115	12,605
Average milk yield per cow (litres)	2,545	2,355	3,065	3,545	4,070	4,765
Average net producer price in 1986 prices (pence per litre)	25.2	29.8	29.1	22.5	18.2	15.0

Source: MMB, *Dairy Facts and Figures* (Thames Ditton, annual), 1960, 1976, 1987.

* = Estimated by dividing milk sales by yield figures from *Dairy Facts and Figures* 1976, tables 25 and 55.
** = 1942 figure.

various regions, and Devon and Cornwall comprised the Far Western region. Dorset, the other county for which we have FMS data, was part of the Mid-Western region, so some of the MMB data that is only available at regional level cannot be used for all three counties, whereas data quoted at county level in *Dairy Facts and Figures* can obviously be used to give a total figure for all three south-western counties (henceforth referred to as 3SW data). Comparing Far Western and 3SW figures for cow numbers, it can be seen that they increase more or less steadily over the whole period, in contrast to the national figures in table 5.1, which show only small increases or decreases after the 1960s. Consequently, whereas only a little over 10 per cent of the national cow herd (both dairy and beef) was found in the 3SW counties in 1939, over 15 per cent of the dairy herd was there in 1985. Producer numbers in the Far Western counties also increased in proportion to the national figure, although, as with the national pattern, the number of farms with cows peaked in the late 1940s/early 1950s in the

Dairy Farming

TABLE 5.2. Changes in dairy farming in south-west England

	1939	1944	1954/5	1965	1975	1985
Far Western cow numbers ('000)	197	226	256	258	305	312
3 SW counties cow numbers ('000)	226	295	335	349	416	424
Far Western producer numbers	14,280	NA	16,890*	13,385	8,332	5,326
3 SW counties producer numbers	NA	NA	NA	15,560	9,807	6,407
Far Western average herd size	10.3**	10.3**	12.5	20	37	58
Far Western milk sales (million litres)	250	NA	677	814	1,213	1,490
3 SW counties milk sales (million litres)	NA	NA	NA	1,126	1,683	2,058
3 SW counties milk sales/cow numbers = yield (litres)	1,272***	NA	2,645***	3,226	4,044	4,855

Sources: 'Far Western' was the MMB region covering Devon and Cornwall. Cow numbers 1939 to 1954/5 are from the county figures in various volumes of MAFF, *Agricultural Statistics, England and Wales* (London, annual) for cows and heifers in milk plus cows in calf, and include both dairy and beef cows. For 1965–85, the data are for cows and heifers in milk plus cows in calf, for dairy cows only, taken from various volumes of MMB, *Dairy Facts and Figures*. All other figures are from MMB, *Dairy Facts and Figures*.

NA – data not available
* = 1958 figure
** = 1942 figure
*** = based on Far Western data only.

south-west too. By 1985, there were only about one-third of the number of registered producers compared with the mid-1950s. Consequently, herd sizes increased, most rapidly after the mid-1960s, as the data for the Far West shows. It is worth noting that herd sizes in the Mid-West region, which includes Dorset, were significantly higher than those in the Far West, and higher than the national average, whereas Far Western herds remained a little smaller than the national average. Whereas national average milk yields increased by about 50 per cent between the mid-1950s and the mid-1980s, sales per cow in the three south-western counties increased by over 80 per cent in the same period, so total milk sales also increased by more than the national average. Whereas the two Far Western counties only accounted for about 5 per cent of national milk supplies at the beginning of the Second World War, by the mid-1980s they produced nearly 12 per cent of English and Welsh milk.

The south-western counties do not, therefore, completely reflect the national pattern of developments in dairy farming. Dairying in the south-west became relatively more important over the second half of the twentieth century. Whereas in 1939 south-western dairy farms were smaller than the national average, and their cows lower-yielding, by the 1980s they had caught up in yields, and almost in herd sizes, and all while milk prices were falling in real terms and the market was increasingly saturated. Dairy farmers could respond to these challenges in three ways: they could try to keep up, by keeping more and higher yielding cows, or they could find ways of reducing costs, or they could get out of dairying. The national average figures in table 5.1 suggest that the overwhelming majority of milk producers in the country as a whole who were in the business in the 1950s simply responded by getting out of dairying by the end of the 1970s. The Donaldsons' remark about the majority of farmers depending on dairying was probably just about accurate when they wrote their book, but it did not remain so for long. The same happened in the south-west, albeit to a lesser extent. This is part of the specialisation and expansion story that we referred to towards the end of the introduction to this section. Since the farmed land area did not increase – in many areas it declined – and the total national cow herd increased very little after 1960, it follows that all the success stories, involving bigger farms and bigger dairy herds, must be accompanied by other stories, much less likely to be told and more difficult to find evidence for, of farms going out of business and milk producers selling their herds.

The average surviving dairy farmer, therefore, kept more cows, more than four times as many in 1985 as at the end of the war, and each cow produced almost twice as much milk in 1985 as her forebears had done at the beginning of the Second World War. The story of technical change in dairy farming is concerned with how this intensification was brought

Dairy Farming

about. It was done by changes in breeds, feeding, housing, and, to a lesser degree, disease control, and we shall deal with each of these in turn.

Breeds and Breeding

By 1985, most dairy farms had black and white cattle, Friesians or Holsteins (which many people saw as simply a type of Friesian). It was not always so. In the 1880s, there were perhaps up to forty established commercial herds of Friesians. The first herdbook for the breed was produced in 1911, later than most other cattle breeds, and they were improved by a consignment of pedigree Dutch cattle that arrived at Tilbury docks three days before the First World War began. But there were not enough of them to be separately counted in the Board of Agriculture's list of the numbers in each breed in 1908, in which about two-thirds of all cattle were identified as Shorthorns.[9] By the middle of the nineteenth century, separate breeds of cattle had been firmly established, and it was widely recognised that some, by virtue of their body conformation and maturity characteristics, were more suitable for beef production, while others, given their predisposition to producing higher milk yields, were seen as dairy breeds. The most numerous breed, the Shorthorn, was seen as a dual-purpose animal, although different strains within the breed were more of a dairy type and others more suitable for beef. In agricultural textbooks written at the end of the war and in the 1960s, cattle breeds were listed according to whether they were for dairy or beef production, or dual-purpose, and in 1934 regulations were introduced requiring breeding bulls to be licensed by Ministry of Agriculture Inspectors.[10] This meant that we have some idea of the changing popularity of the various breeds, as table 5.3 reveals.

As is clear from table 5.3, some of the specialist dairy breeds, such as the Kerry, Gloucester, and Blue Albion, were already disappearing from commercial use by the outbreak of the Second World War. They would be among the breeds of concern to the Rare Breeds Survival Trust when it was established in the early 1970s.[11] The breeds that were seen as dual-purpose as late as 1960 were not only in decline as far as numbers were concerned, but also increasingly seen as beef breeds. The possible exception to this generalisation can be found in the more dairy types of Shorthorn, which, as the table shows, remained in relatively small

---

[9] G.E. Mingay, *British Friesians: An Epic of Progress* (Rickmansworth, 1982), pp. 34, 47; P. Brassley, 'Livestock Breeds', in E.J.T. Collins (ed.), *The Agrarian History of England and Wales*, vol. VII, 1850–1914 (Cambridge, 2000), p. 564.

[10] D.H. Robinson (ed.), *Fream's Elements of Agriculture* (13th edn, London, 1949), p. 571.

[11] L. Alderson and V. Porter, *Saving the Breeds: A History of the Rare Breeds Survival Trust* (Robertsbridge, 1994).

The Real Agricultural Revolution

TABLE 5.3. The changing popularity of cattle breeds in England and Wales

	Licensed bulls in England and Wales, year ended 31 March 1939	Licensed bulls in England and Wales, year ended 31 March 1960	Dairy cow numbers ('000) in 1978/9
Dairy breeds			
Friesian	3,086	7,084	2,939
Ayrshire	554	1,298	201
Guernsey	1,544	468	69
Jersey	498	480	58
Holstein	NA	NA	41
Kerry	14	3	
Gloucester	3	–	
Blue Albion	32	–	
Dual-purpose breeds			
Red Poll	536	172	
South Devon	449	168	
Belted Galloway	6	12	
Shorthorn	23,897	2,156	14
Lincoln Red Shorthorn	1,300	381	
Welsh Black	440	190	
Longhorn	5	–	

Source: J.A.S. Watson and J.A. More, *Agriculture: The Science and Practice of Farming* (Edinburgh), 8th edn, 1945, p. 540 and 11th edn, 1962, p. 484; C. Spedding (ed.), *Fream's Agriculture* (16th edn, London, 1983), p. 210.

numbers in dairy herds into the 1970s. Among the more popular of the specialist dairy breeds, only the Ayrshire increased in popularity in the 1940s and '50s, but by the 1960s it too was giving way to the Friesians, and by the end of the 1970s it can be seen that the Holsteins, which would become much more important in the 1980s and '90s, were beginning to make an impact. The MMB surveyed the distribution of breeds in the dairy herd from time to time, and figures are available relating to 1955 onwards, as table 5.4 shows.

Dairy Farming

TABLE 5.4. National dairy herd breed distribution (percentages)

	England and Wales 1955	Far Western 1955	England and Wales 1965	England and Wales 1973–4	Far Western 1973–4	England and Wales 1985–6
Ayrshire	18.3	10.0	15.7	3.6	2.7	2.2
Friesian	40.6	23.9	64.2	81.0	72.2	85.8
Guernsey	5.3	15.6	5.7	2.8	7.2	1.8
Jersey	2.6	2.4	4.3	2.2	2.8	1.6
Dairy Shorthorn	25.3	17.3	6.3	0.9	0.3	0.4
Holstein and Holstein/Friesian crosses	–	–	–	–	–	7.8
Other breeds and crosses	7.9	30.7	3.8	9.5	14.8	0.3

Source: MMB, *Dairy Facts and Figures*, 1961, 1976, 1986.

Table 5.4 clearly shows the rise to dominance of the Friesians between the 1950s and 1970s, initially at the expense of the Shorthorns and later in replacing Ayrshires and Channel Island cattle. The 1973–4 figure for 'other breeds and crosses' nationally almost certainly includes Holsteins and their crosses. The same pattern of development can be found in the data for the two Far Western counties, but with some interesting differences. A 1950 survey of farms in Devon revealed that a third of the dairy cows in the county were South Devons, another third of crosses or mixed breeds, and the remaining third comprised the Friesians, Ayrshires, Shorthorns, and Channel Island cows.[12] Friesians took over more slowly, even though Shorthorns were probably never as popular as they were in other parts of the country. Mixed breeds and crosses were more common than elsewhere, and the South Devon breed remained in the dairy herd despite being increasingly seen as a beef animal, as the 1973–4 figure for 'other breeds and crosses' in the Far Western region illustrates. As was often the case, therefore, the national picture became more complex when examined at a regional level, and more complex still at the individual farm level.

[12] Devon Agriculture Study Group, *Devon Farming*, pp. 20–3.

In the 1950s, as table 5.4 shows, many dairy farmers in the south-west were using Ayrshire, Channel Island, or Shorthorn cows in their dairy herds. Only one of the twenty farmers who discussed cow breeds in their interviews could solely remember milking Friesians, and often herds were made up of a mixture of breeds. Farms 109 in mid-Devon and 2/7 in Dorset, for example, kept both Ayrshires and Shorthorns, and farm 576 in east Cornwall remembered having 'some South Devons, probably some Shorthorns ... We had a couple of Guernseys because I learned to hand milk on a Guernsey ... We had a little flirt with Ayrshires when cows were dear and Ayrshires were a bit cheaper.' On farm 162, on the edge of Exmoor, the farmer remembered his father in the 1950s

> milking about ten beef-type cows, ... Devons and Herefords, but as I was showing a bit of interest father bought two Ayrshires and two Friesians as well. It wouldn't have been much more than a churn – ten gallons a day. A lot of the milk was always used for calf rearing. He would hand milk the cows and then let the calves in afterwards.

On farm 842 in south-east Devon between the wars they were 'hand-milking Devons, Red Rubies [i.e. North Devons], in my grandfather's day', but by 1952 there was a herd of thirty-five Shorthorns. In north Devon, on farm 570, they were unimpressed by Shorthorns: they had Red Rubies in 1940, 'and the Ministry came along ... and they said "If you cross them with Shorthorns you'll get milk *and* beef", and everybody did that and they found by the 1950s that Shorthorns didn't produce milk *or* beef'.

Only two of these twenty farmers failed, in the end, to go over to Friesians, and they both went out of dairying, one (162) in the 1960s and the other (826) in 1972. For many, the change started in the 1950s. Not all farmers went straight to Friesians ('father kept Shorthorns, then he gradually changed over to Ayrshires and Friesians' – farm 692), and the change could take a long time. On farm 243 in east Devon,

> Father kept Shorthorns, and we changed over about 1955 or '56, and what happened was he couldn't find a decent Shorthorn bull, because it was all AI by then, and he had to go to the Shorthorn Society, and they said they were going to import some from Denmark or Sweden I believe, but my neighbour had a quiet Friesian bull, so we put him on the Shorthorns, brilliant milkers, so then we put him on the Friesians, absolutely useless, second cross was absolutely useless, so we started buying in Friesian heifers. It would be about 1981 or '82 before all the Shorthorns were gone from the herd. We had one cow that had seventeen calves and was still milking well.

Farm 669 in North Devon was another of those that mixed milk and beef production up to the 1950s:

In 1944 the cows were producing 249 gallons per cow, in 1984 they were producing 1,100, nearly 1,150 gallons per cow. A lot of it's breeding, and better diet. We went over to Friesians, before it was Devons, North Devons, and a lot of the milk went to the calves, so we were selling the surplus. We gradually went over to Friesians over three or four years after we got married [in 1953] ... By 1960-odd we were entirely Friesian.

It is worth noticing here, in passing, that a major farm management decision was associated with a major family change. Similarly, on farm 272 in east Cornwall, the farmer remembered taking over the farm 'in 1956 when we were married ... We used to have some South Devons that I took over from Father. Friesians were coming in then. We bought some. It was gradual.' On farm 466, also in east Cornwall, the change was associated with the son becoming a partner, in 1961, at about the same time as the farm acquired a new milking parlour:

I remember father doing the weekend milking in the summer when half the cows were dry, and he said 'It took me longer to bring the cows in and wash up after than to do the milking.' I said 'blame it on me, we'll go to black and whites'. The trouble with South Devons was, as a milk breed there was too much wastage, calving troubles, mastitis troubles, shapeless udders, fine for beef, but no good for milk. There was a big argument in the breed about which way they should go, to beef or milk. There was a premium for many years for butterfat, if you could keep above 4 per cent, so you were chopping out cows that gave below 4 per cent and the herd never expanded very fast, you couldn't make it expand, whereas when we got Friesians you could breed your own replacements and scale up gradually. The Friesians came in about 1961, we needed more cows if we were going to scale up to save labour, that pushed us to black and whites.

The demise of the South Devon as a dairy breed was accepted in their home area, and among the education and advisory community, by 1960. On farm 744, a few miles south of Dartmoor,

I remember when ... was lecturer in management at Seale-Hayne, he put his arm round my shoulder and said 'Take it from me, milk from South Devons is finished', I can hear him saying it now, and I took notice of what he said. We steadily bought in Friesians and bred from them. We didn't breed up from South Devons, nobody did that. Quite a few of the herds around us were Ayrshires, and they did it, but we never did, we steadily bought Friesians and bred pure Friesians.

Friesians were therefore the dominant breed until about the mid-1980s, when they began to be challenged by Holsteins. The farmer on farm 139 in east Devon remembered 'when my father first saw Holsteins he said "little hat racks" [i.e. bony, with little flesh], but they've certainly pushed yields, from about the mid-80s some Holstein blood was coming in, before that it would be straight Friesian'. Nevertheless, it would be a mistake to think that farmers were only interested in milk production, and that beef played no part in their decisions. On farm 209, in west Cornwall, the change from Shorthorns to Friesians began in 1952 or 1953, but a significant proportion of the cows were still put to a beef bull,

> a Hereford, all the good calves went to market to make a good price, and all the poorer ones we kept to sell as stores, although if the calf price was down we'd keep them all, and sell them as stores. But back then Hereford cross Friesians would sell like hot cakes, as long as they were colour marked. We were still using Herefords up to the 1980s, then we went over to Charolais, that was the first, and Welsh Black for the cow you couldn't get in calf, then we went Simmental in the '80s and '90s. We never went to Holsteins, we stuck to traditional British Friesians because you got a good beef calf out of it. Beef has always been an important part of the business.

Similarly, on farm 272, although Holsteins began to come in from the mid-1980s, the decision was later made to start 'going back the other way, because some of the more extreme Holsteins you have to feed a lot, and they have feet problems, they haven't got the longevity'. These husbandry factors, and others such as ease of calving and handling, were also important to farmers in deciding upon a choice of breed. On farm 101, in mid-Devon, a particular Charolais bull was used

> because he was easy calving, and all his calves looked like peas in a pod, I didn't like Limousins, a farmer next door had Limousins, they were flighty things, and I'd be in a field and look at them and they'd be gone, talk about nervous, another neighbour used them on some Jerseys, and they just about tried to jump through the front of the lorry, and I thought 'I'm not having any of that.'

Once the decision had been made to change over to Friesians, the next question was how it should be done. The alternatives were to buy cows, to buy a bull, or to use AI. As the previous quotations indicate, producing Friesian/South Devon crosses was rarely if ever done, but 'grading up' as it was called, by using a Friesian sire on Ayrshire or Shorthorn cows, and another on their crossbred daughters, and so on until the herd was effectively Friesian, was more common. On farm 209, for example, 'the Shorthorns were graded up using Friesian AI. We also bought a Friesian bull, but it was mostly AI.' The way things were often done comes over vividly from the account of experiences on farm 3/1 in the Blackmore Vale of Dorset:

> We still had one or two Ayrshires left when I came back in 1976, but we were certainly serving British Friesians then. We graded up the Ayrshires by grading up with a Friesian bull, we used to keep Friesian

bulls for that purpose, it was the way a lot of people did it, AI was still a relatively new concept then, and an expensive one. We first used AI after I came back, late 1970s the first AI man was on the farm, for the best cows, it was expensive to buy semen straws then, so we kept Friesian bulls to do the main work. We never kept a beef bull then, it was just Friesians. Everybody has the same stories about Friesian bulls, about being cornered, and having to run out of the field, they were a nightmare. Then we kept some beef bulls, after that, things like Simmentals, which were no good in our climate, but then AI was becoming the way you did it. From the 1980s we used AI on everything, with a bull just kept to sweep up those that didn't hold to AI. So we kept Friesian bulls for quite a long time in the 1960s and '70s.

Compared with some others, this farm was a relatively late adopter of AI. On the edge of Cranborne Chase in Dorset, on farm 2/7, 'We used AI, we had a bull ... In about 1970, he was the last one, then we went fully over to AI. We had a Hereford quite often for running with the young stock, and then he would go in with the dairy cows sometimes.' On this relatively large farm – nearly seven hundred acres and two hundred cows by 1980 – there was considerable interest in breeding:

> in 1950-odd my father started to go pedigree with Friesians, and I got the bug, which is why there are so many herd books over there, we tried to buy a few pedigree ones, and we went through the grading up system, and in the end half the cows were fully pedigree.

Farms such as this were in the minority, but there was general agreement about the importance of breeding: 'The main part of your profitability with dairying is genetics, if you get the right animal for your farm. That's more important than the feed, it's your basic stepping stone ...' (farm 3/1). The significance of AI was that it enabled the best bulls to be used on a much wider range of cows than would have been possible with natural service. As experience on farm 139 in east Devon demonstrated,

> the stock bull's been a beef breed for sweeping up, and we've mainly used AI, ... The genetics through AI has been immense, the ability to select, as a general farmer, not a pedigree breeder, we had access to some of the best bloodline in the world, and that wasn't happening before.

Another farmer (466), explaining the effect of importing Holstein semen from the USA to students from the local agricultural college (probably around 1990), claimed that 'we've made more genetic progress in one jump than my father did in his whole life. You say a thing like that, and I turned to ... [the Principal of the college] and said "Is that possible?" and he said "I think you're probably right."'

The MMB began its AI service in 1944 and by 1960 was operating at twenty-two centres. There were other centres operated by independent organisations and the Ministry of Agriculture. From twelve thousand first inseminations in 1944–5, the number increased rapidly to over a million in England and Wales only ten years later, and by the early 1960s it had reached the level, at between 1.6 and 1.8 million first inseminations per year, that it would maintain into the mid-1980s. There were in this period between about 2.4 and 2.6 million cows in the national dairy herd (see table 5.1), and the non-return percentage (the percentage of cows that became pregnant as a result of the first insemination) was about 75 per cent, so from the 1960s onwards it follows that about half of the calves produced were the result of AI. In 1960, 63.4 per cent of dairy herds only used AI, with 13.1 per cent of herds only using natural mating, and these proportions were virtually unchanged in 1985. In the Far Western MMB region, AI was more popular than the national average, with 73.2 per cent of herds only using AI by 1960, whereas in the Mid-Western region (which included Dorset), where the average herd size was significantly larger, the proportion of herds only using AI was a little below the national average.[13]

From these figures, it might appear that the introduction of AI in dairy cattle was rapid, problem-free, and concerned with genetic improvement. Not surprisingly, the reality was a little more complex. Speaking at the end of 1944, the Minister of Agriculture noted the shortage of trained staff and suitable buildings, the dangers of over-rapid expansion, and the need for caution, notwithstanding his 'great hopes' for the future. His remarks were quoted in an article in the Ministry's Journal early the following year, which noted not only the value of AI for livestock improvement 'particularly among the smaller herds which cannot normally command the services of a high-class bull', but also its value in preventing the spread of trichomoniasis and other diseases communicated by bulls on mating.[14] As Sarah Wilmot's detailed study makes clear, although the expansion of AI may have been rapid after the 1940s, it had taken at least twenty years to reach that point. Some AI techniques were being explored in the UK in the 1920s, and on a much larger scale in the USSR and Argentina at the same time, but pedigree breeders in Britain were either indifferent or opposed to its widespread use. As Wilmot argues, 'for a very long time scientists did not succeed in capturing the interest of the agricultural industry or government in this technology and their research on AI stayed inside the laboratory walls'. Both the National Cattle Breeders' Association and the NFU were opposed to the MMB's efforts to establish a national service in the 1940s.[15] As we have seen,

[13] MMB, *Dairy Facts and Figures*, 1960, 1963, 1970, 1986 editions.
[14] Anon, 'Artificial Insemination of Cattle', *Agriculture* 51 (1945), pp. 529–32.
[15] S. Wilmot, 'From "Public Service" to Artificial Insemination: Animal Breeding

however, the MMB managed to get things going, in part – considerable part, it is often argued – thanks to the efforts of Dr Joseph Edwards, who moved from the Cambridge University School of Agriculture, where much of the original research on AI in Britain had been done, to the MMB. Edwards and his colleagues were responsible for much of the subsequent technical development that went along with AI: techniques for freezing semen, which meant that it was possible to evaluate the performance of bulls over a long enough period before using them on a wide range of cows, and eventually for embryo transfer to multiply the influence of the best cows.[16] Cows could be bred to produce much more milk, provided that the farmer could get enough nutrients into them.

Feeds and Feeding

Feed was the major cost of milk production, on average 60 per cent of gross costs per cow in 1956–7, according to MMB calculations, and never less than half in subsequent years.[17] Since they were ruminants, cows, unlike pigs or chickens, could eat bulky, fibrous foods such as grass, hay, straw, or silage, which were relatively cheap. On the other hand, they needed to take in enough energy and protein to meet the physiological demands of lactation and pregnancy, which often required concentrated feeds, which were relatively expensive. This was the balancing act that was constantly on the mind of the dairy farmer: maintain, and if possible increase output, but limit costs; maximise the use of grass, but not at the expense of milk yield. In 1974, it was estimated that 57 per cent of the energy input of UK ruminants came from grass or rough grazing. Most of the rest came from other feeds, principally cereals.[18]

Grass was usually the principal feed for dairy cows from the spring to the autumn, but how well it performed this task could vary considerably from one farm to another. Its productivity depended upon the varieties and fertilisers used, and the grazing management decisions of the farmer. Between the 1940s and the 1980s, new varieties became available, and fertiliser use increased, but the variability in grassland management skills from one farmer to another appears to have remained in place. A comparison between agricultural textbooks written in the 1940s and those written in the 1980s suggests that the basic species in use changed

---

Science and Reproductive Research in Early Twentieth-Century Britain', *Studies in the History and Philosophy of Biological and Biomedical Sciences* 38 (2007), pp. 411–41.

[16] Q. Seddon, *The Silent Revolution: Farming and the Countryside into the 21st Century* (London, 1989), pp. 41–55.

[17] MMB, *Dairy Facts and Figures*, various years.

[18] J.S. Brockman, 'Grassland', in R.J. Halley (ed.), *The Agricultural Notebook* (17th edn, London, 1982), pp. 173–202.

little, although the varieties of those species changed considerably. In the 1940s, for example, the species identified as being of agricultural significance were principally Italian ryegrass, perennial ryegrass, cocksfoot, timothy, and meadow fescue, with a mention of rough-stalked meadow grass and crested dogstail, which appeared in some pastures. A seeds mixture for establishing a ley, or temporary grassland, designed to last for more than three years, therefore involved a mixture of four varieties of perennial ryegrass, two of cocksfoot, two of timothy, two varieties of white clover, and one of red clover.[19] A similar list of species, and several identical varieties in the recommended seeds mixture, could be found in a book entirely devoted to grass and grassland written by an agricultural academic with long experience of grassland management in the 1960s. The long-established Cockle Park mixture, for example, which had been developed at the experimental station of that name in Northumberland in the 1930s, contained perennial ryegrass, cocksfoot, timothy, and three kinds of clover.[20] Agricultural scientists and seed firms were developing new varieties from at least the 1950s onwards, and brought them to the market. Among the significant innovations was the development of tetraploid varieties of perennial and Italian ryegrasses, because they were more palatable and digestible. They first appeared on the NIAB recommended list in 1964.[21] By the early 1980s, the seeds mixture suggested for a medium-term grazing ley had become simpler, consisting of two varieties of Italian ryegrass (one of which was tetraploid), four of perennial (one tetraploid), and one variety of white clover.[22]

The desirable qualities of a seeds mixture depended upon whether the resultant sward was to be used for grazing, mowing, or both, and within each species different varieties could be selected for variations in persistence and date of maturity. Farmers might therefore be expected to consider such factors carefully, and indeed some did so. On farm 466 in east Cornwall,

> We changed the grass varieties. We went from Cockle Park mixtures to pure ryegrass, and as the herd grew we had permanent ryegrass round the buildings for the cows to graze and Italian ryegrass further out that you would renew, and we would make most of the silage from that, and those fields would be subject to a kind of rotation, because we would grow maize out there, and forage peas, so you had an arable part of the farm further out and permanent pasture with ryegrass, and it became specialist ryegrass rather than mixed, we forgot about timothy and cocksfoot, forgot about clover of course, so all those technologies were moving together with what we were doing with the breeding. The

[19] Robinson, *Fream's Elements of Agriculture* (13th edn), pp. 259–69.
[20] H.I. Moore, *Grass and Grasslands* (London, 1966), pp. 51–9.
[21] NIAB, *Varieties of Ryegrass*, Farmers' Leaflet no. 16 (Cambridge, 1964).
[22] Brockman, 'Grassland', p. 185.

merchants were selling the new varieties and we were receptive to the new ideas.

Farm 7/8, in Dorset, took advice from NAAS (and later ADAS), 'they gave us advice on certain leys to use. We'd ring the District Adviser.' On farm 744 in south Devon, however, although the farmer was a member of the Devon Grassland Society, which held discussions and conducted visits on grassland topics, 'We bought varieties by the advice of the seedsman, we didn't know enough about it.' Farmer 193 in north Devon felt the same: 'I can't claim to have put much thought to grass varieties. As long as there was plenty of clover there I left it up to the merchant.' So too did farm 3/1 in Dorset: 'you'd ask the seeds rep – often the cake rep, the same firm – and he'd say "I'll send you some bags of No.4." Everybody had a firm they dealt with.' Similarly, on farm 243 in east Devon, grass seed was bought according to the merchant's brand: 'We used Mole Valley Gold grass seed. There were three or four types of ryegrass and two sorts of white clover, and quite a bit of timothy in it.'

Increasing fertiliser use, especially of nitrogen, reduced the value of clover, the extent to which it was used in seeds mixtures, and its survival in pastures. The 1949 edition of *Fream's Elements of Agriculture* described an intensive grassland production system that involved the use of between three and four hundredweights per acre of ammonium sulphate or nitro-chalk, which, depending upon which was used, would be equivalent to between seventy and 115 kilogrammes per hectare.[23] Clearly it was not expected that the average farm would use this much. In contrast, a textbook written thirty years later could assume the use of over three hundred kilogrammes of nitrogen per hectare in some circumstances.[24] These were only recommendations. What happened in practice can be gauged from a report of the Royal Commission on Environmental Pollution, which demonstrated that the total quantity of nitrogen used on UK farms rose from less than two hundred thousand tons in the late 1940s to over a million tons by the late 1970s, two-thirds of which was applied to the grass crop.[25] By 1984, Nix's *Farm Management Pocketbook* was assuming that a dairy farm at the *average* level of performance would be stocking 1.85 cows per forage hectare and using two hundred kilogrammes of nitrogen per hectare.[26]

On farms in the south-west, this increase in nitrogen use took some time to get going. Figure 5.1, based on all analysed farms, demonstrates that although there was a steady rise in nitrogen (N) use in the post-war

---

23 Robinson, *Fream's Elements of Agriculture* (13th edn), p. 278.
24 Brockman, 'Grassland', p. 187.
25 *Royal Commission on Environmental Pollution, Seventh Report: Agriculture and Pollution*, Cmnd.7644 (1979).
26 J. Nix, *Farm Management Pocketbook* (14th edn, Ashford, 1984), p. 25.

period it was in the early-mid 1970s that N use increased significantly. Figure 5.2 confirms what we would expect, that dairy farms were applying larger quantities of N per acre. Interestingly, until the mid-1950s there was little difference in N use on dairy and non-dairy farms. Thereafter, although both groups of farms increased N use, dairy farms became relatively more intensive (using N/acre as a measure of intensity). Figure 5.3 indicates how the trend of N intensification varied according to farm tenure. Clearly N use rose on all farms regardless of tenure but from the early/mid-1970s it is apparent that N use on wholly owned farms did not rise to the same extent as on wholly rented and mixed tenure farms. Mixed tenure farms were the most intensive in terms of applications of N/acre. This may be for a number of reasons. Contemporary research indicates that mixed tenure farms are often much more dynamic and expansionary than wholly owned and wholly rented farms, and so it may be expected that in the 1970s and '80s they were also the most intensive farms. In addition, there is a strong statistical association (using Chi Squared) between owner-occupiers and being a non-dairy farm, which, as we have already seen, tend to use less N.

Farm 162, on the edge of Exmoor, saw fertiliser use double between 1968 and 1978, just at the time when the farmer's son was returning to work on the farm: 'we were building up the numbers, it was a matter of keeping me on and interested'. Fertiliser use increased on farm 570 in north Devon as a result of the farmer's son attending college, but it was not without problems.

> In 1960 my Dad said I ought to be educated a bit so I went off to day release classes on Wednesday to learn more about farming, and that was the thing then, put more fertiliser on, coming home from Bicton I said to Dad the latest thing is nitrogen, you could buy a bag of nitrogen, lovely bright blue colour and little granules ran out, and we tried it out, we had a little three acre field down there and we put this nitrogen on and the grass grew and we were all so pleased, and we put the calves in there and they wouldn't eat it, there was too much nitrogen in it, and then if they did eat it they would scour like mad, you could use that for your silage, it was lovely for silage, but we found that what Dad had been using was a fish fertiliser made down in Penzance and it was the offal of the fish and the fishes heads and seaweed and ashes and all sorts of things mixed together and it was a really wonderful thing, and that used to come in hundredweight and a quarter bags, and it was very dusty, and you'd stand up in a trailer throwing it into a spinner behind, and you had to be careful to keep your balance, but didn't it make the grass grow, and the grass was sweet, it was a fish fertiliser, but it's all been banned now. That would be in the 1950s, then we changed over to these artificials, to Nitram. But we used a lot of lime, and basic slag, we had lime quarries in the village, we used to get a lot from down there, and a lot of basic slag from the iron ore works. It went on into the 1960s.

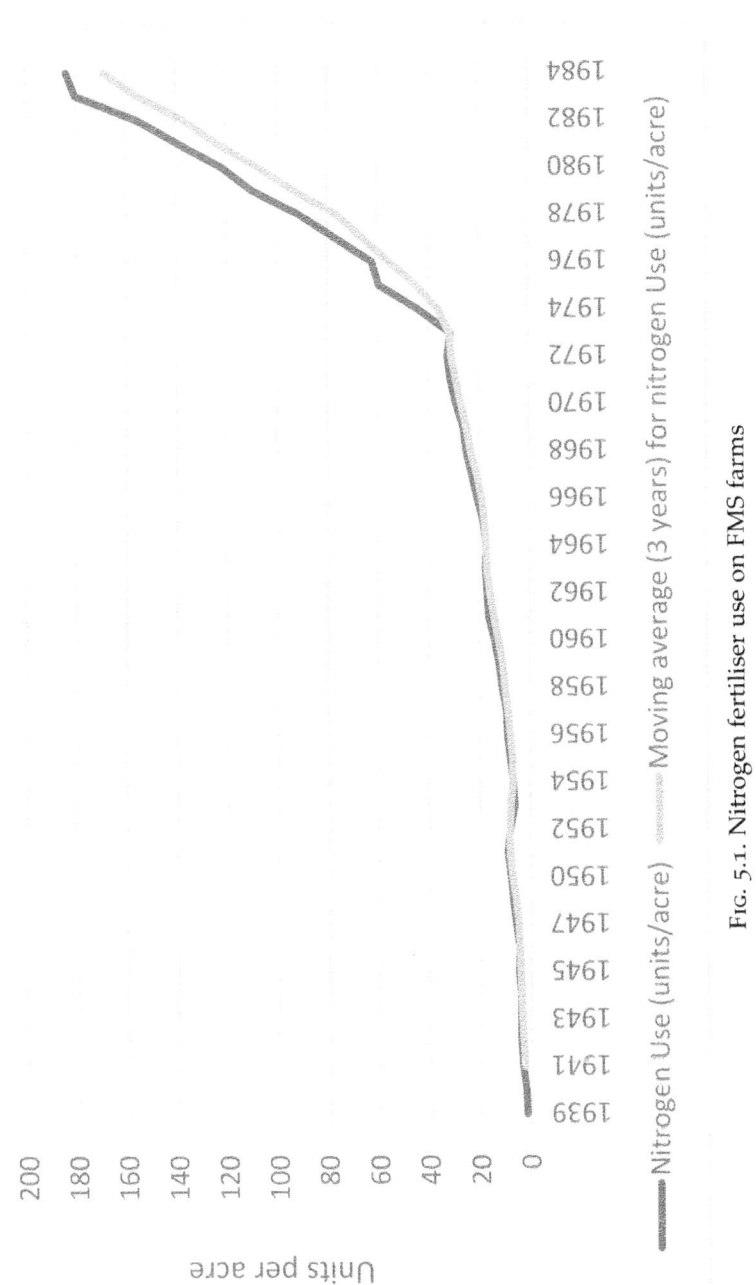

FIG. 5.1. Nitrogen fertiliser use on FMS farms

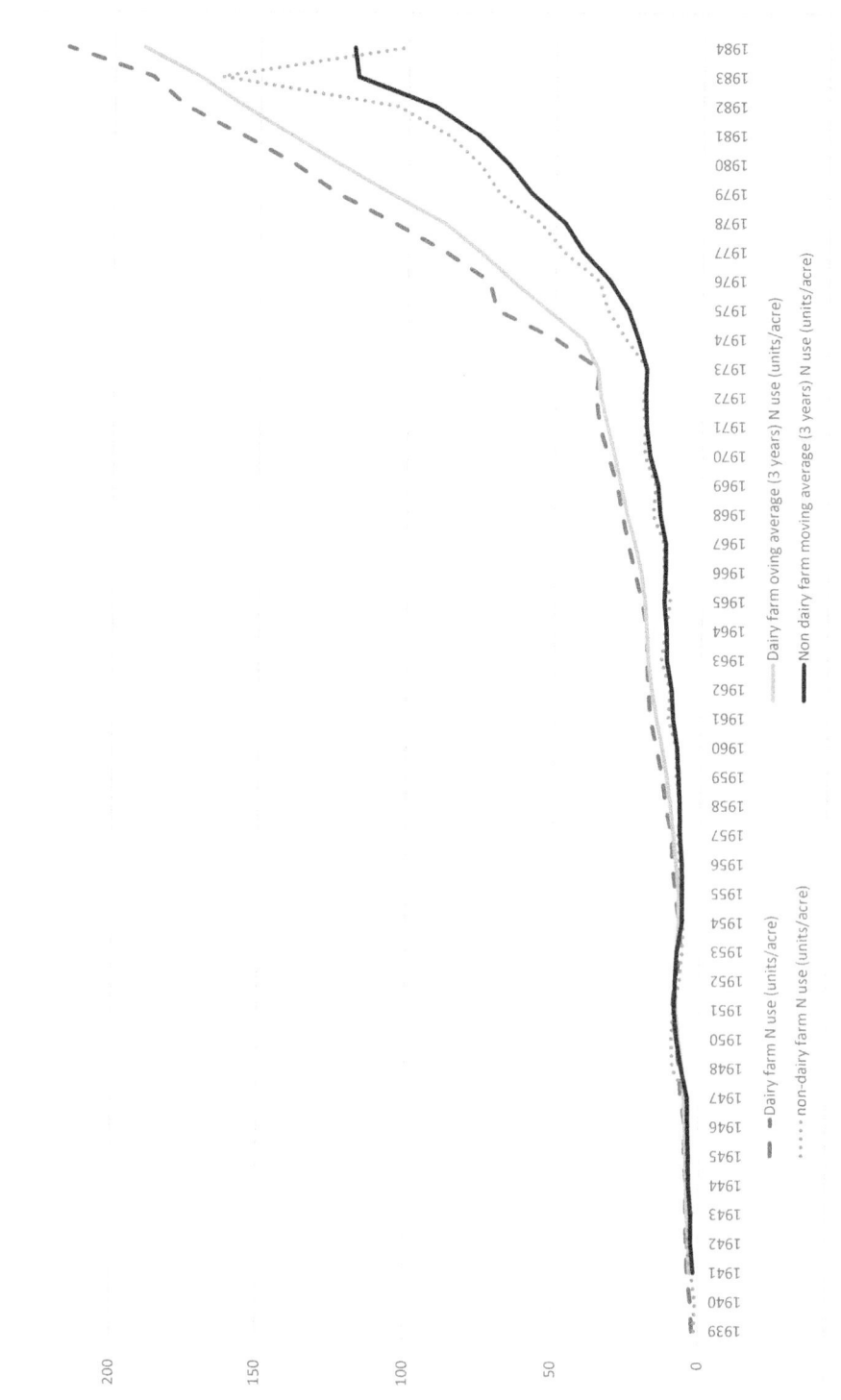

Fig. 5.2. Nitrogen fertiliser use on FMS dairy and non-dairy farms

Fig. 5.3. Nitrogen fertiliser use on FMS farms of different tenure types

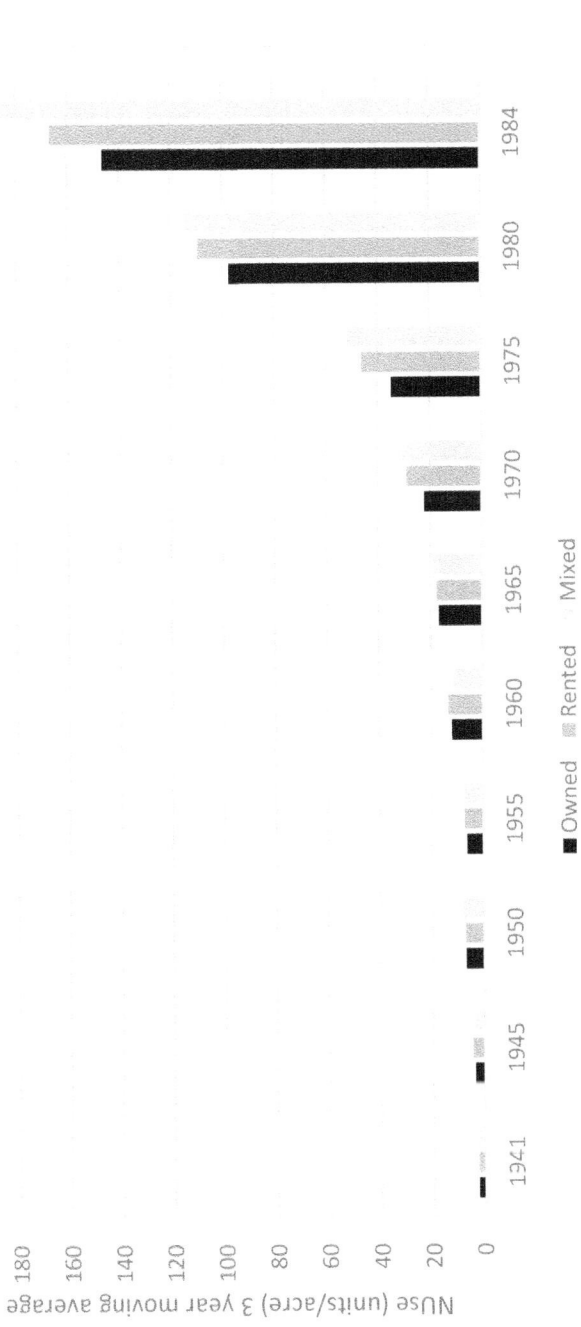

British Rail used to bring it out when we were haymaking. British Rail used to have a three-wheel tractor unit with a trailer, and this chap would come out from Tiverton with two ton at a time, big fat chap with a red face, and mother used to keep taking him a metal container of tea, because she felt sorry for him, having to unload it, there was nobody to help him because we were haymaking. Then it came in bigger lorries and we put sleepers in the field and unloaded it. We had our own slag spreader, a second hand one made in Tivertons, Twoses, and that was a long metal roller with some zig-zag metal on top so that it dribbled out all the time. We put 7 cwt on at a time. There was a lot of basic slag used. All our neighbours used it, it was about £5 a ton.

Farmer 570's wife sounded a note of caution:

We went to an ICI experimental farm near Dorchester on a farmers' outing from Liscombe. One of the employees at Liscombe used to live in Bampton, and we became friends with him and his wife and he got up a farmers' discussion group, about the early 1970s. I couldn't believe ... I was quite young at the time ... To keep putting more and more fertiliser on, to get more and more grass, and more and more milk, it seemed to me to be a vicious circle, and when I came home I said to [my husband] 'That can't be right, this isn't right for the cows. If you've got somebody working for you and you work them twenty hours a day, it's not right, work them at a gentler pace.' But after that they eased back a little bit. As long as you've got enough money coming in ... just go along at a gentler rate. I was horrified. As I said at the beginning of this conversation, we go along in a traditional way, we haven't been in the rat race. It's like vegetables, we don't put fertiliser on our vegetables. It's not right for the soil either. But you had to in those days. It was a time of change.

Nonetheless, compared with the textbook recommendations, nitrogen use on FMS dairy farms was not enormous, only reaching about one hundred units per acre (roughly equivalent to one hundred kilogrammes per hectare) in the mid-1970s. Even in the 1980s on farm 243, 'where the cows fed they got about a hundredweight of Nitram. And you've also got a lot of shit, mind.' As farmer 3/1 remembered, 'When I came back in 1976, for the whole grazing season, we'd only have been putting on about four bags of Nitram, about 120 units.' On farm 7/8, also in Dorset, where both cow numbers and yields doubled between 1945 and 1985,

We had more medium-term leys rather than permanent pasture, and better use of fertiliser, more fertiliser. We used to work a thirty-day rotation, and we used to put a couple of hundredweight of Nitram on every thirty days through the summer [i.e. sixty-nine units every thirty days]; it was a lot of fertiliser, and of course in those days fertiliser wasn't so dear as it is now, you couldn't do that now, and a couple of the dressings were of complete fertiliser, 20-10-10.

It should also be remembered that some farms had other sources of nutrients, and land that was climatically suited to growing grass, as, for example, farm 209 in west Cornwall:

> The big thing that's enabled us to expand the herd is that it's incredibly good grass growing land here. We have ryegrass and clover leys. We were never incredibly high N users. In the 1960s if we put on four applications of thirty units, about 120 in total, that would be somewhere around it. Possibly a bit more rather than less, and some P [phosphorus] and K [potassium]. And we had pig manure back then. The grass here will grow for more than eight months a year.

Improved grass varieties and increased fertiliser applications were of little use, however, unless the grazing was properly managed. 'Grass management is the hardest thing', said farmer 787, and while some farmers were good at it, many were not. The textbooks published at the end of the war perhaps suggest why. Although they were agreed that 'the severity of the grazing throughout the season affects the persistency of the grasses, the yield and nutritive quantity of the herbage, and the seasonal distribution of growth', and that 'the aim of the grazier should be to secure a succession of flushes of young grass for consumption at the stage of their maximum feeding value', they were less clear about the management regime that would produce the correct severity of grazing to maximise the succession of flushes of digestible grass.[27] Writing in the mid-1950s, Professor Cooper agreed with the basic principle ('If a pasture is to be fully productive it must be kept juvenile') but had little confidence in the average farmer's capacity to achieve it:

> The indifference of the average British farmer to his grassland is a heritage of the bad old days between the wars when concentrates were cheap and plentiful ... It did not pay then to exploit grass for the dairy herd. Provided grass gave maintenance and leg-room, and a little more perhaps in the early summer, it was doing its job. There was no sustained effort to extend the grazing season or to provide concentrate-sparing herbage for seven or eight months of the year.[28]

While admitting that the wartime plough-up policy had given a boost to Professor Stapledon's ideas about ley farming, and that, to judge from the topics of their meetings farmers had become 'grassland conscious' by 1950, he felt that there was little real improvement. If dairy farmers fed fewer rationed concentrates, 'the main effort had been one of substituting home-grown for purchased concentrates. ... Only 55 per cent of the nutrients required for milk production were being obtained from grass,

---

[27] Watson and More, *Agriculture* (8th edn), p. 403; Robinson, *Fream's Elements of Agriculture* (13th edn), p. 273.
[28] M.McG. Cooper, *Competitive Farming* (London, 1956), p. 25.

as compared with a Dutch figure of over 80 per cent.' Although there were some notable and praiseworthy exceptions, 'the general run of dairy farmers did not have confidence in grass'.[29]

Thirty years later, some things had changed, as the existence of organisations such as the Devon Grassland Society and the Grasshopper Club in Hampshire suggests. The textbooks of the early 1980s discussed the relative merits of traditional set stocking compared with paddocks, block grazing, and strip grazing, without arriving at any clear conclusion that one was preferable to another.[30] Much would depend upon the individual circumstances of the farm. In 1961, both the three-year perennial ryegrass leys and the permanent pasture on Pump Farm, Whitford, in east Devon were strip-grazed by the dairy herd from early March onwards and were found to be equally productive as long as they had the same manurial treatment.[31] On farm 466, the cows grazed permanent grassland, predominantly ryegrass, around the buildings, with the more distant grass fields being kept for silage. Few of the farmers interviewed discussed the details of summer grazing management, and it seems likely that most relied on set stocking. Whatever methods were used, though, farmer 7/8's view that grassland management improved between the 1960s and the 1980s was widely accepted.

The other aspect of summer cow nutrition was the cake that was fed at milking time, but it is not easy to assess the extent to which that changed, because data for concentrate use is normally collected for the whole year, and it was not a topic that farmers discussed much. There is some evidence to suggest that farmers were not always aware of how much their cows received. An investigation by the NAAS found that, of a sample of twenty farmers, eleven fed more concentrates than they intended and four fed less.[32] At Pump Farm, in east Devon, it was felt that the grass was enough for maintenance plus four gallons, but cows yielding more than four gallons per day were fed a mixture of barley and oats in addition.[33] The use of home-grown grain was widespread. On farm 744 in south Devon, 'we fed our own grain, home mill and mix, our cereals and some bought-in protein', and on farm 2/7 in Dorset 'we fed all the cows on a home-grown meal. We used to have one chap who worked nearly all the time in the barn, milling and mixing, and then delivering it to three different dairies.' This, however, was probably as much for

[29] Cooper, *Competitive Farming*, pp. 25–7.
[30] Brockman, 'Grassland', pp. 190–2; Spedding, *Fream's Agriculture* (16th edn), pp. 559–61.
[31] Anon, 'Summer Milk in the South West', *Dairy Farmer*, May 1961, p. 26.
[32] MAFF, *The Farm as a Business: Aids to Management No. 8, Dairying* (London, 1967), p. 8.
[33] Anon, 'Summer Milk'.

Dairy Farming

winter as for summer feeding, and the way in which cows were fed over winter changed to a much greater extent.

Writing at the end of the 1930s, two academics in the Cambridge University School of Agriculture gave an example of a winter ration that would provide for the maintenance of an average-yielding dairy cow. It required twelve pounds of medium-quality meadow hay and forty pounds of roots, preferably mangolds, although the reader was reminded that they were 'considered unsafe for feeding till after Christmas on account of their amide content'. Before Christmas, swedes could be used instead of mangolds, but they were more likely to taint the milk. In addition, there were a variety of production rations, to be fed at either 3.5 or four pounds per gallon of milk produced, which involved various combinations of cereals, such as crushed oats or barley, or cracked maize, together with a protein source such as cracked beans, linseed cake, or decorticated groundnut cake. However, on small farms, or grassland farms where no cereals were grown, they found that there was a good case for buying proprietary concentrates. They worked out the nutrient content of each ration in terms of its starch equivalent and protein equivalent and pointed out that the costs of different rations could vary considerably from year to year as the ingredient prices fluctuated.[34] The same starch and protein equivalent system was still in use in 1960 when MAFF produced the fifteenth edition (the first had appeared in 1921) of its Bulletin no. 48, *Rations for Livestock*. It recommended the same kind of ration as Halnan and Garner. For maintenance and the first gallon of milk from typical dairy cows, for example, it suggested fifteen pounds of good hay plus forty pounds of kale or cabbage, or seven pounds of Lucerne hay plus ten pounds of good hay plus fifty pounds of mangolds.[35]

Examples of this kind of ration were commonly found on many of the farms in the south-west in the 1940s and '50s. Farms would have perhaps two or three acres of turnips and swedes, an acre or two of mangolds, and another of flat poll cabbages. Since mixed farming was predominant, not all of these were destined to feed the dairy herd, but they certainly formed a part of the cows' diet. The survey of Devon agriculture published in 1952 revealed that the area of fodder crops (a combination of turnips, swedes, mangolds, rape, cabbage, kale, savoys, and kohl rabi) peaked in 1945 at nearly eighty thousand acres, roughly 20 per cent of the total tillage area. By 1950, it had declined to a little over sixty thousand acres (62,036), but still formed about the same proportion of the total tillage. The commentary noted that

---

[34] E.T. Halnan and F.H. Garner, *The Principles and Practice of Feeding Farm Animals* (2nd edn, London, 1944), pp. 188–97.
[35] R.E. Evans, *Rations for Livestock*, Ministry of Agriculture, Fisheries and Food, Bulletin no. 48 (London, 1960), p. 58.

> The acreage of mangolds has remained remarkably constant since 1939, ... Green fodder crops which are predominantly kales have shown an enormous uninterrupted increase ... this is in large measure due to the spread of the practice of grazing cattle on un-singled kale using an electric fence which saves labour both in the Spring and in the Autumn.[36]

On farm 744 in south Devon, where 'we never dreamed that we wouldn't be making hay or growing roots', they grew 3.5 acres of mangolds, 4.5 acres of turnips and swedes, and a quarter of an acre of fodder cabbage in 1947, and this pattern of cropping was still roughly similar in 1969. On farm 692 in mid-Devon, 'I remember father grew mangolds, flatpolls [fodder cabbage] and swedes' (indeed, in 1944 the farm had two acres of mangolds, one of swedes, one of kale, and one of cabbage, a pattern that lasted into the 1960s), and 'I remember going out with a horse and buck cart when I was still at school, on Saturday morning, bringing in enough mangolds and flatpolls for the week, pull them by hand.'

These fodder crops involved a great deal of hard manual work. On farm 535 in north Devon, the cereals were undersown with a mixture of rape, turnips, and grass seed using a fiddle drill (a small hand-held device for broadcasting seed): 'father would walk miles and I would come behind with the horse and drags'. Mangolds were sown in single drills on a ridge, and flatpoll cabbage plants were purchased and planted out manually. On farm 782, on the eastern edge of Dartmoor,

> Father grew mangolds, which are about 90 per cent water [depending on the variety, between 86 and 90 per cent water – 'but it's good water, boy' as an old farmer said to one of the authors (PB) many years ago], we used to pull them and put them in a trench. It was always done by hand, never mechanised. We used to do it all ourselves, with all the hoeing and singling.

The labour requirement was one of the principal disadvantages of such crops. On farm 162, on the edge of Exmoor, lifting mangolds by hand

> was back breaking, pulling them by hand over two to three acres. I grew them for two years after father retired, and he used to come out and hoe them, that was ten days' work twice a year, and you have to single them, ... he stopped hoeing after about three years I should think, and I didn't grow them again, because I didn't fancy hoeing them.

An acre of mangolds, another acre and a half of turnips and swedes, and an acre of cabbage was being grown in 1944 on farm 669, in north Devon, but eventually it was decided that too much labour was involved, and by the mid-1960s the fodder cropping had been simplified to 4.5 acres of kale, which

---

[36] Devon Agriculture Study Group, *Devon Farming*, p. 11.

wasn't too bad because you only had to put up an electric fence, until you get a really bad winter. We had one or two bad winters that put us off, the frost came in and spoiled a lot, and the cows were out and getting dirty, and it took a lot out of them.

Farmer 787, interviewed in a wet January, agreed: 'Kale is a wonderful feed when its dry, but now they'd be up to their hocks.' On farm 842 in east Devon, where roots were also replaced by kale,

> as the herds got larger, we were cutting kale and bringing it in, and that got harder, then we were driving the cows to the kale, but they got so muddy, the time you spent washing them made that very difficult. It was a matter of increasing herd size and decreasing labour, and the labour being me, unwilling to go and chop kale and freeze your hands to death doing it ... these things were so labour intensive.

Similarly, in east Cornwall, on farm 466,

> The kale was for the cows, and that worked well when you had seventy South Devons, but you can imagine one hundred cows treading around in this, we gave up autumn grazing of kale. The kale fitted with the potatoes, because we dug early potatoes in June or July and then put the kale in the ground, and when it was a small herd of cows it worked well, but not when we got serious.

Writing a last-ditch defence of fodder crops in 1972, a lecturer in crop husbandry at Seale-Hayne College in Devon explained their decline as a result of 'the frequent heavy manual labour involved in production, especially of roots, problems in controlling weeds, acute difficulties of utilisation, and the great advances made in the growing and mechanical handling of the grass crop in recent years'. The fodder crop acreage had declined from about 10 per cent of the tillage area of England and Wales in 1950 to less than 4 per cent in 1970.[37] Between the 1940s and the 1970s, therefore, it is possible to discern a common pattern in which the bulk winter diet for dairy cows changed from a mixture of hay and roots to one in which hay and kale were more important, and finally to one in which silage replaced both, as the figures in table 5.5 suggest. The figures for kale in the 1940s and '50s include flatpoll cabbage for stockfeed, but by the 1970s cabbage was on the way out, with less than two thousand acres in cultivation across the three counties. The kale area peaked in the 1950s, fell thereafter, and was back to its wartime level by 1979. It is also worth noting that between 1939 and 1979 the area of rough grazing in the three south-western counties fell from nearly 550,000 acres to 356,000 acres, and it seems likely that much of this went into permanent grass.

---

[37] R.D. Toosey, *Profitable Fodder Cropping* (Ipswich, 1972), pp. 15–16.

TABLE 5.5. Forage crop acreages in Cornwall, Devon, and Dorset ('000 acres)

	Temporary grass	Total grass	Temporary grass as a % of total grass	Roots (turnips, swedes, and mangolds)	Kale (includes fodder cabbage)
1939	410	1,441	29	62	9
1944	352	1,296	27	75	22
1954	542	1,642	33	52	49
1964	635	1,689	38	25	46
1974	643	1,737	37	13	30

Source: MAFF, *Agricultural Statistics, England and Wales*, various years.

By the 1980s, not only had the suggested winter ration changed, but so had the method of calculating its nutrient content. It was assumed that the bulk food would be silage, and that on the flat-rate feeding system all of the cows would be fed the same daily amount of concentrates, regardless of yield, throughout the winter. A variant of this was complete diet feeding, in which the bulk food and concentrates would be mixed together. In larger herds, it was suggested, the cows could be split into three groups depending upon the stage of lactation they were in and fed accordingly. Rations were no longer calculated in terms of starch and protein equivalents, but in terms of metabolisable energy (ME) and digestible crude protein.[38] This was a system that that been developed in the 1960s as a result of considerable experimental work on animal nutrition, much of it carried out at the Hannah Dairy Research Institute in Ayrshire and the Rowett Research Station near Aberdeen.[39] It concluded that the old starch equivalent system had provided more energy than the cow needed at low levels of milk production, but not enough at higher levels.[40] Farmers therefore had some significant technical changes to consider, and, unsurprisingly, there were considerable variations in the speed with which they did so.

The major change, especially for dairy farmers, was the move from hay to silage as the basis of grass conservation for winter feed. Farmer 466 found a view that summarised the whole process:

---

[38] J. Kirk, 'Cattle', in R.J. Halley (ed.), *The Agricultural Notebook* (17th edn, London, 1982), pp. 351–74.
[39] P. McDonald, R.A. Edwards, and J.F.D. Greenhalgh, *Animal Nutrition* (Edinburgh, 1966); K.L. Blaxter and N. Robertson, *From Dearth to Plenty: The Modern Revolution in Food Production* (Cambridge, 1995), pp. 229–33.
[40] ARC, *The Nutrient Requirements of Farm Livestock, No. 2, Ruminants: Technical Reviews and Summaries* (London, 1965), p. 239.

I remember coming down by the village one day, and there were three grass fields together, one had been cut early and was already greening up, and one had been cut a bit later and there hadn't been enough rain to make it come green, and one was hay waiting for the rain, and you could see how the technology had changed in that way, from hay to late cut silage to early-cut nutritious silage.

As this suggests, the change from hay to silage did not happen overnight; in fact, it took nearly a century. There were examples of farmers in the south of England and East Anglia producing silage in the 1870s, and in 1884 the *Journal* of the Royal Agricultural Society of England published a long report on the state of silage making. It had its detractors too. In his diary in 1905, the agricultural writer Primrose McConnell, normally an enthusiast for any new method, remembered that 'I made a stack of grass ensilage once, but only once, and never more.' The fermentation went wrong, 'It put the milk off the cows ... how could you progress in a case like this, with a smell as bad as ten motor cars?'[41] Between the wars, silage making was more successful in attracting the interest of agricultural scientists to explain the biochemistry and microbiology of the process than in attracting the interest of farmers. During the Second World War, official opinion saw silage as a means of saving imports ('every ton of silage made has liberated one ton of shipping space'), but for most farmers 'silage making remained a complicated and uncertain process, offering little perceived advantage over haymaking which fitted in well with the existing labour force, equipment and facilities of most farms'.[42]

After the war, agricultural scientists, pioneering farmers such as Rex Paterson in Hampshire, CAECs, and official opinion in general continued to expound the virtues of silage by many different means, from radio programmes to grant schemes. A 1957 survey found that dairy farmers were more likely than other livestock farmers to make silage; nearly half of those in the Midlands did so, and over England and Wales as a whole about a third of dairy farmers made it.[43] On farm 787 in north Devon, 'the first person that my father saw do silage was his father in law, and we're going back into the 1940s, he did silage then', and further south in mid-Devon on farm 101 'Father made silage in the 1950s, it's in the diaries, I'm not sure he didn't make some earlier than that.' For other farmers, however, the dating of the first silage cut was very specific,

---

[41] P. Brassley, 'Silage in Britain, 1880–1990: The Delayed Adoption of an Innovation', *Agric. Hist. Rev.* 44 (1996), pp. 66–71, 77.

[42] Brassley, 'Silage in Britain', p. 74; M. Riley, '"Silage for Self-sufficiency"? The Wartime Promotion of Silage and Its Use in the Peak District', in B. Short, C. Watkins, and J. Martin (eds), *The Front Line of Freedom: British Farming in the Second World War* (Exeter, 2007), pp. 87–8.

[43] *Report of the Committee on Grassland Utilisation*, Cmnd.547 (1958), pp. 55–6.

suggesting that it was part of a certain, purposeful, and significant change in the management and practices on the farm. On farm 2/7 in Dorset, 'We started silage in 1948, which was early for around here. It was about getting a product that was fresher and better than old frowsty hay. You cut it at an earlier stage you get a better protein content.' In the Teign Valley in Devon in 1961, as part of a research project in advisory work, the Nuffield Foundation sponsored the establishment of a number of machinery groups for silage making, and found a general trend towards silage making, albeit limited by steep land and difficult farm layouts.[44] At about the same time, a survey of twenty-seven Devon farms found an average of 22.6 acres in every hundred devoted to hay, compared with 14.7 used for silage, which suggests that the silage area in Devon was probably greater than in the country as a whole.[45]

Nationally, silage production expanded gradually in the 1950s and '60s, but as table 5.6 demonstrates, hay production did not reach a peak until 1971, and 1970 was the first year in which silage production exceeded hay production.

TABLE 5.6. Hay and silage production (million tons)

	Hay (UK)	Silage (Great Britain)
1940	8.0	0.25
1960	8.3	4.8
1970	8.0	9.4
1971	9.6	11.1
1979	7.4	25.7
1985	4.6	42.3

Source: hay data from Marks and Britton, *British Food and Farming*, p. 197; silage data from Brassley, 'Silage in Britain', p. 72.

The data are not perfectly comparable, because the hay figures are for the UK as a whole, while the silage data is for Great Britain only, but their meaning is clear. After 1971, hay production fell consistently, while silage production rose dramatically. It should also be remembered that since hay is about 85 per cent dry matter, whereas silage, certainly as it was

[44] J. Bradley, *Co-operation: A Report on an Experiment in Setting Up Co-operative Groups for the Purpose of Making Grass Silage*, University of Bristol, Department of Economics (Agricultural Economics), Bristol II Province, Report no. 125 (Newton Abbot, 1961).

[45] V.H. Beynon, *Grassland Management: An Economic Study in Devon*, University of Exeter, Department of Economics (Agricultural Economics), Report no. 138 (Newton Abbot, 1963), p. 6.

made in the 1970s, would be between 25 and 30 per cent dry matter, about three tons of silage would be equivalent to one ton of hay in dry matter terms. By 1979, therefore, as table 5.6 shows, silage output exceeded hay in dry matter terms too. These figures are fascinating, but they are not self-explanatory. What we need to know, from our study of south-western farms, is why the widespread adoption of silage was so delayed when farmers had been encouraged for so long to produce it, and what stimulated its rapid expansion in production from the 1970s onwards.

As the earlier discussion of feeds suggests, a ration of hay, roots, and concentrates suited most farmers in the 1940s and '50s. They knew how to make hay, and had the labour and equipment to do so, concentrates were reasonably cheap and very often produced as part of the arable rotation on what remained small mixed farms, and root crops were valued not only for the fodder they produced but also as cleaning crops, which could be hoed, several times if necessary, to destroy emergent weeds, and thus clean the land for subsequent years in the cropping cycle. Once herbicides became more widely available and more useful for weed control, and labour was less available, and farms specialised more in grass and dairy production, these factors weighed less heavily, but all that took time.

Several farmers remembered making silage in the 1950s, almost as an experiment, without adopting it permanently or on a large scale. On farm 193 in west Devon, 'My father did make a little silage. He had one of those little above-ground circular silos made of concrete sections, it all had to be heaved in by hand, I remember going round with a watering can of molasses and treading it down, when I was fairly young.' Treading down and adding molasses were ways of removing air and adding fermentable carbohydrates in order to produce the desirable lactic acid fermentation necessary to produce good silage. In mid-Devon, on farm 101, in the early 1950s, 'father had a little concrete tower, concrete slabs, all fitted together. The trouble was it wasn't airtight, so there was a lot of waste.' On occasion, the waste could be almost total; farmer 836 in south Devon recalled his father 'building an outdoor clamp, no plastic sheet over or anything, and it all went in the dung swiller'.

What many farmers remembered more than waste and quality problems was the amount of labour needed for silage making and feeding in the 1950s and '60s. It was, perhaps, because many of those interviewed were in their youth during those decades, and therefore formed part, if not all, of the labour force doing the heavy work. In Dorset, on farm 7/8,

> there was a green crop loader, and my God wasn't that hard work! Grass used to come up in a blanket and you had to shift it, to move it about the trailer, and it was long grass – that was hard work. That came in between the 1940s and the early 1950s, you had to cut it with a mower and then pick it up from the swath, I remember shouting down to the tractor driver 'Go slower!'.

There were similar memories on farm 272 in east Cornwall:

> we had a green crop loader to drop it on the trailer and somebody had to make a load, that was hard work, green grass, with it falling on top of you and you had to make a load. We didn't let it wilt at all, it had to be picked up immediately, and that caused a lot of effluent, and I'm afraid some of it came out in the road and we weren't very popular.

And on farm 101 in mid-Devon:

> we got a green crop loader, one of those things you tow behind the trailer, and the chap on the trailer has to chuck it to the front, and build the load on the trailer, very hard work, green grass, and if you get some red clover and long ryegrass, tangled together, and then of course it was all hand work, it was before the days of buckrakes, it was about 1958 that people started using buckrakes very much.

On a national scale, in fact, buckrakes had appeared rather earlier. They were invented or developed by Rex Paterson in Hampshire in the late 1940s. Something like a buckrake, called a haysweep, was used before the war, mounted on the front of a tractor or an old car, but Paterson's buckrake, mounted on the three-point linkage at the rear of a tractor, was much more manoeuvrable, and with it a heap of grass could be picked up from the swath and rapidly driven to a clamp made at the side of the field. The problem in tracing its adoption is that buckrakes were enumerated along with haysweeps and sometimes hay loaders in Ministry machinery censuses until 1968, but by then there were nearly sixty thousand of them in the UK.[46] There was also much labour involved in feeding the silage during the winter in the 1950s. On farm 2/7 in Dorset,

> we had large clamps or pits out in the field ... then cut out by hand, not self-fed. We had two men who spent all day cutting out silage and putting it on a trailer and taking it out, and taking a trailer load out every night to every herd of cows, and they might have two trailer loads a day, spread out on the field, and at the end of the winter you would have a vast acreage to plough up and put into corn because the cows would make an awful mess.

The basic problem was that silage, with its high moisture content and consequent heavy weight, did not mix well with manual labour. That, coupled with quality and effluent problems, held back the adoption of silage in the first two decades after the war.

Another difficulty was that farmers were also beginning to experience problems with hay by the mid-1960s. If all went well, haymaking could be a pleasant occupation producing a useful feed, but as a Lake

---

[46] Brassley, 'Silage in Britain', p. 84.

Dairy Farming

District farmer, writing more recently, pungently put it: 'Making hay in daydreams tends to be idyllic and sunny, but in real life it can be a bitch of a thing ... You need nearly a week of dry and sunny weather to make hay ... What could possibly go wrong in one of the wettest places in England?'[47] The south-west of England is not quite as wet, but not every June or early July could be relied upon to provide the necessary few continuous days of sunshine. And by that traditional haymaking time the grass was nearing maturity, with an increased fibre and lower protein content. Increased fertiliser use and leafier tetraploid ryegrasses, whose expanded use has been discussed earlier, made the problem worse because more wilting was required before they would make hay. Despite the best efforts of machinery manufacturers in producing tedders, conditioners, balers, bale sledges, elevators, and barn drying fans, there was always pressure to get the hay under cover as quickly as possible before the weather broke, and it was a job that needed all the labour available. On farm 209, in west Cornwall, after an experiment with silage in the 1950s, 'we went back to quality hay, not barn dried, but we would cut hay and have it baled by the end of May'. Then

> every bale was a small bale and you threw the lot. We never had a bale sledge, we left them singly until we had a trailed sledge. [My wife] would drive the tractor, and we just threw them up by hand on to the trailer, one person on the trailer, just building up to four rings [layers], that's much easier than going up seven or eight. If we bought some grass a couple of miles away we might go up higher, but if you're only three or four fields away, just put up four or five rings, then off with them and up again.

But while there were 777,000 employed workers on farms in England and Wales at the post-war peak in 1947, there were only 562,000 in 1960, and by 1985 that number had halved again.[48] The experience of farm 193 epitomised the problem:

> handling so many little hay bales was getting beyond a reduced labour force, so we went to self-feed silage, we got up to about nine thousand little bales of hay in a season – it was just getting too much. If there was extra labour about, we might get some in, but it wasn't always available, so the hay harvest could take some time.

As more effective machinery began to be introduced, silage was seen as a way of saving labour. On farm 243 in east Devon, where the winter fodder had been

---

[47] J. Rebanks, *The Shepherd's Life: A Tale of the Lake District* (London, 2016), pp. 67–8.
[48] Marks and Britton, *British Food and Farming*, p. 140.

all hay, we used to make about ten thousand bales a year ... We changed over to silage in 1978, after my father died. My neighbour up the road changed over to it and I used to help him, because we helped each other haymaking, and I thought 'this saves a lot of labour', and he changed in 1977 and I changed in 1978.

As the problems with hay mounted, therefore, some of the silage problems began to be solved. Changes in machinery, in the techniques of making and of feeding silage, and building developments, all combined to overcome some of the problems that had held silage back in the 1950s and '60s and make the 1970s the decade in which it became the dominant form of fodder conservation. On farm 466, with two big dairy herds in east Cornwall, this was precisely identified as the time of change:

> In the 1970s we went over to self-feed silage, before that it hadn't been a big part of forage conservation. By that time mechanisation had advanced to the point where you began to think of a second cut. In earlier days it was a substitute for haymaking, so you got over-mature silage in the middle of June, whereas by the 1970s we were thinking of making a cut in May and cutting again in June or July, and being conscious of D values [the digestibility of the grass] and things like that ... Now you would never have done that unless you had the machinery to cope with it. We were buying forage harvesters, and, later, feeder wagons. Tipping trailers – all in the early 1970s.

In west Cornwall, on farm 209, they made the change at about the same time:

> we said until we can afford a forage harvester, a nice simple Kidd and a couple of trailers, we'll stick with the hay, and then as soon as we could afford it, about 1971, when the silage barn went up, we foraged our own grass and self-fed it. There was an improvement in milk quality and cattle condition, and you didn't have to use so much concentrate, because there's a lot more feed value in well-made silage than in well-made hay. When we were on hay we were on kale and rape as well, strip grazing through the winter, and once we went on to silage those fodder crops gradually went.

Again the point is made about the effect on the general cropping pattern, on the improvement in the standard of nutrition, on the change in the way in which the silage was fed, and on the importance of the forage harvester, the widespread adoption of which was 'the major factor which helped to bring about the decline in the acreage of fodder crops'.[49]

The forage harvester, which cut the grass and blew it into a trailer that could then be taken to the silage clamp and tipped, was not a completely new invention in the 1970s, but it was by then much improved from its

---

[49] Toosey, *Profitable Fodder Cropping*, p. 17.

initial versions. One of the earliest was called the Hayter 'Silerator', and it was slow and noisy, as they discovered on farm 7/8, where 'we bought a Silerator in 1953, which could be heard all over north Dorset, and you'd be lucky if you did a field a day. You'd have some complaints about the noise now ...' The importance of the machinery for silage quality was identified on farm 744 in south Devon, where 'we had a pick-up harvester, a forage wagon, but it didn't chop it fine enough, so it didn't make good silage'. In this context, the effect of a new generation taking over was vividly illustrated on farm 570 in north Devon:

> I took over in 1975 when my father died, ... silage making, that was all done with machinery. We were the first ones [in this district] to use forage harvesters, and double chop forage harvesters. Before that it was done with a buck rake. There's a nine-acre meadow here and I've done that with a buckrake, just keep going along and loading up a buckrake full and coming in the shed and squeezing it down, but there was a lot of wastage with that system, you couldn't get it down, but as soon as they had forage harvesters with a little bit of chop it would go down better.

The official national statistics collected for the farm machinery surveys show how types like the 'nice simple Kidd' were gradually replaced by larger and more complex machines. When the figures were first collected, in 1959, all forage harvesters were listed together; by the mid-1970s, there were enough different types for greater detail to be worthwhile, and as table 5.7 demonstrates, it was the types that produced a shorter length of chopped grass that were increasing in popularity.

TABLE 5.7. Number of forage harvesters in England and Wales

Type	1959	1971	1976	1987
Loader wagons			5,570	8,390
Simple flail			12,190	6,160
Double chop			9,740	8,370
Metered chop			4,940	13,050
Total	7,920	23,690	32,440	35,970

Source: Brassley, 'Silage in Britain', p. 85.

It was not only the machinery that changed. Silage making methods were improving too. Tower silos, of various designs, coupled with mechanised feeding systems, had been in use since at least the 1960s, but although they usually produced high-quality silage, they required a large capital investment, and by 1971 there were only 1,560 of them in operation across the country as a whole.⁵⁰ The major breakthrough was a simple system developed by the Dorset farmer Richard Waltham in the early 1960s. It involved stacking the grass rapidly in a wedge shape and covering it overnight with a polythene sheet to prevent warm air rising from the grass and being replaced by cold oxygen-laden air entering from the bottom. Cheap polythene sheeting was by now available, and from the mid-1960s onwards this was the system of silage making promoted by the Grassland Research Institute, the advisory services, and the fertiliser manufacturers (at least one of which also made the polythene sheeting).⁵¹ Silage made in this way was usually self-fed by the cows themselves from the clamp, thus overcoming the other labour problem of cutting into the silage and taking it to the cows. By the beginning of the 1970s, the techniques necessary for the average farmer to adopt silage were in place. The final piece in the jigsaw for some farmers was the development of big-bale silage, initially in plastic bags and subsequently by wrapping bales, which was not available until the 1980s. A county council smallholder (farm 782) keeping forty-five cows on seventy acres provided a succinct account of the whole process:

> we switched over to silage in 1985 when the county council built us a silage clamp, it was all hay before that. We were keen to change over to silage because the benefits were quite obvious, from a labour point of view, and all sorts of reasons, it meant we didn't have to load and unload about four thousand bales of hay a year, because it was self-feed silage, plus the frustrations of the weather with haymaking, and the ease of feeding the cows through the winter, we had a walled clamp and we had an electric fence wire that we moved on a few inches every day and the cows helped themselves, they were in the cubicles and they came from the door to the cubicles straight to the silage clamp, so they could have a feed when they wanted, and it was a much better system. ... Most of our neighbours switched at the same time. My neighbour was retiring about that time, and for the last two years he was there he went to big bale silage ... Big bale silage got going in the early 1980s, that was a great invention. We would maximise the first cut to fill the clamp, and after that we would use big bales, and use them to start with before we opened the clamp, we put them in circular feeders. When the grass quality was starting to go down we would start a little bit of silage, and that seemed a good way of doing it to start with, and some of the young stock we used to feed. But the big bales were a great invention. It was a contractor's job.

By the mid-1980s, silage making was a far cry from self-built clamps on the sides of fields and boys with watering cans of molasses. As farmer 466 notes: 'The nutritional system changed in this country. We not only

---

50   Brassley, 'Silage in Britain', p. 85.
51   Seddon, *Silent Revolution*, pp. 29–32; Brassley, 'Silage in Britain', pp. 85–6.

Dairy Farming

went to litres of milk, but we also went to ME [Metabolisable Energy] and that kind of thing.' By the end of our period of study, therefore, silage had moved from being one of enthusiastic experimentation to being a science-led activity that required increasingly complex and expensive machinery, and a good deal of precision. For a lot of farmers, this meant that they turned to contractors to undertake the task of silage harvesting. On farm 576 in east Cornwall, where the tractor 'was not big enough or posh enough' to do an effective job of silage harvesting, they began to use contractors in the early 1980s, as did farm 782 on Dartmoor. On farm 744, it was all about the precision and speed that the contractors could deliver:

> We tried [making silage] a time or two ... but it was too wasteful, it wasn't on. We did it with a buckrake, then we had a pick-up harvester, a forage wagon, but it didn't chop it fine enough, so it didn't make good silage. No comparison to the speed [the contractor] does it now.

Increasingly for farmers, the combined requirements of very expensive machinery and skilled labour over a shorter window of time has meant that the widespread use of contractors can perhaps be seen as the necessary and inevitable outcome of the way in which technology, and in particular machinery, changed. The experience of farm 787 in north Devon can stand for many south-western farms by 1985:

> I use a contractor now, because we had got to the point when it was taking us a fortnight or three weeks [to do the silage harvest]. There were just the three of us here, and the grass was going past its best, so I thought about going from our Kidd double chop to a precision chop and rowing it – doing it properly – and I looked at what that would cost, because you need a bigger tractor as well, and that would cost £30,000 to £33,000, second hand. I bumped into a local contractor and asked him what it would cost to do the whole job on our first cut, and he said 'About £3,000.' And I have to find people to drive the tractors, and [what with] the diesel, and interest rates then were about 10 per cent, you couldn't compare. And he did it in four days. That was in the mid-80s, and we've had it done by contractor ever since.

What should be clear from this account of changes in the way dairy cattle were fed is that it was not a linear process. Although the graphs and the figures in the tables above tell a consistent story of gradual, or in some cases rapid change in the same direction, what emerges from the accounts of those individuals whose lives and businesses were involved in the story is more complicated. Not all farmers immediately thought that it was a good idea to change from hay and roots to silage, and even if they did there could be capital shortages or landlord investment decisions holding them back. Not all farmers immediately knew how to make good silage even if they had access to the right equipment. The fact that many farmers tried silage in the 1950s suggests that there was no lack of enterprise or initiative, but equally the fact that they went back to making hay revealed what they felt would work at the time. And finally, what mattered for many of them was that a change from hay to silage often also meant a change in machinery and especially in buildings, as we shall examine in the following section.

Housing

Silage was only one component of a system change. Winter forage, the way that the cows were housed, and the way that their manure was handled were all linked. The traditional cowshed in which cows were tied up individually, bedded on straw, fed on hay, roots, and concentrates, and milked, initially by hand, and then into a milking machine bucket that was moved around the shed by the milker, gave way to milking in a parlour, with cows (self-) feeding on silage, and living in cubicles, with their dung going into a slurry store. While this was happening, the collection system changed from one in which all milk was sent to the dairy in ten-gallon churns to one in which it was collected from bulk tanks on the farm by a fleet of MMB tankers. All this required considerable capital expenditure by farmers, and while, for some, it was something they were prepared or even anxious to do in order to keep up to date and maintain the profitability of their farms, for others it was a challenge they did not wish, or were unable, to meet, and consequently they ceased to be milk producers. For those who remained as milk producers, changing milking and housing methods affected labour requirements and consequently the number of cows that could be kept. Not all farmers changed in the same way or at the same time. As with changes in breeds and feeds, there was a considerable variety in the ways in which farmers changed and the time at which they did so.

The traditional cowshed or shippon was not without its attractions. On a cold winter's morning, it was a cosy and warm place to work, to do the morning milking, the first job of the day, amid the comforting smells of cows, hay, and cattle cake. The cows were often bedded on straw, which, given that, as we have seen, most farms were mixed in the 1940s and '50s, was produced on the farm, and as it gradually became mixed with cow dung, and was cleared out, formed good farmyard manure. When herds were small, and family labour was available, it was a good use for traditional buildings, and in some places new cowsheds were still being built. Although effective milking machines were available by the late 1920s, 90 per cent of herds in England and Wales were still being hand-milked in 1939.[52] Some farmers just preferred it that way. On farm 826 in the Culm Valley of east Devon,

---

[52] P. Brassley, 'Output and Technical Change in Twentieth-Century British Agriculture', *Agric. Hist. Rev.* 48 (2000), p. 73.

Dairy Farming

> My father was a fairly traditional sort of farmer and long after electricity came he would still take his paraffin lamps out to milk his cows ... He was still milking cows by hand then, and so was I when I first came home [in 1950]. The milking machine was installed when I was still at [university], and he refused to use it, and never used it. We got up to about twenty, milked by hand. My mother used to milk a lot, when I first came home from [university] I would help too, so we were milking about half a dozen cows each. How long it took depended on the cows and how many buckets were kicked over in the process. It took about two hours, I expect.

Family labour was used and useful: 'They used to milk ten to fifteen cows, because when I was about six or seven I used to have to milk two of them before I went to school' (farm 243). On farm 782, 'when we were hand milking cows ... we used to milk about ten cows, in the old shippon, we had two of the old Aladdin paraffin lights, hung one at each end of the shippon, and milk away, it was pretty primitive, in the semi-darkness'. It was the same story of a small herd milked by hand in a small building with limited equipment for many years on farm 162 on the edge of Exmoor:

> The first milking machine was 1961 – before that we milked by hand, which was partly why we only milked a few cows, we only ever milked ten, which was all the shippon would hold. Three of us would be milking when I started, mum dad and me, two or three cows each, straight into churns and then put the cooler on top of it, it had a hose attached and the pressure of the water turned the cooler round.

In the 1940s and '50s, the cowshed was the usual accommodation in which the cows were housed, fed, and milked. As with feeding methods (see above), the agricultural textbooks of the time reveal what was just on the advanced side of normal. The 1945 edition of Watson and More's *Agriculture* assumes that the cows will be housed in a cowshed and states that 'a good milker may be expected to milk from seven to ten average cows in an hour and a half, the time ordinarily allotted for the work', although it adds 'Milking machines of the latest types with skilled supervision give very satisfactory results.' In other words, the typical herd was hand-milked in a cowshed, although the existence of milking parlours ('a shed with special stalls ...') and bails (i.e. 'a movable set of milking stalls with milking machine and cooler built in') for herds kept out of doors for the whole year was also mentioned. Only four years later, however, Watson and More's rival textbook, *Fream's Elements of Agriculture*, noted that recently 'the mechanism of the milking machine has been so improved that in most average-sized herds machine milking is both economically desirable and essential as a means of easing labour problems'. It also noted the development of loose housing in yards with parlour milking.[53]

By the mid-1950s, the conversion to machine milking was in full swing. Professor Cooper noted a 'two-and-a-half fold increase in the number of milking machines' between 1944 and 1952 but observed that the 'full benefit of such developments is not being realised because farmers have to persevere with buildings which belong to the days of hand-milking'. He too was an advocate of the yard and parlour system but observed that 'the erection of a yard and parlour costs money which usually the landlord or tenant cannot easily find'.[54] By the time the eleventh edition of Watson and More appeared in 1962, revised by James McMillan, recently retired from the Directorship of the NAAS, it was necessary to allocate much more text to the discussion of milking machines, milk handling, and comparisons of the relative merits and labour requirements of cowsheds and various different designs of milking parlour (abreast, tandem, herringbone). The development of the bulk tank, to replace milk churns, was also noted.[55]

The extent to which these innovations were adopted by farmers across England and Wales as a whole is demonstrated in table 5.8. Unfortunately, this detailed information is only available from MMB publications, and the statistical series only begins in 1964. It would be fascinating to have comparable figures for the two previous decades. However, closer inspection of the table suggests that while this might be desirable, it may not be absolutely necessary, because the 1964 figures show how little had changed from the position described in the post-war textbooks. Clearly, the major change by 1964 was in the adoption of machine milking. Whereas only about 10 per cent of herds had been machine-milked in 1939, less than 10 per cent were still being hand-milked in 1964. To some degree, this was linked with the spread of mains electricity in the countryside.[56] On farm 782, on the edge of Dartmoor, 'We had the first milking machine in 1961 after the electricity came in, that transformed what you could do.' Mains electricity was not essential, however. A basic bucket milking plant only needed a vacuum to make the pulsator work, and the necessary vacuum pump could be, and often was, powered by a small stationary petrol or oil engine, or an electric motor powered by an on-farm generator. In east Devon, on farm 243, 'Father started with a milking machine in 1945 or '46, he definitely had one in that bad winter of 1947, it was a little Petter engine and a bucket plant.' On farm 162 on

---

53 Watson and More, *Agriculture* (8th edn), pp. 568–9; Robinson, *Fream's Elements of Agriculture* (13th edn), p. 605.
54 Cooper, *Competitive Farming*, p. 123.
55 Watson and More, *Agriculture* (11th edn), pp. 515–52.
56 P. Brassley, J. Burchardt, and K. Sayer, *Transforming the Countryside: The Electrification of Rural Britain* (Abingdon, 2017).

TABLE 5.8. Milking systems in England and Wales

	1964 No. of herds	1964 % of herds	1964 Cows per herd	1975 No. of systems	1975 % of systems	1985 No. of systems	1985 % of systems
COWSHED							
Hand	9,015	8.6	8	1,371	2.4	148	0.4
Bucket	78,213	74.4	23	20,780	36.0	3,804	9.9
Pipeline	3,112	3.0	42	10,281	17.8	6,964	18.0
Total Cowshed	90,340	86.0	23	32,432	56.2	10,16	28.3
PARLOUR							
Abreast	9,007	8.6	49	13,112	22.7	11,208	29.0
Herringbone	804	0.8	72	10,298	17.8	15,695	40.6
Tandem & Chute	1,203	1.1	51	950	1.6	378	1.0
Rotary	NA			371	0.6	195	0.5
Total Parlour	11,014	10.5	51	24,731	42.7	27,476	71.1
BAIL	2,537	2.4	34	632	1.1	230	0.6
OTHERS	1,140	1.1	39	NA		NA	
TOTAL	105,031	100.0	26	57,795	100.0	38,622	100.0

Source: MMB, *Dairy Facts and Figures*, 1965 (p. 36); 1976 (p. 36); 1986 (p. 21).

the edge of Exmoor, 'the generator did the job pretty adequately, and it did the house as well. But the television was better with the mains – less voltage surge and drop.'

In contrast to the adoption of machinery, however, changes to buildings took longer. If we can assume that very few herds were milked through a parlour in the 1940s, table 5.8 shows that over eleven thousand herds had changed over to this system by 1964, and these were likely to be the bigger herds, with twice the number of cows on average as cowshed-milked herds. But they still only represented a little over 10 per cent of all the herds in the country, and most of them were using abreast parlours, which even by then were beginning to be seen as outdated and inferior to herringbone parlours by some farmers. In east Devon, on farm 842,

> In 1967 we had a new milking parlour. I'd taken on the farm and I thought we needed something different. I went on a farm walk with the Farmers' Union and I came back and said 'I know what we're going to have.' So we ordered a new herringbone parlour, one of the early ones. I went on this farm walk and I thought it was such a good idea, if you were going to put one in, that was the one. It was the simplicity, and the cows were at a sensible level to put the clusters on without continually bending, there was less risk of being kicked and it made milking quicker and easier. Most people were still putting in abreast parlours at that time.

However, the overwhelming majority of herds – 86 per cent – were still being milked in a cowshed in 1964. As a comparison with table 5.1 indicates, the number of producers had declined by about fifty thousand since the end of the war, when it was at its peak, and most of these would have been small, hand-milked, cowshed-housed herds, but the average herd was still small in 1964, and most cows probably still had their individual names.

The 1975 and 1985 figures in table 5.8 are for milking systems rather than herds, but as it was rare to find herds that were milked through two or more different systems, the numbers of systems, herds, and producers were very similar, as a comparison of tables 5.1 and 5.8 confirms. Between 1964 and 1975, table 5.8 shows how the number of herds milked in parlours more than doubled, with herringbone parlours accounting for most of the increase. By 1985, herringbone and abreast parlours together were accounting for the majority of milking systems. Even for the really big herds, herringbone parlours were effective, as the small (and by 1985 declining) numbers of high-capital rotary parlours suggests. In contrast, the system of bucket milking in cowsheds, by far the most common milking method in 1964, accounted for less than 10 per cent of systems by 1985. Some farmers with cowsheds installed pipeline systems between 1964 and 1975. With these, a plastic tube was installed alongside the vacuum pipe to take the milk direct from the teat cup cluster on the cow to the dairy or milk room where it was delivered into churns or a bulk tank, so saving much labour in lifting buckets. Installing such a system clearly represented a much smaller capital investment than going over to a parlour. The change that really stands out in table 5.8 is that the number of cowsheds decreased by over eighty thousand between 1964 and 1985, more than the decrease of some sixty thousand or more in the total number of herds.

The other system change that occurred from the 1960s onwards was the introduction of bulk tanks. Milk churns, in which milk was transported from the farm to the bottling dairy, had been introduced in the nineteenth century when milk was first transported by rail from the farms to the cities, and by the post-war years a roadside platform with a number of churns waiting for a lorry to collect them was a familiar sight all over the country. From the beginning of the 1960s, as table 5.9 indicates, the MMB began to introduce daily collection by tanker lorry direct from refrigerated tanks on farms, and by 1980 churns had been phased out and all milk was collected in bulk.

TABLE 5.9. Bulk milk collection in England and Wales

	Tank numbers in England and Wales	% of milk collected in bulk	Number of bulk tanks in the Far West MMB region
1960	NA	0.4	0
1964	2,493	5.7	0
1969	12,676	30.1	187 (1.6% of producers in the region)
1975	33,065	79.7	3,083 (49.4% of producers in the region)
1980	45,045	100.0	5,564

Source: MMB, *Dairy Facts and Figures*, 1965, 1969, 1975, 1980.

The expansion of bulk collection took place at different times in different MMB regions. It only began in the Far Western region in 1967, by which time there were already thousands of tanks in the north-west of England and the West Midlands. As farmer 576 observed,

> We were later on bulk down here because the farms were small and getting the tankers into some of the farms was a bit problematic, because the dairies weren't always where you could get the lorry to, but we didn't have that problem, although we've widened that gate down there [at the end of the farm drive] two or three times.

The change to a bulk tank 'made life easier, because you had to watch it with a plate cooler, filling the churns, because you couldn't see the churns from the parlour' (farm 576 again). There were schemes operated by the MMB and many of the tank manufacturers to provide loans for their purchase, but nevertheless the option, and eventually the requirement, to install a tank was often a factor that made farmers think about whether it made sense to remain in dairying. On farm 109 in mid-Devon, for example, the decision to get out of dairying rather than to buy a bulk tank was made in 1972.

Often at the same time, a farmer who concluded that the cowshed was no longer adequate for the dairy herd had the choice of investing in an alternative system, almost inevitably a parlour of some kind, or ceasing to be a dairy farmer at all, and clearly about half of all dairy farmers took that course of action between 1964 and 1975, and even more in the following ten years. Bulk tanks, housing, changing over to silage, or a new generation taking over the farm were all potential crisis points that could produce major impacts on the management of a farm. In practice, on many farms, several of these crisis points all came at once. On small south-western farms, increasing the cow numbers usually meant reducing the cereal acreage, so straw was no longer so cheaply available for bedding. Changing from hay to self-feed silage often required a new farmyard layout. On some farms, the change might be gradual, with an initial move from cowshed to loose housing in a yard, with straw bedding, and parlour milking, before changing to a system of cubicles with the dung handled as slurry. On other farms, all these changes could come at once, with a change from hay to silage and cowshed to cubicles.

The changes were often made either in the 1960s or 1970s rather than earlier, but there were almost as many differences in detail as there were individual farms. On farm 576, for example:

> In 1968 we bodged up a few cubicles in a corner, then in 1971 we put up a new parlour and eighty cubicles, that was before bulk tanks, but the cows went up and we only had a two-unit chute parlour, and the shed was only for thirty cows, so when we got to forty it was time to do something. We put in a herringbone, only four units to start with, but we made it big enough to take five, so then the fifth unit went in, then it went to eight then to eleven or twelve by the time we finished. That's when we'd gone specialised.

Changing to a silage-based system in the 1970s nearly always coincided with a big investment in machinery and buildings, even on the smaller farms, such as the 124-acre farm 272 in east Cornwall, where silage, cubicles, and slurry arrived together:

> We put an abreast parlour in when [our son] came home [in about 1980], before that in the early–mid '70s we put in a milk pipe [i.e. a

Dairy Farming

pipeline in the cowshed]. We borrowed from the bank for the bulk tank. We had a cubicle house in 1980, with a grant from the FHDS [Farm and Horticultural Development Scheme]. The cubicle house was the thing of the day, never thought about a loose house, we didn't have enough straw, it's what everyone around here was doing. We put in a slurry store and silage clamps at the same time.

On farm 787 in north Devon, there were two crisis points at which changes were made. The first was caused by rising cow numbers:

In 1975 we had a new parlour, so the shippon lasted until then. There was an ultimatum. Our cow numbers were going up to about a hundred, it's all right milking fifty in the shippon, but milking one hundred was pushing it a bit, so we said either the cows go or we have a parlour, it [i.e. milking] was taking so long. ... We looked at some parlours and went ahead. It's the same parlour as is there now, a 14-14 herringbone.

The second major change came at the point when the new generation took over the farm:

In 1981 when my brother and I took over ... we were only going to do a silage pit to start with, so I got [a builder and family friend] ... and I said the original plan was to put in a silage pit now and put cubicles in later, and he said 'Why not do it all at once?', and I said 'I can't afford to do it all', and he said 'Don't worry about that, do it all now and pay me when you can', and he meant it ... it was all meant to be done in three years, but we did it in six months.

On a large farm (2/21) in Dorset, the decisions about expansion and the role of the succeeding generation came together with a perception about the demand for milk and government grant policy in driving an investment decision:

There was the Farm Improvement Grant scheme, at a time when the government wanted more and more produced, they were giving fifty per cent capital grants, ... and we spent a lot of money, £80,000, which in those days was a lot of money, moving the dairy up there and equipping it with big silage barns, ... it was a time when [my son] was at Seale-Hayne himself, and was talking of going to New Zealand, and I remember asking him then if he had any serious intention of coming back, because I didn't want to get involved in any extensive capital development on this scale if he didn't intend to carry on himself, and that was the beginning of major development, which he eventually took over. The new dairy opened in 1979, and it was an 8-8 herringbone parlour, and we increased our cows and increased our production considerably, we moved from forty to fifty down here to about 120-130 up there.

In west Cornwall, where farm 209 was increasing its acreage and cow numbers in the 1970s, the changes in machinery, buildings, forage conservation, and manure handling methods all came at once. Inflationary economic circumstances and the provision of capital grants all helped:

> When we got our tenancy, we invested in a bulk tank and cubicles. The main thing was to expand the herd to earn money, because things were going well then. It was a Hosier herringbone parlour, we extended it again in 1977, it's still there ... [we] borrowed £70,000 from Barclays to put in a milking parlour, a cubicle house, silage barn – we had grant on it – and that was big borrowing back then, but in a year or two, with inflation, you could stop worrying about it. ... and there weren't any contractors doing foraging then, you had to have your own tackle, we said until we can afford a forage harvester, a nice simple Kidd and a couple of trailers, we'll stick with the hay, and then as soon as we could afford it, about 1971, when the silage barn went up, we foraged our own grass and self-fed it. ...

On the sixty-eight-acre farm 243 in east Devon, it was the desire to keep more cows and the need to change to a bulk tank, with the aid of an MMB grant, that precipitated the first round of investment:

> I went over to the bulk tank in 1973 ... I wanted to keep more cows, so that meant altering the cowsheds, so we put in different plant, a pipeline straight into the bulk tank. We never had a parlour, the cowsheds are still down there to this day. We had twenty-six standings, we used to milk about fifty cows, so we had to change over a couple of times, once the cows got used to it, it didn't take long to change over, half the cows you didn't have to tie up.

Then in 1978 came the change to silage:

> we built a cubicle house right beside the silage barn. Common sense told me that if you were going to self-feed silage it made sense to put the cows next to it, so you had the silage barn and the cubicle house and the slurry pit. ... I had to get grants for the silage barn and cubicles, and I put up a big shed down the bottom there, I had a grant for that from the Farm Capital Grant Scheme. ... For buildings it was 70 per cent. For the rest, we borrowed a bit from the bank, no trouble at all. Right up until the mid-1990s you could borrow whatever you wanted. I would go in to ... in Lloyds in Cullompton and say I want to borrow £20,000 and he'd say 'Right, you can have it', quick as that, no problem. They made a profit out of you.

Farm 243 had been owner-occupied since 1960, so the bank manager had the security of the land to set against the loan, but this phase of hay-to-silage transition is also, perhaps, where investing landlords had the chance to show their support for their tenant's agricultural improvement plans – or were otherwise found wanting. On an estate in east Devon, the landlord of farm 139 put in a new parlour, silage pit, and Dutch barn in 1971, and later paid part of the costs for further improvements to the silage system. Farm 466 rented land from both a large estate and a small private landowner. In the early 1970s, the estate paid for a cubicle house to go alongside a silage building, but the tenants financed the developments on the private landlord's holding in order to maintain their expansion. 'In 1972 I hadn't quite taken over from father, but it happened progressively. We went over to cubicles and self-feed silage; we put up cubicles on the private landlord's farm as it then was. Between the mid-60s and the mid-1970s we went from sixty to 320 cows.' On farm 782, however, the much-desired change to silage could not come until

> 1985 when the county council built us a silage clamp, … [after which the cows] … were in the cubicles and they came from the door to the cubicles straight to the silage clamp, so they could have a feed when they wanted, and it was a much better system. Before then it was all baled hay.

The importance of housing as part of this new system of buildings, machinery, and forage conservation is emphasised by the experience of farm 2/7: 'As soon as the idea of keeping cows in barns came along, that must be when forage harvesters came along, because that was when we went over to self-feed [silage].'

Cubicles were an especially important part of the system in the southwest because it was a grassland area, so sufficient straw for bedding was less likely to be available on all-grass farms or those that had only a few acres of cereals, and when it was bought in from other parts of the country it had to bear the transport costs. If there was an alternative, it was worth making an investment, as the case of farm 3/1 in the Blackmore Vale illustrates.

> We … had some form of cubicles before 1966, before that they were loose housed on straw. The cost of straw made it worth going over to cubicles. On an all-grass farm we had to buy every last bit of straw in, so it became expensive. We've always had a simple slurry handling system here, we pile it up on a hard concrete base and spread it throughout the winter. We had to invest in a dirty water system after 1984. The extra cubicles in the 1970s just reflect the expansion of the herd, and barns to put the cubicles in. And we could get sawdust to put in the cubicles very cheaply, it was considered a waste product then, we could go over to Mere brush factory and get sawdust very cheaply, it was a local waste product, marvellous, we used that for years and years, then the chipboard manufacturers came and bought it so all of a sudden it became a tradable commodity, and out of our reach. Then we went back to straw, there was no option. Rubber mats were a later concept for cubicles.

By the late 1970s, therefore, with a few exceptions such as farm 782, most of the farmers that had decided to stay in dairying had changed from feeding hay in cowsheds and making farmyard manure to a silage-cubicle-slurry system. Those who were unwilling or unable to make the change had very often ceased to produce milk. In some cases, as on farm 162, it was because the next generation was unenthusiastic about milking: 'as a small child I was a bit interested in milking cows, but as I got nearer to working on the farm it didn't seem so attractive'. In others, as on farm 109 in mid-Devon, the crunch came when the decision had to be made about whether or not to invest in a bulk tank. For others, it came when a decision had to be made about investing in a new milking parlour. Given the reduction in dairy producer numbers (see table 5.2), those difficult decisions affected a high proportion of the farms in the three south-western counties. Perhaps surprisingly, however, none of the farmers interviewed mentioned herd health problems as a major factor in their decision-making.

Dairy Herd Health and Disease

In 1940, a committee of the National Veterinary Medical Association (the forerunner of the British Veterinary Association) estimated that two hundred million gallons of milk, worth £17 million, were lost each year from the combined effects of brucellosis, sterility, mastitis, and Johne's disease, a chronic wasting condition of cattle.[57] In addition, there were the effects of bovine tuberculosis (bTB), the pre-war campaign against which had had to be suspended through lack of labour and laboratory equipment.[58] Over the following forty years, farmers and vets either dealt with, or learned to live with, each of these diseases, although by the middle of the 1980s the problem of bTB was beginning to reappear.[59] None of the farmers interviewed for this book identified animal disease as a major farm management issue, or the solutions found for it as an important contribution to increased output. Nevertheless, it is worth paying some attention to developments in cattle disease control on the grounds that things might have been worse in their absence.

The output of herds in which brucellosis, otherwise known as contagious abortion, occurred was obviously reduced because cows did not deliver their calves and so begin their lactations. Vaccines, especially

---

[57] A. Woods, 'The Farm as Clinic', *Studies in the History and Philosophy of Biological and Biomedical Sciences* 38 (2007), p. 474.

[58] A. Woods, 'A Historical Synopsis of Farm Animal Disease and Public Policy in Twentieth-Century Britain', *Philosophical Transactions of the Royal Society, Series B: Biological Sciences* 366/1573 (2011), p. 1947.

[59] A. Cassidy, *Vermin, Victims and Disease: British Debates over Bovine Tuberculosis and Badgers* (Basingstoke, 2019).

Dairy Farming

the new S19 vaccine developed in the United States, helped to keep the problem under control during the war, but there were other causes of infertility that could only be addressed with professional veterinary assistance.[60] Once the war was over, it was not necessary to maintain every possible animal to contribute to the food supply, and the money was available, it was possible to contemplate health campaigns based on the slaughter, with compensation, of affected animals. The first disease to be attacked was bovine tuberculosis. Before and during the war, herds could be tuberculin-tested, with those free of the disease being given accredited TT status, but there was no compulsion to slaughter those cows that reacted to the test. An Area Eradication scheme was introduced in 1950, involving compulsory testing of all herds and the slaughter of reactors, and by 1960 the whole country was declared attested, with bTB close to eradication. The scheme had cost £250 million. From the early 1970s, there was a similar scheme to eradicate brucellosis, resulting in the whole country being declared attested in 1981.[61] Johne's disease appeared in the 1940 survey because leading veterinary scientists, given its similarities to bTB, were interested in it, but it remained of much less concern to most farmers and practising farm vets.[62]

For many of the wide range of other diseases that potentially affected farm animals, the post-war years saw the gradual introduction of more and more vaccines and therapeutic drugs. Vaccination, for example, could deal with the effects of the various *Clostridium* bacteria, and there was a range of anthelmintics to treat parasitic worms.[63] Vaccination and drug use became part of the routine of animal husbandry, and in some cases the decision about whether such treatments should be used was more a matter of economics than therapeutics. For dairy farmers, the big disease problem was mastitis, or inflammation of the udder. Despite considerable state-funded research, and initiatives by pharmaceutical companies and the MMB, the incidence of mastitis seemed to remain more or less constant. In the 1930s, it was estimated that 30 per cent of cattle were affected; in 1980, a third of the dairy herd had mastitis. But it was a different kind of mastitis. The principal causal organism in the 1930s was the bacterium *Streptococcus agalactiae*. It was susceptible to treatment with penicillin, which was made available in single-use intra-mammary tubes, and by 1956 it was implicated in less than 4 per cent of cases. By that time, another bacterium, *Staphylococcus aureus*, was becoming responsible for more cases of mastitis, and by the early 1960s

---

[60] Woods, 'The Farm as Clinic', pp. 475–80.
[61] Cassidy, *Vermin, Victims and Disease*, p. 22; Woods, 'A Historical Synopsis', p. 1948.
[62] A. Woods, personal communication.
[63] I. Fincham, 'Animal Health', in R.J. Halley (ed.), *The Agricultural Notebook* (17th edn, London, 1982), pp. 446–81.

it was estimated that about a quarter of the dairy herd had sub-clinical mastitis at any one time. Antibiotic resistance began to increase, and in 1963 11 per cent of milk samples contained antibiotic residues. A joint initiative of the NFU, the MMB, the British Veterinary Association, and the pharmaceutical companies looked for an alternative approach and from the early 1970s promoted a 'five-point plan' for mastitis control: teat dipping in disinfectant after milking, antibiotics for clinical cases, antibiotic treatment at the end of the lactation, culling of chronically infected cows, and annual testing of milking machines. Its effectiveness would be judged by a monthly bulk milk cell count (BMCC) to assess the mastitis status of the herd. As with many of the other technical changes that we have examined, it took time for this plan to be widely adopted, but by the early 1980s the proportion of infected cows in the national herd had been reduced from 50 per cent to 32 per cent, and the national BMCC had been reduced by a third.[64]

There seems to be little doubt that the intensification of dairy production, with more cows in bigger herds each giving more milk on less land, was associated with the prevalence of mastitis, and that mastitis was the main disease problem with which dairy farmers had to contend in this period. Equally, as Professor Woods argues, the efforts of the scientists to find ways of combatting the problem enabled this intensification to go ahead without being overwhelmed by the disease.[65]

Conclusion

British farming as a whole adopted new technologies and as a result expanded its output during the Second World War and in the four decades after it. Different sectors of the agricultural industry were affected by different technical changes. The major influences on cereal farming were new varieties, pesticides, and more powerful and capable machinery. Intensive livestock production was transformed by breeding and housing changes. Beef cattle probably changed less than other sectors, but even they were changed by the introduction of continental breeds. The dairy industry, as we have seen in this chapter, was transformed by new breeds of cattle and new ways of feeding and housing them. We have examined these in detail because, as we argued at the beginning, dairy farming was, in terms of the number of people involved and the value of its output, the most important sector of the national agricultural industry. It was also the one for which we have most detailed evidence for the south-western counties.

This detail enables us to demonstrate not only the effects on the farm

---

[64] A. Woods, 'Science, Disease and Dairy Production in Britain, c.1927 to 1980', *Agric. Hist. Rev.* 62 (2014), pp. 294–314.
[65] Woods, 'Science, Disease and Dairy Production', pp. 313–14.

of technical changes that can be identified statistically, as in tables 5.3 to 5.9 in this chapter, but also to show what national and even regional or county statistics hide: the interdependency of technical changes, and the enormous variety in the ways in which individual farmers responded to technical change. The on-farm effects of new technology were summed up neatly, in the case of silage, by farmer 466, when he said:

> In earlier days it was a substitute for haymaking, so you got overmature silage in the middle of June, whereas by the 1970s we were thinking of making a cut in May and cutting again in June or July, and being conscious of D values and things like that. ... it then became obvious that the quality of the forages was crucial ... it became obvious that if you had better quality silage the cow would eat more, and every kilogramme she ate would nourish her more, so there was a double whammy in the right direction.

He also saw technical change in a wider context, as he explained to his daughter:

> The most significant technical change in my lifetime, in our case, has been the biology of the cow, but as we said, that's not a single factor. Our daughter was a geneticist, when we were undergraduates they'd only just discovered DNA, Crick and Watson were of our generation. By the time our daughter went to university it was a new subject, and she got a PhD in genetics, ... she was getting disillusioned with the ivory towers of academia, and I said 'come home with me, and I'll take you round the farm and I'll show you what technology and science has done since your grandfather's day'. She was just amazed. She'd been brought up on the farm and she hadn't seen it. The genetics of the cow, all these crops, maize, we couldn't grow maize ten years ago, but now with new varieties, ... and of course all the chemicals, and the breeding of the cow, ... I tried to reassure her that science did in the end get out. We were part of the process of science getting out.

As this highlights, and the examples earlier in this chapter demonstrate, it was the combination of new technologies that was crucial. But it is also worth re-emphasising that 'the process of science getting out' took time. Many of the new technologies that were available in the 1960s were still new on some farms in the 1980s. Farmers were unlikely to read about some new development in the *Farmer's Weekly* on Friday evening and ring up to buy it on Monday morning. The point at which old equipment wore out, or buildings needed repairing, or a child became of an age to enter the farm labour force, or a parent died, could all influence the time at which an innovation was adopted. But even if a farmer felt that it was time to make a change, some investment was usually necessary, and the necessary funds were not always available. On occasion, the costs could be minimised by using farm labour, as on farm 787 when 'we built the silage pit ourselves, we got some RSJs and some old wood from an old mill, put plywood round the outside and concreted it, that cost £6,000, but it was still a cheaper way of doing it', and there can be few farmers or farm workers who have not at some time done a bit of building or plumbing work, or even, on occasion, electrical work. For more major developments, however, either the farm's own cash reserves needed to be invested, or money had to be borrowed. The ease with which this could be done depended on several factors, from the availability of government grants and the varying levels of inflation to the ability of owner-occupiers to use the farm as security for a loan or the willingness of landlords to invest in tenanted farms. These factors will be discussed in more detail in the following chapter.

6

Land and Capital

Capital and Land Tenure

As we saw at the end of the last chapter, technical changes often, if not inevitably, needed capital investment of some kind to be put into effect. It is easier to understand why and how changes occurred in this respect between 1939 and 1985 if we remember that capital in agriculture is conventionally divided into several categories, each of which may be provided from different sources.

Capital investment is required on a farm to make the land productive. Some capital items, such as field boundaries and drains, may have been in existence for many years; short-term capital may be needed to pay for storing finished crops until they can be sold. The conventional division is between landlord's capital and tenant's capital. The former consists of the land itself and the buildings, hedges, and fences, roads, drains, and so on upon it, all of which are for all practical purposes inseparable from the land, and the money invested in these items is not available for running the farm business. However, since they are so immobile, such items provide good security against which money can be borrowed. They are usually referred to as *landlord's capital*, since they are normally provided by the landlord on a tenanted farm. More capital is needed to acquire the machinery and breeding livestock, and it too has to be invested for several years and is not available for day-to-day purposes, so like the landlord's capital it forms part of the *fixed capital* of the farm. However, since on a tenanted farm it is normally provided by the tenant, it forms part of the *tenant's capital*. The other part of the tenant's capital is the *working capital*, which is turned over more rapidly. It is used to pay for the necessary labour and feedingstuffs that must be bought before fattening animals can be sold, or the seeds and fertilisers purchased in the spring before a cereal crop is sold in the autumn. Some writers therefore distinguished between long-term and short-term capital and argued that different sources should be used for each type; in other words, that it would be unwise to use a bank loan that can be recalled at any time to finance land purchase.[1]

---

[1] R. Cohen, *The Economics of Agriculture* (Cambridge, 1940), pp. 62–3; J.A.S.

Owner-occupiers had to provide all these kinds of capital, so for them these distinctions probably seemed academic. And since very few farming businesses were limited companies, both owner-occupiers and tenants made little distinction between the money used for the farm business and that used for personal or family purposes. They were familiar with the saying that 'there are three sources of capital for farming – patrimony, matrimony, and parsimony'.[2] For all practical purposes, for both owner-occupiers and tenants, land and capital were bound together. However, there were some important distinctions between them that could affect their investment decisions and abilities. Owner-occupiers were free to plan their farms as they wished, any improvements made to their holdings were to their own advantage, and they had the value of their land to use as collateral if they wished to borrow from the bank. As farmer 243 pointed out, the banks 'knew the farmers, you can't run away from a farm, you can't hide. So they always had the security of the land. I've never known it go down in price.' As the price of land rose, their collateral increased, and in addition to their farming profits they also benefited from the capital appreciation of their land. On the other hand, owner-occupiers who had bought land with borrowed money in times of high land prices and high interest rates could have considerable mortgage repayment obligations, which might result in the under-capitalisation of their farming operations. Tenants, in contrast, only had to find the capital for machinery and livestock, and their security of tenure and the level of rent they had to pay had both been regulated by a series of Agricultural Holdings Acts over many years up to the 1950s. For tenants with landlords who had the desire and ability to invest in new technology, this was therefore in many ways the ideal form of tenure, since they had access to farmland and buildings without the need to find large capital sums. On the other hand, if their landlords were unable or unwilling to invest in new buildings, water supplies, electrification, roads, drainage, or other forms of land improvement, their technical progress could be restricted.[3]

Between the beginning of the Second World War and the mid-1980s, several important factors affecting tenants and owner-occupiers and their access to land and capital changed. The amount of land available

---

Watson and J.A. More, *Agriculture: The Science and Practice of Farming* (8th edn, Edinburgh, 1945), pp. 728–39; K. Dexter and D. Barber, *Farming for Profits* (2nd edn, London, 1967), p. 85.

[2] A quip attributed by Dexter and Barber (*Farming for Profits*, p. 84) to A.W. Ashby, Professor of Agricultural Economics at the University of Aberystwyth for many years between the wars.

[3] A. Edwards, 'Resources in Agriculture: Land', in A. Edwards and A. Rogers (eds), *Agricultural Resources: An Introduction to the Farming Industry of the United Kingdom* (London, 1974), pp. 82–106.

for agriculture, and the proportion of it farmed by tenants, went down. Land prices and inflation rose, changing the real net worth of the agricultural industry. Less quantifiable factors changed too: government policy with regard to grants and subsidies, farmers' attitudes to borrowing, and banks' views on lending to farmers, and we shall consider each of these in the following pages.

Some idea of the capital position of British agriculture in 1939 – and, indeed, ten years later – emerges from a single sentence in *Fream's*: 'Existing buildings ... usually date from the early part of the nineteenth century ...', a state of affairs that is attributed to 'the severe depressions through which the agricultural industry has passed'.[4] The exact extent of the depression was a matter of some discussion at the time and has remained so subsequently. There were certainly examples of farmers who found ways of changing their farming systems to meet the challenges of low and fluctuating prices in the interwar years, but overall the country's net farm income between 1923 and 1935, after allowing for inflation, was less than it had been in the first decade of the twentieth century.[5] There was a perceived shortage of credit for tenant farmers, most of whose assets were 'of an insufficiently durable nature to be acceptable to the bank as security', so that the government had stepped in with various schemes under the Agricultural Credits Act of 1928, which among other initiatives established the Agricultural Mortgage Corporation. The number of owner-occupied holdings had increased from roughly 10 per cent of the national total in 1910 to about one-third of the total in 1939, although farmers who purchased land after the First World War found things difficult, especially if they had borrowed heavily in order to do so. By 1939, there was no widespread demand on the part of farmers to own their own farms.[6] But the real problem was the lack of investment by landlords:

> In consequence, estates have been allowed to run down, buildings have not been repaired, drains not relaid, farm roads not mended ... there is little doubt that there has been a gradual wastage of much of the fixed capital of agriculture. Landlords no longer have resources equal to the task, tenant farmers are impoverished after years of falling prices and in any case require their savings to bring their own equipment into line with modern developments.[7]

[4] D.H. Robinson (ed.), *Fream's Elements of Agriculture* (13th edn, London, 1949), p. 52.
[5] P. Brassley, 'British Farming between the Wars', in P. Brassley, J. Burchardt, and L. Thompson (eds), *The English Countryside between the Wars: Regeneration or Decline?* (Woodbridge, 2006), pp. 195–8.
[6] Viscount Astor and B. S. Rowntree, *British Agriculture: The Principles of Future Policy* (Harmondsworth, 1939), pp. 239–42, 245.
[7] Astor and Rowntree, *British Agriculture*, p. 246.

Over the following forty years, for many farmers, this picture would change dramatically.

Land

As farmer 209 understood only too well, 'if you haven't got land you can't farm', and the wartime and post-war demand for land for purposes other than agriculture was considerable. During the war, it was for airfields and military training areas. After the war, the main competitor for the better land was urban development, and for marginal agricultural land it was forestry. Between 1950 and 1965, the area of land lost to urban development and forestry in the UK totalled 545,000 hectares, slightly more than half of which went to forestry. This represented about 2.7 per cent of the agricultural land at the time, but, more importantly, because the urban expansion was mainly on the better land it was calculated to be equivalent to about 3.6 per cent of the production potential over the fifteen years, or 0.24 per cent per year. However, since the gross output of agriculture was increasing by between 2 and 3 per cent per year during those years, it was argued that one year's productivity gain offset ten years' land loss.[8] As the figures for England as a whole and the three south-western counties (Cornwall, Devon, and Dorset) shown in table 6.1 suggest, this was part of a complex argument. The land classified as arable (which includes temporary grass or leys) actually increased over these years, whereas the total area of crops and grass fell, by an average of nearly twenty-nine thousand acres per year over England as a whole.

TABLE 6.1. Changes in the area of agricultural land in England and the three south-western counties, 1939–79 ('000 acres)

	England, 1939	3SW 1939	England 1979	3SW 1979
Arable	8,397	840	10,320	1,130
Crops and Grass	21,947	2,151	20,792	2,016
Rough Grazing	3,795	548	2,929	356

Source: MAFF, *Agricultural Statistics 1939–1944, England and Wales, Part 1* (London, 1947), p. 110; MAFF, *Agricultural Statistics England, 1978/9* (London, 1981), p. 2.

---

[8] A.G. Champion, 'Competition for Agricultural Land', in Edwards and Rogers, *Agricultural Resources*, p. 236.

This apparent contradiction is easily explained, because a lot of potentially arable land was in permanent grass in 1939 and was incorporated into the arable area during and after the war. However, perhaps the greatest relative change was in the area of rough grazing, of which nearly nine hundred thousand acres were converted to other uses during these forty years, some incorporated into the farmed land, and some planted up into forestry. By the 1970s, the question of whether or not agricultural land was being lost too rapidly or not was becoming politically sensitive. The Centre for Agricultural Strategy at the University of Reading, seen by many people as a pro-agriculture think tank, produced a report suggesting that 'there is a danger of land scarcity in the near future', and Richard (later Sir Richard) Body, MP for the agricultural constituency of Holland with Boston in Lincolnshire, highlighted the conversion of rough grazing to farmland (with some exaggeration of the figures), claiming that the price, in terms of agricultural subsidies, high food prices, and loss of access to recreational land, 'has been shameful'.[9] Shameful or not, it was part of an ongoing discussion about whether farmers could get access to land in order to farm.

Land Tenure

The other part of the discussion involved tenancy. Astor and Rowntree's comment about the lack of demand for landownership notwithstanding, the proportion of owner-occupied land and holdings increased more or less continuously from 1914 onwards, as table 6.2 reveals. Tenants may not have been anxious to buy before the Second World War, but landowners were increasingly happy to sell. The social prestige derived from landownership was decreasing, successive Agricultural Holdings Acts restricted the way in which estates could be managed, inheritance taxes had been imposed, and the interwar depression reduced the level of non-agricultural income that could be re-invested in land. The costs of landownership increased with little or no corresponding increases in farm rents.[10] Rather than seeing their farms sold to another owner, with unpredictable consequences, many tenants took advantage of the opportunity to buy their farms as sitting tenants, with the corresponding price advantage. Between 1914 and 1927, it is generally accepted that over six million acres were transferred from landlords to tenants, although there remain academic arguments over precisely when the bulk of the transfer

---

9 Centre for Agricultural Strategy, *Land for Agriculture*, CAS Report no. 1 (Reading, 1976), p. 12; R. Body, *Agriculture: The Triumph and the Shame* (London, 1982), p. 40.
10 E. Thomas, *An Introduction to Agricultural Economics* (London, 1949), pp. 166–9; A. Martin, *Economics and Agriculture* (London, 1958), pp. 145–7.

occurred.[11] As Astor and Rowntree suggest, and table 6.2 confirms, the process slowed or even reversed in the 1930s, but thereafter continued throughout the post-war decades.

TABLE 6.2. The proportion of the agricultural area and of holdings held by owner-occupiers in England and Wales, 1914–83

	% of holdings	% of area
1914	11.3	10.9
1927	36.6	36.0
1941	34.6	32.7
1960	56.7	49.2
1983	70.4	60.2

Source: D. Grigg, *English Agriculture: An Historical Perspective* (Oxford, 1989), p. 104.

Even after the war, farms could still be an unattractive investment for landlords. On farm 744, where a new tenant took over after the Second World War, 'the farms were run down, unproductive, over-run with rabbits, silly low rents, even after the war, I paid £150 a year, a pound an acre'. Under the provisions of the 1948 Agricultural Holdings Act, tenants had increased security of tenure, so landlords found it increasingly difficult to dispossess tenants in order to sell with vacant possession, and a vacant possession premium developed, to the advantage of sitting tenants wishing to purchase their farms. In addition, they benefitted from lower Estate Duties on death. As a result, very few new agricultural tenancies were established after the 1950s. When land fell vacant, landowners were often more interested in putting in managers rather than tenants, or incorporating the land into their home farms. When estates were sold, the new owners were increasingly interested in having them farmed by farm management companies.[12] Concerns began to grow about access to farms for ordinary farmers and their children wishing to obtain access to land in order to farm. There were particular concerns about the number of estates being purchased by financial institutions and foreign buyers. By the late 1970s, these had reached a point at which the Minister of Agriculture decided to appoint a Committee of Inquiry into the Acquisition and Occupancy of Agricultural Land, chaired by Lord Northfield. The Committee found that institutional and foreign owners

---

[11] J. Beckett and M. Turner, 'End of the Old Order? F.M.L. Thompson, the Land Question, and the Burden of Ownership in England, c.1880–c.1925', *Agric. Hist. Rev.* 55 (2007), pp. 280, 288; F.M.L. Thompson, 'The Land Market, 1880–1925: A Reappraisal Reappraised', *Agric. Hist. Rev.* 55 (2007), p. 293.

[12] Edwards, 'Resources in Agriculture: Land', pp. 92–3.

Land and Capital

between them owned only a little over 2 per cent of agricultural land, and that this did not constitute a problem, but recognised that 'young people wishing to farm face considerable difficulties because of the shortage of tenancies and the high cost of establishment as an owner-occupier'.[13]

As the differences between the holdings and area figures indicate, the average size of the owner-occupied holdings was a little less than that of tenanted holdings. These figures simplify the reality of the changes, because the sources from which they are derived specify land as being 'owned or mainly owned', and one of the major expanding categories was of farms on which some of the land was owned and some rented.

TABLE 6.3. The proportion of holdings and of the agricultural area held under different tenure types, England and Wales, 1960–83

	% of all holdings			% of total area		
	All rented	Mixed	All owner-occupied	All rented	Mixed	All owner-occupied
1960	37.1	15.6	47.3	41.6	21.7	36.7
1975	25.5	30.5	44.0	27.2	40.8	32.0
1983	20.4	22.3	57.4	24.4	34.4	41.3

Source: Grigg, *English Agriculture*, p. 107.

Only about 15 per cent of holdings had this mix of owner-occupied and tenanted land in 1960, but in the 1960s and early '70s it was the most rapidly expanding sector, and even after the further growth of owner-occupation from the late 1970s it still accounted for more than a fifth of the holdings and a third of the land, as table 6.3 shows. It was presumably a response to the problem of acquiring more land to farm. Owner-occupiers expanded by taking on tenanted land where they could; tenants by buying land when they had the ability and opportunity to do so. As figure 6.1 shows, this national trend was replicated among the farms in south-west England included in the FMS sample, of which about half were held in mixed tenure, and only about 15 per cent entirely rented, by 1985. The history of farm 744 provides a typical example of the way in which a mixed tenure farm could evolve. Beginning with 150 rented acres in 1946,

> We bought a bit of land in 1970, and also a bit from a neighbouring farmer, to get it up to 220 acres, and [my son] still rents a bit even now.

---

[13] *Report of the Committee of Inquiry into the Acquisition and Occupancy of Agricultural Land*, Cmnd.7599 (1979), pp. 10–11.

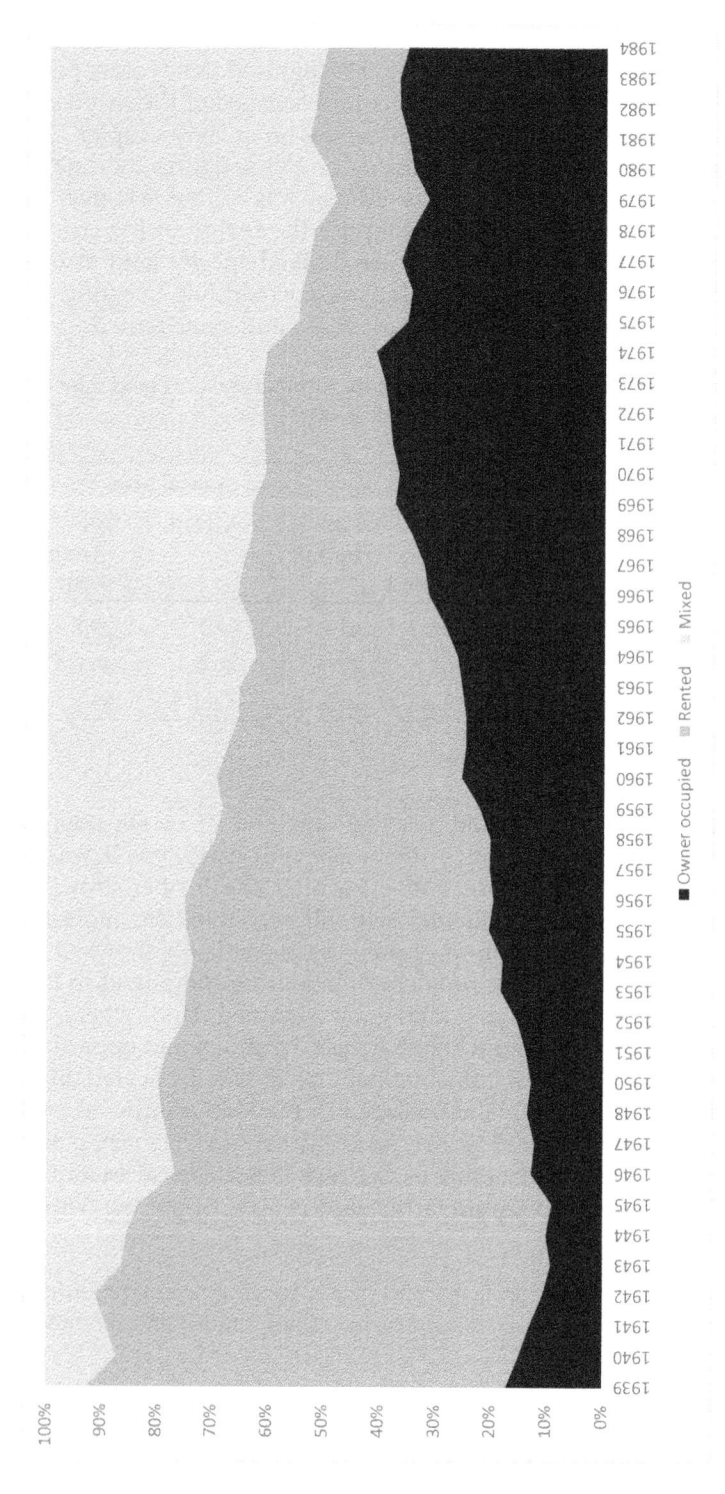

FIG. 6.1. Changes in tenure types on FMS farms

> [The main] farm is still rented from the Church Commissioners, but there's about eighty-seven acres we own. [My son] has some grass from a neighbour.

This is not to say that all farmers preferred to be owner-occupiers rather than tenants. As farmer 744 found, 'the tenant farming situation was a good way to farm, it gave people with limited capital like myself a chance to farm, if you have to find the capital today to buy the farm it's beyond what you can do'. Farm 787 was a 305-acre tenanted farm on a large private estate in 1948, and when it came up for sale in 1957 the neighbours who could remain as tenants were pleased to do so: 'the people who didn't have to buy were rubbing their hands'. Landlords could sometimes sell off less good land to concentrate their resources where they would be more profitable. In mid-Devon, for example, the owners of farm 109 had previously been tenants of another farm on better land on the same estate: 'they sold us the worst to get us out of the best'.

For many farmers, however, buying land was desirable, if not a necessity. At the end of the war and just after land could still be bought cheaply, as in the case of farm 2/21, near the coast in Dorset:

> My father-in-law bought the farm in 1948, when it was a very run down farm. It hadn't received any support during the war. There was no road here, no electricity [and] no telephone. It was regarded as too much of a challenge even for the War Agricultural Committee to undertake. Covered in scrub ... it was a very rough shooting area, and father-in-law bought it for a song in 1948.

Also in Dorset, for part of the land of farm 2/7, 'In 1943 my father bought five hundred acres of the 610, and in 1944 my uncle bought the remaining 108 acres [sic] because my father didn't have enough money to buy it, and he persuaded my uncle to buy it and rent it to him.' The way in which the decision was influenced by personal interests and family dynamics is further illustrated by the history of farm 209 in west Cornwall, which was a thirty-four-acre rented farm from the late 1850s until it was purchased by the current farmer's father in 1943. By the mid-1950s, the father's interest in farming was waning as much as the son's was waxing:

> Dad by 1956 became a county councillor, and that was the love of his life. ... his interest in expanding or modernising had gone, so I had a battle on my hands, all I wanted to do was go farming, and I knew that if I didn't expand I wouldn't be farming much longer, because things were taking off by 1956, go-ahead people were taking off by 1950, we missed some of the local land coming up for sale, and Dad was a popular man, and although he didn't have a big farm it was intensive with two staff and pigs and poultry and suchlike, nineteen cows on thirty-four acres was going some then, and he was well liked, and there were local people who were wanting to sell and said to Dad, if [your

son is] coming home on the farm you will have the first chance, and I couldn't persuade him to take them. I was only seventeen and you think you know everything, but I did know something, I knew they weren't making any more land in the world, so that was the thing to invest in, because if you haven't got land you can't farm. By the time we were in partnership we persuaded him to buy another fifty acres next door, and then a few years later another sixty acres came up next door, then Dad was tailing off and I was married … in 1961 and we became tenants of Mum and Dad, and then [my wife] and myself could make our own decisions.

By the mid-1960s, they had bought enough land to get the farm up to 270 acres, but after 1980 it expanded further by renting land from several different landlords, so that by the early twenty-first century the family was farming over seven hundred acres.

As with many other farmers, farmer 209 recognised the importance of acquiring neighbouring land when it became available, and the rarity with which it did so: 'We've had two chances to buy two little blocks of land … but very often you only get one chance in a generation.' Neighbouring farmers were normally those most interested in acquiring any parcel of land, and most able to do so, because they could often farm it without needing to invest in extra buildings or machinery. When the farm next to farm 101 was advertised for sale one Friday in 1967, '[we] heard on Saturday, by Tuesday all signed and sealed. We'd co-operated with him since the war, it was our longest border. Father just bought it.' Similarly, on farm 272, a typical owner-occupied family dairy farm in east Cornwall,

> We took over in 1956 when we were married. An extra twenty-six acres were rented … making it 101 acres. In 1974, we then bought that land, plus another twenty-four, so we were up to 124 by 1984, we bought another fifty acres in 1997–8. We wanted the extra land to expand the business, and it was all adjoining, more convenient to us than anyone else.

Where this option was unavailable, it was a matter of regret, as on farm 2/7 in Dorset:

> There was never enough money, or land available, to increase the acreage, because we wanted neighbouring land. … land round here rarely comes up within tractor distance. Just east of here there are three large estates, but most of the farms round here are long-established family farms.

Land and Capital

With the transfer of land to owner-occupation, the net worth and the creditworthiness of farmers increasingly depended upon the value of their land. There were no official estimates of the balance sheet of UK agriculture before 1970, but there were occasional estimates before that. Table 6.4 has been constructed from these sources and has two important features: it shows that the total assets of agriculture were increasingly dependent upon the value of land and buildings, and that these assets far outstripped the industry's liabilities, in the form of loans from the Agricultural Mortgage Corporation and the banks, and merchant credit. Thus the net worth (assets minus liabilities) of the industry was high and tended to increase over time. However, since it was increasingly dependent upon land values, it fluctuated as these changed after 1970, whereas it had been rising fairly steadily before then.[14]

TABLE 6.4. The balance sheet of UK agriculture, 1953–85 (£ million)

	1953	1963	1975	1985
Land and Buildings	1,850	3,000	12,350	37,000
Total Assets	3,465	5,200	19,500	52,350
Land and buildings as a % of total assets	53.4	57.7	63.3	70.7
Total Liabilities	880	1,190	2,200	8,150
Net Worth	2,585	4,010	17,300	44,200
Net worth as a % of total assets	74.6	77.1	88.7	84.4

Source: A. Burrell, B. Hill and J. Medland, *Agrifacts: A Handbook of UK and EEC Agricultural and Food Statistics* (London, 1990), p. 65; Centre for Agricultural Strategy, *Land for Agriculture*, pp. 23, 29.

Table 6.5, which highlights years of significant change, shows the more or less continuous increase in land prices in current price terms, and the way in which it peaked in the 1970s in real terms. There was much discussion over the reasons for rising land prices and their fluctuation. Before the Second World War, land prices generally reflected the profitability of agriculture, and with guaranteed prices and rising farm incomes after the war they continued to do so. But there were other factors at work too.

---

[14] B. Hill, *Farm Incomes, Wealth and Agricultural Policy* (3rd edn, Aldershot, 2000), p. 289.

TABLE 6.5. Land prices (£ per hectare)

	Price (in current prices)	Retail Price Index (1986 = 100)	Price (in £ 1986 values)
1944	93	7.4	1,257
1950	153	9.23	1,658
1957	155	12.32	1,258
1961	265	13.21	2,006
1968	517	16.89	3,061
1971	620	20.75	2,988
1972	1,238	22.22	5,572
1973	1,643	24.21	6,786
1979	3,227	57.8	5,583
1985	3,871	97.07	3,988

Source: Burrell et al., *Agrifacts*, p. 29; P. Brassley, 'Output and Technical Change in Twentieth-Century British Agriculture', *Agric. Hist. Rev.* 48 (2000), p. 81. Note that prices for 1968 and earlier are for all land, whereas those for 1971 and later are for land with vacant possession.

Regulations increasing security of tenure produced an increasing premium for land with vacant possession, the estate duty relief of 45 per cent on the value of farmland, the amenity value of rural property, and, in particular, as we have seen in the cases of farms 209 and 272, the premium that neighbouring farmers were prepared to pay for land that they could farm from their existing holdings, were all advanced as reasons for rising land values.[15]

The reasons for land price increases need not concern us further, for what mattered more as far as the history of technical change was concerned was the impact of changing land prices and net worth on capital formation in agriculture. The implication of agriculture's high net worth is that the industry provided much of its own capital, so that when profits were high farmers invested in buildings and bought machinery; when they weren't, they didn't. Table 6.6 provides some support for this idea in that the investment (i.e. Gross Fixed Capital Formation (GFCF)) figures peaked in real terms in the 1970s after the high-income years of 1970 and 1973, although the relationship is not strong. A study covering an earlier period found that the Farm Improvement Scheme, a part of the 1957 Agriculture Act, was responsible for the considerable increase in investment in farm buildings between 1955 and 1960.

[15] Edwards, 'Resources in Agriculture: Land', pp. 97–100.

Land and Capital

TABLE 6.6. Gross Fixed Capital Formation in UK agriculture

	Buildings and works, current £m	Plant vehicles and machinery current £m	Total agricultural GFCF Current £m	Real investment index (deflated by RPI) 1980 = 100	Real Income Index 1985 = 100
1955	26	78	104	71	251
1960	45	96	141	83	240
1965	67	117	184	88	284
1970	117	133	250	99	291
1971–5	198	247	445	117	288
1976–80	352	529	881	111	217
1981–5	591	639	1230	97	161

Source: Burrell et al., *Agrifacts*, pp. 59, 135. Note that the real income figure for 1955 is the average of 1954/5 and 1955/6, and for 1960 is the average of 1959/60 and 1960/1.

It provided grants for one-third of the approved expenditure. A survey of the country as a whole concluded that grants contributed one-quarter of agriculture's spending on building and works in 1967/8. A study carried out in Buckinghamshire in 1967 found that owner-occupiers were responsible for two-thirds of spending on buildings and fixed equipment, landlords for a quarter, with tenants financing the remainder.[16]

Tenants were usually reluctant to invest in fixed equipment because the benefit might accrue to the landowner. One tenant (farm 162) observed that

> Some people took it on themselves and built sheds on the estate's land, but I was reluctant to do that because after seven years it becomes the estate's, and then they can say 'well there's a jolly nice shed' and increase your rent because it's there, even though you built it yourself, so I didn't think that was the way to go, … they invited me to build my own sheds, so we know what the answer to that is. This estate has always gone on the low-cost system.

Farm 162 was on a relatively small estate, but some of the bigger institutional landlords could also be either unwilling or unable to invest. The landlord's plans, desires, and expectations were not always at one with those of the tenant. On a big institutional estate with farms all over the country, the landlord regarded farm 744 'as not being viable, as one

[16] B. Hill, 'Resources in Agriculture: Capital', in Edwards and Rogers, *Agricultural Resources*, pp. 152–3, 162.

of the lesser, poorer farms, they had it in their minds that we would be one of the first to go and be amalgamated', which is perhaps why they increased the rent without putting in much investment. However, the tenant responded by increasing output: 'I never really saw ... as a dairy farm, ... economics was such that as the landlords wanted a bit more rent we had to get a bit more income, and we thought the best way to do it was from cows.' As a result, there was little investment from the estate before 1970. The tenant had to do it himself: 'we put up that deep litter house by ourselves and a shed ourselves that was done as cheaply as we could'. Finally, the landlord relented. 'We went over to a parlour in 1971 or '72, when we went over to a bulk tank – we'd often thought of changing but it was difficult to get the [landlords] to do the investment, but in the end they did do and paid for most of it.' Farm 466 rented part of its land from a large institutional landowner in Cornwall and part from a much smaller private landowner, and by the mid-1980s the institutional landlord 'wasn't interested in putting much money in, and the private landlord hadn't got the means'. Earlier, however, the institutional landlord and the tenant had co-operated in modifying the buildings for the dairy herd. 'The [landlord] put up the shed, and father would have invested in the parlour and the rest of it.'

Just as the vagaries of family life and fortune could affect the management of farms, so they could also determine the management of estates, with consequent effects on their tenants. The estate in east Devon on which farm 139 was located

> went through dodgy times ... they were one of the poorer estates until they sold the land for building. They sold fifty or sixty acres for building in [the local town], and that transformed their finances. They just didn't have the money to spend, so you had to do it.

This probably took place after 1985, so it is really beyond the scope of this study, but it is a good example of a more widespread phenomenon. What happened next is also instructive in showing some of the difficulties of farming tenanted land:

> after they sold the land for building, and they went round to the farms ... they updated some of the farms. We had the least amount of updates to any of them, [but] we did a manure management plan, and I said 'we're going to have to store some slurry, what budget did you have?' They said '£5,000'. Well that wasn't going to do a lot, so they put in a blooming great slurry lagoon, and I looked at the agent and said 'You shouldn't be doing this – you're going to spend forty or fifty grand on a unit that's twenty years old, ... it would be a better idea to say let's build up a whole new unit and go from there, and we would contribute towards it', and he said 'That's not in the plan.' That's the only time I've ever felt held back by them, we would have put a new unit up rather

than tacking the lagoon on the old unit. Because once that was there, the die was cast. Not only is it a big fixed cost, it's a big thing you can't move, we could have set ourselves up for the next thirty years, and the herd would have got bigger then.

This reveals a good deal of complexity and depth to the relationships between landlords and tenants; differing attitudes to investment and differing access to funds. In some cases, the existence of a tenancy might delay technical change, through a landlord either not having the capital for investment or not having the inclination. As late as 1960, a study of land tenure made the point that 'landlords have been unable to build up capital from the present low level of rents and will not be prepared indefinitely to inject fresh capital into the industry if it continues to yield such a poor return'.[17]

Borrowing and Other Sources of Capital

Even when a landlord with capital was pro-active in their investment plans, such plans might be limiting in their scope and lacking in awareness of the requirements of specific farm businesses. The clear inference from this is that it was easier for owner-occupiers to raise money for investment, and to make the investments that they needed. This was a new and important development, probably from the later 1950s onwards. A study of post-war agricultural economics bemoaned 'the inherent conservatism of farmers in money matters ... manifested in a general mistrust of borrowing ... Farmers as a class do not regard the use of credit as a legitimate business means for implementing the planned investment of their farms.'[18] In complete contrast, as we have already seen, on farm 243 in east Devon, which had been 'bought as sitting tenant when [the landlord] died' in about 1959, the attitude had completely changed by the 1960s, when the farmer frequently went to borrow from Lloyds Bank in Cullompton. As an owner-occupier, a farmer was in a relatively strong position to secure a loan for technical investment, particularly at certain times (such as the 1960s and 1970s) when there was relatively high inflation. Farm 209 in west Cornwall expanded considerably in this period, and

> all these land purchases were financed off borrowed money: Barclays Bank. They were very positive. Back then the bank manager knew that we always paid off our debts, and land price inflation helped ... we had a good relationship with the bank manager, he was brilliantly helpful. At one stage [my wife] and myself borrowed £70,000 from Barclays to put in a milking parlour, a cubicle house, silage barn – we had grant on

17   G. Hallett, *The Economics of Agricultural Land Tenure* (London, 1960), p. 25.
18   Thomas, *Introduction to Agricultural Economics*, p. 48.

it – and that was big borrowing back then, but in a year or two, with inflation, you could stop worrying about it.

Nevertheless, attitudes to risk varied considerably, and not all owner-occupiers wanted to borrow. Farm 692, with 130 acres in mid-Devon, was at one extreme:

> I would never go and buy machinery unless I could afford it. The only loan I took out was when I took over the cows from father, and I took over twenty cows from father and paid £100 each, and I went to the bank and borrowed £2,000, and I paid it back within two years, and that was the only time I ever borrowed money. My brother always said 'Go to the bank and borrow money, they've got plenty.' But I said 'You've got to pay it back.' My brother would do it but I didn't like borrowing money, if I couldn't afford it I'd do without.

Differing attitudes within the same family were also revealed on farm 836, in the South Hams of Devon:

> [My father] was a great believer in the idea that you should never have anything unless you can pay for it. If I stuck to that, I wouldn't be where I am now, because, ... I had to borrow a lot. But I don't like to get out of depth – my comfort zone.

Some farmers were clearly encouraged to leave their comfort zones. On farm 826 in east Devon:

> I specialised in poultry because I thought it was going to make money, but it was my biggest mistake ever. At the time when the banks were throwing money at you, they said 'You must get bigger.' And I got up to about sixteen or seventeen thousand hens I suppose, which is nothing these days, and increasingly got more and more in debt until it was terribly serious ... The annual visit to the bank manager was important. The wretched bloke would encourage you to borrow more money, and like a sucker I would say 'Yes', until the day dawns when you have to pay it back.

However, it would also be a mistake to think that banks were always eager to lend in any circumstances, as the experience of farm 2/7 demonstrates:

> I had a bank manager on my back. I started farming in 1960-odd with an overdraft of £15,000–£20,000, and it gradually got bigger and bigger. I used to console myself with the fact that when we had a £200,000 or £250,000 overdraft I could wipe that off by selling the cows, because they were worth a lot. I had one bank manager in [the local town] who would give me all I wanted, for about ten years, so the overdraft went up and up, and he got moved on because he was loaning too much, and the hatchet man came in and looked me straight in the eye and said

'You've got to reduce it', and that was when I sold one of the herds of cows and made sure that one man was milking twice as many.

As the national data suggests, banks were not the only source of funds for investment. On farm 2/7, an uncle was persuaded by the interviewee's father to buy land and rent it to them in order to make the transition from tenancy to ownership. Such family arrangements in one form or other was actually quite common. Farmer 2/21 began farming 450 acres in 1955 as a tenant of his father-in-law. In around 1959, his father-in-law sold the farm to him and his wife for the same price that he had paid for it in 1948:

> Of course there wasn't inflation in those days. It wasn't quite as generous as you might suppose, but it was nevertheless a good start. And he put in quite a few improvements. ... When he was wanting to retire he asked if we would come into the farming limited company with him and benefit tax-wise from the losses the company had attracted, so that was quite an attraction because it meant we could make reasonable profits without being taxed for some years.

Farmer 576 also worked closely with his parents-in-law, buying land together and swapping land between them in order to amalgamate their holdings, while farmer 836's father borrowed money from his brothers to allow him to buy land. Farmer 787 rented fifty acres of land from their mother 'as grass keep so it doesn't show in the accounts', and he is also one instance of a farmer benefitting from the informal generosity of a family friend:

> the original plan was to put in a silage pit now and put cubicles in later, and he said 'Why not do it all at once?', and I said 'I can't afford to do it all', and he said 'Don't worry about that, do it all now and pay me when you can', and he meant it.

Capital Grants

To go along with these informal or family sources of funding, there were also grants, providing an incentive for various kinds of capital investment from 1940 onwards. The most important ones are listed in table 6.7. It should be emphasised that the rates of grant shown in the table are only those most commonly applied. Most schemes had very detailed rules that changed over time, and different rates of grant could be applied to different kinds of investments. Most notably, field drainage usually appeared to receive a higher rate of grant than many other investments, probably because many farmers would not have invested in it without grant aid.

TABLE 6.7. Capital grants available for UK farmers

Grant scheme	Period of operation	Most common rate of grant
Field drainage	1940–70	50%
Farm water supply	1941–70	50%
Silo subsidy	1956–66	50%
Farm Improvement Scheme	1957–70	One-third
Small Farmer Scheme	1959–65	Maximum £1,000
Farm Capital Grant Scheme	1971–80	30% (50% for drainage)
Farm and Horticulture Development Scheme	1974–80	25% (60% for drainage)
Agriculture and Horticulture Development Scheme	From 1980	32.5% (50% for drainage)

Source: S.P. Bingham, *A Guide to the Development of Grants for Agriculture and Horticulture for England and Wales 1940–1982*, London: MAFF, Economics Division III, internal publication (London, no date, probably 1982); MAFF, *At the Farmer's Service* (London, 1976–7); J. Nix, *Farm Management Pocketbook* (12th edn, Ashford, 1981), pp. 134–5.

In the 1990s, by which time drainage grant rates had fallen to 15 per cent, only about ten thousand hectares were being drained each year, compared with ten times that amount in the 1970s when grant rates were higher.[19] On farm 193 in north Devon, which had grants for drainage in 1977 and 1981 ('plastic by that time, done by contractor, quite a few acres, maybe seventy to eighty'), the farmer admitted that 'I think it was doubtful from an economic point of view. I wouldn't have done it without the grant.' Conversely, in east Devon, on farm 243, 'as the fields started to dry out you grew more grass, because it's beautiful earth. Several times we had two hundred bales an acre of hay, no trouble at all. Some was done with grant, some wasn't. It was worth doing whether you had a grant or not.'

As with drainage, some farmers felt ambivalent about capital grants for buildings. Farm 466 had 'a lot of grant aid on one of the farms, Farm Improvement Scheme, the ... farm buildings were largely grant aided. I don't know if we would have done it without it or not.' In general, however, and unsurprisingly, farmers felt more positive towards grant schemes. Farm 2/21's new dairy and silage buildings in the 1970s were grant aided 'at a time when the government wanted more and more produced', and also in Dorset, on farm 2/7, 'We were encouraged by government grant aid to invest. That's why we've got so many groups

[19] Brassley, 'Output and Technical Change', p. 68.

of buildings and so many barns on this farm. We had 33 per cent grant on any building we could put up, so they sprang up all over the farm.' Perhaps the most ringing endorsement of the impact of grants came from the experience of farm 209 in west Cornwall, a farm that began with thirty-five acres and eventually expanded to seven hundred:

> It would all have been a lot more difficult without grants. We got 40 per cent grants, if we'd locked in to the Farm Amalgamation we'd have had 60 per cent, but we had 40 per cent and that was pretty good, and it was very important, especially as we were borrowing all the money to do it. It was all Farm Capital Grant Scheme. It modernised British agriculture pretty well, and it had a big impact on what we could do here.

From a more dispassionate standpoint, an academic assessment of the impact of grants found it 'highly unlikely that all the post-1957 grant-aided investment would have occurred in the absence of the Farm Improvement Scheme, and the adoption of technological advances with expansion in output and simultaneous reduction in the agricultural labour force might not then have been possible', although it admitted that 'no overwhelming evidence exists by which the encouragement of capital investment in agriculture can be judged in relation to investment in other sectors of the economy'.[20] Writing at the end of our period, one agricultural economist found that 'The direct grants for farm investments in drainage, other land improvements, farm roads, fencing, plant, buildings and machinery plus the considerable fiscal incentives for such investments, have clearly been of great importance in lowering the real user cost of capital', and he therefore suggested that 'these structural and fiscal measures may well be more important in determining the extent, pace and nature of technical and structural change in farming than the price support measures'.[21]

Conclusions

As this chapter demonstrates, UK farming entered the Second World War with a long history of quite understandable underinvestment in farm buildings and a cautious attitude to borrowing and investment on the part of farmers. The following forty years saw some significant changes. Overall, land was lost to building and forestry, but for farming the effect of the loss was offset by bringing more than 20 per cent of the rough grazing area into the acreage of crops and grass, and by producing more from each of the farmed acres. The way in which the farmed land was organised changed too, with an increase in the proportion farmed

---

[20] Hill, 'Resources in Agriculture: Capital', p. 163.
[21] A. Buckwell, 'Economic Signals, Farmers' Response, and Environmental Change', *Journal of Rural Studies* 5 (1989), p. 157.

by owner-occupiers and an increase in the number of mixed-tenure farms, with the owner-occupied area supplemented with rented land. The effect was often for farms to increase in size, either by buying neighbouring fields as they came on to the market or by renting as landowners reorganised their estates. Farmers were now able to buy land, take on extra rental obligations, and invest in buildings and machinery because they were being encouraged to do so by government agricultural policy in the form of grants and subsidies and were seen as creditworthy by lending institutions. Moreover, by the late 1960s, and in particular in the 1970s, the effect of inflation meant that loans could be repaid in devalued pounds. Nevertheless, it is important to recognise that there remained considerable differences between individual farms and farmers.

In understanding the process of technical change, the role of, attitude to, and nature of dealing with investment and finance is of crucial importance. On the whole, it appears that tenancies delayed investment, with several farmers showing signs of frustration that they were not permitted (or had no incentive) to make technical investments that they recognised as necessary. The attitude of farmers was also of crucial importance. In some instances, a desire to buy more land actually led to technical change being delayed, as the purchase of new machinery was put off while loan repayments were made. More commonly, it was owner-occupiers who were able to use their land-based creditworthiness to innovate before tenants often could. As with the technical changes themselves, the stories of individual farms reveal as much about the variation from one farm to another as they do about the overall trends. But the overall trend was clear. After the war, government grant assistance, increasing confidence, and increasing creditworthiness arising in large part from the increasing level of owner-occupation had a big impact on the average farmer's willingness and ability to invest. That in turn affected the use of farm labour, which forms the subject of the following chapter.

7

Labour and Machinery

Labour

In 1939, 4.6 per cent of the working population of Great Britain was engaged in agriculture; by 1975, only 1.65 per cent (of a larger workforce) were still in farming.[1] No account of technical change in agriculture can omit some mention of agricultural labour, for while increased use of capital was the cause of some technical changes, decreasing use of labour was, at least in part, a result of technical change and a cause of increasing labour productivity.

By 1939, the decline in the agricultural labour force from the peak that it had reached in 1851 was a well-established trend. It had especially affected the employed sector, those other than the farmers and their families.[2] A contemporary analysis of the position mentioned the search for better wages and housing conditions among the reasons for 'the rural exodus', and a consequent shortage in both the traditional and new (mechanical) skills needed in farming, together with potential changes in the vitality of village life.[3] Ironically, this was written just as the farm labour force was about to rise for the first time in eighty years in response to the wartime increase in the demand for home-produced food. For today's reader, accustomed to seeing cereals harvested by combine harvester and hearing of automatic milking machines, it is worth remembering how much hand work, from stooking sheaves to milking, was needed during the war. Extra output needed extra labour. The regular labour force increased hardly at all between 1939 and 1944 (by less than 1 per cent), but it was assisted by far more casual workers, members of the Women's Land Army, and eventually prisoners of war, so that the total labour force rose by more than 20 per cent by 1944, although it was not evenly distributed.[4]

[1] E. Thomas, *An Introduction to Agricultural Economics* (London, 1949), p. 64; Central Statistical Office, *Annual Abstract of Statistics, 1976* (London, 1976), p. 151.
[2] D. Grigg, *English Agriculture: An Historical Perspective* (Oxford, 1989), p. 137.
[3] Viscount Astor and B.S. Rowntree, *British Agriculture: The Principles of Future Policy* (Harmondsworth, 1939), pp. 211–18.
[4] G. Clarke, 'The Women's Land Army and Its Recruits, 1938–50', in B. Short, C. Watkins, and J. Martin (eds), *The Front Line of Freedom: British Farming in*

In 1941, the data from the National Farm Survey found that 44 per cent of holdings in England and Wales had no regular labour apart from the farmer and his or her spouse.[5] Numbers of hired workers rose still further with the post-war growth in output, and still included German prisoners of war until 1947.[6] Then after 1951 the long-run decline in the employed labour force resumed, as table 7.1 demonstrates, even more rapidly in the case of those employed for the whole of their working weeks. It also shows that there was little difference in the post-1951 trends between the three south-western counties and England as a whole.

This decline in the employed agricultural labour force, its causes, and its implications attracted the attention of sociologists, economists, and agriculturalists. Williams in his studies of villages in the north-west and south-west of England, Frankenberg on a Welsh village, and Blythe, using a more impressionistic methodology for East Anglia, wrote about the workings of rural society as a whole, whereas Nalson was concerned only with farm families in an unidentified upland area, and Newby only with agricultural workers.[7] As an agriculturalist, Professor Cooper was more concerned with explaining why workers were leaving the land, which he attributed to low wages, increasing mechanisation, and the lack of a ladder of promotion by which ambitious farm workers could aspire to farm on their own account. He also emphasised the importance of increased skill levels as technology changed and the labour force shrank. Farm workers had to be competent not only in a wide range of agricultural skills, from ploughing and other arable tasks to milking and a range of livestock-related jobs, but they also had to be able to maintain machinery, build and repair buildings, and know enough about plumbing, carpentry, and electrical work to keep the farm going without constant recourse to expensive specialists.[8] As new technologies emerged, farm workers had to be trained, sometimes informally on the farm, and sometimes on formal training courses. On farm 139, 'father said "It's

---

the Second World War (Exeter, 2006), pp. 101–16; R. Moore-Colyer, 'Prisoners of War and the Struggle for Food Production, 1939–49', in Short et al., Front Line of Freedom, pp. 117–31.

[5] MAF, National Farm Survey of England and Wales (1941–1943): A Summary Report (London, 1946), p. 48.

[6] J. Custodis, 'Employing the Enemy: The Contribution of German and Italian Prisoners of War to British Agriculture during and after the Second World War', Agric. Hist. Rev. 60 (2012), pp. 243–65.

[7] W.M. Williams, The Sociology of an English Village: Gosforth (London, 1956); W.M. Williams, A West Country Village: Ashworthy (London, 1963); R. Frankenberg, Village on the Border (London, 1957); R. Blythe, Akenfield (London, 1969); J.S. Nalson, Mobility of Farm Families: A Study of Occupational and Residential Mobility in an Upland Area of England (Manchester, 1968); H. Newby, The Deferential Worker (London, 1977).

[8] M.McG. Cooper, Competitive Farming (London, 1956), pp. 151–62.

TABLE 7.1. Numbers of agricultural workers (excluding farmers, partners, and directors) in England and the three south-western counties (Cornwall, Devon, and Dorset), 1939–78

	England			Three south-western counties		
	1939	1951	1978	1939	1951	1978
Whole time	474,483	518,163	152,802	34,368	38,824	12,021
Part-time and casual	90,023	143,389	128,781	7,439	10,923	10,995

Source: MAF, *Agricultural Statistics 1939–1944, England and Wales*, Part 1 (London, 1947), pp. 212–13; MAF, *Agricultural Statistics 1950–1, England and Wales*, Part 1 (London, 1954), pp. 78–9; MAFF, *Agricultural Statistics, England 1978/79* (London, 1981), pp. 80–3. Note that for 1939 and 1951, 'regular male and female' totals are used for the whole-time labour force, and 'casual workers' for the part-time and casual labour force. For 1978, 'regular whole-time family and hired workers, male and female' totals are used for the whole-time labour force, and for the part-time and casual, the total of 'regular part-time and seasonal or casual, family and hired, male and female'.

better for them to go and get trained because if I tell them they won't listen to me." They'd listen to some professional from outside the farm, ATB, merchants, and so on.' Some workers stayed on the same farm for most of their working lives. On farm 3/1, a Blackmore Vale dairy farm, 'We only ever had one full-time worker, … He was with us for forty years …', and not far away on farm 7/8 'we were down to two men – … and … – and the family in 1965. … is still alive – he's eighty-four in August. They both worked their whole working lives on [this] farm.' For some workers, however, the fall in the employed labour force meant that they increasingly worked on their own, with, in a few cases, potentially tragic results. On farm 2/7, a much bigger farm, 'we had a lot of little dairies all over the place, and in 1977 the chap who was milking the cows up at … tried to commit suicide, and that opened my eyes to the fact that it was a very isolated spot up there'.

By the late 1960s, it was generally accepted that farm workers might be both pushed and pulled out of agriculture. The push factors were mechanisation, specialisation, and farm amalgamation. Mechanisation in particular took some of the need for simple physical strength out of farming, as farmer 209 observed:

> If you went back seventy or eighty years a big farm could have twenty staff because the materials handling was enormous. It was better than being a miner, because you were working in decent air, but you were shovelling as many tons. I can remember carrying corn in sheaves … And as far as machinery is concerned, the thing that's transformed

everything is hydraulics, right up to a telescopic loader, we do everything with them, they're wonderful, it affects materials handling, ploughing – hydraulic instead of hand-draulic ... Electricity's another one. A lot of the materials handling you couldn't do without electricity.

A study of the structure of the farm labour force revealed that 19.4 per cent of hired and family workers were under twenty-one years old in 1970. It was clear that many young people went into agriculture after leaving school but then left when they were in their twenties, had acquired some skills, and had greater income needs as they began to think about starting a family. The pull of higher wages, better housing conditions, and shorter hours in urban, or at least non-agricultural, occupations then began to be felt, especially when unemployment levels were low, as they often were in the 1950s and '60s. By 1969, only 27 per cent of all holdings in the UK were still employing full-time hired workers.[9] Very often, it was not so much that farm workers were dismissed or made redundant, but rather that they were not replaced when they left the farm. The experience of farm 193 in north Devon encapsulates the story: 'The labour force got up to five men plus my father in the late 1940s and '50s, on the 220 acres. Some moved on, some retired, they weren't all replaced, we took on a little more machinery and made do with a little less labour.' There was a similar process on farm 466 in Cornwall:

> At one stage when there was a lot of potato planting we were up to eleven men, and by 1965 we were down to five men and a boy, and we had quite a lot of pigs then, and it stayed that way ... The farm labour force dropped off by natural wastage.

On farm 272, the employed worker effectively became a part-timer as far as their farm was concerned, although he remained a full-time agricultural worker: 'In the war it was father and one man from outside the family, ... We had ... for many years, he was here when we were married, and then we started giving him less work and he worked on another farm for a couple of days a week.'

There were, however, examples of simple financial pressures resulting in the reduction of the farm labour force, as on farm 2/7, where nineteen people were employed in 1945:

> By 1968 we were down to nine workers, which then went down more slowly, to about six in 1984. ... I had to sack three or four people, when I was feeling the pinch and trying not to spend so much on labour. There

[9] K. Cowling, D. Metcalf, and A.J. Rayner, *Resource Structure of Agriculture: An Economic Analysis* (Oxford, 1970), pp. 57–64; R. Gasson, 'Resources in Agriculture: Labour', in A. Edwards and A. Rogers (eds), *Agricultural Resources: An Introduction to the Farming Industry of the United Kingdom* (London, 1974), pp. 116–25.

was a tendency to keep people on until they were sixty-five, I remember one man who was only capable of doing the very simple jobs, and I had to give him the push.

The fact that hired workers left agriculture more rapidly than farmers and family workers inevitably meant that labour productivity rose more quickly on the larger farms where they formed a greater proportion of the labour force. One estimate found that the average annual growth in labour productivity (including farmer labour) in UK agriculture between 1954 and 1964 was 5.1 per cent, compared with 2.7 per cent in the construction industry and 1.9 per cent in all manufacturing.[10] It also inevitably meant that farmers and their families formed an increasing proportion of the labour force as time went on. By 1974, farmers formed 44.7 per cent of the regularly employed whole-time labour force on English farms as a whole, and by 1983 more than half of it, although this figure varied considerably from one area to another, as table 7.2 demonstrates.[11] It should be noted that the data in table 7.2 refers only to the full-time labour force.

TABLE 7.2. The full-time labour force on farms in 1974

	Hired	Family	Farmers, partners, and directors	Total full-time labour	Farmers etc. as a % of the total full-time labour force	Farmers etc. plus family workers as a % of the total full-time labour force
England	144,465	34,631	144,616	323,712	44.7	55.4
Cornwall	2,510	1,570	6,384	10,464	61.0	76.0
Devon	4,185	2,343	9,939	16,467	60.4	74.6
Dorset	3,021	627	2,581	6,229	41.4	51.5
Lincolnshire	11,993	1,429	6,882	20,304	33.9	40.9
Norfolk	10,528	1,136	5,076	16,740	30.3	37.1

Source: MAFF, *Agricultural Statistics, England and Wales, 1974* (London, 1976), pp. 96–9.

Adding in the part-time and casual labour force complicates the picture considerably, as a comparison of the full-time and part-time figures in

[10] K. Dexter, 'Productivity in Agriculture', in J. Ashton and S.J. Rogers (eds), *Economic Change and Agriculture* (Edinburgh, 1967) pp. 69, 77–8.
[11] Grigg, *English Agriculture*, p. 146.

table 7.1 demonstrates. The non-full-time part of the labour force changed at a different rate from the full-time workers, but the variability of their employment made it very difficult to assess the impact of the changes over time. While a farmer's wife in Cornwall may have spent a roughly similar time each day working on the farm, a casual worker in Lincolnshire might have spent two or three weeks each year picking potatoes for about six hours per day, and then not worked on a farm at all for the rest of the year. Both would count in the labour statistics as a single part-time or casual worker. The students employed for the whole year on farm 243 might be difficult to classify, because they were not permanently employed on the farm, but worked full time while they were there: 'We had one student a year, from about the last week in August and change over the following year. We made them do every mortal thing.' Farm 101, in Devon, continued to employ casual labour for relief milking into the 1980s, and farmer 535 recalled employing two or three harvest casual workers in the 1950s for stooking and carting, whereas straw bale carting and stacking, one of the common casual jobs in the arable areas of eastern England in the 1960s, gradually disappeared as new machinery became available. It therefore makes more sense to restrict the statistics to the full-time labour force in order compare like with like across different counties.

As would be expected, the conclusion from this comparison, as table 7.2 shows, is that the smaller farms of Devon and Cornwall were far more reliant on the labour of the farmer, and of the farmer's family, which on average formed about 15 per cent of the labour force in those two counties, than the bigger farms of Lincolnshire and Norfolk, which still employed significant numbers of hired full-time workers in 1974. The farms of Dorset, however, fell between these two extremes, and there is little doubt that a still more detailed geographical division would show that the small dairy farms in the Blackmore Vale in that county were closer to Devon, while the big arable farms on the chalk were more like Norfolk, in terms of the balance of farmer, family, and hired labour. There were numerous examples of family replacing hired labour, as on farm 2/9 in Dorset: 'Originally we had three men plus my father, then in 1973 we had one man ... plus my brother and me ... It wasn't a deliberate policy to replace employed by family labour, but it sort of happened.' And on farm 787 in north Devon: 'Father had two men when he started, and now it's me and my brother, and my son's home at the moment.' It was never too early to begin work on the farm, as farmer 243 remembered: 'when I was about six or seven I used to have to milk two [cows, by hand] before I went to school'. The difficulty of discerning the complexity of farm labour arrangements from variations and changes in national official statistics is well-illustrated by the evolution of the workforce on farm 782:

> I left school in 1954, before that father employed a local boy, then I became the boy until I took over in 1970, then we had casual labour

to help with potatoes at busy times, but tried to keep labour to a minimum. Father was only in [the local small town] so he used to see what was going on but he was good at letting me do what I wanted to do. My sister also worked on the farm when she left school in 1957, working a bit of indoors and a bit outside, it was a bit more of the norm in those days, she was there until she married in 1964, a farmer down at [another local small town].

The importance of the contribution made by unmarried daughters is also illustrated on farm 570, where 'My sister looked after the poultry when she left school, along with Mum, but there had always been poultry on the farm because Dad's sister always looked after the poultry, ... they all lived on the farm until they got married.' The changes on farm 744, in south Devon, show not only family labour replacing hired labour, but also the importance of specialist contractors:

> We employed at least three men to start with [in the late 1940s], but then as labour got dearer and the agricultural engineers and scientists got better methods for us, the labour steadily went, in the end it was down to me and [my son], with the help of a good contractor.

Contractors were important for small dairy farms, for the corn harvest in the 1950s and '60s, and later for silage and spraying. They could afford big specialist machinery that would have been under-employed on small farms. On farm 782, where there were a few acres of cereals in the 1950s and '60s, 'The combine would have come from a contractor. ... There were several contractors – ... of Ashton, they did a lot of combining in the 1950s, latterly ... at Christow did a lot for us.' The Christow contractor worked on his own in the 1970s and had a JCB digger with which he did a lot of work in the winter, and a combine harvester that was employed over several of the neighbouring parishes during the corn harvest.

For the historian, there is an additional problem: the annual agricultural census only began to record the number of farmers, partners, and directors from 1970 onwards, so that there is no consistent data source for the whole period from 1939 to 1985 for this crucial variable. As Gasson argues, a rough estimate of the number of farmers can be deduced by assuming that there would be one for each holding.[12] Not all holdings are used for agriculture, and some farms consist of multiple holdings, so the equivalence cannot be completely accurate, although if we can assume that the extent to which these variations occur does not change significantly we can use holding numbers to demonstrate the trends in numbers of farmers. There is a bigger problem in dealing with those who had an alternative source of income or did not work full time on their farms. In 1955, the Ministry of Agriculture defined a full-time farm as one with a

---

[12] Gasson, 'Resources in Agriculture: Labour', p. 109.

labour requirement of 275 Standard Man Days (SMDs), and a Ministry of Agriculture survey in 1958 found that nearly half of all holdings were part time according to this standard.[13] Twenty years later, the number of part-time holdings in England as a whole and in the three south-western counties had fallen to about 24 per cent of the total.[14] The data in table 7.3 therefore assumes that all holdings under five acres or two hectares will be part time, and accepts that many of those over this size will also be part time.

TABLE 7.3. Holdings and farmers in England and the three south-western counties, 1939–78

	1939 holdings over five acres	1950 holdings over five acres	1979 holdings over two hectares	1978 full-time and part-time principal farmers, partners, and directors
England	250,055	247,633	152,693	144,458
3SW	29,048	29,935	21,538	20,427

Source: MAF, *Agricultural Statistics 1939–44*, part 1, pp. 198–9; MAF, *Agricultural Statistics 1950–1*, p. 70; MAFF, *Agricultural Statistics, England 1978/79*, pp. 48 and 84.

Comparing the 1979 and 1978 figures for holding and farmer numbers in this table shows that the number of farmers is about 5 per cent less than the number of holdings, a discrepancy that was also found (and explained) in the 1958 survey.[15] The important conclusion that can be drawn from table 7.3 is that the number of farmers declined between 1950 and 1979, but that it declined less in the south-west (by 28 per cent) than in England as a whole (where it declined by 38 per cent). It seems likely that many of those leaving agriculture were on small or part-time holdings. For the present discussion, what needs to be emphasised is that, as tables 7.1 and 7.3 show, employed labour decreased a lot in the thirty years after 1950, while farmer and family labour decreased too, but to a lesser extent. It is worth remembering that this was not a purely UK phenomenon. In fact, the UK already had a relatively low agricultural population in 1939 and 1950, and whereas the average annual loss of agricultural labour in the UK was 1.73 per cent between 1950 and 1985, in western Europe as a whole it was 3.14 per cent. In Germany, the active agricultural population

---

[13] J. Ashton and B.E. Cracknell, 'Agricultural Holdings and Farm Business Structure in England and Wales', *J. Agric. Econs.* 14 (1961), pp. 472–506.
[14] MAFF, *Agricultural Statistics, England 1978/79*, p. 84.
[15] Ashton and Cracknell, 'Agricultural Holdings and Farm Business Structure'.

fell from more than five million to less than 1.5 million between 1950 and 1982; in France, it fell from more than six million to less than two million in the same period; and in western Europe as a whole from 16.3 million to 5.4 million in 1982, almost exactly one-third of the 1950 figure.[16]

Technical change, in other words, helped to push labour out of agriculture and also allowed farmers to compensate for the labour that was pulled out of the industry. The extent to which it did so can be judged by comparing the standard labour requirements for various agricultural tasks listed in publications from 1945 and 1981.

TABLE 7.4. Labour requirements for crops and livestock in 1945 and 1981

	1945	1981
Crops	SMDs per acre	
Cereals	6	1
Potatoes	30	9
Roots (folded)	12	2
Livestock	SMDs per head	
Dairy Cows (cowshed)	18	7
Dairy Cows (parlour)	N/A	5
Ewes	1	0.5

Source: J.A.S. Watson and J.A. More, *Agriculture: The Science and Practice of Farming* (Edinburgh, 1945), p. 759; J. Nix, *Farm Management Pocketbook* (Ashford, 1981), p. 143. The 1945 figures are expressed in 'Man Labour-Days', which are slightly longer than the Standard Man Days used in 1981.

Some of these are listed in table 7.4 and illustrate the extent to which labour requirements could fall over this period. An alternative estimate by John Nix suggested that labour hours per acre fell by eight times in the case of cereals, and fivefold for potatoes, between 1950 and 1983.[17] The change was clearly greater for crops, for which the labour required fell by a factor of between three and six, whereas for livestock it was generally between two and three. There are no figures for parlour-milked dairy cows in 1945 because, as we saw in chapter 5, very few cows were milked through a parlour until later. The impact of these changes on farms in the FMS sample is shown in figure 7.1. The analysis of farm accounts did not record actual labour numbers for each farm but did record total labour

[16] M. Martín-Retortillo and V. Pinilla, 'Patterns and Causes of the Growth of European Agricultural Production, 1950 to 2005', *Agric. Hist. Rev.* 63 (2015), pp. 147, 152.
[17] Grigg, *English Agriculture*, p. 164.

The Real Agricultural Revolution

costs. Using labour cost data, we can estimate the full-time equivalent labour requirements (FTEs) on each farm, and as figure 7.1 shows, this decreased over time. This is what would be expected, although it should be remembered that the graph shows FTEs per acre, and the stocking rate was increasing, so that two trends – technical change and intensification – are working against each other in this variable. The trend was the same for both dairy and non-dairy farms in the sample, although dairy farms always employed more FTEs per acre, as figure 7.2 demonstrates. The result was that the level of output per £100 of labour cost fell as labour use intensified in the wartime and immediate post-war years, then rose, at first rapidly and then more steadily, until the mid-1970s, when it was probably rising labour costs per hour that pushed the trend down, as figure 7.3 shows. In short, one effect of the technical changes discussed in chapter 5 was to increase farm labour productivity, at least until the mid-1970s, and also to enable those farmers who employed labour to manage their farms with fewer people earning higher wages (although not usually as high as in other industries).

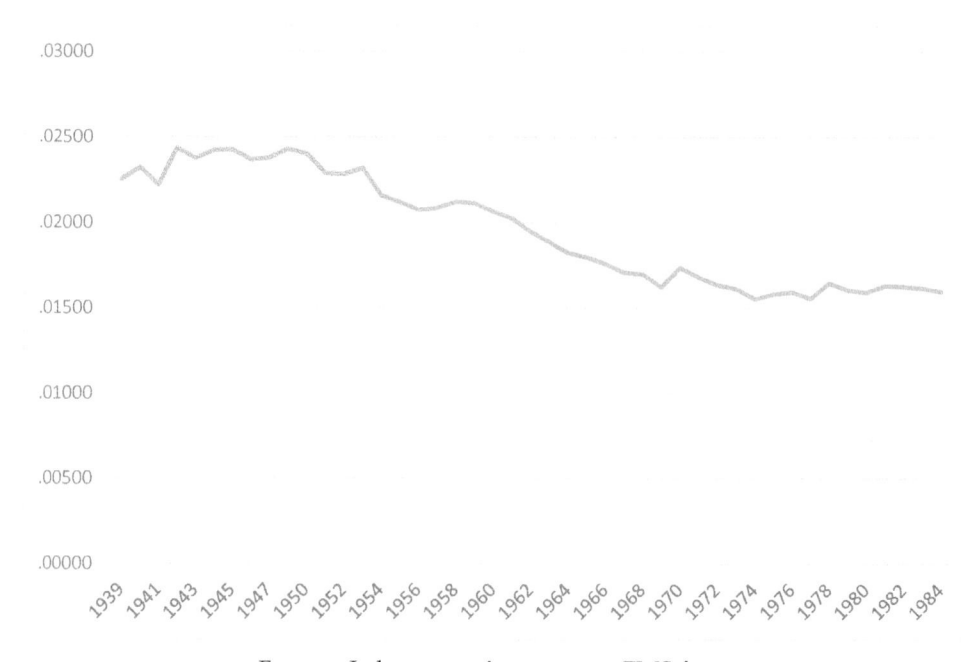

Fig. 7.1. Labour requirements on FMS farms

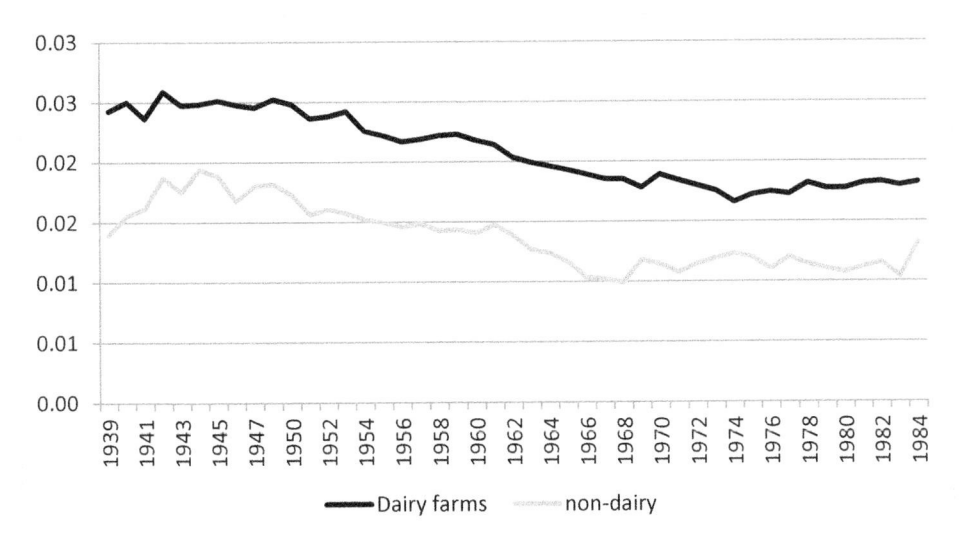

FIG. 7.2. Labour requirements (estimated FTEs) on dairy and non-dairy farms

FIG. 7.3. Output per £100 of labour cost on FMS farms

Machinery

As previous chapters have suggested, it is impossible to explain the decrease in labour numbers in agriculture without reference to technical change. We have already examined the technical changes that were especially important in dairy farming, such as the adoption of the milking machine, the replacement of hay by silage, and the change from cowsheds to parlours and cubicles, but there were other technical changes, relevant to agriculture as a whole, that affected the farms in the FMS sample. They are discussed here under the heading of 'machinery', but, as we shall see, it was not only mechanical changes that enabled farmers to economise on or reduce labour.

In 1939, most farm work was powered by the muscles of people and horses; in 1985, most of the power came from electricity and diesel engines. Despite the landgirls-on-tractors images in wartime propaganda photographs, there were about ten times as many horses on British farms in 1940 as there were tractors.[18] An agricultural textbook written at the end of the 1940s, while admitting that tractors could do 'as well or better than a team of horses', argued that 'it is not usually economic to replace all horses by tractors. There are some jobs which horses do particularly well, especially light haulage work involving frequent stops ... most farmers find it advisable to keep at least one or two horses'.[19] South-western farmers seem to have agreed with this. In a sample of twenty farms in Devon and Cornwall in the FMS sample analysed for this book, seventeen already had tractors by 1950. On ten farms, their tractors had been bought during the war. But all twenty still had horses at the end of the war, and several bought new horse equipment, such as harness or horse hoes, during the war. Even a relatively small farm such as farm 162, with 132 acres on the edge of Exmoor, could keep five horses at one point during the war. Ten years after the war ended, thirteen of the sample were still using horses. The average gap between acquiring the first tractor and dispensing with the last horse was about eighteen years. The last of them, a horse called Derby, was on farm 669, near Holsworthy, until 1967, and the way in which he was used was probably typical:

> We kept horses until 1967. That was when Derby died, that was the last carthorse we had. We had a tractor right from the war years. The tractor did the cutting of the grass, but the horses did the turning and raking and worked the elevator when they used to sweep it in and put it up with grabs, pulled by the horse. We were still doing that, perhaps

[18] Ministry of Information, *Land at War: The Official Story of British Farming 1939–44* (London, 1945), p. 43; P. Brassley, 'Output and Technical Change in Twentieth-Century British Agriculture', *Agric. Hist. Rev.* 48 (2000), p. 74.

[19] D.H. Robinson (ed.), *Fream's Elements of Agriculture* (13th edn, London, 1949), p. 87.

tedding a bit, in the 1960s. The rake was never changed to go with a tractor, although the turner was converted to drawbar, but the other stuff still had shafts.

In the late 1940s and the 1950s, the number of farm horses declined dramatically, while the use of tractors increased correspondingly. By the early 1950s, there were as many tractors as horses, and by 1960 nearly ten times as many. The new tractors were also more powerful, so that the average horsepower of farm tractors increased from 22hp per tractor in 1947 to about 40hp per tractor in 1965; more flexible, because they had rubber tyres rather than the earlier metal wheels; and, through the development of the three-point linkage and live power take-off, more capable.[20] There were only one hundred combine harvesters in Britain in 1939, and farmers (such as 139 and 209) were still buying new binders during the war, but the number of binders in the UK peaked in about 1950, while the number of combines reached something like its present level in 1960, although of course modern machines are much bigger, faster, and more powerful than those of the 1950s. The 1950s also saw the widespread adoption of the baler.[21] These are just the machines for which figures are readily available. There were certainly others that had a significant impact on farm labour requirements. In 1950, for example, there were fewer than a thousand tractor-mounted fore-end loaders on English farms, whereas by 1958 there were nearly fifty thousand.[22] In the 1940s, on farm 570 in north Devon, when there was farmyard manure to be spread, a farm worker who 'was here ever such long hours, all day long, and he took the dung out with a horse and cart in the winter and tipped it in little heaps fifteen yards apart, and then he went out with his dung fork and spread it, and he spread it beautifully'. It had probably been done that way for centuries. By 1958, there were nearly sixty thousand tractor-drawn farmyard manure spreaders – muckspreaders – on English farms.[23] This is not to say that manure handling was completely mechanised by this time. There were still many livestock buildings dating from earlier periods into which it was impossible to get a tractor with a fore-end loader, and consequently still many hours to be spent by farm workers with dung forks loading trailers and muckspreaders, but it gives some idea of the trend and the way in which mechanisation was increasingly replacing hand labour, so that farm workers who retired or moved out of agriculture could be replaced.

[20] Brassley, 'Output and Technical Change', p. 74; Cowling et al., *Resource Structure of Agriculture*, p. 97.
[21] Brassley, 'Output and Technical Change', p. 75.
[22] MAF, *Agricultural Statistics 1950–1, England and Wales*, Part 1, p. 81; MAFF, *Agricultural Statistics 1958–59, England and Wales*, p. 80.
[23] MAFF, *Agricultural Statistics 1958–59, England and Wales*, p. 80.

There were, however, implications for small farms. As farmer 209, who began with thirty-five acres, pointed out:

> I realised that you had to have a larger amount of land to earn a living off, but also to warrant buying the tractors and machinery, spreading costs over a bigger acreage, those people who think farms shouldn't have got bigger aren't thinking it through, because as soon as tractors replaced horses, and bigger tractors replaced smaller tractors, you had to have more land to warrant buying that gear and fully use it.

The other technical change that decreased the demand for field labour was the development of pesticides, and in particular of herbicides. Whereas insecticides and fungicides, by protecting crops from damage, increased yields, herbicides had the additional benefit of saving the labour previously expended in weeding, either by hand or by using a hoe drawn by a horse or tractor. The 1919 edition of McConnell's *Agricultural Notebook* asserted that 'from a third to a half of the field labour on a farm is devoted to the destruction of growing weeds', and while it was unlikely to be as much as this on south-western farms, with their higher proportion of grassland, the figure gives some idea of the potential savings in labour that could result from using herbicides.[24] Not only did they keep cereal crops cleaner, but they also removed the need to grow the labour-intensive root crops that were hitherto the easiest point in the rotation to do the hoeing. As we saw when discussing dairy cow diets, the root acreage fell dramatically in the 1950s and '60s. Selective herbicides for use on cereals, such as 2,4-D and MCPA, were developed in the 1940s, although it took longer for them to be widely adopted by farmers. Precisely how long is difficult to say, because there were no official statistics on their use before 1970. One estimate suggests that 65 per cent of the UK cereal acreage was treated with herbicides by the late 1960s, and most of it by 1975. UK herbicide production trebled between 1961 and 1967, but some of these products were exported rather than being used at home.[25] Overall, however, it is clear that chemicals assisted mechanisation in progressively reducing the need for human and horse muscular activity on farms after the war.

Conclusions

It is possible, if not always easy, to quantify changes in mechanisation, chemical use, and labour numbers, and the outlines of the story are clear enough: a decline in the numbers of full-time non-family workers, less of

[24] P. McConnell, *Notebook of Agricultural Facts and Figures for Farmers and Farm Students* (9th edn, London, 1919), p. 278.
[25] Brassley, 'Output and Technical Change', pp. 68–9; Grigg, *English Agriculture*, p. 74; Cowling et al., *Resource Structure of Agriculture*, p. 138.

a decline in part-time and casual labour, greater reliance on the labour of the farmers and their families; a variety of reasons for the changes; and the replacement of labour by machinery and chemicals, the timing of which was often associated with family dynamics, especially a change in the generation in charge.

It is less easy to quantify the changes required in the farmers and farm workers who remained in agriculture. To the casual outside observer, farm work might sometimes appear to be a matter of simple unskilled labour. Forking manure into a cart or stacking bales on a trailer doesn't look too complicated. But try forking manure for eight hours at a stretch or building a load of bales that will not fall off when the trailer sways along bumpy roads, and it soon becomes clear that there are very few totally unskilled jobs. Moreover, the nature of the skills required by farmers and farm workers changed rapidly over the post-war period. People who had grown up in their teens developing skills with horses in the 1930s might, by the time they retired in the 1980s, be injecting veterinary medicines, maintaining complex machinery, and calculating spray rates for herbicides. Speaking on the radio in 1942, one well-informed observer felt that 'farmers of the last generation had the knack of horsemanship … It will take a few more generations of mechanical power before farmers have the same instinct for tractors and tractor implements.'[26] In the event, one generation seems to have been enough.

'Ah, you should see Cynddylan on a tractor. / Gone the old look that yoked him to the soil; / he's a new man now, part of the machine', wrote the Welsh priest-poet R.S. Thomas in 1952, but in many cases his novelty might have been exaggerated.[27] Although the horse was being replaced by the tractor as the source of power, farmers and their workers had been used to working with a range of machinery since the nineteenth century at least: drills, fertiliser distributors, horse-hoes, mowers, hay tedders, rakes, horse-powered elevators, reaper-binders; several if not all of them could be found on most farms. They were initially designed to be pulled by horses, although they could be converted for a tractor, and the farm labour force was accustomed to maintaining them. As others have argued, there was a difference between mechanisation and motorisation.[28] The steam engine, which transformed nineteenth-century

[26] Anon, *Farming Today Broadcasts: A Series of Agricultural Education and Technical Development Broadcast Talks* (Worcester, 1942), p. 80.
[27] The poem was first published in R.S. Thomas, *An Acre of Land* (Newtown, Montgomery, 1952), and reprinted in *Penguin Modern Poets I* (Harmondsworth, 1962), p. 97.
[28] J. Auderset and P. Moser, 'Mechanisation and Motorisation: Natural Resources, Knowledge, Politics and Technology in 19th- and 20th-Century Agriculture', in C. Martiin, J. Pan-Montojo, and P. Brassley (eds), *Agriculture in Capitalist Europe, 1945–1960: From Food Shortages to Food Surpluses* (London, 2016), pp. 145–64.

urban industry, was ill-suited to work in the fields, but animal-powered machinery was widely adopted in north-west Europe. According to one estimate, eighty thousand reaping machines were cutting over half of the British corn harvest by 1874.[29] Although the number of tractors increased rapidly during and after the Second World War, there was a long period, from the 1920s to the 1960s, in which they coexisted with horses as the sources of power on UK farms, by which time the farm labour force had had the experience of several generations of working with machinery.[30]

Nevertheless, younger people probably took to tractors and other forms of technical change more easily than older workers. Farmer 535, who remembers ploughing with horses, was also the main tractor driver on his father's farm and compares his acquisition of facility with tractors to that of modern children with computers. Farmer 466 reflects on the same process:

> Father never properly retired. He used to look after the grazing young stock, which was very useful, until he got into his eighties, he was born in 07, so we're talking about 1987, so by that time he said 'I don't know what you're on about now, I can't cope with it', and there was a period when we could each go away for holidays and leave the other in charge, because his years were coming up again and the technology was getting beyond him, so having been a technical leader in the 1950s there came a time when he couldn't cope with it, and that will happen to all of us, won't it? Father was brought up in the horse age but learned to live with the internal combustion engine; I was brought up with the internal combustion engine but have learned to live with the computer. Not much better than that.

In part, coping with change was a matter of training, which has been discussed in chapter 3. Nevertheless, the capacity of the general run of farmers and farm workers to adapt to new methods required more than the occasional ATB course, even if they had the time to go to it. It is impossible to quantify, but it was clearly a significant component in the process of technical change. It was probably helped by the trend towards specialisation; the range of new skills required on a specialist dairy farm would be less than that needed on a mixed farm. The specialisation of farming will therefore be investigated in the following chapter.

---

[29] E.J.T. Collins, 'Labour Supply and Demand in European Agriculture 1800–1880', in E.L. Jones and S.J. Woolf (eds), *Agrarian Change and Economic Development: The Historical Problems* (London, 1969), p. 75.
[30] F. McWilliams, 'Equine Machines: Horses and Tractors on British Farms c.1920–1970' (unpublished Ph.D. thesis, King's College, London, 2020).

8

Specialisation and Expansion

In the 1940s and '50s, many English farms were small, although not as small as those of continental Europe (even in 1970, the average farm size in the six original members of the European Union was only 31.4 acres). Cornish farms were especially small; the National Farm Survey of 1941–2 revealed that 82 per cent of them were of less than one hundred acres, compared with 71 per cent in Devon and 64 per cent in Dorset.[1] Over the following three decades, they grew in size, and whereas the average size of a holding in England and Wales in 1944 was 81.7 acres, by 1983 it was 155.3 acres.[2] The size of an average dairy herd grew to an even greater extent, from fifteen cows in 1942 to sixty-seven cows in 1985, as table 5.1 reveals, so it logically follows that farms that remained as milk producers must have specialised and dispensed with some enterprises in order to concentrate on dairy farming. This, as we shall see, resulted in the more effective use of capital equipment and made it easier for farmers and their workers to keep up to date with changing technologies, and to some extent resulted from the desire to achieve these desirable outcomes. This chapter examines these changes in farm size and the process of specialisation.

Farm Size Changes

As table 8.1 shows, the decrease in the number of holdings over time was not evenly spread over the various different farm size groups. It was the smaller farms that tended to go, while the number of farms with more than one hundred acres increased. This applied to the structure of farming in the three south-western counties as much as to the national picture. By 1974, Cornwall still had more than the national average number of farms of less than one hundred acres, but the number of sub-fifty-acre farms

---

[1] D.K. Britton, 'The Structure of Agriculture', in A. Edwards and A. Rogers (eds), *Agricultural Resources: An Introduction to the Farming Industry of the United Kingdom* (London, 1974), p. 23; Ministry of Agriculture and Fisheries, *National Farm Survey of England and Wales (1941–1943): A Summary Report* (London, 1946), p. 92.
[2] D. Grigg, *English Agriculture: An Historical Perspective* (Oxford, 1989), p. 113.

had decreased considerably since 1950. In Devon and Dorset, where there were fewer sub-fifty-acre farms, but more fifty- to one hundred-acre farms than the national average in 1950, it was the smaller farms that disappeared and those with more than 100 acres that grew in number.

TABLE 8.1. Percentages of farms in different size groups, 1950–74

	5–49 acres %	50–99 acres %	100–299 acres %	Over 300 acres %	Total number of holdings
England 1950	52.0	19.7	23.3	5.0	247,633
England 1974	40.5	20.8	28.1	10.7	158,507
Cornwall 1950	61.9	21.3	16.2	0.7	11,218
Cornwall 1974	47.8	24.2	24.6	3.5	7,604
Devon 1950	45.8	26.0	26.9	1.3	14,845
Devon 1974	37.6	26.0	32.3	4.1	11,604
Dorset 1950	44.1	21.1	26.4	8.4	3,872
Dorset 1974	35.1	21.4	29.3	14.3	2,832

Source: MAF, *Agricultural Statistics 1950–1, England and Wales*, Part 1 (London, 1954), pp. 70–1; MAFF, *Agricultural Statistics, England and Wales, 1974* (London, 1976), pp. 58–9.

By the late 1950s, the Ministry of Agriculture was growing increasingly concerned about the preponderance of small farms and the question of whether it was affecting the efficiency of the industry. One effect of this was the recognition that measuring the size of a farm in acres did not necessarily reflect the size of the business that it could support. A few acres entirely devoted to the production of pigs or eggs, with all their feedstuffs purchased from outside, could produce far more sales than a wide expanse of moorland needing several acres to support a single ewe. The concept of the SMD was therefore developed as a measure of farm size, measuring it by the estimated labour requirement. Each sow needed four SMDs per year, each ewe 0.5 SMDs, and each cow eight SMDs per year if milked in a cowshed (but only five if milked in a parlour). An acre of cereals needed three SMDs.[3] Adding together the SMDs required for the cropping and stocking of the whole farm gave a measure of its size. A small farm was therefore seen as one that provided 275 SMDs per year, which was about the amount of work that one person could do. Up to six hundred SMDs needed two people, and over 1,200 required at least four. This system also gave a rough measure of the output of the farm, so adding together the figures for all the farms in the country gave an indication of which farms were responsible for most of the output. Table 8.2 shows the result of this exercise when the Ministry of Agriculture carried out an assessment of the significance of farms in the different size groups in terms of production.

TABLE 8.2. Distribution of holdings and SMDs among size groups in England and Wales in 1965

Size group (SMDs)	% of all holdings	% of total SMDs	% of full-time dairy holdings	% of dairy SMDs
Over 1,200	11	49	15	35
600–1,199	18	27	37	39
275–599	22	17	48	26
Under 275	49	7	–	–

Source: MAFF, *The Structure of Agriculture* (London, 1966), pp. 9, 12.

It revealed that the largest 29 per cent of holdings were responsible for all but 24 per cent of the total output: 'about half of the industry's total output is produced by the 42,000 large farms [in the UK as a whole] which are capable of providing employment for at least four men'.[4] Although nearly half of all holdings were classified as part time (i.e. with less than 275 SMDs), they were virtually insignificant in production terms.

In the same report, the Ministry also examined the distribution of output among the 156,200 full-time holdings (those with more than 275 SMDs) in England and Wales. Of these, 60,800 were classified as dairy holdings, in that more than 50 per cent of their SMDs derived from dairying (compare this figure with over one hundred thousand registered milk producers at the same time – see table 5.1). In fact, about half of these had at least 75 per cent of their total SMDs in dairy farming. As table 8.2 shows, the large (over 1,200 SMD) farms were less significant in dairy farming than in agriculture as a whole, with the small and medium-sized

---

[3] J. Nix, *Farm Management Pocketbook* (9th edn, Ashford, 1978), p. 139.
[4] MAFF, *The Structure of Agriculture*, p. 4.

groups being correspondingly more so.⁵ It seems likely that dairy output on part-time farms would have been more significant than it was in agriculture as a whole, but the report provided no data on these sub-275 SMD dairy holdings.

Another result of the Ministry's concern over small farms and the structure of agriculture was an increased interest in the relationship between size and efficiency in farming. A grant scheme, the 1959 Small Farmer Scheme, had already been introduced to encourage small farmers, defined as those with between twenty and one hundred acres of crops and grass and an SMD total exceeding 275 after the completion of the scheme, to carry out an approved improvement plan to increase profitability (and almost certainly the size of the business).⁶ In 1961, the Office of the Minister for Science took an interest in the subject when the Natural Resources (Technical) Committee set up a Steering Group on Scale of Enterprise. It concluded that costs per £100 of output were greater on small farms (defined as those with less than one hundred acres), largely because of the costs of family labour, but that there were considerable differences between different farm types and that economies of scale did not seem to be evident on farms over four hundred or five hundred acres.⁷ This was the first of a series of studies of the changing structure of agriculture and the relationship between size and efficiency in the industry. The Ministry produced studies of agricultural structure in 1966, 1970, and 1977, and by the early 1970s structural data was regularly reported in the annual agriculture White Paper.⁸ A detailed study of the size/efficiency relationship found 'a kind of "threshold" somewhere between the two-man and three-man size of farm business, and if that size is not attained it is likely that resources, particularly labour, are not being effectively used'.⁹ This conclusion appeared to hold true for the period from the mid-1950s, and later studies confirmed it, but, as one of its authors later argued,

> the notion of efficiency improving with size of farm is of little concern to the farmer; what he is interested in is the profits which can be earned, and he will wish to expand if by doing so his total rewards

---

5   MAFF, *The Structure of Agriculture*, p. 12.
6   S.P. Bingham, *A Guide to the Development of Grants for Agriculture and Horticulture for England and Wales 1940–1982* (London, no date, probably 1982), p. 73.
7   Natural Resources (Technical) Committee. Committee on Agriculture, *Scale of Enterprise in Farming* (London, 1961), p. 64. The Committee was chaired by Professor Ellison, professor of crop husbandry at the University of Aberystwyth.
8   Ministry of Agriculture, Fisheries and Food, *The Changing Structure of Agriculture, 1968–1975* (London, 1977), p. 4.
9   D.K. Britton and B. Hill, *Size and Efficiency in Farming* (Farnborough, 1975), p. 175.

are increased. The efficiency of a farm is usually expressed in terms of the ratio between the value of its output and the value of the resources it uses. The income of the farmer is, however, the difference between these two values ... Efficiency is incidental to structural change, not its driving force.[10]

Farmers thus had an incentive to increase the size of their farm businesses, but if that required more land it was not always easily achieved. It was easier to increase the size of an enterprise, even at the expense of decreasing the size of other enterprises or discontinuing them altogether.

Enterprise Size Changes

Farming is a risky business. The sources of risk may be weather, disease, the market, simple bad luck, or a complex mixture of all four, but many farmers implicitly insured against the risk that one enterprise might fail by operating several. Thus if the cows got foot and mouth disease they could still make some money from the cereals, and if cereal prices went through the floor the pigs might be profitable. Moreover, concentrating on one enterprise made it difficult to find a rotation, whereas the classic rotations were designed to cater for several enterprises and in doing so increase the output of each. Thus the Norfolk four-course rotation had two years of different cereals separated by two years of different fodder crops. Mixed farming was about using the resources of the farm and the people who worked on it, and even when mixed cropping no longer made sense, the idea of maintaining several different enterprises to maximise the returns from the available resources could still be worthwhile. The experience of a small farm (782) on the edge of Dartmoor shows how this could be done, in various ways, into the 1980s:

> Father didn't like too many cows, but we used to keep sheep, and pigs and poultry, so it was much more of a mixed farm, a little bit of everything from the 1940s to the 1960s. He had a system he was happy with and he carried on with that. He even had a field of corn, which I dropped, because I didn't think it was profitable, so it was very much a mixed farm. We used to keep a few pigs, bought as eight-week-old pigs and sold as pork, because we used to make cream as well, and the skimmed milk from that was ideal for the pigs, so we did that for several years, feeding the skim with bought in barley meal. Father sold a little bit of cream, but we increased that side of it. It was clotted cream, we had our own electric separator to separate the skim from the cream, then it was put into a pan which was set into a bigger preserving pan with a couple of inches of water in the bottom, and that would take about a couple of hours, and when it formed a head you would give it

[10] B. Hill and D. Ray, *Economics for Agriculture: Food, Farming and the Rural Economy* (Basingstoke, 1987), p. 245.

a good stir and leave it to form another head, and then take it off and leave it to cool, and there was your clotted cream. We used to sell it in the village, when I delivered potatoes we had cream alongside it. In 1984 when milk quotas came in my wife was keen to do cream teas, so from 1985 she did cream teas, for about eleven years, we had a lot of visitors going past to the reservoirs, and our own homemade strawberry jam, we used to grow some, and buy some strawberries, and that was a nice little sideline, you'd never make a fortune but it was a bit of extra income. Once the quotas were in we had to cut back a bit on the milk we were producing, so we thought we'd try to get a bit higher value for the milk. Father used to make a bit of cream too, and that was where we learned how to do it.

This level of diversification was unusual by the 1980s, but up to the 1960s many farms were mixed to some degree or other. Mixed farming was seen as the traditional system. But it was more than that. It was held to be the *right* system, a system that maintained both soil fertility and employment on the land. This was the view that Astor and Rowntree set out to criticise in their book *Mixed Farming and Muddled Thinking*, published just after the war. It was much more than a simple consideration of alternative farming methods – indeed, it was an argument for a radical change in agricultural policy – but it began with a detailed historically and technically informed critique of mixed farming, and went on to argue that 'specialisation will be able to provide the producers with the large and prosperous agriculture that they are campaigning for', whereas the 'principal advantage' of mixed farming, the insurance it provided against problems with an individual enterprise, would be better provided by various forms of state support.[11]

Then came tractors, more fertilisers, and pesticides. By the 1960s, there was a joke about the new Norfolk four-course rotation: barley, barley, barley, Bermuda. Farms were increasingly specialised, and the old idea of a few pigs in a shed, a few chickens running around the yard, some cereals, a few acres of sugar beet or potatoes, a sheep flock, and a beef herd as well as the cows on a one hundred- or two hundred-acre family holding was disappearing. To set against the idea of risk spreading and rotation, there was the concept of economies of size. If the milking parlour could cope with one hundred cows, it made no sense to keep the herd down to sixty. If the tractor could plough one hundred acres, why restrict it to fifty? Bigger enterprises enabled fixed costs to be spread over a bigger volume of output. This was the view espoused by Dexter and Barber in their *Farming for Profits*, and also by Mac Cooper, a professor of agriculture who could keep a roomful of students awake at 10 o'clock in the morning, and a roomful of farmers from the bar at 10 o'clock at night.

---

[11] Viscount Astor and B. Seebohm Rowntree, *Mixed Farming and Muddled Thinking* (London, 1946), p. 134.

Dismissing the argument that it might be safer not to have all one's eggs in the same basket 'now that we have a system of guaranteed prices for the major commodities', he argued that 'Under present circumstances the greatest safeguard for the individual can come from one main branch of farming in which he is really expert for he will make a living when all the eggs of his diversified neighbours are addled.'[12]

By the 1980s, farmers had grasped this idea for long enough for the results to be measurable from the agricultural statistics. The average number of enterprises per farm fell from 3.18 in 1968 to 2.85 only six years later, and whereas one-third of all the cows were to be found on specialist dairy farms (on which 75 per cent of the SMDs were attributed to dairying) in 1963, the figure was two-thirds in 1977. Another 21 per cent of the cows were on farms with 50 to 75 per cent of the SMDs in dairying, leaving only 13 per cent of cows on non-specialist holdings in 1977.[13] The same trend was apparent in other enterprises.[14] The farm management advisers were pushing the idea of fewer and larger enterprises, and the farmers were taking their advice. Farmer 929, who began farming in the early 1950s on about one hundred acres, and was farming nearly nine hundred acres thirty years later, was asked about the most significant farming changes in his lifetime and replied unhesitatingly:

> Specialisation in particular. In this village in 1950 when I came home farming there were fourteen dairy herds based within the village, and cows were going this way and that way and getting all mixed up. Now there are two dairy herds in the parish. It's a much more specialised and upgraded business scene than it was.

Specialisation is therefore an important dimension of post-war agricultural change, but, as with technical changes, not all farmers saw the point at the same time.

We saw in chapter 5 (see especially the account of dairy cow feeding) that most farms were mixed in the 1940s and '50s. In part, this was inevitable, because most farmers took the view that buying in oats to feed their carthorses or straw for livestock bedding would have been a waste of money when they could grow the oats themselves. Once the horses had gone and the cows were in cubicles, it was no longer so inevitable, but there were still reasons why farmers could maintain several enterprises. One was the availability of labour. Farm 744 was essentially a south Devon dairy farm by the 1970s, but nevertheless some retail income was worthwhile for a time: 'We had a few acres of potatoes into the 1980s. I had two sons home and we had labour to do it, … we used to deliver

---

12 K. Dexter and D. Barber, *Farming for Profits* (London, 1967), pp. 44–6; M.McG. Cooper, *Competitive Farming* (London, 1956), p. 11.
13 Hill and Ray, *Economics for Agriculture*, p. 240.
14 P. Brassley, *Agricultural Economics and the CAP* (Oxford, 1997), p. 70.

them round [the local town] every week, a bit of a time-consuming job.' Some farmers clearly took the view that sons should be kept busy, and that having their own enterprise was the way to do it. On farm 576 in east Cornwall, there was a small poultry enterprise for a time: 'the eggs were to keep me occupied when I came home from school, they were deep litter, there wasn't much margin in it for small quantities'. On other farms, however, such as farm 570 in north Devon, paying the farmer's son very little but allowing him to keep pigs was a way of using youthful energy and enthusiasm to keep down the wage bill in the early 1960s.

It is a truism that poultry were seen by many farmers as an occupation for their wives and daughters, and there were indeed many examples of poultry enterprises that were an important part of the farm business. On farm 570 again:

> My sister looked after the poultry when she left school, along with Mum, but there had always been poultry on the farm because Dad's sister always looked after the poultry, and they had breeding units, they all lived on the farm until they got married. ... My sister wasn't here very long after she left school, about four years, and as soon as she went the poultry went.

Farm 744 also found poultry profitable in the 1950s:

> It doesn't sound much these days but if you kept one hundred birds and they showed you a profit of £1 a bird that was quite something in those days, now it's peanuts, but in those days it was quite a help, and ... my first wife, she was interested in poultry, she'd been to an agricultural college and it was her influence that made me go in for poultry, I didn't know much about it. She mostly did the job.

In some cases, far from just being a few hens scratching around the farmhouse door, the poultry enterprise could grow to a significant size. On the other hand, while admitting that 'Poultry was quite an important part of our enterprise in the early days', one of the larger farmers interviewed, on farm 2/21 in Dorset, was more dismissive:

> I don't think there was any great capital investment in poultry, we were using old buildings, because there was an opportunity of making a buck or two. [My wife] looked after them, it was a farmer's wife job. I've never regarded them as an important part of the business, but it made a few bob.

The history of pigs and poultry is considered in much more detail in the following chapter; the purpose of discussing the examples above is to make the point that the decision to be a mixed farmer or a specialist could be contingent upon the requirements of the whole farm family. When the farm labour force, or a significant part of it, was composed of the family,

Specialisation and Expansion

all of their interests were usually (not inevitably) taken into account. It is also worth remembering that many farming families in the 1940s and '50s expected to live off the resources of the farm to a much greater extent than they would in the 1970s or '80s. As one young farmer's wife on farm 570 found,

> I had one child and I was expecting another, and we were given £5 a week to manage our bills on, and your father said to me 'You've got to be very careful if we're buying this farm', so I couldn't go mad on £5 a week, could I? We'd already been investigated by the taxman because we weren't drawing anything out of the farm to live on. When we got married we had potatoes and gooseberries and rabbits and pheasants and things, the odd pig and chicken, we never spent any money, we never even had a dustbin because we never had anything to put out. Cornflakes packets were burned, we never had a dustbin.

But as well as the extent of specialisation being decided by necessity, it could also be influenced by pleasure. The distinction between work and home, or employment and enjoyment, was often less clear-cut for farmers' families, with enjoyment of particular farming enterprises influencing both the degree of specialisation and enterprise choice.[15] Pigs were part of the business on farm 570 for a time, but they were also a source of pleasure for the farmer's son and his young wife: 'I still love pigs to this day, they're lovely animals. We used to go up to Salisbury buying them if we had a day off from work, we'd go and buy a pedigree boar, up Salisbury, that was a long way years ago.' They were also a source of pleasure for farmer 576's father, who kept Landrace pigs,

> they were pedigree, he used to quite like showing them, at Launceston Show, there was a Callington Show, and he went to the Bath and West when it was down in Plymouth, but that was because it was local, and then Liskeard, I think he took pigs to Camelford, every market town had its show. It was about selling breeding stock. But he enjoyed it, and he had one old sow, she loved shows, she would show off, walk nicely, she enjoyed it, she would get fussed and groomed.

Farmer 243 shared this love of pigs – 'I've always liked pigs. And sheep. But I can't stand poultry' – and a younger farmer, now running farm 139, expressed very clearly the importance of personal preferences in making farm management decisions:

> Specialisation depends on your mentality. Farming isn't just about making money, it's also a way of life, and if you enjoy having pigs

---

[15] D.M. Winter, 'The Survival and Re-emergence of Family Farming: A Study of the Holsworthy Area of West Devon' (unpublished Ph.D. dissertation, Open University, 1986).

around, especially the amount we had, it wasn't a big enterprise, it wasn't going to lose us a lot of money, it wasn't going to make us a lot of money, and if you enjoyed seeing them there, for a farmer to stop doing things it isn't just money, there's got to be another trigger as well.

There were in practice several specialisation triggers apart from money: generational changes, capital and labour constraints, and simple personal preferences. Not that the money was unimportant. Thinking back on the management of farm 744 since the Second World War produced the reflection that 'I never really saw it as a dairy farm, but economics was such that as the landlords wanted a bit more rent we had to get a bit more income, and we thought the best way to do it was from cows.' And specialisation was not always successful, as farmer 826 ruefully recalled: 'I specialised in poultry because I thought it was going to make money, but it was my biggest mistake ever.' For most farmers, however, some kind of specialisation, or at least some rationalisation of the enterprise mix, was worthwhile. Sometimes it was motivated by the farmer's likes and dislikes, as on farm 243, where the farmer's dislike of poultry was perhaps understandable:

> Mother used to keep them in these deep litter houses, and I used to have to go down and turn it, couldn't stand that, all that ammonia, and thousands of rats, ... That was another job put me off poultry when they went on holiday, I had to wash the eggs, I was about ten to twelve years old.

Similarly, farmer 576 failed to share his father's love of pigs, again for understandable reasons:

> Father hadn't got the pigs organised, it was hard work, and I was a bit allergic to the barley meal. It made my nose run, I suppose we could have gone to pellets. Father liked the pigs, but the pig housing needed money spent on it, and we spent the money on the cows instead. We'd got little houses dotted all round the yard, and if you wanted to move them and one got out you'd be chasing them round the yard, they could play ring-a-ring-a-roses round the centre of the yard here.

As the experience of farm 576 suggests, the reasons for specialisation seldom fell into neat categories. A combination of factors was more common. On farm 576, it was the personal antipathy towards pigs, the realisation that the pig housing required capital investment, and a new generation taking over the management of the farm: 'when I came home, I took over the cows in 1964 and then they began to increase, fairly steadily ... By 1967 we were a more or less specialist dairy farm.' On farm 782, 'My father was never keen to keep too many cows, when he retired [in 1970] we were up to about thirty, but after that we got it up to about forty-five.' On farm 692 in mid-Devon, there was a mixture of cattle and sheep up to the early 1970s, but the sheep competed with the cows for the spring grass, so when a new generation took on the farm in 1973, and the sheep 'started breaking out' in the spring, they were sold. Even in the later 1970s some farms were still beginning the process of specialisation. Again, on farm 272 it began with the insertion of a new generation into the farm:

> In 1939 it was a mixed farm, by 1984 it was an all-grass dairy farm. I came home from [agricultural college], where I was in 1978–9, doing an NCA, and I thought we should expand the dairy herd, we had twenty-nine cows then and I could see that we needed sixty-five or seventy cows to make a viable unit. When I came home there were sheep, Mum had some poultry, a small amount of potatoes, beef from the dairy herd. ... And the beef and sheep were taking up acres which could go to the cows, and we needed the old battery house for calves.

Earlier, in the 1960s on farm 209, the new generation had to decide whether to overcome the labour requirements of small pig and poultry enterprises by further investment, or to concentrate on the dairy herd:

> We had the choice to do it properly or get out, but [my wife] and I knew that if we wanted modern dairy, pig, and poultry units we could do it if we had money enough, but we only had money enough to modernise one commodity, so that had to be the dairy. So it was a capital constraint. ... It was so obvious that the dairy herd was the thing to concentrate on.

These are clearly examples of the decisions that farmers all over the south-west, indeed all over the country, were taking from the 1960s onwards. Attempting to quantify the process is not easy. As we saw earlier, Hill and Ray simply used the number of enterprises per farm as a measure of specialisation.[16] This has the merit of simplicity, but it is not necessarily informative. Suppose, for example, that a farmer sells his dairy herd, retaining only a couple of house cows, and concentrates on continuous corn. Clearly, he has specialised, but there are still two enterprises on the farm. An alternative approach, used by the Ministry of Agriculture and in the University of Exeter Farm Management Handbook, is to define specialist dairy farms as those that derive 75 per cent or more of their standard farm gross margin from dairying, but this does not lend itself to measuring changes in the level of specialisation over time. What is needed is a metric that combines the number of enterprises with their significance, so that a farm with 99 per cent of its output from cereals and 1 per cent from dairy cows appears more specialised than one deriving 55 per cent from cereals and 45 per cent from cows. Similarly, the latter should appear to be more specialised than a farm that derives half of

---

[16] Hill and Ray, *Economics for Agriculture*, p. 240.

The Real Agricultural Revolution

its income from cows and the rest from a mixture of corn, potatoes, sugar beet, beef, pigs, and eggs. The way in which an index of farm specialisation (IFS) that summarises these variations can be constructed is described in the appendix at the end of this chapter. The result of calculating the IFS over the full sample of farms analysed from the FMS data is shown in figure 8.1, which confirms the impression gained from the interviews (and from table 5.1) that the process of specialisation was at its most active between the early 1960s and the mid-1970s.

Figure 8.2 sheds light on what this means for our aggregate sample. Aside from year-to-year fluctuations (an issue returned to below), it is quite clear that what in early days was a sample of farms with a wide range of enterprises present, rapidly became a more specialised sample. It is clear that it has always been a dairy/cattle sample, but we can see a very rapid decline in the proportion of farms selling other crops, and then towards the end of the 1960s the precipitous decline in the percentage of farms selling poultry. The decline in commercial pig enterprises was more drawn out and by 1984 had yet to reach the extent of the decline seen in the poultry sector. By the mid-1980s, most farms in the sample were selling cattle and/or milk, and compared to the earlier years of the survey far fewer farms were still selling sheep, although a significant proportion had retained a sheep enterprise.

Useful though this analysis is, it only reports on the incidence of different enterprises and tells us nothing of their economic significance. Figure 8.3 on the other hand looks at specialisation in terms of the contribution of output of individual enterprises to overall output (measured in £s). This presents a picture of more dramatic and rapid change. In the very early years of the survey, dairy output accounted for 20 to 25 per cent of total output but rapidly took on greater significance so that by the early 1960s it accounted for 40 per cent of total output, rising to around 50 per cent in the early 1980s. At the bottom of the chart, we can see a small spike in the contribution of cereals to total output associated with the war years. Subsequently, cereal output declined rapidly with some signs of an increase towards the end of the period, which is presumably a result of farmers growing more of their own feed. In the 1980s, approximately 80 per cent of output is accounted for by just two enterprises (dairy and cattle).

This analysis confirms that cattle and dairy enterprises have always been important in the FMS sample. They have always been there. But in the early years the picture is much more one of mixed farming. In the immediate post-war years, dairying quickly took on greater significance, and from the 1950s cattle and dairying accounted for half or more of total output as the sample became increasingly specialised. As we have already argued, the economic justifications for mixed farming weakened as price guarantees became an apparently fixed feature of farming. The technical

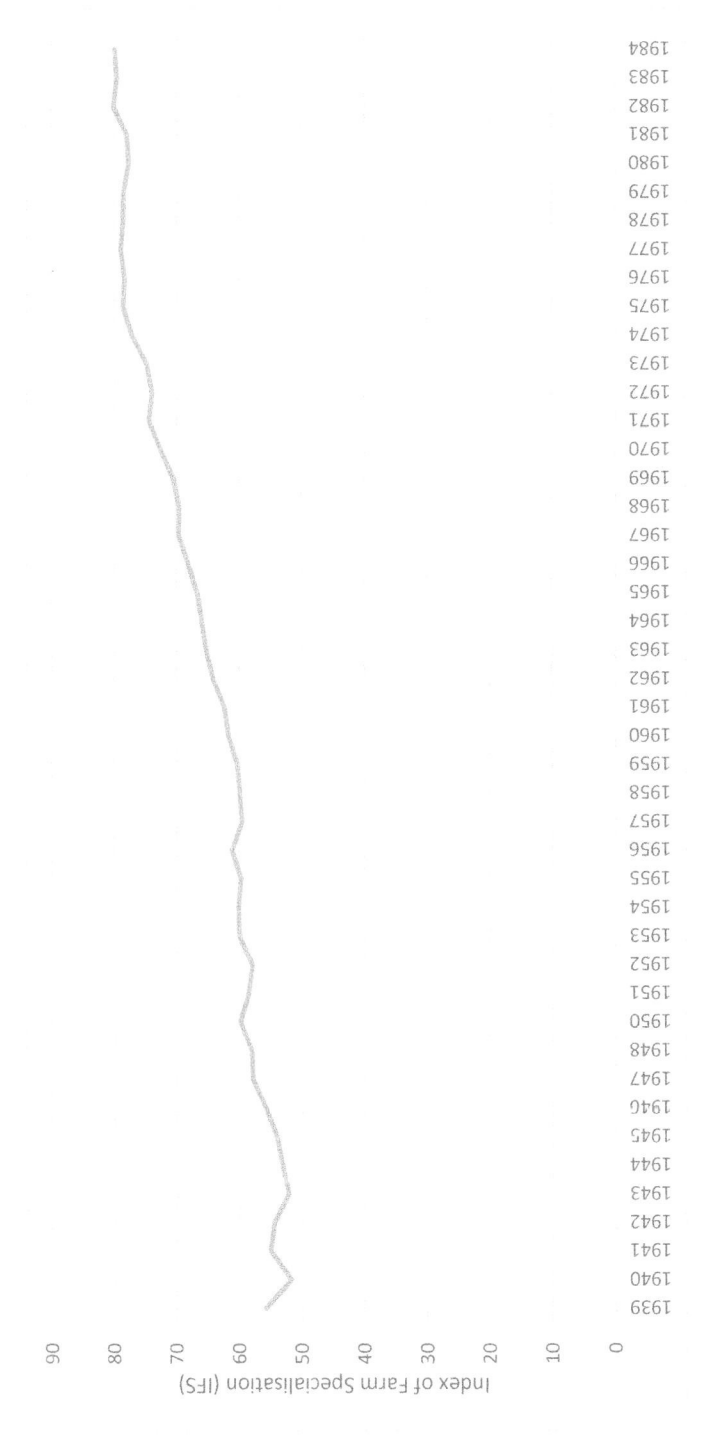

FIG. 8.1. Changes in the level of specialisation on FMS farms

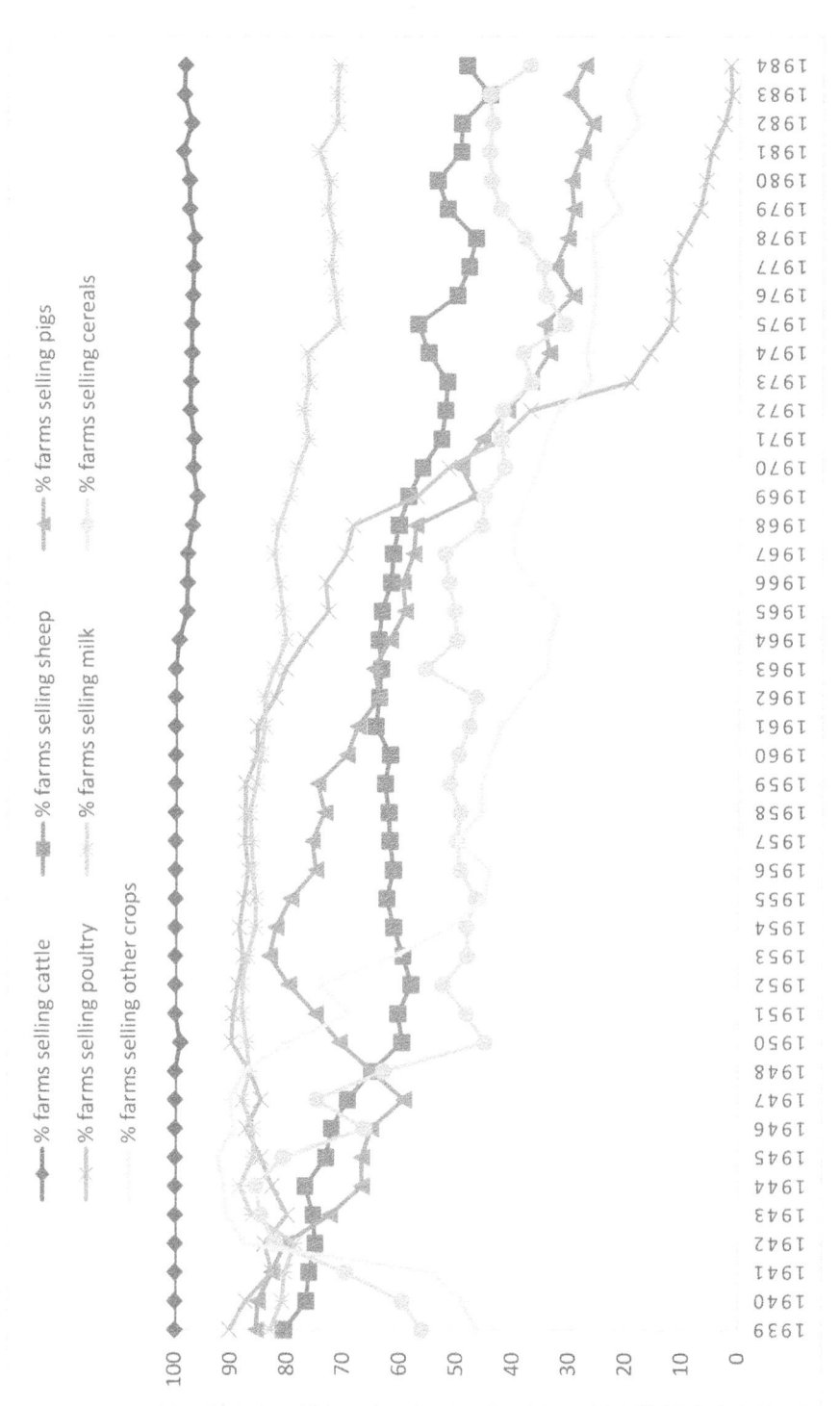

FIG. 8.2. Changes in enterprises on FMS farms

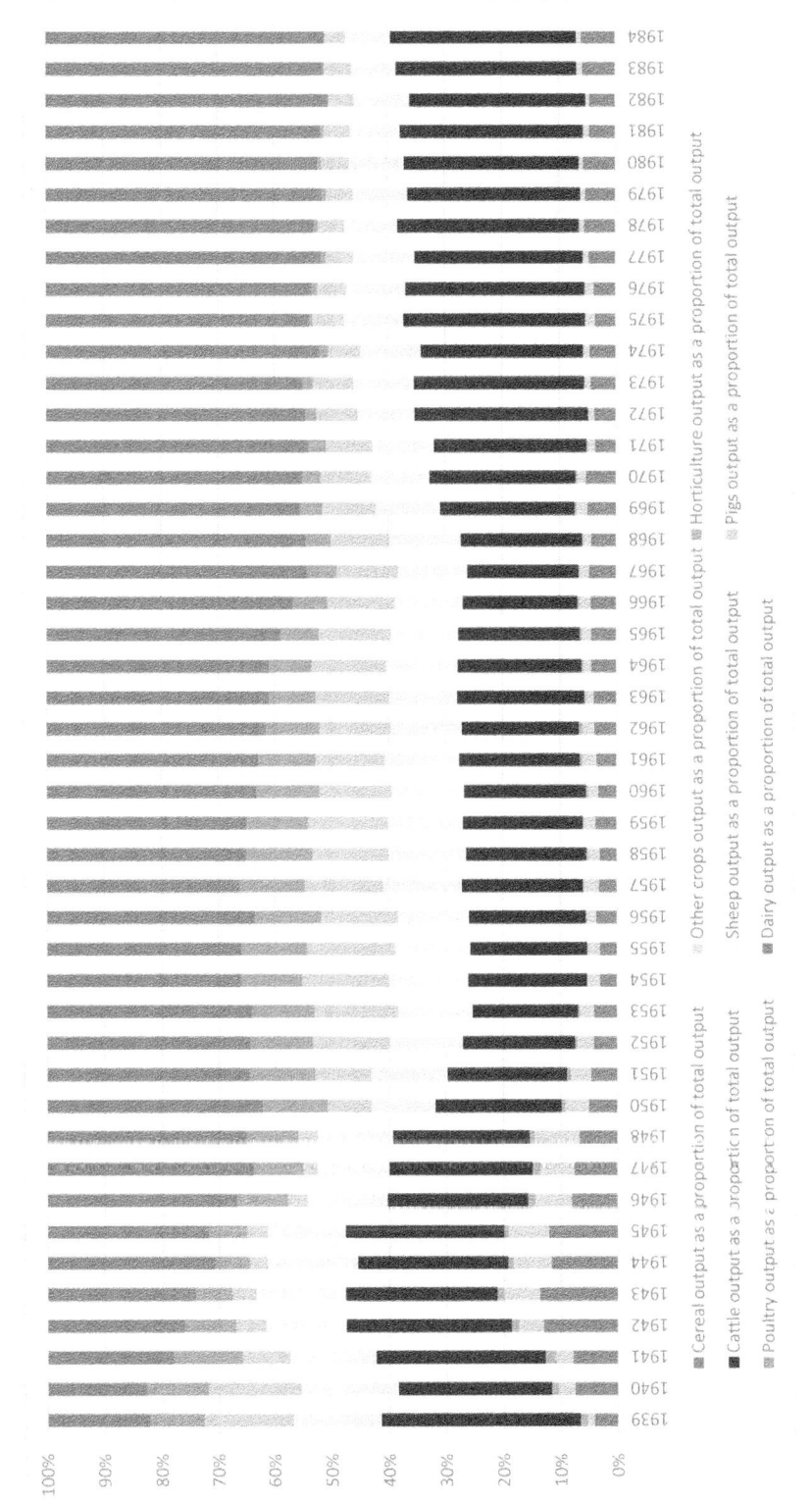

Fig. 8.3. Contributions to total output of individual enterprises on FMS farms

case for producing cereals often disappeared with the horse and its need for oats, and for growing roots with the increase in silage. On many dairy farms, the sheep competed with the cows for grass. These arguments relate to a farm sample dominated by cattle, and for other farming systems and enterprise mixes the technical reasons would be different. But for any farm the desirability of using machinery to its full capacity, and of keeping up to date with changing technologies, would produce the same incentive to specialise. The inevitable corollary was that some enterprises had to be discontinued. As figures 8.2 and 8.3 demonstrate, it was the intensive livestock – pig and poultry – enterprises that were most likely to be abandoned as a result of specialisation, so the following chapter is devoted to a discussion of the other side of the story: why it was these enterprises that disappeared from most south-western farms.

Appendix: The Index of Farm Specialisation (IFS)

Perhaps the clearest indicator of the extent to which a farm is specialised at any one point in time is a simple list of its outputs and the contribution to total output made by each one. For example, compare farm C with farm D:

	Farm C	Farm D
Milk sales (£)	3,728	21,003
Cattle sales (£)	816	1,985
Cereals' sales (£)	0	1,480
Other crops (£)	0	8,404

It is clear from these figures that farm C is a specialist dairy farm selling milk and the resultant calves, heifers, stores, or fat cattle, whereas farm D is still mainly a dairy farm but also has two significant arable enterprises. Thus farm C is more specialised than farm D. But if we wish to measure the extent to which either farm becomes more or less specialised over time, or compare the tendency to specialise of small farms as opposed to large farms, or of farms in Cornwall as opposed to farms in Dorset, simply listing the output of each enterprise, or even the percentage contribution of each to total output, becomes unwieldy. Ideally, what is needed is a single figure that can be calculated from the data available in the FMS field books and compared for an individual farm at different times, or indeed for different farms at the same or different times: an IFS. And, again ideally, the IFS should reflect both the significance of the main enterprise and the number of subsidiary enterprises, it should have a theoretical maximum and a significantly different minimum, it should work irrespective of farm size, and it should be reasonably easy to compute. The method explained below appears to satisfy each of these criteria.

Imagine a farmer who sells only wheat, to the value of £100. Clearly, the farm is completely specialised. Bored by this simple life and needing company, the farmer sacrifices a little of the wheat to feed a few chickens, whose eggs are sold at the farm gate. The farm's output is now wheat to the value of £99 and eggs worth £1. The level of specialisation has decreased, but not much. Alternatively, supposing the farmer cut the wheat production and grew potatoes, so that the farm output was £50 from wheat and £50 from potatoes. As in the previous example, there are still two enterprises, but the level of specialisation is much less. Thirdly, suppose this less specialised system still provides no company, so again a little wheat is sacrificed to feed a few hens, and the farm now has three enterprises, with the biggest still accounting for £50 worth of output. The IFS should be different in each case.

The following calculation is entirely arbitrary but reflects the importance of the largest enterprise and the number of enterprises.

Let O = total farm output (£)
     E_1 = output of the largest enterprise (£)
     n = number of enterprises

Then
$$IFS = [(E_1/O) \times 100] + 1/n\,[(O-E_1)/O \times 100]$$

or, in simpler terms, the percentage share of the largest enterprise plus the share of the remaining enterprises divided by the number of enterprises.

Applying this formula to the examples above, in the first case, when the farm sells only wheat,
$$IFS = (100/100) \times 100 + 1/1[(100-100)/100 \times 100] = 100;$$
When the farm sells £99 of wheat and £1 of eggs
$$IFS = (99/100) \times 100 + \tfrac{1}{2}[(100-99)/100 \times 100] = 99.5$$
But when the output is equally split between wheat and potatoes
$$IFS = (50/100) \times 100 + \tfrac{1}{2}[(100-50)/100 \times 100] = 75$$
And when a small third enterprise – egg production – is added
$$IFS = (50/100) \times 100 + 1/3[(100-50)/100 \times 100] = 66.6'$$
At the opposite end of the scale, when there are twenty enterprises and the largest accounts for only 5 per cent of the total output, IFS = 5 + 95/20 = 9.75.

9

The Declining Enterprises: Pigs and Poultry

This chapter is about both pigs and poultry. From a twenty-first-century perspective, it may not make much sense to write about two separate industries in the same chapter, but until about the 1970s they were often bracketed together. The second edition of Dexter and Barber's classic book on farm management put them into the same chapter but also caught the end of the era:

> Both pigs and poultry are moving into the hands of specialist producers. A few hundred poultry kept on the general farm is becoming a thing of the past ... in general, large-scale units are necessary to make use of the technical know-how required for successful egg production. Pig production has not yet become so specialised. Pigs are still found as a subsidiary enterprise on many farms, and there are few, if any, of the enormous empires commonly associated with commercial egg and poultry production.[1]

What brought them together in the first place was that they could both be kept on small areas of land and be fed either on the by-products of the farm or on purchased feeds.[2] They were also often the first casualties of specialisation in the 1960s and '70s. As mixed farms began to specialise in grassland or arable enterprises, pigs and poultry were found to require more labour and capital than they warranted. As pig and poultry producers specialised, they were able to produce at prices that left little profit for mixed farms. What follows in this chapter is a more detailed account of the evolution of these two intensive livestock enterprises in the United Kingdom in general and south-west England in particular since the beginning of the Second World War.

---

[1] K. Dexter and D. Barber, *Farming for Profits* (2nd edn, London, 1967), pp. 178–9.

[2] The production of both pigs and poultry was reduced dramatically in the Second World War, when purchased feeds were rationed. See K.A.H. Murray, 'Agriculture', in K. Hancock (ed.), *History of the Second World War: United Kingdom Civil Series* (London, 1955), pp. 136–9.

Pig Keeping in the 1940s, '50s, and '60s

There were 4.4 million pigs in the UK in 1939, supplying 82 per cent of the nation's pork consumption but only 37 per cent of its bacon and ham. The latter dominated the imported pigmeat market, with most imported supplies originating in Denmark and the Netherlands, and the UK was the major world importer of pigmeat.[3] By 1947, the pig population had declined to 1.6 million, pork had virtually disappeared from the market, and bacon production had more than halved. During the war, of course, imports from continental Europe ceased. From 1939, all pigs had to be sold to the Ministry of Food at fixed prices, and supplies of pig feed were rationed, which largely explains the dramatic fall in the total number of pigs. But after the war the government responded to rapidly rising world agricultural prices, together with a shortage of foreign exchange, by instituting an agricultural expansion policy. Pigs, with their capacity to increase in numbers more rapidly than cattle or sheep, were targeted as the meat sector to be expanded, and pig prices were 50 per cent higher, in relation to feed prices, than they had been before the war. Pig feed rations were increased after 1947 and feed rationing was discontinued altogether from 1953. In 1954, the Ministry of Food ceased to be the buyer, and the NFU set up the Fatstock Marketing Corporation to provide deadweight grading of meat animals. It soon accounted for about 90 per cent of sales of bacon pigs and provided greater price stability than had prevailed before the war. By 1954, the pig population had risen to over six million, the need to restrict imports from Europe had decreased, and pigmeat consumption was exceeding pre-war levels. Most of the pork was home-produced, but about 60 per cent of the bacon came from imports, mainly from Denmark, Sweden, Eire, and Poland.[4]

Increased numbers notwithstanding, post-war pig farming remained similar to its pre-war antecedent. A textbook writer in 1950 argued that 'pigs are most profitable when co-opted with kindred activities. The

---

[3] H. Marks and D.K. Britton, *A Hundred Years of British Food and Farming: A Statistical Survey* (London, 1989), p. 215; P. Brassley, 'International Trade in Agricultural Products, 1935–1955', in P. Brassley, Y. Segers, and L. Van Molle (eds), *War, Agriculture and Food: Rural Europe from the 1930s to the 1950s* (London, 2012), p. 34.

[4] Marks and Britton, *A Hundred Years of British Food and Farming*, p. 215; E. Burnside and W.M. Strong, *A Comparison of Pig Production before and after the War: With Special Reference to South West England*, University of Bristol, Department of Economics (Agricultural Economics, Bristol II province), Report no. 88 (Newton Abbot, 1955), pp. 1–10; E. Burnside and R.C. Rickard, *An Economic Study of Pig Production in South West England 1953–57*, University of Bristol, Department of Economics (Agricultural Economics), Report no. 105 (Newton Abbot, 1958), pp. 9–12.

economy of dairy and arable farms is not complete without a herd.'[5] In 1955, Estelle Burnside and W.M. Strong of the University of Bristol agricultural economics unit in Newton Abbot published a comparison of pre- and post-war pig production in south-west England. It revealed that pig herds remained small, with an average of 10.2 sows in breeding herds in 1954 compared with 11.1 before the war. Pigs were generally fed on purchased meals and concentrates, with only a few farmers feeding skim milk, presumably reflecting the decline of farmhouse cheese and butter-making before and during the war. Feed conversion ratios varied from about 5:1 before the war to 6:1 in the early 1950s, which Burnside and Strong attributed to high post-war prices attracting new and possibly less skilled farmers into the pig trade after the war. On the other hand, pre-weaning mortality decreased, with the number of pigs weaned per sow per year increasing from 13.2 in 1938 to 14.6 in 1954.[6] Contemporary textbooks extolled the virtues of keeping breeding pigs in moveable fold units on grass fields and estimated that two men could look after about forty sows and their fattening progeny, while admitting that few non-specialist producers achieved that size, and that most fattening pigs were kept indoors.[7]

The Ministry of Agriculture presumably felt that this pattern of pig farming was inadequate to meet the needs of the national market, for in January 1955 the Minister appointed a Committee, chaired by Sir Harold Howitt, to advise on the development of pig production in the UK. In particular, the Committee was asked to advise on the how the pigmeat market was likely to develop, the kinds of pigs that it would require, and the developments in breeding policy that would produce them. The Committee's report, published in the following October, presents a detailed picture of the pig industry at that time, which supports Burnside and Strong's findings of numerous small herds. About two-thirds of all holdings over an acre in size, a total of 198,000 holdings, had pigs, an average of about twenty-seven pigs per farm. The 4.7 million growing pigs recorded in the June census in 1954 had been produced by 726,000 sows, an average of about 6.5 pigs per sow. The report identified four principal types of pig enterprise: pedigree breeders selling breeding boars and gilts; commercial breeders selling weaners or young store pigs; feeders, fattening weaners, and stores; and those farms that had both breeding and fattening herds. Although over 150,000 farmers had breeding stock,

---

5   A. Morley, *The Right Way to Pig Keeping and Breeding* (Kingswood, Surrey, 1950), p. 18.
6   Burnside and Strong, *A Comparison of Pig Production before and after the War*, pp. 14–23.
7   K.W.D. Campbell, 'Production of Bacon and Pork', in J.A. Hanley (ed.), *Progressive Farming: The Maintenance of High Production*, III (London, 1949), pp. 258–64.

only about fourteen thousand were members of breed societies, and many of these sold only one or two pedigree boars or sows each year. At the opposite end of the scale, only 13 per cent of Large White breeders produced more than twenty breeding sows each year, but they accounted for over half of the sows produced. There was a pyramid of breeding, in which a small number of prominent breeders sold stock to a middle tier, who in turn sold breeding stock to the commercial breeding herds. Consequently, a few pigs could have an enormous genetic influence. Over half of the Large White boars registered in the 1955 herd book were grandsons of boars from one of only twelve prominent herds, and not all of these were large herds, so the selection pressure involved in producing breeding stock was not great. Moreover, the identification of superior stock was often by the eye of a judge at an agricultural show, since there was little progeny or performance testing at this point in time. The dominant sire breed was the Large White, as table 9.1 shows, and whereas the saddleback breeds, the Wessex and Essex, had increased in number after the war, they were beginning to give way to the Landrace, the first of which had been imported from Sweden in 1953.[8] Boar licensing had been introduced in 1946, so the figures in this table are likely to be reasonably accurate, and they reveal a late stage in the decline of breeds such as the Berkshire and Middle White that had been prominent in the nineteenth-century pork trade. All of the breeds below the Essex in table 9.1 would be identified as endangered by the Rare Breeds Survival Trust in the 1970s, with the exception of the Lincolnshire Curly Coat, which was extinct, and the Essex and Wessex, which essentially differed only in the colouring of the hind feet, and combined to form the Saddleback breed.[9]

The commercial breeding herds were also generally small: half of the sows were in the 86 per cent of herds with fewer than 10 sows. Many of these sows were cross-breds, put to a pedigree boar. The Howitt Committee found that 'the most common breeding policy commercially was the use of a Large White boar either on a pure-bred "coloured" [i.e. often Saddleback] sow or a first- or second-cross sow of this breeding', so that some 70 per cent of fat pigs 'had some touch of "colour" in their ancestry'.[10] Almost 80 per cent of these herds took pigs on to fattening, but there were also large numbers – over 140,000 – of herds with fewer than fifty fattening pigs at any one time, and the Howitt Report estimated that about a quarter of all pig enterprises bought in weaners or stores, often from auction markets, for fattening. They were often located in the

---

[8] *Development of Pig Production in the United Kingdom: Report of the Advisory Committee on Development of Pig Production in the UK*, Cmd.9588 (London, 1955).

[9] L. Alderson and V. Porter, *Saving the Breeds: A History of the Rare Breeds Survival Trust* (Robertsbridge, 1994).

[10] *Development of Pig Production*, Cmd.9588, p. 11.

TABLE 9.1. Boar breeds in Great Britain

	Number of boars licensed for the first time in 1954
Large White	16,751
Landrace	2,032
Welsh	1,363
Wessex	701
Essex	488
Large Black	269
Berkshire	67
Middle White	97
Tamworth	72
Gloucester Old Spot	44
Long White Lop Eared	29
Cumberland	3
Yorkshire Blue and White	3
Dorset Gold Tip	2
Lincolnshire Curly Coat	2
Oxford Sandy and Black	1

Source: *Development of Pig Production*, Cmd.9588, p. 11.

eastern arable areas and fed on home-grown cereals with supplements. Bacon pigs were most usually sold through the Fatstock Marketing corporation on a deadweight basis, but porkers, cutters, and heavy hogs might also be sold through any one of about five hundred auction markets on a liveweight basis. The Howitt Committee found numerous problems with the industry at the time they reported: it was difficult to find one type of pig that could produce a satisfactory carcase for all requirements, grading and breed society standards did not always reflect market requirements, the separation of breeding and fattening produced health and other problems, and more research was needed on housing and carcase quality.[11]

This national picture was replicated in the south-west of England. A study of the data for Dorset in 1953 found that 55 per cent of the 3,029 full-time farms over one acre in size kept pigs of some sort, and 36 per cent had at least one sow. But most (85 per cent) of the herds had fewer

[11] *Development of Pig Production*, Cmd.9588.

The Declining Enterprises: Pigs and Poultry

than ten sows, and most (89 per cent) had fewer than fifty pigs in total at any one time.[12] Thus there were few specialist pig producers, and most pigs were produced in small numbers on mixed farms, in housing that ranged from Danish-style piggeries to straw bale huts, with converted buildings that led to inefficient labour use predominating. There was no dominant breed, although Wessex sows were often preferred for pork production and Large White or Landrace for bacon. A study of thirty-eight pig producers in Devon, Cornwall, and Dorset in 1956/7 found that the average breeding herd size was eleven sows, and only six of the herds had more than fifteen sows. Most of the feed was purchased, and the average feed conversion rate was 4.2 pounds of meal equivalent per pound of liveweight gain.[13] One of the more successful producers ground his own barley in a hammer mill and mixed it (with a shovel) with weatings, Vitamealo (a protein concentrate), and grass meal. To each ton of this mixture, he added two pounds of the antibiotic Terramycin.[14] The average sow in this sample had 1.9 litters per year in which a total of nineteen piglets were born, 3.1 of which died before weaning, often from being overlain by the sow. The range of performance was considerable. Nearly a quarter of the herds managed to wean fewer than fourteen piglets per sow per year, whereas almost another quarter weaned more than eighteen.[15]

The farms in the FMS replicated this pattern, in that a high proportion of farms had pigs in 1939, many dispensed with them during and shortly after the war, but then went back into pigs after feed rationing ended. As table 9.2 shows, the proportion of farms with pigs peaked in 1953 and thereafter declined steadily, especially in the twenty years between the mid-1950s and the mid-1970s.

---

[12] E. Burnside and R.C. Rickard, *An Economic Study of Pig Production in South West England 1960/61*, University of Exeter, Department of Economics (Agricultural Economics), Report no. 129 (Newton Abbot, 1962), p. 11.

[13] Burnside and Rickard, *An Economic Study of Pig Production in South West England 1953–57*, pp. 16–24.

[14] Writing later, Robert Bud argued that 'since the 1950s, at least a quarter of the antibiotics made have been administered to animals ...' In 1954, the chemotherapist Lawrence Garrod suggested that feeding antibiotics to animals would not produce human health problems, and the 1962 Netherthorpe Committee (Lord Netherthorpe was a former NFU president) agreed, but in 1969 the Swann Committee distinguished between the therapeutic use of antibiotics on farm animals, which they did not see as a problem, and their use as a growth promoter, which was, and this led to the banning of tetracyclines and penicillins as growth promoters. R. Bud, *Penicillin: Triumph and Tragedy* (Oxford, 2007), pp. 163–82.

[15] Burnside and Rickard, *An Economic Study of Pig Production in South West England 1953–57*, pp. 38–9.

TABLE 9.2. Percentage of FMS farms with pigs

1939	85.4
1947	59.3
1953	83.2
1964	61.8
1969	46.6
1974	33.6
1979	29.4
1984	27.4

Source: FMS field books.

Of the thirty-two farms in the FMS that have been studied in more detail, all but two had pigs at some point, but only twenty-four had them after 1964, and only seven after 1974. Only three farms had more than twenty sows, and at least fourteen were the kinds of farms that went in and out of small numbers of pig – say, fewer than twenty per year – often buying weaners or stores and fattening them to pork, or, more often, bacon weights. When interviewed, the farmers often told the same story: they had only a few pigs, taking up more than their fair share of labour, and they had to decide whether to do the job properly or not. Farm 243 in east Devon described a typical management system:

> We had Saddlebacks, and we crossed them with a Landrace or Large White, according to what the bloke down the road who had the weaners wanted. We always kept them outside, but farrowed them inside, but after six to eight weeks when you weaned them they were outside. We finished up with thirty-five to forty sows. It's keeping them clean all the time. If you don't keep them clean they don't do, and you've got to spend time with them, especially when they're little pigs. I've always liked pigs.

The experience of farmer 570, on a mixed livestock farm in north Devon, shows how it was easy to get into pigs in a small way without needing too much capital. His father allowed him to keep a pig to supplement his wages, and …

> well you know what pigs are, you've only got to mate them and then you've got twelve, then you've got twenty four, and in no time I had a hundred, and Dad said 'These pigs are taking over the farm', they were in this field, and that field, and in the orchard, they were doing so well, it was a good time, in 1961, for pigs.

The Declining Enterprises: Pigs and Poultry

On farm 466, in east Cornwall, another farmer's son came back from university in the early 1960s and also expanded the pig herd:

> We kept the pigs on this farm in these converted buildings. They finished up being Landrace and Landrace cross. ... When I came home [in the early 1960s], day to day father managed the cows and the pig herd was my baby, and we got to about one thousand pigs, roughly one hundred sows and taking the progeny to bacon, which at that time was a significant herd, a full time specialist pigman's job, so that was when the Saddlebacks went and we brought in Landraces and crosses. We probably bred up from the Saddleback sows, but the blood soon dilutes, and we used a bit of AI for pigs too, when it became available. We had Landrace, mostly crossed with Large Whites.

The difficulties inherent in keeping pigs in converted or non-specialist buildings is vividly illustrated by the memories of farmer 209, in west Cornwall:

> The pig system was pretty labour consuming. Dad never had pig houses with dunging passages where you could go down with a hand or tractor squeegee, it was always fork, shovel and broom, so that was far too labour consuming. Then he got to the point where he had hardly any sows and bought the weaners, and they were kept in various old concrete block houses, with ten or twenty in a house, and you fought your way in to feed them and fought your way out again, and Friday was always cleaning out pig's houses here and down at ..., so off you went with tractor and muck spreader and fork, shovel, and broom. ... Dad had fifteen sows in the mid-1960s ...

These recollections, together with the regional and national statistics, show the state of the pig industry up to the early or mid-1960s. Indeed, 'industry' seems to be hardly the appropriate term for a sector of agriculture that comprised a large number of mostly small herds of mostly traditional breeds kept in mostly non-specialist environments by mostly non-specialist producers on mixed farms. Professor Woods argues that 'indoor "factory-style" production was already established by the 1930s', but while it is certainly true that some producers kept significant numbers of pigs in specialist housing in the twenty post-war years, it seems clear from the evidence produced here that they were in a minority.[16]

---

[16] A. Woods, 'Rethinking the History of Modern Agriculture: British Pig Production, c.1910–65', *Twentieth Century British History* 23 (2012), p. 168.

Poultry 1940–60

A reading of agricultural textbooks published in the 1940s suggests that poultry would normally be a part of the stocking of the mixed farm found all over England and Wales. Such a farm would normally have land available for free range poultry that could utilise food grown on the farm and spend some profitable time on cereal stubbles. Free range was considered preferable – the general farmer was 'not likely to have much sympathy with' battery houses – but it was important to move the poultry houses regularly to avoid too much damage to grassland and avoid the build-up of disease. The mixed farmer could make better use of the manure produced and spread in such a system than the specialist producer, but the disadvantage of the system was that it produced fewer winter eggs, because it was difficult to provide artificial lighting in small movable houses, which was important when October to December egg prices were twice March to May prices. The maximum recommended stocking rate was 150 birds per acre, and one worker could look after between 1,200 and 1,500 birds. The feed normally included dry or wet mash and a scattering of grain. Hens came into lay at about six or seven months old, and most were only kept for one or two seasons, laying at least 150 eggs in the first season. The White Leghorn, which was the most important of the pure laying breeds, produced white eggs. The heavier dual-purpose (i.e. eggs and meat) Rhode Island Red breed produced brown eggs. Many farmers used cross-bred hens.[17] This was exactly the kind of poultry keeping found in the mid-1950s, in the experience of one of the authors (PB) on a small, tenanted farm in south Lincolnshire, where the laying hens were kept in two or three wooden houses permanently sited on permanent pasture adjacent to the farm buildings. The hens were fed on purchased food, and water was provided in buckets designed to provide a trough when laid on their sides. They wandered at will over the pasture, which was also grazed by the dairy herd. Some of the eggs were sold at the farmhouse door, but most went to a packing station. In the mid-1960s, on a dairy farm in Warwickshire, the hens were kept in the orchard. There were perhaps fifty or sixty of them, and they were shut up at night in three wooden huts that also contained their nest boxes. Every so often, the farm staff would be sent to dig out the droppings that collected on the floors of the houses (the ammonia released in the process was an instant cure for a blocked nose), but otherwise most of the feeding

---

[17] J.A.S. Watson and J.A. More, *Agriculture: The Science and Practice of British Farming* (8th edn, Edinburgh, 1945), pp. 687–704; H. Howes, 'Poultry on the General Farm', in J.A. Hanley (ed.), *Progressive Farming*, IV (London, 1949), pp. 1–40; D.H. Robinson (ed.), *Fream's Elements of Agriculture* (13th edn, London, 1949), pp. 648–51.

and egg collecting were done by the farmer's wife. The eggs were sold at the farmhouse door to a more or less regular clientele.

These two farms were typical of thousands at the time, when eggs were still largely produced by small flocks of hens kept as part of mixed farming systems. But although the author's recollections in the paragraph above might suggest a traditional business, it was in fact one marked by rapid change. As with pigs, poultry numbers declined during the war and subsequently rose as the availability of feed increased. As table 9.3 shows, the number of birds in the country exceeded the pre-war level by the 1950s, and by 1960 egg production was at nearly double the pre-war level, largely at the expense of imports, which had been significant before the war but accounted for no more than 2 per cent of the market by 1960.[18] Consumption of poultrymeat at the end of the war was so insignificant that it was omitted from the meat ration, but as table 9.3 indicates, it expanded rapidly in the 1960s, as a result of the initiation and expansion of the broiler industry from about 1953.[19] At the end of the war, there were therefore three types of farm involved in poultry: those that sold eggs, those that sold chickens to the meat trade, and those that sold breeding stock to the other two. Specialist poultrymeat producers were in a minority in the 1940s, as most of the chickens on the market came from birds that had ended their laying lives – 'spent hens' as they were called. Specialist breeders were an even smaller minority: 2,900 'independent breeding stations' were identified in 1948.[20]

TABLE 9.3. Poultry numbers and production in Great Britain, 1939–60

	Poultry numbers (million)	Egg Production (million dozen)	Poultrymeat Production ('000 tons)	Poultrymeat consumption (kg/head/year)
1939	61.1	556.3	79	2.3
1947	45.9	486.7	52	1.3
1955	74.0	848.6	112	2.9
1960	91.1	1080.0	312	5.3

Source: Marks and Britton, *A Hundred Years of British Food and Farming*, pp. 224, 227–8, 238.

[18] R. Coles, 'Current Developments in the Poultry Industry', *Journal of the Royal Agricultural Society of England* 122 (1961), pp. 39–53.

[19] A. Godley and B. Williams, 'Democratizing Luxury and the Contentious "Invention of the Technological Chicken" in Britain', *Business History Review* 83 (2009), pp. 267–90.

[20] B.M. Short, '"The Art and Craft of Chicken Cramming": Poultry in the Weald of Sussex 1850–1950', *Agric. Hist. Rev.* 30 (1982), p. 29; Coles, 'Current Developments in the Poultry Industry', p. 41.

Since most of the farms in south-west England in this period were egg producers, and since the history of the broiler industry has already been the subject of detailed work by Godley and Williams, the following discussion will concentrate on the former.[21]

As Professor Sayer points out, one of the problems in tracing the history of the laying flock is the difficulty of obtaining useful and accurate statistics.[22] The annual census produced figures for total fowls (see table 9.3), but the number of laying hens was not listed separately until 1960. However, various authors made estimates that tell a reasonably consistent story, in which most farms had a small poultry flock. In 1952, there were nearly 305,000 holdings in England and Wales with adult fowls, representing about 81 per cent of all holdings over one acre, up from just under 294,000 holdings in 1948.[23] At a time when purchased feedstuffs were still rationed, the general mixed farm had an advantage over the specialist producer who had started to take a larger share of the market before the war, but this was not to last, and the decrease in the total number of flocks was largely produced by the decrease in flocks with fewer than two hundred birds, as table 9.4 reveals. Even more pronounced was the decline in the proportion of hens in such flocks, which more than halved between the mid-1950s and the mid-1960s, and the concomitant rise in the importance of flocks of more than five thousand laying birds.

By the mid-1960s, a few flocks – perhaps ten or a dozen – had reached over one hundred thousand laying hens.[24] Already by the mid-1950s it was clear to contemporary writers that the egg production business was undergoing radical change. A detailed costing exercise suggested that many flocks were losing money as demand failed to keep pace with rising production and prices fell. This was forcing some producers out of business, or at least out of egg production, but it was not a rapid process. Lloyd found that those with small farms were often willing to work for lower returns or found that a poultry enterprise balanced labour use and provided an outlet for home-grown cereals, while some turned to breeding and rearing to increase profits. He also argued that it was the farmer's wife who often looked after the poultry and kept the profits, so that even if the hens were losing a little money 'it would be a rash man who would risk matrimonial discord for the sake of a few pounds'.[25]

---

[21] Godley and Williams, 'Democratizing Luxury'; A. Godley, 'The Emergence of Agribusiness in Europe and the Development of the Western European Broiler Chicken Industry, 1945 to 1973', *Agric. Hist. Rev.* 62 (2014), pp. 315–36.
[22] K. Sayer, '"His Footmarks on Her Shoulders": The Place of Women within Poultry Keeping in the British Countryside, c.1880 to c.1980', *Agric. Hist. Rev.* 61 (2013), p. 303.
[23] Lloyd, 'The Economics of the Commercial Egg Production Industry', p. 245.
[24] Coles, 'The Structure of the Poultry Industry', p. 154.
[25] Lloyd, 'The Economics of the Commercial Egg Production Industry', pp. 257–8; see also Sayer, '"His Footmarks on Her Shoulders"'.

TABLE 9.4. The size structure of egg-producing flocks in England and Wales, 1948–65

	Total flocks	Total hens (million)	% of flocks with fewer than two hundred hens	% of hens in flocks of fewer than two hundred	% of hens in flocks of more than five thousand
1948	293,915	19.6	95.2	–	–
1952	304,961	27.8	91.7	–	–
1957	255,022	31.9	82.3	40.2	1.5
1963	187,386	39.1	76.5	19.7	15.1
1965	158,102	40.6	79.0	14.7	31.1

Source: R. Coles, 'The Structure of the Poultry Industry of England and Wales', in W.P. Blount (ed.), *Intensive Livestock Farming* (London, 1968), p. 151; data for 1948 and 1952 from D.H. Lloyd, 'The Economics of the Commercial Egg Production Industry of the UK', *J. Agric. Econs.* VI (1955), p. 245, and Coles, 'Current Developments in the Poultry Industry', p. 40.

There were two basic factors underlying the changes in flock sizes: housing and breeding. At the end of the war, there was a general shortage of building materials, and what was available was expensive, perhaps five times as much as before the war, while new timber could only be acquired under licence. In consequence, an article in the Ministry of Agriculture's journal gave instructions on constructing poultry houses from recycled materials: 'The writer made some serviceable poultry houses out of old A.R.P. folding beds ... orange crates make good nest boxes ... Parts of old aeroplanes, pontoons and boats, old vans and even the bodies of derelict tramcars and railway carriages have been used for making poultry houses.'[26] By the 1950s, however, farmers were beginning to convert farm buildings to poultry housing. The introduction of intensive housing with lighting patterns controlled to stimulate laying was also associated with increased house sizes and mechanisation, so that one operator could manage as many as eight thousand birds, compared with the one thousand to 1,500 possible on free range systems. These changes can readily be perceived from table 9.5, which shows how rapidly free range flocks disappeared in the 1950s. Some farmers clearly replaced them with battery houses, while others went over to deep litter or straw yards (essentially a less intensive form of deep litter), which offered some of the advantages of intensification at a lower capital cost. Many mixed or dairy

[26] J.B. Thorburn, 'Home-Made Poultry Housing', *Agriculture* LVI (1949), pp. 278–9.

TABLE 9.5. *Laying hens in different housing systems as a percentage of the laying population in England and Wales, 1948–59*

	Range systems	Batteries	Deep litter and straw yards
1948	95	5	–
1952	83	10	7
1955	45	25	30
1959	30	37	33

Source: Coles, 'Current Developments in the Poultry Industry', p. 40. Lloyd, 'The Economics of the Commercial Egg Production Industry', p. 246 has some earlier data suggesting that range systems accounted for a higher proportion of the laying flock, and batteries and deep litter etc. a lower proportion, in the mid-1950s.

farmers found that a small deep litter enterprise was a useful addition to output. As farmer 570, in north Devon, recalled, deep litter

> was all the rage then [late 1950s/early 1960s], the farmers' daughters were leaving school and coming home and it was a time of expansion when this deep litter business came in, so any shed that you could put eighteen inches of sawdust in was used, with these time switches for the lights to come on, and then you'd get eggs all the year round.

In east Devon, farmer 826 found that 'poultry was very profitable when I started. This was in the fifties, I bought sixty cages and we could go to France on the profits, from sixty hens'. On farm 272, in east Cornwall, the farmer's wife recalled that

> we had deep litter in that house, and I used to rear my baby chicks in there, then we had the deep litter and bought them at point of lay, then we put batteries in there, I used to do that. ... we used to buy them at point of lay and I didn't rear them then, just looked after the egg production.

It was also a job for the farmer's wife in east Devon, on farm 243, where the farmer remembered his mother, in the 1950s, keeping poultry 'in these deep litter houses, ... down by the river, two or three houses, I suppose in the end she kept getting on for 2,000 layers'. For many farms, as for example on farm 209 in west Cornwall,

> just after the war pigs and chickens were an important part of the business. Poultry were on a deep litter system, for eggs, about five or six houses. Looking back they weren't bad little systems for egg production, deep litter, some had dropping boards and some didn't,

The Declining Enterprises: Pigs and Poultry

Mum washed the eggs, and they went through a packing station, a local firm that bought the eggs.

The farmers who provided these examples of small poultry enterprises in converted buildings did not mention breed changes, but at the same time that housing changes were occurring, traditional breeders were moving away from selling pure breeds and were increasingly selling hybrid birds, a process that was taken even further by breeding companies such as Shaver and Thornber, which by the mid-1960s were producing strains with brand names such as the Thornber 909 or the Shaver Starcross 288. Increasingly, traditional breeders became multipliers for these companies. Whereas there were 2,900 independent breeding stations in 1948, there were only 2,435 in 1960, but also an additional 1,060 breeders enfranchised by the breeding companies.[27] The most significant impact of this breeding activity was on egg yields. Whereas the average UK hen produced 120 eggs each year in 1948, she laid 204 in 1964–5.[28] This level of technical change, together with the possibility of putting two or three hens in a battery cage, attracted big specialist firms such as J.B. Eastwood into egg production. Starting in 1964, Eastwood was the largest single producer of eggs in the world by 1975.[29]

The other important sector of the poultry industry, meat production, does not appear to have been so common on west country farms. In contrast to Sussex, where there was a well-established pre-war poultrymeat trade, table chickens were largely a by-product of egg production. Drivers collecting eggs for the packing stations would bring back surplus birds, but the fact that Lloyd Maunder, Devon's biggest egg packer in the 1930s, processed only twenty or thirty chickens per day in its Tiverton plant gives some idea of the small scale of the operation. Godley and Williams have produced a detailed and convincing account of the way in which poultrymeat production changed in the thirty years or so after the war, largely as a result of the adoption of technologies of breeding, housing, disease control, and processing originating in the USA. By 1963, what they describe as a 'stable technological platform' for producing and marketing broiler chicken was in place, and the results could be seen not only in the expansion of production (see table 9.3 above) but also in the emergence of a few large flocks. By 1966, nearly half of all broilers were kept in flocks of more than fifty thousand birds, and indeed a third were in flocks of more than one hundred thousand. They were kept in specialised buildings with low lighting and about a square foot per bird,

---

[27] Coles, 'Current Developments in the Poultry Industry', p. 41; Sayer, '"His Footmarks on Her Shoulders"', pp. 322–3.
[28] Marks and Britton, *A Hundred Years of British Food and Farming*, p. 237.
[29] Q. Seddon, *The Silent Revolution: Farming and the Countryside into the 21st Century* (London, 1989), p. 110.

with mechanised distribution of feed containing coccidiostats and antibiotics. The extent to which this type of poultry production was carried on in south-west England is unclear, although the fact that Lloyd Maunder was one of Sainsbury's major suppliers suggests that it must have been present to some extent at least.[30]

Intensive Livestock from the 1960s to the 1980s

As the above accounts suggest, by the early 1960s it was increasingly evident that significant changes were occurring in the pig and poultry industries. They were greatest in broiler production and least in the pig business at that point in time, but they were sufficient to lead to increasing public interest in both animal welfare and the human health implications of animal feed additives, the results of which were to produce further information on these changes.

By the late 1950s, the Royal Society for the Prevention of Cruelty to Animals was concerned about laying hens in batteries and, to a lesser extent, on deep litter. In 1962, Rachel Carson published *Silent Spring*, condemning the effect of pesticides in US agriculture. Godley and Williams contend that Carson's book inspired the British author Ruth Harrison to write *Animal Machines*, which was published in 1964 and immediately attracted considerable public attention.[31] In her book, Harrison wrote about the animal welfare implications of broilers, poultry slaughterhouses, laying hens in batteries and veal calves in crates, and pigs in sweat boxes. She was also concerned with the visual impact of these forms of farming. She included a photograph of a traditional farm, with the comment 'whatever its supposed inefficiencies, the traditional farm has contributed to the visual pleasure of the countryside'. Underneath this was a photograph of a farm with intensive livestock buildings, against which she commented:

> The new type of farm is like a straggling factory. The buildings jar on the eye and rob the countryside of much of its charm. These long sheds are completely utilitarian, each with its giant feed hopper to meet the needs of the animals permanently enclosed within. The new type of farm is a factory run on completely commercial lines by people who are businessmen rather than farmers ... With the increasing disappearance of animals from the countryside our children lose a very precious heritage.[32]

---

[30] Short, '"The Art and Craft of Chicken Cramming"'; Godley and Williams, 'Democratizing Luxury'.

[31] Godley and Williams, 'Democratizing Luxury', p. 285; R. Carson, *Silent Spring* (London, 1963). It was first published in the USA a year earlier.

[32] R. Harrison, *Animal Machines: The New Factory Farming Industry* (London, 1964), figs. 2 and 3.

The Declining Enterprises: Pigs and Poultry

Very quickly, at the end of June 1964, the government responded to the animal welfare concerns raised by the book (although, interestingly, not to the landscape and socio-cultural points implicit in the photograph caption) by appointing a Committee of Inquiry, chaired by F.W. Rogers Brambell, professor of zoology at Bangor university, and made up of three MAFF civil servants, two vets, the Reader in animal behaviour at Cambridge University, and Lady Isobel Barnett, a medical doctor and television personality. From 1965 June census data, they found that nearly 80 per cent of the forty-five million laying hens in Great Britain were kept in intensive systems, and 35 per cent in batteries, mostly at more than one bird per cage. Indoor flocks produced 85 per cent of the eggs. They pointed out that battery cages were claimed to eliminate the pecking order and so produce better performance from weaker birds while allowing better identification and culling of the poorer performing hens. Deep litter housing had spread simply because it facilitated simpler cleaning and so reduced labour costs, but it was not without problems, such as feather pecking, cannibalism, and the build-up of disease organisms in wet litter. Big research and breeding programmes, benefitting from the short generation interval and prolificacy of poultry, had produced high performance genetic strains, resulting in 'the virtual disappearance both of the traditional breeds and the small-scale breeder and the dominance of specialist hybrid stock bred by large commercial organisations'. The Committee felt that 'Similar developments, already discernible with pigs and sheep', might follow, but more slowly. The welfare issue with which they were most concerned in pigs was the 'sweat box'. Although, as they pointed out, there were probably no more than twenty-five to thirty true sweat boxes in Britain, they had attracted Harrison's attention, and since they involved high stocking rates the pigs' normal behaviour of avoiding their dunging area was impossible. Consequently, they were unable to keep themselves clean, and some horrendous photographs of sweat boxes were published – 'aesthetically repugnant' was Brambell's phrase. In theory the high temperature and humidity produced by the high stocking rate was claimed to discourage respiratory disease, but in practice the working conditions they produced for farm labour would have been enough to restrict their widespread adoption even if they had been good for the pigs.[33]

By the mid 1960s, therefore, it was clear that the poultry industry had already changed significantly and that the pig industry was beginning to do so. Writing in 1968, D.B. Bellis, chief pig adviser for the feed firm BOCM, emphasised the importance of pre-war work on producing

---

[33] *Report of the Technical Committee to Enquire into the Welfare of Animals Kept under Intensive Livestock Husbandry Systems*, Cmnd.2836 (London, 1965), pp. 5, 16, 28–34; T. Beresford, *We Plough the Fields: British Farming Today* (Harmondsworth, 1975), plate 21.

synthetic vitamins and the post-war synthesis of amino acids, especially lysine, so that feed companies could use less fishmeal and more soya and groundnut meal in pig rations. They had also discovered that copper supplementation gave them some of the advantages of antibiotic supplements for intensively housed pigs. Improved piglet feed formulation allowed earlier weaning and thus earlier mating of sows and so more pigs per sow per year. Ideas about pig housing were also changing and had 'moved far from the cottager's sty of old, and indeed from the Danish houses that were erected in the 1930s'. The choice of production system remained much as it had before: small farmers tended either to sell weaners or to breed and fatten, and while there were many large units that also bred and fattened, those that bought in weaners to fatten tended to be the larger units. However, the role of auction markets was diminishing, and about forty per cent of all weaners were sold direct to fatteners, often through weaner groups that organised collection from several farms and delivery to fatteners. Although dry sows were still often kept outdoors in small herds, large herds were increasingly being kept in yards, and sow stalls had made an appearance. And the previous five years had been especially 'notable for the development of pig breeding on a large scale by both independent groups of farmers and commercial companies'.[34]

A profitable pig is one that grows quickly, uses feed efficiently, and reaches slaughter weight without putting on too much backfat. Its mother should also produce large litters. Traditional pedigree breeders in the post-war years judged the value of a pig in the show ring by eye, but few if any judges could estimate growth rate and feed conversion rate that way, and so although, as the Howitt Committee found (see above), a few breeders were genetically influential, they were not producing better pigs.[35] By this time, however, the necessary genetic theories, based on inbreeding lines and then crossing them, had been well established by Professor Jay Lush and his colleagues at Iowa State University, brought to Britain and explored further at Edinburgh University with its Animal Breeding Research Organisation (ABRO), and even applied in the poultry industry. This was the position in the late 1950s when Douglas Thornton, an agricultural economist at Reading University, organised a monthly discussion group of local pig farmers, which usually met at the White Hart public house in Nettlebed, Oxfordshire. They began to talk about how they might produce better stock, and one of them, Ken Woolley, went to ABRO and on his return said 'The [pedigree] breeders have got the pigs, but they haven't a bloody clue about pig breeding. The scientists

---

[34] D.B. Bellis, 'Pig Farming in the United Kingdom: Its Development and Future Trends', *Journal of the Royal Agricultural Society of England* 129 (1968), pp. 35–40.
[35] *Development of Pig Production in the United Kingdom*, p. 8.

The Declining Enterprises: Pigs and Poultry

know how to do it, but haven't got any pigs and are too lazy to get out of their ivory towers and get some – so that's where we come in.'[36]

That was the start of the PIC, in 1962. They picked up on the scientific work of the geneticists who at that time were analysing data to provide heritability estimates and developing crossbreeding theory and selection programmes. In 1966, Woolley decided that PIC needed a consultant geneticist and recruited Dr Maurice Bichard, then a lecturer at the University of Newcastle, to work as a consultant for a day or so each month. Bichard became the firm's full-time Technical Director in 1974 and remained with them until he retired in the 1990s. He explained why they were able to use a combination of genetic theory and measurable characteristics to produce improved pigs:

> With pigs you've got this big female reproductive rate – you have 200 sows but you can sell a lot of progeny out of them – ten gilts per year and you can sell nearly all of them. And it's fairly easy to define what your improvement goals are in the pig industry, because all of your customers are sitting there with a building, buying feed, so feed efficiency is important, speed of growth is important because he's farrowing all year and the slaughterhouse wants them every month, and carcase quality, pigs have always been graded and paid according to grade, and a lot were sold deadweight not liveweight, and that's something you can measure on the hoof because we had ultrasonic machines, developed during the war looking for faults in pipelines as I understand it but fairly soon adapted to pigs, but before that in America they used a scalpel and probe – you cut down in the backline and press a blunt ruler down until it hits the eye muscle. So defining what the customer wanted was relatively easy, and he's measuring his technical performance, they know how old those pigs are and what the carcase returns are.[37]

From the beginning, PIC also had a Minimal Disease herd,

> which meant that every pig we brought in here was brought in through hysterectomy, buying pregnant sows, slaughtering them the day before they were due to farrow, whipping out the piglets through a disinfectant bath, rearing them initially artificially, which can be an awful business because mortality can be very high ... you needed a good patient stockman. When they first started they brought in about thirty sows from around the country. There was a lab in Cambridge that was doing this commercially – artificially rearing pigs. And then we had extreme measures – fencing, compulsory showering, trying to keep

---

[36] J. Montgomery, *Small in Number – Big in Spirit: The History of the First 30-odd Years of the Pig Improvement Company* (privately printed, 1999), p. 14. We are grateful to Dr Maurice Bichard for the loan of this book.

[37] M. Bichard, interview with Paul Brassley, 30 August 2011.

pathogens out. The big one was virus pneumonia – enzootic pneumonia it's called now.[38]

Disease-free stock grew much faster – Bichard concluded that 'Disease control was as big an element in our success as a company as the genetics' – and he also identified improved weaner diets as an important factor in productivity improvement. Traditionally, weaning took place

> at eight weeks, then we all went to three weeks which made a huge difference to sow productivity, which was always twelve to fourteen pigs per sow per year, and then we showed that you could do twenty, and a few people are hitting thirty – that's a huge difference. This was from the study of digestion in young pigs, and the processing plant to produce palatable diets … The development of early weaning diets was very important.[39]

Professor Peter Brooks, who worked as a university-based pig scientist for forty years or so, agreed on the importance of the PIC:

> When I was a kid, my dad, once he got up to about ten or fifteen sows had a boar, and that boar was the boar for the area, and other farmers brought sows to our boar. What changed when Ken Woolley and the like got going was that good tested (performance tested) boars came in. Performance testing could tell you about growth rate and FCR [feed conversion ratio], and the next step was ultrasonic testing to tell you about backfat thickness on the live pig, which you could then correlate with its final carcase. So very quickly we got good performance tested boars coming on to the market at a reasonable price, and that really accelerated the process. My younger brother worked for PIC as his first job, which was going around tame breeders doing boar selection, which was based on the paper records of the boars and giving them a point score, so you paid your money and got your points, and the more money you spent the more points you got – brilliant shorthand for buyers, because as their herds improved they could buy better boars and see the improvement. So that made a huge difference. That came from PIC – Woolley was not the only player, but the most influential.[40]

Brooks also agrees with Bichard on the importance of early weaning and changes in feed, but argues that antibiotic feed additives, which attracted so much attention from a human health viewpoint in the 1960s, were not very effective:

> The other people who wanted to sell into this large pig market, apart from the feed companies, were the drug companies. I did contract

---

[38] Bichard interview.
[39] Bichard interview.
[40] P. Brooks, interview with Paul Brassley, 25 August 2011.

research at Seale-Hayne [College, later a faculty of the University of Plymouth] for thirty years, and many times we were looking at the latest antibiotic growth promoter that some firm or other had come up with, and that was not the best unit, with hundreds of students walking through it. In all the trials that we ran we never even saw a positive response from the market leader, which we were using as a control. When in Denmark they discontinued antibiotic use, in many units they saw no difference. Infectious diseases weren't as much of a problem as coliform scours, because they knock your performance, and that's what the antibiotics were controlling – but probably only in the two weeks after weaning. But the drug companies wanted sales, and producers were often led by the nose by them. And big drug companies were talking to big animal feed companies, and the feed companies wanted to put it in all the diet or none of it. The use of antibiotics will rarely improve on good husbandry; what they will do is permit bad husbandry. You could have bad husbandry and get away with it, which in reality is what made the difference. But it's interesting how many units now have better performance than when they had access to these products.[41]

Professor Brooks praised PIDA, the Pig Industry Development Authority, which later became part of the MLC. For young pig scientists, it provided invaluable contacts:

PIDA had a tremendous impact – made a huge investment in people. They had a conference every year for PIDA scholars and their supervisors, and you could have sixty to seventy people in the room, so we all got to know each other, and I know people from those days now. Your network was created before you'd finished your training – you could always pick up the phone to somebody.[42]

However, the MLC, he felt, had only a little more money than PIDA but had to deal with the requirements of the whole meat industry, and so could support less long-term research and fewer postgraduate students.

The result of these changes in breeding, feeding, and housing on mixed and dairy farms in south-west England was predictable: pig and poultry producers got bigger or got out, although the reasons they remember for doing so were not always to do with lower prices or increased capital costs. For some small-scale egg producers, it was about time and convenience. As farmer 744, in south Devon, explained, 'when Watts's of Torquay came around every week to collect the eggs it was fine, but when they decided that we had to take the eggs to Newton Abbot every week it was an extra bore and it wasn't worth carrying on.' Farmer 272's wife, in east Cornwall, made a similar point: 'At the start it was the packing station

---

[41] Brooks interview.
[42] Brooks interview.

in Launceston, and we supplied Butcher Mardon, then it came that it was a job to get rid of them because they all had to be graded, and they were so particular, so we gave it up.' In the Blackmore Vale of Dorset, farmer 3/1 remembers what was probably a common story of a farmer's wife's enterprise: 'We had poultry on deep litter for egg production, they weren't prepared to invest a lot of money in egg production, but he wanted to be more intensive than free range. This was really Mum's enterprise, she was keen on poultry, but in the end it just proved uneconomic.' Farmer 576, in east Cornwall, also felt that he had to make a choice about how scarce investment funds would be allocated: 'The eggs were to keep me occupied when I came home from school, they were deep litter, there wasn't much margin in it for small quantities, it would have meant building proper houses, and I preferred the cows.'

Other farmers found it worthwhile to try to stay in egg production during the 1950s and 1960s but eventually found it difficult to compete with bigger producers, as farmer 101, whose family farm is near Exeter, explained:

> there was a group of farmers who got together and thought 'we don't like the egg price', and we can do something about it, and they didn't have their own packing station, but there was a packing station out Honiton way that would do it for them, and keep the eggs separate, and they made enough money to put up the packing station and store down in Crediton, it must have been going for twenty years before they were bought out by Sun Valley Eggs, I think it was, from Kent. That's when we got out of eggs, we just weren't big enough, that's the trouble with supermarkets, you've got to be so big, but it was very profitable.

In east Devon, farmer 826 did specialise in poultry for a time, but by the end of the 1980s even he found that he was not operating on a large enough scale:

> I specialised in poultry because I thought it was going to make money, but it was my biggest mistake ever, at the time when the banks were throwing money at you, they said 'You must get bigger', and I got up to about sixteen or seventeen thousand hens I suppose, which is nothing these days, and increasingly got more and more in debt until it was terribly serious, and then I suddenly thought 'Why am I producing eggs when I could buy them?', so from that time, which was about twenty years ago I suppose, I just bought all the eggs I wanted from a friend in Culmstock, and at one stage I had the contract for a quarter of Devon's schools and old people's homes, you can't lose money if you buy and sell, you buy cheaply and sell more expensively, so from that time forward my bank balance improved, but I wished I'd done it twenty years before. ... The broilers and capons were a disaster as well. Economics finished broilers. I was producing batches of two thousand, that's miniscule compared with what the big boys could do.

The Declining Enterprises: Pigs and Poultry

The result of decisions like these, spread over the whole region, was that egg production eventually decreased, although the increase in eggs per hen was probably enough to compensate for the decrease in the number of birds until the end of the 1970s, as the estimates in table 9.6 indicate. Although egg production in the UK peaked in the late 1970s, the decline in the south-west, certainly from 1980 onwards, was more pronounced.

TABLE 9.6. Egg production in south-west (SW) England (Cornwall, Devon, Dorset, and Somerset) and the UK

	(1) Total SW Poultry (million)	(2) Estimated SW laying hens (million)	(3) UK annual egg yield per hen	(4) Estimated SW Egg production (million dozen)	(5) UK Egg production (million dozen)
1966	9.704	4.208	207	72.6	1,089.2
1970	10.860	4.225	220	77.5	1,157.8
1975	10.534	3.845	229	73.4	1,147.6
1980	10.639	3.660	248	75.6	1,100.5
1985	9.651	3.001	258	64.5	1,017.5

Source: column 1: SW poultry numbers from MAFF, *Agricultural Statistics* (annual); column 2 estimated by multiplying column 1 numbers by the ratio of UK laying hens to UK total poultry numbers, data from Marks and Britton, *A Hundred Years of British Food and Farming*, pp. 225, 237; columns 3 and 5 from Marks and Britton, *A Hundred Years of British Food and Farming*, pp. 237–8; column 4 calculated from column 2 × column 3 divided by 12.

This, and the even clearer decline in south-western laying hen numbers, was probably associated with changes in housing systems. The trend towards battery production in the 1950s (see table 9.5 above) continued in the following two decades, and 92 per cent of UK egg production came from battery-housed hens by the middle of the 1970s, with both free-range and deep litter systems in decline.[43] At the same time, egg yields increased and the food required to produce them decreased. Whereas an average hen in the 1950s might produce 150 eggs in her annual laying season, by 1968 farm management specialists were building an assumption of 210 eggs per year into their calculations, and by 1986 the figure was 264 for caged birds (the national average figure for all layers was a little lower at 258 eggs per bird). Between 1968 and 1986, the figure for the annual

[43] J. Portsmouth and T. Marangos, 'Poultry', in R.J. Soffe (ed.), *The Agricultural Notebook* (20th edn, Oxford, 2003), p. 560.

average feed consumption decreased from 47.25 kilogrammes per year to forty-four kilogrammes per year.[44] The impact of the change to more intensive systems on the size structure of the national egg laying flock was dramatic. There were over 180,000 flocks in 1964 but only 35,110 in 1986. The number of flocks with over ten thousand birds just about doubled, from 317 to 621, in the same period, while at the same time flocks with fewer than one hundred birds decreased from over 112,000 to about thirty thousand, most of which had fewer than twenty-five birds.[45] Much of this change took place between the mid-1960s and the mid-1970s, which accords with the FMS evidence for the disappearance of small farm flocks in the south-west of England, although not with the egg production figures in table 9.6, perhaps because a rise in the number of medium-sized producers maintained production until the mid-1970s.

The choice between investing in what was probably always going to be a secondary enterprise and focusing expertise, attention, and investment on the principal enterprise of the farm also affected those with small, and even some not so small pig herds. On farm 209, near Truro in Cornwall, the hens went in 1970 and the pigs the following year:

> [The pig enterprise] wasn't a very big unit and keeping going with an uneconomic unit would affect the whole business. We had to buy in the feed for the pigs and chickens, apart from a bit of grain for the poultry, so getting rid of them was an easier decision. It was so obvious that the dairy herd was the thing to concentrate on.

Farmer 466, further east in Cornwall, made the same point: 'We gave up pigs because they too needed investment. They were in converted buildings, ... converted cheaply, they were not efficient for feed because of insulation and the like, and they were inconvenient to work, so cows won on the investment decision.' And farmer 7/8 in Dorset, on the edge of the Blackmore Vale, said much the same:

> The pigs were getting in the way of the dairy, and we weren't pigmen, we weren't making a very good job of it. At the height we had about twenty sows, which was nothing by the 1960s, and it was all manual cleaning out in the sties we had. It was labour intensive, and faced with the choice between investing in pigs and cattle, the cattle won.

On a few farms, it was the pigs that won. Farm 929 in north Devon was a dairy farm with just over one hundred acres when the previous farmer's son took over in 1957. By 1981, he had over nine hundred acres and no cows. The intensive livestock enterprises initially concentrated on

---

44   J. Nix, *Farm Management Pocketbook* (2nd edn, Ashford, 1968), p. 49, and (17th edn, Ashford, 1986), p. 67; Marks and Britton, *A Hundred Years of British Food and Farming*, p. 237.

45   Marks and Britton, *A Hundred Years of British Food and Farming*, p. 237.

poultry, with one thousand hens in 1958, but this enterprise was running down by the late 1960s, to be replaced by pigs. Starting with twenty-seven sows in 1963, this enterprise grew rapidly. There were eighty sows by the end of 1968, over one hundred five years later, and 250 by 1981, when the farm was selling over five thousand fat pigs per year. It was a decision based simply on profit maximisation:

> the poultry enterprise, the requirements had outgrown the buildings we had, and the pigs came along and forced the poultry unit out. The scope for the poultry enterprise was limited down here, so it would have meant development on another farm to have the space available, and there was more money in pigs – they were developing and the poultry were running down in the early 1960s. … I started off here at … Farm with traditional buildings, some of which I knocked down and then built with the aid of grant more specialist pig buildings – Solari farrowing pens, and then more up to date farrowing rooms in the existing buildings, plus some other new buildings to go alongside. Originally for a period we sold weaners, but then I went into the finished product, and the finishing accommodation was developed at …, and continued up until recent times. There was no room here for fattening accommodation – it wasn't about biosecurity. Grants were quite important in all that, because the pig buildings were very dependent upon borrowed capital, and if there was grant to help, it made it easier. We put in drying and storage and milling facilities. All our cereal production went towards the pig enterprise. We bought in protein. In the end we were producing mainly wheat, and that was going through the pigs.

At an elevation of nearly one thousand feet on Dartmoor, and with only about fifty acres of land, Geoff Hearnden did not have the same option of producing most of the feed for his pigs. He bought the farm in 1960

> and gradually built up a small herd of Ayrshires because that's what all the educational establishment said one could do in those days was to have a dairy herd because then you got a milk cheque every month, and there was a market that took everything. After the winter of 1963, at which point we had a few sows, … we took the decision to get out of cows because the farm was really too small and went into pigs where we could actually buy in acres. [The herd] … grew very rapidly from twenty or thirty sows because we kept some gilts back prior to selling the cows, perhaps thirty-odd, and we built up to one hundred sows fairly quickly. In those days it was quite a big unit.[46]

These examples notwithstanding, overall more south-western farmers chose to specialise in grazing livestock, with the result that the percentage of FMS farms with pigs decreased from the mid-1950s onwards (see

[46] G. Hearnden, interview with Paul Brassley, 18 February 2005.

table 9.2). However, the number of pigs in Devon, Cornwall, and Dorset continued to increase for almost another ten years, reaching a peak in 1963, as table 9.7 shows. Subsequently, however, numbers fell steadily, and the south-western pig herd also formed a smaller part of the national pig herd in England and Wales, as pig production in the eastern counties grew.

TABLE 9.7. Pig numbers in Devon, Cornwall, and Dorset, 1953–83

	No. of breeding sows	Breeding sows as % of total in England and Wales	All pigs	All pigs as % of pigs in England and Wales
1953	51,448	9.3	370,419	9.4
1958	75,834	11.4	56,686,73	10.9
1963	86,777	12.4	618,539	11.8
1968	70,397	9.9	539,885	9.3
1973	68,254	8.2	562,580	7.7
1978	47,569	6.9*	418,334	6.6*
1983	47,593	6.7*	463,689	6.8*

Source: E. Burnside and R.C. Rickard, *An Economic Study of Pig Production in South West England 1964/65,* University of Exeter, Department of Economics (Agricultural Economics) Report no. 158 (Newton Abbot, 1966), p. 22; W.J.K. Thomas and E. Burnside, *Pig Production: Results of a Study in South West England in 1972–73,* University of Exeter, Agricultural Economics Unit, Economic Report no. 26 (Exeter, 1974), p. 38; E. Burnside and A. Sheppard, *Pig Production in South West England 1983–84,* Exeter: University of Exeter, Agricultural Economics Unit, Economic Report no. 93 (Exeter, 1985), p. 53.

* = % of sows or pigs in England only.

Cornish pig production was particularly affected. Pig numbers there reached a peak in the mid-1960s and then decreased so that by 1985 there was only one-third as many pigs as there had been twenty years earlier. In Dorset, in contrast, where there was only one-third of the number of pigs as there were in Cornwall in the 1950s, numbers rose consistently, so that by 1985 the county had twice as many pigs as Cornwall. In both Devon and Somerset, pig numbers peaked in the early 1970s.[47] The implication of fewer herds in the FMS survey while pig numbers still increased is obviously that herd sizes were growing. While data for all the farms keeping pigs in the south-west is absent, some indication of the trend is given by the average herd sizes on farms costed by the University of

[47] MAFF, *Agricultural Statistics, England and Wales* (London, various years).

The Declining Enterprises: Pigs and Poultry

Exeter, which show sow numbers on breeding and fattening herds rising from eight in 1953/4 to 23.5 ten years later, fifty-six in the early 1970s, and 111 in 1983–4.[48] These figures should be used with care, because they are taken only from the farms visited in the university's pig survey, which were probably farms with an interest or specialisation in pigs, but they give some idea of the rapidity of changes in herd size as pig production became a more specialised activity. Another way of demonstrating this is by examining the changes in the structure of the national pig herd (table 9.8), which clearly show the demise of the small herd and the growth of larger herds. By 1986, there were 151 herds in England and Wales with over five hundred sows.[49]

TABLE 9.8. Number of holdings in England and Wales by size of total pig herd

Size of herd (all pigs)	1960	1966	1975	1986
Fewer than 50	90,000	56,000	17,417	8,333
50–199	17,400	19,300	8,329	3,344
200–999	3,650	6,600	6,267	3,895
Over 1,000	100	400	1,278	1,874

Source: Bellis, 'Pig Farming in the United Kingdom', p. 34; Marks and Britton, *A Hundred Years of British Food and Farming*, p. 216.

The larger pig producers, such as farmer 929, were interested in changing the genetic composition of their herds to improve performance and often did so by buying in boars from the breeding companies such as Cotswold or PIC. Bichard of PIC points out that

> the breeding company looks for the traits important to the commercial producer, and that you can measure, and that have a reasonably high heritability. So we didn't do anything about litter size for many years because the heritability is low, say 10 per cent, so you concentrate on growth rate, feed efficiency and backfat.[50]

The extent to which commercial producers were successful in getting more surviving pigs each year and feeding them more effectively can be seen in table 9.9, which is based on data from farms in the Exeter University pig costings scheme. As Bichard suggests was likely to happen, there was

---

[48] Burnside and Rickard, *Pig Production in South West England 1953–57*; Burnside and Rickard, *Pig Production in South West England 1964/65*; Thomas and Burnside, *Pig Production: Results of a Study in South West England in 1972–73*; Burnside and Sheppard, *Pig Production in South West England 1983–84*.
[49] Marks and Britton, *A Hundred Years of British Food and Farming*, p. 216.
[50] Bichard interview.

little change over thirty years in the pigs born per litter, but more of them survived to weaning because better farrowing accommodation meant that fewer were squashed by the sow, and farmers were more aware of problems such as iron deficiency that could easily be cured by dosing with iron supplements.

TABLE 9.9. Pig performance data on farms in south-west England, 1953–84

	1953–7	1972–3	1983–4	% change 1953–84
Pigs born per litter	10.1	No data	10.4	2.97
Pigs weaned per litter	8.4	8.4	9.2	9.52
Litters per sow per year	1.9	1.99	2.24	17.89
Pigs weaned per sow per year	15.9	16.6	20.6	29.56
Feed conversion ratio (kilogramme feed per kilogramme pigmeat, feeding herds)	4.2	3.65	3.29	21.67

Source: Burnside and Rickard, *Pig Production in South West England 1953–57*, pp. 23, 52; Thomas and Burnside, *Pig Production: Results of a Study in South West England in 1972–73*, pp. 11, 13; Burnside and Sheppard, *Pig Production in South West England 1983–84*, pp. 18–19.

Improved weaner diets allowed earlier weaning, which allowed sows to go to the boar earlier, with the considerable increase in litters per sow per year as a consequence. Overall, therefore, each sow produced nearly 30 per cent more pigs in 1983–4 than her predecessor had in the mid-1950s. And because they grew faster and had better diets and housing, the feed conversion ratio improved by over 20 per cent. What table 9.9 does not measure is the improvement in the conformation of the pigs sent to the slaughterhouses, but farmers could see this for themselves in their grading returns, as they looked at the figures for backfat and length of carcase.[51]

Conclusion

Up to about 1970, as we have attempted to demonstrate in this chapter, pig and poultry production was dominated, not only in south-west England but also in the rest of the United Kingdom, by small enterprises on mixed farms keeping traditional breeds in non-specialist buildings.

[51] Hearnden interview.

The Declining Enterprises: Pigs and Poultry

In the post-war years, when purchased feed was de-rationed, many farmers took the opportunity to expand pig and/or poultry production as a way of increasing output using family labour when it was available. Then from the early 1960s there began to be changes. Initially, they were seen in broiler production, but laying hens and pigs then followed, with specialist housing and breeding stock produced by specialist commercial companies. Although there were big variations between farms in the timing of their responses, the overall trend was more or less the same across the country.

Professor Woods might regard this account as teleological: 'Authors tend to regard intensive farming as an end point and set out to determine how it was reached', producing linear accounts that ignore changes that do not fit into the general trajectory.[52] She makes the point that there were pig herds and poultry flocks that were kept indoors before the Second World War, and also those that remained outdoors after the war. Moreover, several pig farmers chose to mix the two systems, keeping dry sows and in-pig gilts outside in paddocks with simple shelters, bringing them in for farrowing and lactation, and then keeping their fattening offspring indoors. A few opted for a completely outdoor system. There were probably almost as many variations in detail as there were pig herds. Nevertheless, it seems apparent from the individual, regional, and national data examined in this account that large and indoor herds of pigs, or flocks of poultry, were in a minority before the war, even though they may have made a disproportionate contribution to production. Equally, it is clear that small herds and flocks on mixed farms disappeared rapidly in the 1960s and '70s, while the number of specialists operating on a large scale increased. It also seems undeniable that these specialist producers adopted new breeds, feeds, housing systems, and methods of disease control, and probably did so to a greater extent than the decreasing number of mixed farmers who chose to retain a small pig or poultry unit. This was not without the landscape and animal welfare effects predicted by Harrison and Professor Brambell's Committee in the mid-1960s, as the continuing debate over sow stalls, and the later (after 1985) renaissance in free-range egg production, demonstrates. But examining the evidence of farms recorded in the FMS, as well as the national and regional statistics, it is impossible to escape the conclusion that the place of pigs and poultry on most farms changed radically in the forty years after the Second World War, and that the pigs and poultry remaining in the hands of specialist producers were very different animals from their pre-war predecessors. Teleology or not, that was what happened.

---

52 Woods, 'Rethinking the History of Modern Agriculture', p. 166.

10

Conclusions

The first four chapters of this book demonstrate that new technologies became available between the mid-1930s and the mid-1980s and that their production and adoption were encouraged by government policy; the remaining chapters explain why their adoption took time. Before attempting to draw more general conclusions, it is worth summarising the story as told so far.

Summarising Agricultural Change 1939–85

Chapter 2 examined research and development in agriculture. Much of this was funded directly by government through the ARC or indirectly by its support for university-based researchers. As this chapter demonstrates, the funding was not given uncritically or unthinkingly. Throughout these fifty years, to a greater or lesser extent, government ministers and civil servants, as well as others outside the direct policy-forming network, questioned the amount of money going into agricultural research and the purposes to which it was put. Despite this questioning, funding for agricultural research was maintained, at least into the 1970s. The kind of research that was funded was constantly under tension. In general, scientists argued that it was best to carry out fundamental research to explain how plants and animals worked, at a molecular or cellular level if necessary. Knowledge of this sort, they felt, could then be applied to practical problems. Research funders and farmers, on the other hand, were often more interested in finding immediate answers to current problems. It was not a dilemma that was confined to this period or this country. As Jonathan Harwood has pointed out, academics in German agricultural colleges in the late nineteenth and early twentieth centuries often felt that the way to increase their professional standing was to engage in more academic research at the expense of an immediately practical focus.[1] Nevertheless, the scientists could certainly cite several examples of fundamental research being transmuted with reasonable rapidity into

---

[1] J. Harwood, *Technology's Dilemma: Agricultural Colleges between Science and Practice in Germany, 1860–1934* (Bern, 2005).

Conclusions

practical application. The work on the biochemistry and physiology of ruminant digestion carried out at the Hannah Dairy Research Institute and the Rowett Research Institute in the late 1950s and early 1960s, for example, led to a reformulation of feeding standards for cattle and sheep by the late 1960s. Studies of spermatogenesis at Cambridge led not only to improved methods of artificial insemination in cattle but also to the application of AI to pigs, and ultimately to work on embryo transfer, cloning of animals, and in vitro fertilisation for humans. The Welsh Plant Breeding Station at Aberystwyth became widely known among farmers for its new grass varieties from the 1930s onwards.

It is, as we saw, less easy to quantify the research expenditure of private firms, but they clearly made a significant contribution to developments in machinery and pesticides in particular. Not that they always worked alone: as we saw, there was co-operation, co-ordinated by the Ministry of Agriculture, between university researchers and pesticide manufacturers, and although there were government-funded agricultural engineering institutes in England and Scotland, much of the machinery development work, most notably the development of the three-point linkage for tractors, was carried out by the manufacturers.[2]

There was also a kind of three-point linkage in the guidance and administration of agricultural research, between government, researchers, and farmers, as we have discussed in chapter 3. This could be seen both in institutional and personal terms. In other words, there were institutions such as the AIC, EHFs, and education and advisory organisations, each of which included government representatives, farmers, and scientists among their membership and guiding Councils. Whereas the ARC was normally dominated by scientists, its chair was often a prominent landowner such as the Duke of Northumberland (chair 1958–68) or Lord Porchester (chair from 1978). The president of the NFU was a member of the AIC, and when it was relaunched as the AAC in 1963 six of its members were large-scale farmers, landowners, or land agents. The EHFs were launched in the 1940s specifically to make a link between research and farming practice, and one of the principal functions of the various forms of agricultural education, and the advisory services, was to ensure that farmers were aware of technical developments relevant to their farming. The role of the National Institute for Agricultural Botany was to assess new varieties, and the MMB was a major source of technical information. For many farmers, however, the major source of technical information remained the farming press, assisted, probably to a lesser extent, by radio and television broadcasts, and conversations with their farming neighbours.

2   P. Dewey, 'Iron Harvests of the Field': The Making of Farm Machinery in Britain since 1800 (Lancaster, 2008), pp. 276–84.

In concluding chapter 3, we argued that in agriculture, as in many other industries, the process of changing new science to accepted technology involved multiple stages, each involving different kinds of institutions and people, often using different languages (discourses) and transmitting ideas in different media. As Peter Jones, among others, has demonstrated, this was by no means a complete novelty as far as farming was concerned, although of course the details differed considerably.[3] Moreover, it could be argued that at least some of the innovations that were widely adopted after 1945 could have been taken up before 1939. Friesian cows, fertilisers, milking machines, and tractors are obvious examples. But to a greater extent than ever before technical change was reinforced and encouraged by government policy after 1939. As we have argued in chapter 4, there were only a few years in the 1939–85 period, from the early 1950s to the early 1960s, when government price and other policies were inimical to output expansion. In the 1950s, extra output had overcome the immediate post-war crisis, and relatively cheap food was available on the world market. For much of the rest of the time, the accent was on expansion, for a variety of reasons. In the early post-war years, it was a matter of maximising production to overcome rationing without using scarce foreign exchange. From 1960, the farmers convinced the Ministry of Agriculture, if not always the Treasury, that increased domestic output could make a worthwhile contribution to the perennial balance of payments problems, and after UK entry into what became the European Union, increased farm output reduced the UK budget contribution. This, therefore, is the scientific, technical, and policy context within which farmers had to make decisions about the use of new technologies, and those are the issues to which we turn in the remaining chapters of the book.

In examining technical change, we have chosen to focus, in chapter 5, on dairy farming, partly for pragmatic reasons, in that it is the farming type for which we have detailed data, but also because it is a farming system. In other words, we have studied the combination of technical changes on specialist dairy and mainly dairy farms, which is what most of the farms for which we have detailed data were, at least at the beginning of our study period. This contrasts with some previous detailed studies of technical change, which have examined changes in a single technique, such as silage making, AI in cattle, AI in pigs, or herringbone parlours.[4] It also reflects reality, in that farmers made decisions about

---

[3] P.M. Jones, *Agricultural Enlightenment: Knowledge, Technology, and Nature, 1750–1840* (Oxford, 2016).

[4] P. Brassley, 'Silage in Britain, 1880–1990: The Delayed Adoption of an Innovation', *Agric. Hist. Rev.* 44 (1996), pp. 63–87; M. Riley and D.C. Harvey, 'Oral Histories, Farm Practice and Uncovering Meaning in the Countryside', *Social and Cultural Geography* 8 (2007), pp. 391–415; P. Brassley, 'Cutting across Nature? The History of Artificial Insemination in Pigs in the UK', *Studies in the*

Conclusions

new technologies in the context of their whole farming businesses. There remains, therefore, an opportunity for comparative studies of arable farming systems, or hill farming systems, or intensive livestock systems, although we have discussed some of the major changes in pig and poultry production in chapter 9 because they had an impact on the way in which dairy farms operated. The process of specialisation and expansion, which we discuss in chapter 8, can thus be seen as the result of changes in both dairying and pig and poultry production, all of which were occurring at the same time. We argue, however, at the beginning of chapter 5, that dairy farming is a good farm type to choose for this kind of study simply because it was practised on such a large proportion of English and Welsh farms at the beginning of our study period. Furthermore, the increase in yield per acre and per unit of labour, which was one of the major effects of technical change on dairy farms, parallels the increase in crop yields per acre and labour unit that were found on arable farms, and arose from a similar complex of technical and organisational changes, while obviously differing in detail.

The dramatic contrasts between pre- and post-Second World War farming have concentrated much historical attention on the six wartime years.[5] More recent historians have suggested that the war years were not especially remarkable in terms of technical change or changes in output, but essentially produced a relatively small output increase at the expense of a big increase in land and labour inputs.[6] Ten years after the war, a prominent academic could still make trenchant criticisms of the breeding, feeding, and housing systems on dairy farms.[7] By then, however, the major changes that affected dairying over the forty years after the war – increasing total milk output and yield per cow, increasing herd sizes, decreasing numbers of producers, and falling farm gate milk prices – were already in train, albeit slowly. In the 1960s and '70s, total cow numbers in the country as a whole changed little, so clearly the extra milk production came from yield increases. In Cornwall, Devon, and Dorset, the story is a little more complex because cow numbers rose

---

History and Philosophy of Biological and Biomedical Sciences 38 (2007), pp. 442–61; S. Wilmot, 'From "Public Service" to Artificial Insemination: Animal Breeding Science and Productive Research in Early Twentieth-Century Britain', *Studies in the History and Philosophy of Biological and Biomedical Sciences* 38 (2007), pp 411–41; O. Grant, *The Diffusion of the Herringbone Parlour: A Case Study in the History of Agricultural Technology*, University of Oxford Discussion Papers in Economic and Social History, no. 27 (Oxford, 1998).

[5] Initially in K.A.H. Murray, *Agriculture*, in K. Hancock (ed.), *History of the Second World War: United Kingdom Civil Series* (London, 1955).

[6] See, for example, B. Short, C. Watkins, and J. Martin (eds), *The Front Line of Freedom: British Farming in the Second World War* (Exeter, 2007).

[7] See references to M.McG. Cooper, *Competitive Farming* (London, 1956) in chapter 5.

as the region specialised further in dairy farming and other parts of the country concentrated on other enterprises. But many small producers in the three south-western counties left dairy farming as they did in the rest of the country, and other changes replicated those further north and east. There was a major change in the dominant dairy breed as Friesians took over from Shorthorns, Ayrshires, and Channel Island cattle, although again the south-west was slightly different in that the South Devon was a more popular breed among dairy farmers there, and still maintained a significant minority of the cows in the dairy herd into the 1970s. The region was similar to elsewhere, however, in its adoption of AI, not only as a means of access to improved genetic material but also as a way of grading up non-Friesian herds to Friesian. It is also worth noting that the change to a new breed was often associated with a new generation taking over the farm.

It is difficult to be certain about the extent to which grassland management improved. In the 1930s, and even later, English farmers were often criticised for their reliance on cheap purchased concentrate feeds at the expense of maximising the use of grass. By the 1960s, farmers in the south-west and elsewhere recognised the importance of grassland management but also admitted to big variations in individual competence levels. This is not something that is easy to quantify. As far as summer grazing is concerned, even if reliable data on changes in stocking levels were available, they would not mean much without considering other variables. For want of anything better, it is often tempting to examine levels of nitrogen (N) fertiliser use on grassland as a proxy for changes in grazing management, but this carries its own dangers. While it might be the case that increased N use went along with improved grass varieties and better grazing management, it could also be used as a substitute for both. Whatever it means, we can see that the use of increased N levels came late – beginning in the early 1970s – to the south-west but was then adopted rapidly, although big variations between farms remained.

It is easier to identify and quantify changes in winter feeding methods for cows. The hay and roots diet that was standard in the 1950s and fitted well into a mixed farming system gave way initially to a mixture of hay and kale and increasingly from the 1970s to a system that relied mainly on silage. The multiplicity of reasons that delayed the adoption of silage has been investigated in some detail before, and there is no need to repeat the analysis here, except to emphasise the importance of improved forage harvesters for both labour saving and silage quality.[8] It is more important to point out that the move to silage, especially self-feed silage, often precipitated a reorganisation or modernisation of the farm buildings. While the change from hand milking to machine milking could be

---

[8] A previous investigation was Brassley, 'Silage in Britain, 1880–1990'.

accomplished at relatively low capital cost with only minor modifications to the virtually ubiquitous cowshed, the introduction of silage was often associated, from the late 1960s onwards, with more extensive changes to the whole dairy set-up, involving milking parlours, bulk tanks, housing in cubicles, and manure handling as slurry. Naturally, such major changes were also often associated with generational change, and most importantly they required significant capital investments.

The willingness and ability of farmers to make investments was influenced, if not determined, by their tenurial status. As we point out in chapter 6, the interwar years had been marked by low levels of investment, in both landlord's and tenant's capital. Post-war legislation restricting the landlord's ability to increase rents, and taxing those received at relatively high levels, reduced incentives to invest. Landlords responded in various ways. Some took land back in hand when they could and farmed it themselves. Others simply sold up, usually to their sitting tenants, and some carried on as before, although often without much enthusiasm for investing in their farms, or sometimes with little ability to do so. Owner-occupiers, who in theory might have found it more difficult to find capital, because they had to finance land purchases as well as paying for their own buildings, in fact seem to have found the acquisition of funds easier than many tenants. In part, as the comments of farmers recorded in chapter 6 reveal, it was because bank managers saw farms as safe and profitable locations for loans in the 1960s and '70s. For those who borrowed, the prevailing high rates of inflation were more of a solution than a problem, as they paid off their loans in an effectively devalued currency. Many owner-occupiers were especially anxious to acquire neighbouring land or farms when they could, whether to buy or rent, since such land could often be farmed without further investments in machinery, and with an already-existing labour force. Consequently, as the data in chapter 6 show, the number of mixed-tenure farms increased considerably. The other major factor affecting the willingness to invest was the availability of various government grant schemes, introduced when agricultural policies were promoting increased domestic production.

All these factors are identifiable, and to some extent quantifiable, and we have attempted to identify and quantify them in chapters 5 and 6, but there is another important variable that is much harder to measure, but no less important, and that is confidence. By the 1960s, farmers seem to have become convinced that governments would not allow what they thought of as the bad old days of the 1920s and '30s to re-occur. In fact, the early 1920s and the later 1930s saw increasing farm incomes, farmers produced as much as not more in volume terms, especially of livestock products, and the industry's total factor productivity increased. But over the whole period the lean years outnumbered the fat, and that was what farmers remembered.⁹ As we saw in chapter 4, both immediately after the war and in 1960 their representatives went to great lengths to make sure that national agricultural policy was output-expanding, and their success in doing so was presumably reflected in the average farmer's confidence that investment would be worthwhile, at least until the introduction of milk quotas in April 1984.

The increasing capital investment on farms was accompanied by a decrease in the use of labour, especially the permanently employed labour force, as we demonstrate in chapter 7. It was the traditional farm workers that left in the greatest numbers, attracted by higher wages in other occupations, or not replaced when they retired. Farmers and their families did a greater proportion of the physical work on the farms, assisted by contractors, and by a variety of part-time and casual labour. They learned a new set of skills to cope with increased mechanisation, as horses and horse tackle were replaced by tractors and tractor implements, together with the products of the chemical industry, from fertilisers and pesticides to veterinary medicines. But stockmanship skills remained important. The number of farmers in the south-west declined less than in other regions, presumably as a result of the greater emphasis on dairying, which made it easier for small farmers to survive. The number of small farms did decrease, but, as we argue in chapter 8, many farmers found it easier to increase the size of their main enterprise than to increase the size of their farm. There was a double logic in doing so. It was partly to make full use of the capacity of any specialist machinery, and partly a matter of expertise. If new methods required new knowledge and training, it was easier to become expert in one enterprise rather than several. Furthermore, the traditional argument for mixed farming, apart from technical complementarities, was that it spread the risk of price fluctuations over several products, a risk that was reduced by the prevalence of guaranteed prices. Again, this was something that was often influenced by family dynamics, with major decisions about specialisation often following a change in generations or the entry of a new generation into the family labour force.

It was the intensive livestock enterprises – pigs and poultry – that were most affected by this trend. As with the employed labour force, there were push and pull factors involved, as we show in chapter 9. As specialist pig and poultry producers grew in size, they could achieve

9   P. Brassley, 'British Farming between the Wars', in P. Brassley, J. Burchardt, and L. Thompson (eds), *The English Countryside between the Wars: Regeneration or Decline?* (Woodbridge, 2006), pp. 187–99; P. Brassley, 'Agricultural Output, Costs and Incomes in the United Kingdom, 1919–1940', in J.-M. Chevet and G. Béaur (eds), *Measuring Agricultural Growth: Land and Labour Productivity in Western Europe from the Middle Ages to the Twentieth Century (England, France and Spain)* (Turnhout, 2014), pp. 181–91.

economies in labour use that were denied to the farmer with a few animals in non-specialist buildings. Faced with the decision to get bigger, which usually required capital investment, or get out, many dairy farmers decided that whatever capital investment they could manage was best devoted to their main enterprise, the cows, so they got out of pigs and/or poultry. Those that remained often went the other way, and specialised in either pigs or poultry, so that intensive livestock production continued in the south-west and increased in technical efficiency, as the data in chapter 9 suggest, but it was no longer spread evenly across all of the farms in the region.

Economics and Technical Change

We cannot claim to be the first to study technical change or its causes and effects in wartime and post-war UK agriculture. Agricultural economists have been making detailed studies of the industry since well before the Second World War, and technical change was usually among the topics that they found important.[10] The standard model they developed to explain changes in the supply of a farm product identified the price of the product, the price of other products that the farm might produce, costs, the state of technology, and the goals of the farmer as the important variables. A price increase would be expected to increase supply, and vice versa, and an increase in the cost of inputs would be expected to reduce supply. The paradox they faced was that, for much of the post-war period, prices, after allowing for inflation, were falling, costs of labour and often of land were rising, yet output increased. They resolved the paradox by pointing out that the state of technology was not constant, and that farmers were on a 'treadmill' with respect to technical change. This was a concept developed by the American economist Willard W. Cochrane.[11] He pointed out that in an industry with many producers, none of which supplied a significant proportion of the industry's total output, an individual farmer could adopt an output-increasing technology without having much or any effect on the market price, and thereby increase his profits. However, when large numbers of farmers, attracted by these higher profits, adopt the new technology, the price will fall, because the

---

[10] R. Cohen, *The Economics of Agriculture* (Cambridge, 1940); E. Thomas, *An Introduction to Agricultural Economics* (London, 1949); J. Ashton and S.J. Rogers (eds), *Economic Change and Agriculture* (Edinburgh, 1968); M. Capstick, *The Economics of Agriculture* (London, 1970); C. Ritson, *Agricultural Economics: Principles and Policy* (London, 1977); B.E. Hill and K. Ingersent, *An Economic Analysis of Agriculture* (London, 1977); and B. Hill and D. Ray, *Economics for Agriculture: Food, Farming and the Rural Economy* (Basingstoke, 1987) were among some of the texts in the UK.

[11] W.W. Cochrane, *Farm Prices, Myth and Reality* (Minneapolis, 1958).

demand for food is relatively constant. This lower price will then make the older techniques increasingly unprofitable, so eventually all farmers will have a considerable incentive to introduce the innovation, so reducing the market price still further. The initial innovators will then search for further new technologies, and the whole process will begin again, but with the treadmill, in Cochrane's image, revolving a little faster.[12] There was also an 'asset fixity' theory, which was a further elaboration of this idea, explaining that output expansion at times of rising prices would not necessarily be followed by contraction when prices fell because durable assets would then have a low salvage value.[13] For example, if some farmers expanded their dairy herds because receipts from milk rose, they would find, when receipts fell, that they had fallen for other farmers too, so that nobody would wish to pay decent prices for any surplus cows they might wish to sell off. In consequence, larger dairy herds would remain so. But what really mattered was the constant pressure to adopt new technology.

According to economic theory, as soon as the marginal (i.e. extra) return from implementing an innovation exceeded the marginal cost of doing so, the profit-maximising farmer would adopt the new technology. Farm management advisers used the same idea in assessing the effects of small changes in the management of the farm. They called it partial budgeting.[14] The difficulty lay in assessing marginal costs and returns, both of which might vary over time and with the individual circumstances of a particular farm or farming family. The work of the agricultural economists was mostly devoted to explaining the behaviour of the agricultural industry as a whole, as has been the work of the historians. They, too have emphasised the importance of technical change in the UK and, like the economists, have mostly concentrated their analysis at the national level or upon the typical farmer.[15]

Inside the Black Box

Analysing technical change in agriculture at the national level or by examining the behaviour of a notional 'typical farmer' is reminiscent

---

[12] Hill and Ray, *Economics for Agriculture*, pp. 282–3.
[13] Hill and Ingersent, *An Economic Analysis of Agriculture*, p. 52.
[14] G.W. Furness, 'Farm Business Management', in R.J. Halley (ed.), *The Agricultural Notebook* (17th edn, London, 1982), pp. 602–3.
[15] See, e.g., B.A. Holderness, 'Apropos the Third Agricultural Revolution: How Productive Was British Agriculture in the Long Boom, 1954–1973?', in P. Mathias and J.A. Davis (eds), *Agriculture and Industrialization from the Eighteenth Century to the Present Day* (Oxford, 1996); J. Martin, *The Development of Modern Agriculture: British Farming since 1931* (Basingstoke, 2000); P. Brassley, 'Output and Technical Change in Twentieth-Century British Agriculture', *Agric. Hist. Rev.* 48 (2000), pp. 60–84.

of what Rosenberg has characterised as the 'black box' problem.[16] What he meant by this was that economists (and the criticism probably applies less to historians) have often treated the details of technical change as unimportant, concentrating only on its consequences. In other words, it might as well have gone on inside a black box, the contents of which remained uninvestigated. But, he argued, the specific features of individual technologies are important, because they can affect all kinds of variables, from the rate of productivity change and the nature of the underlying learning process to the speed of technology transfer and the effectiveness of the relevant government policies. He suggested that the cost reductions resulting from the improvement of an innovation could be greater than those arising from the introduction of the innovation in the first place, and surveyed other studies suggesting that technical decisions taken at one point in time could affect later learning processes or adoption decisions (the path dependency idea), that there would always be a range of production possibilities within the existing knowledge framework, and that high profits resulted in rapid diffusion of new technologies whereas local conditions could impede them. In short, the technical details mattered as far as the speed of innovation and adoption, and their effect, were concerned.[17] Most of the studies on which he relied were about individual technical changes and their impact on agriculture (e.g. the introduction of the self-binding reaper in the nineteenth century, or hybrid corn in Iowa in the early twentieth century), but we maintain that the principle of looking inside the black box applies equally well to our work on the impact on the whole agricultural industry of a combination of changes occurring and interacting contemporaneously.

The implication of this is that the extent to which, and the speed with which, technical innovations were adopted depended on the characteristics of both the innovation and the adopting farmers. Innovations that required a lot of capital and were complex or hard to manage should therefore have been adopted more slowly than those that were simple and easily understood. Labour-saving innovations should have been adopted more rapidly on big farms with lots of non-family labour and more slowly on small family farms. Output-increasing or land-saving innovations should have been especially attractive to small farmers. Consequently, new varieties of cereals or grasses, which required no new capital equipment and produced higher yields than those they replaced, should have been adopted more rapidly than tractors, which required farm workers to learn new skills and farmers to find capital, rather than breeding their own carthorse replacements on the farm. AI for dairy cows should have expanded more rapidly than AI for sows, on the grounds

---

[16] N. Rosenberg, *Inside the Black Box: Technology and Economics* (Cambridge, 1982).
[17] Rosenberg, *Inside the Black Box*, pp. vii, 8–22.

that cows were treated by travelling trained specialists whereas farmers and farm workers had to be trained to use AI for sows.[18]

To some extent, these predictions were borne out by historical reality. As we saw in chapters 5 and 9, the use of AI in dairy herds expanded rapidly after the war, while the use of AI in pigs expanded more slowly and never attained the same level of penetration. New cereal varieties were adopted relatively soon after they were introduced, although it is important to recognise that there were systemic differences between the kind of long-strawed varieties that were popular before the war and the shorter-strawed higher yielding varieties that took over from the 1950s onwards. Long-strawed varieties could not cope with very high levels of fertility without lodging, but the kind of straw that they produced was well-adapted to thatching ricks; short-strawed varieties could use mineral fertilisers more effectively and were more easily harvested by combines. Thus changing from one short-strawed variety to another was simple, whereas the change from long-strawed to short-strawed varieties was more complex. For dairy farmers, grass varieties were more important, and as we saw in chapter 5 the introduction of lusher tetraploid ryegrasses produced difficulties in haymaking, since they took longer to desiccate. On the other hand, they were well-suited to silage making. Again, therefore, a systemic change was required. However, it is interesting to note (in chapter 5) that few of the farmers that we interviewed attached much importance to the personal selection of grass seed varieties; the majority seemed happy to accept the suggestions or recommendations of their merchants. The adoption of tractors occurred much more rapidly after the war than the capital/complexity model would have predicted. So far, therefore, although we appear to have identified some significant variables, we cannot claim to have explained the process of post-war technical adoption.

Obviously, some technologies, such as pesticides, antibiotics, and forage harvesters, were not available before the war, but many important ones were. An earlier analysis identified the importance of post-war adoption of pre-existing technology.[19] This implies that such technology existed before the Second World War and so could have been adopted then, but for some reason was not, or at least not to the same extent that it was adopted post-war. There are, at least at first sight, numerous examples. Mineral fertilisers, initially superphosphate and later nitrogen and potassium sources, were available in the nineteenth century. Their use doubled in the fifty years before the First World War, when about a million tons were being sold each year in the UK and increased by about 40 per cent again by the end of the 1930s. This increase, however, seems

---

[18] For the reasons why this was so, see Brassley, 'Cutting across Nature?'.
[19] Brassley, 'Output and Technical Change in Twentieth-Century British Agriculture', p. 77.

insignificant in comparison with the post-war increases. By the early 1950s, over four million tons per year were used, and their use plateaued from the early 1970s at about seven million tons per year. Similarly with purchased feedingstuffs, another nineteenth-century introduction: annual sales of six million tons before the First World War became nine million in the late 1930s but nearly fourteen million by 1970 and over sixteen million tons in the UK in 1985.[20] Friesian cows, milking machines, milking parlours, tractors, and silage could all have been found on British farms before the Second World War, and so could the kind of specialisation that we identified as an important component of post-war change in chapter 9. In Norfolk, for example, the Alley brothers had an all-cereal farm near Fakenham, and on the downlands of southern England the Hosier brothers and Rex Paterson, among others, had specialist dairy farms.[21]

It is true that not all of these comparisons are strictly fair. As argued above, increased fertiliser use on the cereal crop went along with new varieties. Replacing older breeds with Friesian cows was accomplished most easily with the aid of AI, and although successful AI techniques were known before 1939, its widespread adoption required a national framework of collecting stations and trained operatives.[22] The major problems in milking machine technology had been solved by the late 1920s, but producing the necessary vacuum was clearly made easier when a mains electricity supply was available, and for most farms that did not come until after the war. Silage was a good example of the sort of learning-by-doing incremental improvements discussed by Rosenberg, and clearly benefitted from the increased availability of mechanical handling from the 1960s onwards. Pre-war tractors, with relatively low power outputs, metal spud wheels that were illegal on roads, and no three-point linkage, were less flexible and less useful than even the smaller early post-war tractors such as the Ferguson TE-20.[23] Opening the technology black box for more detailed internal inspection therefore takes us some way to explaining the pre-/post-war differences, but the fact remains that the sort of radical changes pioneered by the Alley or Hosier brothers stood out because they were not widely emulated before the war.

If a more detailed examination of technical change per se only goes so far, can we go further by complementing it with a study of the remaining

---

[20] Brassley, 'Output and Technical Change in Twentieth-Century British Agriculture', p. 72.

[21] Brassley, 'British Farming between the Wars', p. 196; J. Martin, 'Rex Paterson (1903–1978): Pioneer of Grassland Dairy Farming and Agricultural Innovator', in R.W. Hoyle (ed.), *The Farmer in England, 1650–1980* (Farnham, 2013), pp. 295–324.

[22] Wilmot, 'From "Public Service" to Artificial Insemination', pp. 411–41.

[23] Dewey, 'Iron Harvests of the Field', p. 217.

variable in the economist's supply model, the goals or objectives of the farmer? The standard economic model assumes that the objective of the entrepreneur is profit maximisation, and other things being equal there is likely to be a relationship between technical change and profitability, or its counterpart, loss minimisation, although in practice the relationship is not a simple one, because innovators can sometimes find themselves bearing the costs of experimentation or development or simply trying out an idea that turns out not to work, as farmer 576 recognised: 'I think we kept up with technical development, but we weren't at the forefront, partly because I wanted somebody else to make the mistakes.' Farmer 466, who confessed to being 'too interested in technology to make real money', reflected on this after he had given up farming:

> I think that if I had life again I would change the emphasis, I'd be much more serious about budgeting and financial management and treat the technology as serving the accountancy, whereas for most of my days I went for technology and let the accountant … do the accounts at the end of the year.

The assumption of profit maximisation also needs to be qualified. There were certainly some farmers who expressed their objectives in this way, such as farmer 3/1, who, thinking back to his father and grandfather, felt that he and they had much the same objective:

> The common ground was that we all strived to make the farm profitable, but by different means. So we all looked beyond the pale to make it profitable, Dad had his own way of doing it, I've got my way, so in that way we were similar. Infrastructure was Dad's way, he was building up the value of the farm all the time, perfectly good business practice, saving money, OK the technical side of the cows wasn't very good, but it didn't need to be.

The difference in attitudes to technology and profitability expressed between these two farmers encapsulates the difficulty in generalisation, even between farmers who both had profitability in mind as an objective.

Other farmers expressed their objectives differently, in terms of simply keeping the farm going, or increasing its size, of having something to pass on to the next generation, or maintaining a comfortable lifestyle, or farming well. Asked what made a good farmer, farmer 243 replied 'First thing is they've got to be tidy, no rubbish littered everywhere, keep hedges tidy and gutters clean', and the desire to be thought well of, or respected, by fellow farmers and their families was clearly an important objective for many farmers: 'We all want to be seen to be doing a successful job, and having a new tractor every year is a symbol of that' (farmer 2/7). In these circumstances, profit maximisation became less important than other objectives. At its most extreme, it was expressed by a farmer (farmer

Conclusions

2/7's daughter) who took over from her father after the end of our study period: 'we do it because we're mad or we love it. We don't do it for the money.' For her, therefore, job satisfaction is clearly important:

> I couldn't do anything else now, no two days are the same, you're working outdoors, you're your own boss, my office is a square mile of beautiful countryside, OK the roof leaks sometimes and it can be bitterly cold, but it's a great working environment, the job satisfaction's vast, the financial rewards aren't so great, as I say, we're all mad.

Her father, who did farm in our study period, expressed the same idea in a milder form: 'I think the lifestyle is just as important as the financial side. We have a good living because everything's paid for through the farm.' The need to balance lifestyle and profitability was also expressed by farmer 782, who farmed on a smaller scale as a tenant on poorer land:

> I was trying to make a reasonable living and farm in a sustainable way that could be carried on, and to keep the farm looking tidy, there was a lot of satisfaction from that. Father probably felt the same, but I think I had a little more ambition than him. If it had been practical to take on more land, if it was close by, I would have done. I was actually offered two other ... farms while we were there, and we went and looked at them, but because we had this good retail outlet, for the potatoes and the cream, so when we weighed everything up it didn't seem worthwhile to move, so we decided there was no advantage in moving. The retail side was a fair proportion of our incomes.

The idea of balancing lifestyle and profitability, and taking a long-term view, was encapsulated in the traditional saying quoted with approval by farmer 535: 'you should live as if you'll die tomorrow and farm as if you'll live for ever'. He argued that

> A successful farmer would be one who has gone through his life and is as happy at the end as he was when he went into farming. If he's happy at the end he's been successful through that period of time. ... Father might have looked back and thought he might have been more successful, but he was always relaxed and wasn't wanting what he hadn't got.

A similar recognition of the importance of balancing profitability and lifestyle, tradition and change, was found in farmer 570's reflections on his neighbours and his own experience:

> They were good farmers, they looked after the animals, the crops, the grass. Most people moved with the times. A lot of it's been forced by law, like dehorning cattle or having a safety cab on the tractor, people used to put their waste down streams, you can't do that, they've either died out or changed, like I said just now about gobbling up their

neighbour's farms. I sit on the fence, because a lot of things go round, I tend to be a bit traditional. There was more of a community atmosphere years ago. My Dad's brother had a thrashing machine, so that used to go round the farms in the winter and everyone had a few ricks of corn, and the neighbours would send their men to help, so that was all communal, and Mother would take food up, and they'd sit down and laugh and chatter, it was all part of country life, it was the same with haymaking, she'd bring a kettle up in the field and light a fire under the plough.

Clearly, therefore, the assumption of profit maximisation goes nowhere near capturing the variety of goals or objectives to be found among the post-war farming community.[24] The effects of this variety, and of other personal characteristics, on the way in which technical adoption decisions were taken was identified at the time by rural sociologists and used by agricultural economists. Factors such as age, education, farm size, and sources of advice were identified as different between those who adopted innovations early and those who took longer to do so.[25] Perhaps unsurprisingly, these are the factors that have often been mentioned in connection with technical change decisions in this book. Although younger farmers might have been more open to change than older, what has emerged most often in previous chapters has been the importance of a generational change. A new generation taking over the management of the farm, at whatever age (and in some cases sons could be well into middle age before taking over from fathers), or a child leaving school and beginning to work on the farm, was often the trigger for a technical change or a change in the enterprise mix, and this appears to be as likely to have happened in the 1950s as in the 1980s.

In comparison with generational change, education levels appear to have been less important. In general (and as chapter 3 shows, this was typical of agriculture as a whole), the level of formal education among the farmers we interviewed was not high. Only one farmer had a degree in agriculture, although two others had degrees in other subjects. There were more who had studied at agricultural colleges, or farm institutes, or undertaken part-time or day-release courses. Farmer 272's son, who completed his formal agricultural education in the early 1980s, felt that 'Having had some training made it easier to pick up on new ideas', but overall it was difficult to make a clear connection between the level of

---

[24] And not only in the later twentieth century. Farmers in late eighteenth-century Denmark could be identified, according to one historian, as either 'strivers' or 'fatalists', with the former being quick to commute labour services when they had the opportunity to do so and consequently introducing new farming methods, while the fatalists were scorned by estate officials for their lack of ambition. See Jones, *Agricultural Enlightenment*, p. 224.

[25] Hill and Ray, *Economics for Agriculture*, pp. 292–3.

Conclusions

formal education and the uptake of new technology. In part, this was because there was an overlap between education and what might today be identified as continuing professional development: in other words, the use of training courses and advisory services. Their use was discussed in detail at the end of chapter 3, from which it emerged that there was a clear difference between farmers that preferred more formal sources of information and advice and those that preferred to use less formal networks. On the whole, it seems likely that those using formal sources were more likely to adopt new technology earlier than those using informal networks, but there was considerable overlap, and what might be important in relation to one technical change might be less so for another.

In contrast, variables such as farm size and specialisation, and whether a farm was tenanted or owner-occupied, had a clearer relationship with technical change. As chapters 6 and 8 demonstrate, owner-occupiers found it easier to make innovations requiring significant capital inputs at a time that suited them, rather than a landlord's business plan. Similarly, bigger or more specialised farms were more likely to be aware of new technology, but again, in both cases there was considerable overlap between categories. Thus farm 109, which was owner-occupied, appeared to be less involved in technical change than farm 782, which was half its size and tenanted.

As Picon points out, 'Technological thought is a complex system functioning at different levels. For each actor in the process of production, it comprises a mixture of know-how and interiorized rules of decision-making and action.'[26] Thus, as Mokyr has argued in discussing economic growth in early modern England, change was dependent, at least in part, upon 'what people knew and believed, and how those beliefs affected their economic behaviour'.[27] Developments in science and technology, coupled with education and advice, changed what farmers knew; agricultural policy changed their beliefs. In identifying the differences between the pre- and post-war periods, the factor that stands out is the change in attitudes to risk and the confidence that farmers felt in investing. Farmer 929, who began with 107 acres in the late 1950s and was farming nine hundred acres by 1981, all acquired by purchase with money borrowed from the Midland Bank, said, in response to a remark that not many farmers had managed such a level of expansion, 'Several have gone bust trying to do so. You've got to be a gambler. At the time I didn't even analyse it. I just went on merrily, I enjoyed the scene.' Those who did

---

[26] A. Picon, 'Towards a History of Technological Thought', in R. Fox (ed.), *Technological Change: Methods and Themes in the History of Technology* (Amsterdam, 1996), p. 40.

[27] J. Mokyr, *The Enlightened Economy: An Economic History of Britain, 1750–1850* (New Haven, CT, 2009), introduction.

analyse it attributed much to government policy. In another part of the country, Tony Harman, who farmed in Buckinghamshire between 1931 and the 1980s, and was much involved in the original importation of Charolais cattle into the UK, concluded that

> we made no *real* [his italics] progress until after the war. Then we did come into a period of very rapid development and opportunity and very good farming ... When the war ended and farmers weren't immediately dropped, as they had been at the end of the First World War, but continued to be supported by the government, my confidence increased still further. It seemed to me, at that point, that everything was possible.[28]

Farmer 466, quoted earlier as being 'too interested in technology to make any real money', then justified his attitude as a sensible one in the 1960s, '70s, and '80s: 'in those days you could survive and even prosper doing that, it was the policy environment within which we were working'. The economist Allan Buckwell, writing only shortly after this period, emphasised the same thing:

> Producer expectations are clearly influenced by the existence of elaborate, statutorily entrenched support policies. Over a long period of time such measures encourage a sense of security and protection which is likely to modify the risk behaviour of farmers encouraging them to greater investment than they would undertake if exposed to the uncertainties of unsupported markets.[29]

Unanswered Questions

When the policy environment changed, one would expect the investment behaviour and the attitude of farmers to new technology to change also. The first signs of a change in the policy environment came in 1984. By then, there was a surplus of milk products within the CAP countries that had significant budgetary and foreign trade implications. In an attempt to control or reduce the surplus, milk quotas were introduced in April 1984. Milk producers were allocated a production quota and penalised if they exceeded it. For the first time since 1939, therefore (with the possible exception of some vaguer signals operating for a short time in the late 1950s), farmers were officially discouraged from expanding their output. Subsequent policy went further and by the twenty-first century had altered completely. The effect of this on technical change would obviously make a fascinating comparison with our study of the pre-1985

---

[28] T. Harman, *Seventy Summers: The Story of a Farm* (London, 1986), pp. 186–7.
[29] A. Buckwell, 'Economic Signals, Farmers' Response, and Environmental Change', *Journal of Rural Studies* 5 (1989), p. 156.

period, but it is beyond the scope of this book. Much was written about it at the time, and the official archives for the post-1985 period are now becoming increasingly available under the thirty-year rule. Like much of the pre-1985 archive material, they remain largely unexplored, perhaps because there has been so much published material to engage the attention of historians. Further work on them, and on the archives of the pre-1985 period, remains an exciting prospect.

There is also considerable scope for further oral history work in other UK regions. Several years ago, Alec Douet interviewed a sample of East Anglian farmers, much whose evidence concerned the period before the Second World War.[30] It is now important to capture the reflections of the generation that remembers farming before 1970 before it is too late. And not only farming. As we have seen, agriculture became increasingly informed and influenced by science in the post-war years, and the work of science historians, both oral- and archive-based, has become correspondingly important and relevant to agricultural history in recent years.[31] However, while the connection between science and technical change may be obvious, it should also be clear from these conclusions that the appearance and adoption of new technologies was intimately and indivisibly associated with all the other facets of farming, from the structures of agricultural landholding to the development and training of the labour force, the capital structure of farming and landholding, agricultural and environmental policy, and so on, so the future research plans of agricultural historians need to be comprehensive enough to reflect this.

It would also be well worth comparing developments in the UK with those in other European and other developed countries.[32] Comparative work is still in its infancy but has been enormously assisted by the emergence of several international networks: the Flemish CORN (Comparative Rural History of the North Sea Area) network, which began in 1995; the COST Action A35 with European funding in the following

---

[30] A. Douet, *Breaking New Ground: Agriculture in Norfolk 1914–1972* (Aylsham, 2012).

[31] See, e.g., A. Woods, 'Science, Disease and Dairy Production in Britain, c.1927–1980', *Agric. Hist. Rev.* 62 (2014), pp. 294–314; D. Phillips and S. Kingsland (eds), *New Perspectives on the History of Life Sciences and Agriculture* (Cham, Switzerland, 2015); D. Berry, 'Historiography of Plant Breeding and Agriculture', in M. Dietrich, M. Borello, and O. Harman (eds), *Handbook of the Historiography of Biology* (Cham, Switzerland, 2019), pp. 1–22 and the references therein.

[32] See, e.g., B.L. Gardner, *American Agriculture in the Twentieth Century: How It Flourished and What It Cost* (Cambridge, MA, 2002); L. Fernández Prieto, *El Apagón Tecnológico del Franquismo: Estado e innovación en la agricultura Española del siglo XX* (Valencia, 2007); H. Antonson and U. Jansson (eds), *Agriculture and Forestry in Sweden since 1900: Geographical and Historical Studies* (Stockholm, 2011).

decade; and the formation in 2010 of the European Rural History Organisation (EURHO). While the timing and the details vary from place to place, the work done so far, on a European and a global scale, is enough to suggest that the evolution of UK farming, and its technical development in particular since the war, is by no means unique.[33] If the 1939–85 period was one of agricultural revolution, it was a revolution across the developed world.

We are conscious that one important voice remains largely unheard in our account, and that is the voice of those who did *not* take part in this process of change. As we have seen in chapter 7, the number of full-time farmers in England declined by as much as a third in our period, but to find these people, and to explore why they left, and to what extent it affected or was affected by technical change, is more difficult than finding those who survived or thrived and remained in the FMS sample. We found one former member of the sample (farmer 692) who left agriculture, but as he left for health reasons he may not have been typical. Those of us who have been involved with the agricultural industry for many years have known farmers who failed and left. Some went through simple bad luck, some because they made poor management decisions and lost money, some because their interest in extra-marital affairs exceeded their interest in agricultural affairs, and some because they found they could make more money by using their land and buildings for non-agricultural purposes, which should presumably not count as failure. But with the possible exception of the last group, it is difficult to find many surviving examples of these people, and even more difficult to persuade them to talk about their non-participation in the revolution.

The Real Agricultural Revolution?

Whether or not we call it a revolution is in some sense a matter of semantics. Revolution, evolution, rapid change; whatever term we use, what is clear is that agricultural output increased at an unprecedented rate, and that much of the increase was the result of new technology. Whether it was worth the capital and environmental cost is beyond the scope of this book, which is about what happened and why it happened.

[33] D. Grigg, *The Transformation of Agriculture in the West* (Oxford, 1992); S.R. Schrepfer and P. Scranton (eds), *Industrializing Agriculture: Introducing Evolutionary History* (New York, 2004); G. Federico, *Feeding the World: An Economic History of Agriculture 1800–2000* (Princeton, NJ, 2005); P. Lains and V. Pinilla (eds), *Agriculture and Economic Development in Europe since 1870* (London, 2009); E. Thoen and T. Soens (eds), *Struggling with the Environment: Land Use and Productivity; Rural Economy and Society in North-Western Europe, 500–2000* (Turnhout, 2015); C. Martiin, J. Pan-Montojo, and P. Brassley (eds), *Agriculture in Capitalist Europe, 1945–1960: From Food Shortages to Food Surplus* (London, 2016).

Conclusions

For practical reasons, we have concentrated on one region and mostly on farms involved in milk production, but we have attempted to set these in a national and general farming context, and we have argued that the factors that produced change in this region and type of farming are paralleled in other types of farming and other UK regions – indeed, in other European regions. We would not claim that this is a new or different conclusion. What we have attempted to demonstrate is that behind the national and international statistics are thousands of individual stories, and that the process of technical change cannot be understood without some recognition of this variety. For each technical change that was invented, developed, and adopted, quickly in some cases and less so in others, individual farmers had to decide what suited their individual, family, and farming requirements, and make their adoption decisions accordingly. Most typical, perhaps, was farmer 744, who began farming at the end of the war and was in his nineties when interviewed:

> I was neither a leader or a follower in technical change – 'Be not the first to try the new or last to cast the old askew', although I didn't think about it at the time. We were never quite the first in, but not the last in either, once you saw the advantages you did it. But I would never have imagined in my early days that we would be keeping one hundred cows ... and treating them like they do, would never have thought about it, didn't seem possible. I started with twenty cows tied up by the neck and you had to carry the feed to them and clean them out with a wheelbarrow.

BIBLIOGRAPHY

Archive Sources

The Farm Management Survey Fieldbook archive is stored in the Centre for Rural Policy Research, University of Exeter.

Electronic copies of the interviews with farmers are stored in the Essex University UK Data Archive, reference SN851111, 'Processes of Technical Change in British Agriculture: Innovation in the Farming of South West England, 1935–1985' (http://doi.org/10.5255/UKDA-SN-851111).

Other archive sources (marked TNA in the text) are from the UK National Archives, Kew, under the following references:

MAF 38/38, League of Nations European Conference on Rural Life.

MAF38/198, FMS proposals 1928–31.

MAF 113/656, Agricultural Advisory Council: 43rd–48th meetings, 1972–3.

MAF 113/659, Advisory Committee for Agriculture and Horticulture: bulls and public footpaths, 1975–6.

MAF 114/241, South Western Province, Advisory Services, HQ Administration, Devon County Report 1952–3.

MAF 114/275, Agricultural Public Relations: policy, 1951.

MAF 114/332, Report on NAAS 1946–54.

MAF114/747, South Western Province, Advisory Services, HQ Administration, Devon County Report 1962–3.

MAF 114/807, NAAS and the Farmer: A Follow-Up Report to the First Eight Years of NAAS.

MAF117/199, ARC, statements of staff employed on agricultural research.

MAF 117/343, ARC, Post-War Programme, June 1946.

MAF117/409, Agricultural Research Bill 1956: papers.

MAF117/544, Research and Development: Proposed MAFF Organisation Consequent upon Implementation of Rothschild Report Recommendations.

MAF 132/40, press release 24 January 1963, A New Look at Research and Experiment.

MAF 189/655, AIC experimental husbandry committee minutes.

MAF 197/15, Public Relations: Policy, 1949–52.

MAF 197/18, Food Production Drive Publicity Working Party: Minutes of Meetings, 1952–3.

MAF 197/40, BBC Audience Research Report, 1961.

Bibliography

MAF 197/44, Minutes of the BBC Central Agricultural Advisory Committee 21 January 1965.
MAF 197/84, BBC: Morning Broadcasts; Policy.
TNA, MAF 200/142, Report of the ARC 1965–6.
MAF 250/154, Ministry of Agriculture and Fisheries, Departmental Defence Plans Committee, 1951–4.
MAF 253/75, Minutes of the 79th Meeting of the AIC for England and Wales, 28 November 1956.
MAF 253/105, Minutes and Papers of AAC Council Meetings June to October 1963.
MAF 317/63, 1960, Government Talks with Farmers' Unions.
MAF458, Review of Non-Departmental Public Bodies, 1979–80.
T161/487 (Survey of Farm Management), Middleton to Barnes 10 June 1931.
T224/342, 1960, Discussions between MAFF and the NFUs on Agricultural Guarantee Policy.
T224/343, 1960 Discussions between MAFF and the NFUs on Agricultural Guarantee Policy.

Primary Sources

The Interim Report of the Royal Commission Appointed to Inquire into the Economic Prospects of the Agricultural Industry in Great Britain, Cmd.473 (1919).
Report of the Committee on Post-War Agricultural Education in England and Wales, 1943, Cmd.6433 (1943).
Report of the Committee on Agricultural Education in Scotland, Cmd.6704 (1945).
Report of the Committee on Higher Agricultural Education in England and Wales, Cmnd.6728 (1946).
Guarantees for Home Grown Cereals, Cmd.8947 (1953).
Development of Pig Production in the United Kingdom: Report of the Advisory Committee on Development of Pig Production in the UK, Cmd.9588 (London, 1955).
Long Term Assurances for Agriculture, Cmnd.23 (1956).
Report of the Committee on Grassland Utilisation, Cmnd.547 (1958).
Report of the Committee on Further Education for Agriculture Provided by Local Education Authorities, Cmnd.614 (1958).
Agriculture: Report on Talks between the Agriculture Departments and the Farmers' Unions, June–December 1960, Cmnd.1249 (1960).
Report of the Interdepartmental Committee on the Demand for Agricultural Graduates, Cmnd.2419 (1964).
Report of the Technical Committee to Enquire into the Welfare of Animals Kept under Intensive Livestock Husbandry Systems, Cmnd.2836 (London, 1965).

Bibliography

Agriculture Acts 1947 and 1957: Annual Review and Determination of Guarantees 1971, Cmnd.4623 (1971).
Framework for Government Research and Development, Cmnd.5046 (1971–2).
Food from Our Own Resources, Cmnd.6020 (1975).
Farming and the Nation, Cmnd.7458 (1979).
Report of the Committee of Inquiry into the Acquisition and Occupancy of Agricultural Land, Cmnd.7599 (1979).
Royal Commission on Environmental Pollution, Seventh Report: Agriculture and Pollution, Cmnd.7644 (1979).
Agriculture EDC (Economic Development Committee), *The Adoption of Technology in Agriculture: Opportunities for Improvement* (London, 1985).
Agricultural Economics Research Institute, *Agricultural Economics, 1913–1938: Being the Twenty-Fifth Annual Report of the Agricultural Economics Research Institute* (Oxford, 1938).
ARC (Agricultural Research Council), *Index of Agricultural Research 1953–4* (London, 1954).
ARC, *Index of Agricultural Research 1964* (London, 1965).
ARC, *The Nutrient Requirements of Farm Livestock, No.2, Ruminants: Technical Reviews and Summaries* (London, 1965).
Anon, 'Agricultural Improvement Council for England and Wales', *Agriculture* L (1944), pp. 464–68.
— — 'Agricultural Improvement Council for England and Wales: Second Note on Progress', *Agriculture* LI (1945), pp. 514–18.
— — 'Artificial Insemination of Cattle', *Agriculture* 51 (1945), pp. 529–32.
— — *Farming Today Broadcasts: A Series of Agricultural Education and Technical Development Broadcast Talks* (Worcester, 7 volumes published between 1942 and 1948).
— — 'Summer Milk in the South West', *Dairy Farmer*, May 1961, p. 26.
— — *Agriculture in Britain*, Central Office of Information Reference Pamphlet 43 (London, 1965).
Astor, Viscount, and B.S. Rowntree, *British Agriculture: The Principles of Future Policy* (Harmondsworth, 1939).
— — *Mixed Farming and Muddled Thinking* (London, 1946).
Barnard C.S., and J.S. Nix, *Farm Planning and Control* (Cambridge, 1973).
Bell, A., *Corduroy* (London, 1930).
Bellis, D.B., 'Pig Farming in the United Kingdom: Its Development and Future Trends', *Journal of the Royal Agricultural Society of England* 129 (1968), pp. 35–40.
Beresford, T., *We Plough the Fields: British Farming Today* (Harmondsworth, 1975).
Beynon, V.H., *Grassland Management: An Economic Study in Devon*, University of Exeter, Department of Economics (Agricultural Economics) Report no. 138 (Newton Abbot, 1963).
Bingham, S.P., *A Guide to the Development of Grants for Agriculture and*

Bibliography

Horticulture for England and Wales 1940–1982, London: Ministry of Agriculture, Fisheries and Food, Economics Division III, internal publication (London, no date, probably 1982).

Blythe, R., *Akenfield* (London, 1969).

Board of Agriculture and Fisheries, *The Agricultural Output of Great Britain*, Cd.6277 (1912).

Body, R., *Agriculture: The Triumph and the Shame* (London, 1982).

Bradley, J., *Co-operation: A Report on an Experiment in Setting Up Co-operative Groups for the Purpose of Making Grass Silage*, University of Bristol, Department of Economics (Agricultural Economics), Bristol II Province, Report no.125 (Newton Abbot, 1961).

British Council and Department of Scientific and Industrial Research, *Scientific Research in British Universities 1949–51* (London, 1950).

British Library, *Scientific Research in British Universities and Colleges, 1974–5*, vol. II, *Biological Sciences* (London, 1975).

Brockman, J.S., 'Grassland', in R.J. Halley (ed.), *The Agricultural Notebook* (17th edn, London, 1982), pp. 173–202.

Burnside, E., and W.M. Strong, *A Comparison of Pig Production before and after the War: With Special Reference to South West England*, University of Bristol, Department of Economics (Agricultural Economics, Bristol II province), report no. 88 (Newton Abbot, 1955).

Burnside, E., and R.C. Rickard, *An Economic Study of Pig Production in South West England 1953–57*, University of Bristol, Department of Economics (Agricultural Economics), Report no. 105 (Newton Abbot, 1958).

— — *An Economic Study of Pig Production in South West England 1960/61*, University of Exeter, Department of Economics (Agricultural Economics), report no. 129 (Newton Abbot, 1962).

— — *An Economic Study of Pig Production in South West England 1964/65*, University of Exeter, Department of Economics (Agricultural Economics), report no. 158 (Newton Abbot, 1966).

Burnside, E., and A. Sheppard, *Pig Production in South West England 1983–84*, Exeter: University of Exeter, Agricultural Economics Unit, Economic Report no. 93 (Exeter, 1985).

Campbell, K.W.D., 'Production of Bacon and Pork', in J.A. Hanley (ed.), *Progressive Farming: The Maintenance of High Production*, III (London, 1949), pp. 258–64.

Carson, R., *Silent Spring* (London, 1963).

Central Statistical Office, *Annual Abstract of Statistics* (London, annual).

Cherrington, J., *On the Smell of an Oily Rag* (London, 1979).

Cochrane, W.W., *Farm Prices, Myth and Reality* (Minneapolis, 1958).

Cohen, R., *The Economics of Agriculture* (Cambridge, 1940).

Coles, R., 'Current Developments in the Poultry Industry', *Journal of the Royal Agricultural Society of England* 122 (1961), pp. 39–53.

―― 'The Structure of the Poultry Industry of England and Wales', in W.P. Blount (ed.), *Intensive Livestock Farming* (London, 1968), pp. 150–6.
Comber, N.M., 'Discussion on the Organisation of Agricultural Research', *Agricultural Progress* 22 (1947), p. 20.
Committee of the Privy Council for the Organisation and Development of Agricultural Research, *Agricultural Research in Great Britain*, Cmd.6421 (1943).
Cooper, M.McG., *Competitive Farming* (London, 1956).
Court, A., *Seedtime to Harvest: A Farmer's Life* (Bradford on Avon, 1987).
Culpin, C., *Farm Machinery* (London, 1938).
Currie, J.R., and W. Harwood Long, *An Agricultural Survey in South Devon* (Newton Abbot and Totnes, 1929).
Dainton, F., *The Future of the Research Council System*, in Anon, *A Framework for Government Research and Development*, Cmnd.4814, 1971–2.
Devon Agriculture Study Group, *Devon Farming: A First Study* (no place of publication recorded, 1952).
Dexter, K., and D. Barber, *Farming for Profits* (2nd edn, London, 1967).
DSIR (Department of Scientific and Industrial Research) and British Council, *Scientific Research in British Universities and Colleges, 1963–4* (London, 1964).
Evans, R.E., *Rations for Livestock,* Ministry of Agriculture, Fisheries and Food, Bulletin no. 48 (London, 1960).
Fincham, I., 'Animal Health', in R.J. Halley (ed.), *The Agricultural Notebook* (17th edn, London, 1982), pp. 446–81.
Fryer, J., 'The Organisation for Agricultural Research', *Agricultural Progress* 22 (1947), pp. 9–19.
Furness, G.W., 'Farm Business Management', in R.J. Halley (ed.), *The Agricultural Notebook* (17th edn, London, 1982), pp. 585–619.
Hallett, G., *The Economics of Agricultural Land Tenure* (London, 1960).
Halnan, E.T., and F.H. Garner, *The Principles and Practice of Feeding Farm Animals* (2nd edn, London, 1944).
Harman, T., *Seventy Summers: The Story of a Farm* (London, 1986).
Harrison, R., *Animal Machines: The New Factory Farming Industry* (London, 1964).
Heath, W.E., 'Price Fixing Policies in Agriculture', *J. Agric. Econs.* 8 (1948), pp. 4–19.
Henderson, G., *The Farming Ladder* (London, 1944).
House of Commons, *Parliamentary Debates: Standing Committees*, Session 1946-7, vol. II, Agriculture Bill, 11 February–24 April 1947.
Howes, H., 'Poultry on the General Farm', in J.A. Hanley (ed.), *Progressive Farming: The Maintenance of High Production*, IV (London, 1949), pp. 1–40.
King, J., *Cost Accounting as Applied to Agriculture* (London, 1927).

Bibliography

Kirk, J., 'Cattle', in R.J. Halley (ed.), *The Agricultural Notebook* (17th edn, London, 1982), pp. 351–74.

League of Nations, *European Conference on Rural Life: Report of the Preparatory Committee on the Work of Its First Session, April 4–7, 1938* (Geneva, 1938).

Lloyd, D.H., 'The Economics of the Commercial Egg Production Industry of the UK', *J. Agric. Econs.* VI (1955), pp. 242–59.

McConnell, P., *Notebook of Agricultural Facts and Figures for Farmers and Farm Students* (9th edn, London, 1919).

McDonald, P., R.A. Edwards, and J.F.D. Greenhalgh, *Animal Nutrition* (Edinburgh, 1966).

Macmillan, J.A., 'Experimental Farms and Stations of the NAAS, (1) Experimental Husbandry Farms', *Agriculture* LIX (1952), pp. 421–4.

— — 'Experimental Husbandry Farms: Review of Progress', *Agriculture* LIX (1953), pp. 459–62.

Macmillan J.A., and C.E. Hudson, 'NAAS Experimental Husbandry Farms and Horticulture Stations', *Agriculture* LXIII/5 (1956).

Martin, A., *Economics and Agriculture* (London, 1958).

Maxton, J., *The Survey Method of Research in Farm Economics* (London, 1929).

MAF (Ministry of Agriculture and Fisheries), *National Farm Survey of England and Wales (1941–1943): A Summary Report* (London, 1946),

MAFF (Ministry of Agriculture, Fisheries, and Food), *Agricultural Statistics, England and Wales* (London, annual)

— — *The Structure of Agriculture* (London, 1966).

— — *Aids to Management No.8: Dairying* (London, 1967).

— — *At the Farmer's Service* (Pinner, 1968).

— — *The Changing Structure of Agriculture, 1968–1975* (London, 1977).

Ministry of Information, *Land at War: The Official Story of British Farming 1939–1944* (London, 1945).

MMB (Milk Marketing Board), *Dairy Facts and Figures* (Thames Ditton, annual).

Moore, H.I., *Grass and Grasslands* (London, 1966).

Morley, A., *The Right Way to Pig Keeping and Breeding* (Kingswood, Surrey, 1950).

NEDO (National Economic Development Office), *Agriculture's Import Saving Role: A Report by the Economic Development Committee for the Agricultural Industry* (London, 1968).

NIAB (National Institute of Agricultural Botany), *Varieties of Ryegrass*, Farmers' Leaflet no. 16 (Cambridge, 1964).

Natural Resources (Technical) Committee. Committee on Agriculture, *Scale of Enterprise in Farming* (London, 1961).

Nix, J., *Farm Management Pocketbook* (Ashford, 2nd edn 1968, 14th edn 1984).

Orwin, C.S., *Farm Accounts* (Cambridge, 1914).
— — *The Determination of Farming Costs* (Oxford, 1917).
— — *Farming Costs* (Oxford, 1921).
Polge, C., 'AI May Soon Help You to Breed Better Pigs', *Pig Farming* (November 1954), p. 27.
Pryse Howell, J., *The Productivity of Hill Farming* (Oxford, 1922).
Raeburn, J.R., 'The Food Economy of the UK in Relation to International Balance-Of-Payment Problems', *J. Agric. Econs.* 8 (1948), pp. 20–47.
Rebanks, J., *The Shepherd's Life: A Tale of the Lake District* (London, 2016).
Roberts, E.J., 'Production of Milk', in J.A. Hanley (ed.), *Progressive Farming: The Maintenance of High Production* (London, 1949).
Robinson, D.H. (ed.), *Fream's Elements of Agriculture* (13th edn, London, 1949).
Rothschild, Lord, *The Organisation and Management of Government R & D*, in Anon, *A Framework for Government Research and Development*, Cmnd.4814, 1971–2.
Ruck, R.J., *Place of Stones* (London, 1961).
— — *Hill Farm Story* (London, 1966).
Spedding, C.R.W. (ed.), *Fream's Agriculture* (16th edn, London, 1983).
Stamp, L.D., *The Land of Britain: Its Use and Misuse* (London, 1948).
Stapledon, G., *Farming and Mechanised Agriculture* (4th edn, London, 1950).
Street, A.G., *Farmer's Glory* (London, 1932).
— — *Farming England* (London, 1937).
— — *Farmer's Glory* (2nd edn with postscript, Harmondsworth, 1951).
Templeman, W.G., 'Low Volume Sprayers for Weed Control', *Agriculture* LV/10 (1949), pp. 441–3.
Thomas, E., *An Introduction to Agricultural Economics* (London, 1949).
Thomas, R.S., *An Acre of Land* (Newtown, Montgomery, 1952).
Thomas, W.J.K., and E. Burnside, *Pig Production: Results of a Study in South West England in 1972–73*, University of Exeter, Agricultural Economics Unit, Economic Report no. 26 (Exeter, 1974).
Thorburn, J.B., 'Home-Made Poultry Housing', *Agriculture* LVI (1949), pp. 278–9.
Toosey, R.D., *Profitable Fodder Cropping* (Ipswich, 1972).
Trend, Sir Burke (chair), *Committee of Enquiry into the Organisation of Civil Science*, Cmnd.2171 (1963–4).
Universities of Bristol and Exeter, *Farm Management Handbook* (Exeter, 1968).
University of Cambridge, Farm Economics Branch, *An Economic Survey of Hertfordshire Agriculture*, Report no. 18 (Cambridge, 1931).
University of Exeter, *Farm Management Handbook* (Exeter, 1985).
Venn, J.A., *The Foundations of Agricultural Economics* (Cambridge, 1933).

Bibliography

Watson, J.A. Scott, 'The National Agricultural Advisory Service', *Agriculture* LIII (1946).
Watson, J.A. Scott, and J.A. More, *Agriculture* (11th edn, Edinburgh, 1962).
Whetham, E.H., 'The Agricultural Expansion Programme, 1947–51', *J. Agric. Econs.* 11 (1955), pp. 313–19.
Yates, P. Lamartine, *Food Production in Western Europe: An Economic Survey of Agriculture in Six Countries* (London, 1940).

Secondary Sources

Alderson, L., and V. Porter, *Saving the Breeds: A History of the Rare Breeds Survival Trust* (Robertsbridge, 1994).
Amadi, J., J. Piesse, and C. Thirtle, 'Crop Level Productivity in the Eastern Counties of England, 1970–97', *J. Agric. Econs.* 55 (2004), pp. 367–83.
Antonson, H., and U. Jansson (eds), *Agriculture and Forestry in Sweden since 1900: Geographical and Historical Studies* (Stockholm, 2011).
Aparicio, G., V. Pinilla, and R. Serrano, 'Europe and the International Trade in Agricultural and Food Products, 1870–2000', in P. Lains and V. Pinilla (eds), *Agriculture and Economic Development in Europe since 1870* (Abingdon, 2009), pp. 52–75.
Ashton, J., and B.E. Cracknell, 'Agricultural Holdings and Farm Business Structure in England and Wales', *J. Agric. Econs.* 14 (1961), pp. 472–506.
Ashton, J., and S.J. Rogers (eds), *Economic Change and Agriculture* (Edinburgh, 1968).
Auderset, J., and P. Moser, 'Mechanisation and Motorisation: Natural Resources, Knowledge, Politics and Technology in 19th- and 20th-Century Agriculture', in C. Martiin, J. Pan-Montojo, and P. Brassley (eds), *Agriculture in Capitalist Europe, 1945–1960: From Food Shortages to Food Surpluses* (London, 2016), pp. 145–64.
Bailey, A., K. Balcombe, C. Thirtle, and L. Jenkins, 'ME Estimation of Input and Output Biases of Technical and Policy Change in UK Agriculture, 1953–2000', *J. Agric. Econs.* 55 (2004), pp. 385–400.
Baker, S., *Milk to Market: Forty Years of Milk Marketing* (London, 1973), pp. 230–33.
Beale, C., and G. Owen, *Writtle College: The First Hundred Years 1893–1993* (Chelmsford, 1993).
Beckett, J., and M. Turner, 'End of the Old Order? F.M.L. Thompson, the Land Question, and the Burden of Ownership in England, c.1880–c.1925', *Agric. Hist. Rev.* 55 (2007), pp. 269–88.
Berry, D.J., 'Genetics, Statistics, and Regulation at the National Institute of Agricultural Botany, 1919 – 1969' (unpublished Ph.D. dissertation, University of Leeds, 2014).
—— 'Historiography of Plant Breeding and Agriculture', in M. Dietrich,

M. Borello, and O. Harman (eds), *Handbook of the Historiography of Biology* (Cham, Switzerland, 2019), pp. 1–22.

Bieleman, J., *Five Centuries of Farming: A Short History of Dutch Agriculture 1500–2000* (Wageningen, 2010).

Blaxter, K., and N. Robertson, *From Dearth to Plenty: The Modern Revolution in Food Production* (Cambridge, 1995).

Bowers, J., 'British Agricultural Policy since the Second World War', *Agric. Hist. Rev.* 33 (1985), pp. 66–76.

Brassley, P., 'The Common Agricultural Policy of the European Economic Community', in R.J. Halley (ed.), *The Agricultural Notebook* (17th edn, London, 1982), pp. 575–84.

—— 'The Common Agricultural Policy of the European Union', in R.J. Soffe (ed.), *The Agricultural Notebook* (19th edn, Oxford, 1995), pp. 3–16.

—— 'Silage in Britain 1880–1990: The Delayed Adoption of an Innovation', *Agric. Hist. Rev.* 44 (1996), pp. 46–62.

—— *Agricultural Economics and the CAP: An Introduction* (Oxford, 1997).

—— 'Output and Technical Change in Twentieth-Century British agriculture', *Agric. Hist. Rev.* 48 (2000), pp. 60–84.

—— 'Crop Varieties', in E.J.T. Collins (ed.), *The Agrarian History of England and Wales*, vol. VII, *1850–1914* (Cambridge, 2000), pp. 522–32.

—— 'Livestock Breeds', in E.J.T. Collins (ed.), *The Agrarian History of England and Wales*, vol. VII, *1850–1914* (Cambridge, 2000), pp. 555–69.

—— 'Agricultural Science and Education', in E.J.T. Collins (ed.), *The Agrarian History of England and Wales*, vol. VII, *1850–1914*, part 1 (Cambridge, 2000), pp. 594–649.

—— 'The Professionalisation of English Agriculture?', *Rural History* 16 (2005), pp. 235–51.

—— 'British Farming between the Wars', in P. Brassley, J. Burchardt, and L. Thompson (eds), *The English Countryside between the Wars: Regeneration or Decline?* (Woodbridge, 2006), pp. 187–99.

—— 'Wartime Productivity and Innovation, 1939-45', in B. Short, C. Watkins, and J. Martin (eds), *The Front Line of Freedom: British Farming in the Second World War* (Exeter, 2006), pp. 36–54.

—— 'Cutting across Nature? The History of Artificial Insemination in Pigs in the UK', *Studies in the History and Philosophy of Biological and Biomedical Science* 38 (2007), pp. 462–87.

—— 'International Trade in Agricultural Products, 1935–1955', in P. Brassley, L. Van Molle, and Y. Segers (eds), *War, Agriculture and Food: Rural Europe from the 1930s to the 1950s* (New York, 2012), pp. 33–51.

—— 'Agricultural Output, Costs and Incomes in the United Kingdom, 1919–1940', in J.-M. Chevet and G. Béaur (eds), *Measuring Agricultural Growth: Land and Labour Productivity in Western Europe from the Middle Ages to the Twentieth Century (England, France and Spain)* (Turnhout, 2014), pp. 181–91.

Bibliography

—— 'Electrifying Farms in England', in P. Brassley, J. Burchardt, and K. Sayer (eds), *Transforming the Countryside: The Electrification of Rural Britain* (Abingdon, 2017).
Brassley, P., L. Van Molle, and Y. Segers (eds), *War, Agriculture and Food: Rural Europe from the 1930s to the 1950s* (New York, 2012).
Brassley, P., D. Harvey, M. Lobley, and M. Winter, 'Accounting for Agriculture: The Origins of the Farm Management Survey', *Agric. Hist. Rev.* 61 (2013)
Brassley, P., C. Martiin, and J. Pan-Montojo, 'European Agriculture, 1945–1960: An Introduction', in C. Martiin, J. Pan-Montojo, and P. Brassley (eds), *Agriculture in Capitalist Europe, 1945–1960: From Food Shortages to Food Surpluses* (Abingdon, 2016), pp. 1–20.
Briggs, A., *The BBC: The First Fifty Years* (Oxford, 1985).
Britton, D.K., 'The Structure of Agriculture', in A. Edwards and A. Rogers (eds), *Agricultural Resources: An Introduction to the Farming Industry of the United Kingdom* (London, 1974), pp. 16–35.
Britton, D.K., and B. Hill, *Size and Efficiency in Farming* (Farnborough, 1975).
Broadberry, S., B.M.S. Campbell, A. Klein, M. Overton, and B. van Leeuwen, *British Economic Growth 1270–1870* (Cambridge, 2015).
Buckwell, A., 'Economic Signals, Farmers' Response, and Environmental Change', *Journal of Rural Studies* 5 (1989), pp. 149–60.
Bud, R., *Penicillin: Triumph and Tragedy* (Oxford, 2007).
Burrell, A., B. Hill, and J. Medland, *Agrifacts: A Handbook of UK and EEC Agricultural and Food Statistics* (London, 1990).
Cameron, R., *A Concise Economic History of the World: From Palaeolithic Times to the Present* (London, 1993).
Capstick, M., *The Economics of Agriculture* (London, 1970).
Cassidy, A., *Vermin, Victims and Disease: British Debates over Bovine Tuberculosis and Badgers* (Basingstoke, 2019).
Centre for Agricultural Strategy, *Land for Agriculture*, CAS Report no. 1 (Reading, 1976).
Champion. A.G., 'Competition for Agricultural Land', in A. Edwards and A. Rogers (eds), *Agricultural Resources: An Introduction to the Farming Industry of the United Kingdom* (London, 1974), pp. 229–47.
Clarke, A.E., *Disciplining Reproduction: Modernity, American Life Sciences, and 'the Problems of Sex'* (Berkeley, CA, 1998).
Clarke, G., 'The Women's Land Army and Its Recruits, 1938–50', in B. Short, C. Watkins, and J. Martin (eds), *The Front Line of Freedom: British Farming in the Second World War* (Exeter, 2006), pp. 101–16.
Clarke, P., *Hope and Glory: Britain 1900–1990* (London, 1996).
Clarke, S., 'The Research Council System and the Politics of Medical and Agricultural Research for the British Colonial Empire, 1940–1952', *Medical History* 57 (2013), pp. 338–58.

Collingham, L., *The Taste of War: World War Two and the Battle for Food* (London, 2011).
Collins, E.J.T., 'Labour Supply and Demand in European Agriculture 1800–1880', in E.L. Jones and S.J. Woolf (eds), *Agrarian Change and Economic Development: The Historical Problems* (London, 1969), pp. 61–94.
Colyer, R., *Man's Proper Study: A History of Agricultural Education in Aberystwyth, 1878–1978* (Llandysul, 1982).
Cooper, A.F., *British Agricultural Policy, 1912–36: A Study in Conservative Politics* (Manchester, 1989).
Cowling, K., D. Metcalf, and A.J. Rayner, *Resource Structure of Agriculture: An Economic Analysis* (Oxford, 1970).
Craig, G.M., J.L. Jollans, and A. Korbey (eds), *The Case for Agriculture: An Independent Assessment*, CAS Report no. 10 (Reading, 1986).
Craigie, P.G., 'Notes on the Subjects Discussed at the St. Petersburg Meeting of the International Statistical Institute', *Journal of the Royal Statistical Society* 60 (1897), pp. 735–88.
Custodis, J., 'Employing the Enemy: The Contribution of German and Italian Prisoners of War to British Agriculture during and after the Second World War', *Agric. Hist. Rev.* 60 (2012), pp. 243–65.
Dalton, G.E., 'In Memoriam: Professor John R. Raeburn CBE, FRSE (1912–2006)', *J. Agric. Econs.* 58 (2007), pp. 396–8.
Dancey, R.J., 'The Evolution of Agricultural Extension in England and Wales', *J. Agric. Econs.* 44 (1993), pp. 375–93.
Daston, L., and P. Galison, *Objectivity* (New York, 2007).
Desrosières, A., 'The Part in Relation to the Whole: How to Generalise? The Prehistory of Representative Sampling', in M. Bulmer, K. Bales, and K.K. Sklar (eds), *The Social Survey in Historical Perspective 1880–1940* (Cambridge, 1991), pp. 217–18.
— — 'Managing the Economy', in T.M. Porter and D. Ross (eds), *The Cambridge History of Science, vol. VII, The Modern Social Sciences* (Cambridge, 2003).
Dewey, P., *British Agriculture in the First World War* (London, 1989).
— — *'Iron Harvests of the Field': The Making of Farm Machinery in Britain since 1800* (Lancaster, 2008).
Dexter, K., 'Productivity in Agriculture', in J. Ashton and S.J. Rogers (eds), *Economic Change and Agriculture* (Edinburgh, 1967), pp. 65–82.
Donaldson, J.G.S. and F., with D. Barber, *Farming in Britain Today* (Harmondsworth, 1972).
D'Onofrio, F., *Observing Agriculture in Early Twentieth-Century Italy: Agricultural Economists and Statistics* (Abingdon, 2016).
— — 'Agricultural Numbers: The Statistics of the International Institute of Agriculture in the Interwar Period', *Agric. Hist. Rev.* 65 (2017), pp. 277–96.

Douet, A., *Breaking New Ground: Agriculture in Norfolk 1914–1972* (Aylsham, 2012).
Doyle, C.J., and M.S. Ridout, 'The Impact of Scientific Research on UK Agricultural Productivity', *Research Policy* 14 (1985), pp. 109–16.
Edwards, A., 'Resources in Agriculture: Land', in A. Edwards and A. Rogers (eds), *Agricultural Resources: An Introduction to the Farming Industry of the United Kingdom* (London, 1974), pp. 82–106.
Evans, N., C. Morris, and M. Winter, 'Conceptualizing Agriculture: A Critique of Post-productivism as the New Orthodoxy', *Progress in Human Geography* 26 (2002), pp. 313–32.
Federico, G., *Feeding the World: An Economic History of Agriculture, 1800–2000* (Princeton, NJ, 2005).
Fernández Prieto, L., *El Apagón Tecnológico del Franquismo: Estado e innovación en la agricultura Española del siglo XX* (Valencia, 2007).
Fisher, J.R., 'Agrarian Politics', in E.J.T. Collins (ed.), *The Agrarian History of England and Wales*, vol. VII, *1850–1914* (Cambridge, 2000), pp. 321–57.
Foreman, S., *Loaves and Fishes: An Illustrated History of the Ministry of Agriculture, Fisheries and Food, 1889–1989* (London, 1989).
Frankenberg, R., *Village on the Border* (London, 1957).
Gardner, B.L., *American Agriculture in the Twentieth Century: How It Flourished and What It Cost* (Cambridge, MA, 2002).
Gasson, R., 'Resources in Agriculture: Labour', in A. Edwards and A. Rogers (eds), *Agricultural Resources: An Introduction to the Farming Industry of the United Kingdom* (London, 1974), pp. 116–25.
Geroski, P., 'Models of Technology Diffusion', *Research Policy* 29 (2000), pp. 603–25.
Giles, A.K., and F.D. Mills, *The Farm Managers* (Coventry, 1970).
Goddard, N., *Harvests of Change: The Royal Agricultural Society of England 1838–1988* (London, 1988).
— — 'Agricultural Institutions: Societies, Associations and the Press', in E.J.T. Collins (ed.), *The Agrarian History of England and Wales*, vol. VII, *1850–1914* (Cambridge, 2000), pp. 650–90.
Godley, A., 'The Emergence of Agribusiness in Europe and the Development of the Western European Broiler Chicken Industry, 1945 to 1973', *Agric. Hist. Rev.* 62 (2014), pp. 315–36.
Godley, A., and B. Williams, 'Democratizing Luxury and the Contentious "Invention of the Technological Chicken" in Britain', *Business History Review* 83 (2009), pp. 267–90.
Grant, O., *The Diffusion of the Herringbone Parlour: A Case Study in the History of Agricultural Technology*, University of Oxford Discussion Papers in Economic and Social History, no. 27 (Oxford, 1998).
Griffiths, C., 'Farming in the Public Interest: Constructing and Reconstructing Agriculture on the Political Left', in P. Brassley, J.

Burchardt, and L. Thompson (eds), *The English Countryside between the Wars: Regeneration or Decline?* (Woodbridge, 2006), pp. 164–75.

—— 'Heroes of the Reconstruction? Images of British Farmers in War and Peace', in P. Brassley, L. Van Molle, and Y. Segers (eds), *War, Agriculture and Food: Rural Europe from the 1930s to the 1950s* (New York, 2012), pp. 209–28.

Grigg, D., *English Agriculture: An Historical Perspective* (Oxford, 1989).

—— *The Transformation of Agriculture in the West* (Oxford, 1992).

Gummett, P., *Scientists in Whitehall* (Manchester, 1980).

Harley, C.K., 'The World Food Economy and Pre-World War I Argentina', in S.N. Broadberry and N.F.R. Crafts (eds), *Britain in the International Economy* (Cambridge, 1992), pp. 244–68.

Harris, P., *The Silent Fields: One Hundred Years of Agricultural Education at Reading* (Reading, 1993).

Harris, S., *The World Commodity Scene and the Common Agricultural Policy* (Ashford, 1975).

Harvey, D.C. and M. Riley, 'Country Stories: The Use of Oral Histories of the Countryside to Challenge the Sciences of the Past and Future', *Interdisciplinary Science Reviews* 30 (2005), pp. 19–32.

—— '"Fighting from the Fields": Developing the British "National Farm" in the Second World War', *Journal of Historical Geography* 35 (2009), pp. 495–516.

Harwood, J., *Technology's Dilemma: Agricultural Colleges between Science and Practice in Germany, 1860–1934* (Bern, 2005).

Hayami, Y., and V. Ruttan, *Agricultural Development: An International Perspective* (Baltimore, MD, 1985).

Henderson, W., 'British Agricultural Research and the Agricultural Research Council: A Personal Historical Account', in G.W. Cooke (ed.), *Agricultural Research 1931–1981: A History of the Agricultural Research Council and a Review of Developments in Agricultural Science during the last Fifty Years* (London, 1981), pp. 3–113.

Hennessy, P., *Whitehall* (London, 1990).

Hill, B., 'Resources in Agriculture: Capital', in A. Edwards and A. Rogers (eds), *Agricultural Resources: An Introduction to the Farming Industry of the United Kingdom* (London, 1974), pp. 145–64.

—— *Farm Incomes, Wealth and Agricultural Policy* (3rd edn, Aldershot, 2000).

Hill, B., and D. Ray, *Economics for Agriculture: Food, Farming and the Rural Economy* (Basingstoke, 1987).

Hill, B.E., and K. Ingersent, *An Economic Analysis of Agriculture* (London, 1977).

Holderness, B.A., 'Apropos the Third Agricultural Revolution: How Productive Was British agriculture in the Long Boom, 1954–1973?', in

P. Mathias and J.A. Davis (eds), *Agriculture and Industrialization from the Eighteenth Century to the Present Day* (Oxford, 1996).

Holmes, C.J., 'Science and the Farmer: The Development of the Agricultural Advisory Service in England and Wales, 1900–1939', *Agric. Hist. Rev.* 36 (1988), pp. 77–86.

Howkins, A., *The Death of Rural England: A Social History of the Countryside since 1900* (London, 2003).

Howlett, P., and A. Velkar, 'Technology Transfer and Travelling Facts: A Perspective from Indian Agriculture', in P. Howlett and M.S. Morgan (eds), *How Well do Facts Travel? The Dissemination of Reliable Knowledge* (Cambridge, 2011), pp. 273–300.

Hoyle, R., 'Introduction: Recovering the Farmer', in R. Hoyle (ed.), *The Farmer in England, 1650–1980* (Farnham, 2013).

Humphries, A., *Seeds of Change: 100 Years' Contribution to Rural Economy, Society and the Environment* (Penrith, 1996).

Ilbery, B., and I. Bowler, 'From Agricultural Productivism to Post-productivism', in B. Ilbery (ed.), *The Geography of Rural Change* (Harlow, 1998), pp. 57–84.

Jones, P.M., *Agricultural Enlightenment: Knowledge, Technology, and Nature, 1750–1840* (Oxford, 2016).

Koppel, B.M., *Induced Innovation Theory and International Agricultural Development: A Reassessment* (Baltimore, MD, 1995).

Laing, S., 'Images of the Rural in Popular Culture', in B. Short (ed.), *The English Rural Community: Image and Analysis* (Cambridge, 1992).

Lains, P., and V. Pinilla (eds), *Agriculture and Economic Development in Europe since 1870* (London, 2009).

Leydesdorff, L., 'The Triple Helix: An Evolutionary Model of Innovations', *Research Policy* 29 (2000), pp. 243–55.

McCann, N.F., *The Story of the National Agricultural Advisory Service: A Mainspring of Agricultural Revival 1946–1971* (Ely, 1989).

Macdonald, M., 'The Secularization of Suicide in England', *Past and Present* 111 (1986), pp. 50–100.

Mackenzie, D.A., *Statistics in Britain, 1865–1930: The Social Construction of Scientific Knowledge* (Edinburgh, 1981).

McWilliams, F., 'Equine Machines: Horses and Tractors on British Farms c.1920–1970' (unpublished Ph.D. thesis, King's College, London, 2020).

Marie, J., 'For Science, Love, and Money: The Social Worlds of Poultry and Rabbit Breeding in Britain, 1900–1940', *Social Studies of Science* 36 (2008), pp. 919–36.

Marks, H., and D.K. Britton, *A Hundred Years of British Food and Farming: A Statistical Survey* (London, 1989).

Martiin, C., J. Pan-Montojo, and P. Brassley (eds), *Agriculture in Capitalist Europe, 1945–1960: From Food Shortages to Food Surpluses* (Abingdon, 2016).

Martin, J., *The Development of Modern Agriculture: British Farming since 1931* (Basingstoke, 2000).

— — 'Rex Paterson (1903–1978): Pioneer of Grassland Dairy Farming and Agricultural Innovator', in R.W. Hoyle (ed.), *The Farmer in England, 1650–1980* (Farnham, 2013), pp. 295–324.

Martín-Retortillo, M, and V. Pinilla, 'Patterns and Causes of the Growth of European Agricultural Production, 1950 to 2005', *Agric. Hist. Rev.* 63 (2015), pp. 132–59.

Mignemi, N., 'Italian Agricultural Experts as Transnational Mediators: The Creation of the International Institute of Agriculture, 1905 to 1908', *Agric. Hist. Rev.* 65 (2017), pp. 254–76.

Mingay, G.E., *British Friesians: An Epic of Progress* (Rickmansworth, 1982).

MAFF (Ministry of Agriculture, Fisheries and Food), *A Century of Agricultural Statistics: Great Britain 1866–1966* (London, 1968).

Mokyr, J., *The Enlightened Economy: An Economic History of Britain, 1750–1850* (New Haven, CT, 2009).

Montague, D., *Farming, Food, and Politics: The Merchant's Tale* (Dublin, 2000).

Montgomery, J., *Small in Number – Big in Spirit: The History of the First 30-odd Years of the Pig Improvement Company* (privately printed, 1999).

Moore-Colyer, R., 'Prisoners of War and the Struggle for Food Production, 1939–49', in B. Short, C. Watkins, and J. Martin (eds), *The Front Line of Freedom: British Farming in the Second World War* (Exeter, 2006), pp. 117–31.

— — *Farming in Wales 1936–2011* (Talybont, 2011).

Morgan, *The People's Peace: British History 1945–1990* (Oxford, 1992).

Murdoch, J., T. Marsden, and J. Banks, 'Quality, Nature and Embeddedness: Some Theoretical Considerations in the Context of the Food Sector', *Economic Geography* 76 (2000), pp. 107–25.

Murray, K.A.H., *Agriculture (History of the Second World War: UK Civil Series)* (London, 1955).

— — *Higher Agricultural Education in England and Wales* (the George Johnstone Lecture, Seale-Hayne College) (Newton Abbot, 1962).

Nalson, J.S., *Mobility of Farm Families: A Study of Occupational and Residential Mobility in an Upland Area of England* (Manchester, 1968).

Newby, H., *The Deferential Worker* (London, 1977).

Newby, H., C. Bell, D. Rose, and P. Saunders, *Property, Paternalism and Power: Class and Control in Rural England* (London, 1978).

Nix, J.S., 'Farm Management: The State of the Art (or Science)', *J. Agric. Econs.* 30 (1979), pp. 277–92.

Ordish, G., *The Constant Pest* (London, 1976).

Oudshoorn, N., and T. Pinch, *How Users Matter: The Co-construction of Users and Technologies* (Cambridge, MA, 2003).

Palladino, P., 'Wizards and Devotees: On the Mendelian Theory of

Inheritance and the Professionalization of Agricultural Science in Great Britain and the United States 1880–1930', *History of Science* XXXII (1994), pp. 409–44.

Pan-Montojo, J., 'International Institutions and European Agriculture: From the IIA to the FAO', in C. Martiin, J. Pan-Montojo, and P. Brassley (eds), *Agriculture in Capitalist Europe, 1945–1960: From Food Shortages to Food Surpluses* (London, 2016), pp. 23–43.

Parolini, G., '"Making Sense of Figures": Statistics, Computing and Information Technologies in Agriculture and Biology in Britain, 1920s–1960s' (unpublished Dottorato di Ricerca thesis, Università di Bologna, 2013).

Peacock, F.C., (ed.), *Jealott's Hill: Fifty Years of Agricultural Research 1928–1978* (Bracknell, 1978).

Penning-Rowsell, E.C., 'Who "Betrayed" Whom? Power and Politics in the 1920/1 Agricultural Crisis', *Agric. Hist. Rev.* 45 (1997), pp. 176–94.

Phillips, D., and S. Kingsland (eds), *New Perspectives on the History of Life Sciences and Agriculture* (Cham, Switzerland, 2015).

Picon, A., 'Towards a History of Technological Thought', in R. Fox (ed.), *Technological Change: Methods and Themes in the History of Technology* (Amsterdam, 1996), pp. 37–50.

Pinch, T., 'The Social Construction of Technology: A Review', in R. Fox (ed.), *Technological Change: Methods and Themes in the History of Technology* (Amsterdam, 1996), pp. 17–35.

Porter, D., '"Never-Never Land": Britain under the Conservatives 1951–1964', in N. Tiratsoo (ed.), *From Blitz to Blair: A New History of Britain since 1939* (London, 1997), pp. 102–31.

Porter, T.M., *Trust in Numbers: The Pursuit of Objectivity in Science and Public Life* (Princeton, NJ, 1995).

— — 'Statistics and Statistical Methods', in T.M. Porter and D. Ross (eds), *The Cambridge History of Science, vol. VII, The Modern Social Sciences* (Cambridge, 2003).

Portsmouth, J., and T. Marangos, 'Poultry', in R.J. Soffe (ed.), *The Agricultural Notebook* (20th edn, Oxford, 2003), pp. 555–65.

Richards, S., *Wye College and Its World: A Centenary History* (Ashford, 1994).

Riley, M., '"Ask the Fellows Who Cut the Hay": Farm Practices, Oral History and Nature Conservation', *Journal of the Oral History Society* 32 (2004), pp. 42–51.

— — '"Silage for Self-sufficiency"? The Wartime Promotion of Silage and Its Use in the Peak District', in B. Short, C. Watkins, and J. Martin (eds), *The Front Line of Freedom: British Farming in the Second World War* (Exeter, 2007), pp. 77–88.

Riley, M., and D.C. Harvey, 'Oral Histories, Farm Practice and Uncovering

Meaning in the Countryside', *Social and Cultural Geography* 8 (2007), pp. 391–415.
Ritson, C., *Agricultural Economics: Principles and Policy* (London, 1977).
Rogers, A., *The Most Revolutionary Measure: A History of the Rural Development Commission, 1909–99* (Salisbury, 1999).
Rogers, E.M., *Diffusion of Innovations* (New York, 1962).
Rosenberg, N., *Inside the Black Box: Technology and Economics* (Cambridge, 1982).
Russell, E.J., *A History of Agricultural Science in Great Britain* (London, 1966).
Sayer, K., '"His Footmarks on Her Shoulders": The Place of Women within Poultry Keeping in the British Countryside, c.1880 to c.1980', *Agric. Hist. Rev.* 61 (2013), pp. 301–29.
Schrepfer, S.R., and P. Scranton (eds), *Industrializing Agriculture: Introducing Evolutionary History* (New York, 2004).
Seddon, Q., *The Silent Revolution: Farming and the Countryside into the 21st Century* (London, 1989).
Self, P., and H. Storing, *The State and the Farmer* (London, 1962).
Shabas, M., 'British Economic Theory from Locke to Marshall', in T.M. Porter and D. Ross (eds), *The Cambridge History of Science, vol. VII, The Modern Social Sciences* (Cambridge, 2003).
Sheail, J., 'The White Paper, *Agricultural Policy*, of 1926: Its Context and Significance', *Agric. Hist. Rev.* 58 (2010), pp. 236–54.
Shinn, T., 'The Triple Helix and the New Production of Knowledge: Prepackaged Thinking on Science and Technology', *Social Studies of Science* 32 (2002), pp. 599–614.
Short, B.M., '"The Art and Craft of Chicken Cramming": Poultry in the Weald of Sussex 1850–1950', *Agric. Hist. Rev.* 30 (1982), pp. 17–30.
— — *The Battle of the Fields: Rural Community and Authority in Britain during the Second World War* (Woodbridge, 2014).
Short, B.M., C. Watkins, W. Foot, and P. Kinsman, *The National Farm Survey 1941–1943: State Surveillance and the Countryside in England and Wales in the Second World War* (Wallingford, 2000).
Short, B.M., C. Watkins, and J. Martin (eds), *The Front Line of Freedom: British Farming in the Second World War* (Exeter, 2007).
Silvey, V., 'The Contribution of New Varieties to Increasing Cereal Yield in England and Wales', *Journal of the National Institute of Agricultural Botany* 14 (1978), pp. 367–84.
Thiemeyer, G., 'The Failure of the Green Pool and the Success of the CAP: Long Term Structures in European Agricultural Integration in the 1950s and 1960s', in K.K. Patel (ed.), *Fertile Ground for Europe? The History of European Integration and the Common Agricultural Policy since 1945* (Baden-Baden, 2009), pp. 47–51.
Thirsk, J., 'Agricultural Policy: Public Debate and Legislation', in J. Thirsk

(ed.), *The Agrarian History of England and Wales*, vol. V (ii), 1640–1750 (Cambridge, 1985), pp. 298–388.

Thirtle, C., P. Palladino, and J. Piesse, 'On the Organisation of Agricultural Research in the United Kingdom, 1945–1994: A Quantitative Description and Appraisal of Recent Reforms', *Research Policy* 26 (1997), pp. 557–76.

Thirtle, C., L. Lin, J. Holding, L. Jenkins, and J. Piesse, 'Explaining the Decline in UK Agricultural Productivity Growth', *J. Agric. Econs.* 55 (2004), pp. 343–66.

Thoen, E., and T. Soens (eds), *Struggling with the Environment: Land Use and Productivity; Rural Economy and Society in North-Western Europe, 500–2000* (Turnhout, 2015).

Thompson, F.M.L., 'The Land Market, 1880–1925: A Reappraisal Reappraised', *Agric. Hist. Rev.* 55 (2007), pp. 289–300.

Van der Laan, A.L., and M. Boenink, 'Beyond Bench and Bedside: Disentangling the Concept of Translational Research', *Health Care Analysis* 23 (2015), pp. 32–49.

Whetham, E.H., 'The Agriculture Act, 1920, and Its Repeal: The "Great Betrayal"', *Agric. Hist. Rev.* 22 (1974), pp. 36–49.

— — *The Agrarian History of England and Wales*, vol. VIII, 1914–1939 (Cambridge, 1978).

— — *Agricultural Economists in Britain, 1900–1940* (London, 1981).

Wilkins, R., S. Jarvis, and M. Blackwell (eds), *The Hurley and North Wyke Story: 60 Years of Grassland Research, 1949-2009* (Okehampton, 2009).

Williams, H.T. (ed.), *Principles for British Agricultural Policy* (London, 1960).

Williams, H., *The Lure of the Land: A Century of Education at Harper Adams* (Newport, Shropshire, 2001).

Williams, W.M., *The Sociology of an English Village: Gosforth* (London, 1956).

— — *A West Country Village: Ashworthy* (London, 1963).

Wilmot, S., 'From "Public Service" to Artificial Insemination: Animal Breeding Science and Reproductive Research in Early Twentieth-Century Britain', *Studies in the History and Philosophy of Biological and Biomedical Sciences* 38 (2007), pp. 411–41.

Wilt, A., *Food for War: Agriculture and Rearmament in Britain before the Second World War* (Oxford, 2001).

Winter, M., 'The Survival and Re-emergence of Family Farming: A Study of the Holsworthy Area of West Devon' (unpublished Ph.D. dissertation, Open University, 1986).

— — *Rural Politics: Policies for Agriculture, Forestry and the Environment* (London, 1996).

Woods, A., 'The Farm as Clinic', *Studies in the History and Philosophy of Biological and Biomedical Sciences* 38 (2007), pp. 462–87.

— — 'A Historical Synopsis of Farm Animal Disease and Public Policy

in Twentieth-Century Britain', *Philosophical Transactions of the Royal Society, Series B: Biological Sciences* 366/1573 (2011), pp. 1943–54.
— — 'Rethinking the History of Modern Agriculture: British Pig Production, c.1910–65', *Twentieth Century British History* 23 (2012), pp. 165–91.
— — 'Science, Disease and Dairy Production in Britain, c.1927 to 1980', *Agric. Hist. Rev.* 62 (2014), pp. 294–314.
Wormell, P., *Anatomy of Agriculture: A Study of Britain's Greatest Industry* (London, 1978).

INDEX

Acts of Parliament, re agriculture 89, 90, 92, 94–8,164–5
adoption of innovations 7–11, 253–5; *see also* technical change in agriculture
Advisory Council for Agriculture and Horticulture 49
agricultural colleges
 county *see* farm institutes
 national 51, 56–61
Agricultural Advisory Council 48–9, 50, 85
Agricultural and Food Research Council (AFRC) 39
Agricultural Development and Advisory Service (ADAS) 67, 78, 80
Agricultural Economics Society 98
agricultural education and training 46, 51–61, 155
 Committees of Enquiry into, *see* Alness, Bosanquet, De La Warr, Loveday, Luxmoore
 See also Agricultural Training Board, University Departments of Agriculture, agricultural colleges, farm institutes, students in agriculture
Agricultural Education Association 49
Agricultural Executive Committees *see* County (War) Agricultural Executive Committees
agricultural extension and advice 46, 61–9; *see also* Agricultural Development and Advisory Service, National Agricultural Advisory Service

Agricultural Improvement Councils (AICs) 36, 39, 46–8, 66, 82, 85, 245
Agricultural Land Service 67
Agricultural Mortgage Corporation 173
agricultural output 3–7, 10, 93, 99–102, 106, 109, 262–3
agricultural policy 23, 80, 88–110, 260
agricultural press and publications 62, 69–71, 77–80
agricultural research *see* research, agricultural
Agricultural Research Act 1956 31, 36
Agricultural Research Council (ARC) 26–39, 42–4, 46–50, 82–6, 244–5
 1946 report on post-war needs 26–7
agricultural shows 68–9, 79–80
agricultural surpluses 109–10
Agricultural Training Board (ATB) 67–8, 81, 185
Agricultural Wages Board 62, 89
Alness Committee 52
Animal Breeding Research Organisation 30, 85, 232
animal feeds and nutrition 33, 50, 221, 224, 232
 and antibiotics 50, 221, 235, 254
 see also cattle, feeding
Animal Virus Research Institute 30
animal welfare 230–1
ARC *see* Agricultural Research Council
artificial insemination 33, 67, 82, 112, 122–5, 245, 248

balance of payments, UK 94–5, 105–6

283

Index

banks and borrowing 156, 164–5, 177–9, 249; *see also* capital in agriculture, inflation
Barber, Derek (Baron Barber of Tewkesbury) 70, 216
Barnard, C. 66
Baseley, Godfrey 71
Bayer Agriculture 40
beef production 122–3, 160
Beef Recording Association 67
Bell, Adrian 3
Bichard, Dr Maurice 233–4
Bingham, Dr John 33
Biotechnology and Biological Sciences Research Council (BBSRC) 39
Black Box theories of technical change 10, 253–5
Blaxter, Sir Kenneth 24, 33
Board of Agriculture 89–90
BOCM (British Oil and Cake Mills) 77
Body, Sir Richard 167
borrowing *see* banks and borrowing
Bosanquet Committee 55, 58
Brambell, Professor F.W.Rogers 231, 243
breed societies 78
British Broadcasting Corporation (BBC) 48, 71–6, 100
  Agricultural Broadcasting Advisory Committee 71–5
British Crop Protection Council 42
British Sugar Corporation 67
broadcasts (radio, television and films), agricultural 61–2, 71–6, 78, 80, 245
broiler chicken *see* poultry farming
Brooks, Professor Peter 234–5
brucellosis 158–9
bulk milk collection 153–4, 176, 249
bull and boar licensing 65, 98, 219

Camm, Brian 66
CAP *see* Common Agricultural Policy
capital in agriculture 22, 111, 163–5, 173–82, 249–50
  grants 179–81,
  inflation 177–9, 249
  sources 163–5, 173–82

Carrington, Lord Peter 101
Carson, Rachel 230
cattle
  breeds and breeding 66, 83, 111, 117–25, 248, 255
  feeding 111, 125–48, 248
  health and disease 158–60
  housing 111, 148–58; *see also* farm buildings
  metabolisable energy calculations 138, 147
Central Veterinary Laboratory 30
Cherrington, John 72
Cochrane, W.W. 251–2
Collison, Harold (Baron Collison) 47–8
Comber, Professor N. 35
Combined Food Board (World War II) 96
Common Agricultural Policy of the EEC (later the European Union) 105–9
contractors, agricultural 189
Cooper, Professor M.McG 48, 112–13, 133, 150, 184, 204–5, 247
County Agricultural Organisers (pre-World War II) 62
County (War) Agricultural Executive Committees 5, 52, 62–3, 65, 89, 92, 100–1, 106
cow cubicles 154–8, 249
cowsheds 148–53
Culpin, Claude 48
'cultural amphibians' in knowledge networks 87

dairy cow breeds *see* cattle, breeding
dairy farming 22, 111–62
  cow numbers 113–17
  herd size 113–17,
  producer numbers 112–14, 152, 154
  see also cattle
Dartington (Devon) 16
deficiency payments *see* prices, guaranteed
De La Warr Committee 54–5
Department of Scientific and Industrial Research 34–5
Development Commission 26,, 28, 89

284

Index

Devon Grassland Society 81, 127, 134
Dexter, Dr Keith 70, 216
District Advisory Officers *see* National Agricultural Advisory Service
Drainage 179–80
DSIR *see* Department of Scientific and Industrial Research
Duckham, Professor A.N. 99–101

Eastwood, Sir John 229
Economic Development Committee for Agriculture 84–5
education *see* agricultural education and training
Edwards, Dr Joseph 125
egg production *see* poultry farming
electrification 72, 73, 186
employment
  in agriculture *see* labour, agricultural
  in associated industries and professions 62–3
Engledow, Sir Frank 47
Engholm, Sir Basil 38
enterprise size 114, 116, 203–14; *see also* farm size, size and efficiency
European Economic Community (EEC) (later EU) 94, 97, 106–10, 246
Exeter University 17–18
Experimental Husbandry Farms 49–51, 66, 132, 245

farm accounts 14–16
farm buildings 27, 248–9; *see also* housing, dairy cattle
Farm Improvement Scheme 66, 103, 106, 180–1
farm institutes 51–2, 56–7, 59
farm machinery 141–8, 185–6, 194–8, 248
farm machinery suppliers 79
Farm Management Survey 12–21, 78, 81, 111
  fieldbooks 17–18
  for historical research 17–21
farm managers 60
farm safety 74
farm size 199–203, 259
  size and efficiency 202–3

farm training visits 80
Farmer and Stockbreeder magazine 62, 69, 79–80, 99
farmers
  and the agricultural press 70, 245
  and broadcasting 73, 78, 80–1, 245
  confidence 249–50, 259–60 *see also* risk in agriculture
  demand for advice, education and training 77–81
  discussion groups 81, 127, 134
  education, qualifications and training 51–60, 67–8, 258–9
  generational change 258
  informal discussions on technical change 78–9
  memoirs 3
  numbers of 114–16, 187, 189–90
  objectives 256–8
  oral histories 12, 18–21, 261
  professional status 59–61
  use of advisory services 64–6, 78–81
  See also adoption of innovations
Farmers Weekly magazine 62, 69–70, 78, 80
Farming Today broadcasts 71–2
Fatstock Marketing Corporation 217
Ferguson tractors 83
Fergusson, Sir Donald 46
fertilisers and manures 41, 50, 83, 127–33, 248, 254–5
Fisher, Sir R.A. 27
Fisons Ltd 40–1, 77, 83
fodder crops 135–8; *see also* cattle, feeding
forage harvesters 144–5, 254
Friesian cattle *see* cattle, breeds and breeding
Fryer, Sir John 42, 49

grants and subsidies 97–8, 103–4, 106, 179–81, 202, 249; *see also* capital in agriculture, grants
grass and grazing 125–34
  grassland management 126, 133–4, 248
  research 27
  varieties and seeds mixtures 126–7, 245

285

Index

See also fertilisers and manures, silage
Grassland Improvement Station, Drayton 27
Grassland Research Institute 30, 83

Haddon, Sir Richard 99, 101
Hall, Sir Daniel 14
Hammond, Sir John 48
Hankey Committee 1941 31
Hannah Dairy Research Institute 33
Harrison, Ruth 230–1, 243
hay 138–41
Hearnden, Geoffrey 239
herbicides 40–2
Hill Farming Research Organisation 30
Home Grown Cereals Authority 67
horses 194–7
Hot Springs Conference, 1943 96
housing, dairy cattle 148–58
Howitt Committee on pig production 218–20
Hudson, Robert 63, 97
Hurd, Anthony 94, 98

ICI *see* Imperial Chemical Industries
Imperial Chemical Industries (ICI) 40–2, 77, 83, 132
Index of Farm Specialisation (IFS) 210–11, 214–15; *see also* specialisation in agriculture
insecticides 41
Institute of Animal Physiology 30
International Institute of Agriculture 13, 95
international trade in agricultural products 4, 90–2, 95–7, 105–6, 108–10

Jealott's Hill (ICI) 41–2
Jones, W.Emrys 50

knowledge networks 6–7, 24–5, 46–87, 100
theories of 24–5, 81–3, 86–7
Korean War 99

labour, agricultural 6, 22, 101, 183–93, 196–8, 250

numbers 183–5, 187–8
part-time and casual 187–8
productivity 187, 191–3
land, agricultural 166–77, 182–2
mixed tenure 169–72, 249
owner-occupied 167–9, 249, 259
prices 165, 171, 173–4
tenanted 164–72, 249
see also Northfield Committee
landlord-tenant relationships 175–7
Long Ashton Research Station, Bristol 38
Loveday Committee 52–4
Low Cost Production scheme (MMB) 81
Lucas, Professor Ian 48
Lupton, Dr Francis. 33
Luxmoore Committee 52, 63

machinery, agricultural, *see* Farm machinery
MAF/MAFF *see* Ministry of Agriculture, Fisheries and Food
mastitis 159–60
May and Baker Ltd 40, 83
Meat and Livestock Commission 43, 67, 235
Middleton, Sir Thomas 46
Milk Marketing Board (MMB) 5, 43, 67, 103, 112, 118, 124–5, 159–60, 245
milk quotas 110
milk yield 50, 112–16
milking, by hand 149–50
milking machines 66, 84, 150–1, 248, 255
milking parlours 80, 150–6, 176, 191, 246, 249, 255
Ministry of Agriculture and Fisheries (MAF) (to 1955) *see* Ministry of Agriculture, Fisheries and Food
Ministry of Agriculture, Fisheries and Food (MAFF) 37, 48, 52, 61, 70–1, 74–5, 89–92, 98, 103–7, 200, 245
public relations policy 99–102
research 26, 37–9, 42–3
Ministry of Food 89–92, 97, 103, 217
Ministry of Information 93
MMB *see* Milk Marketing Board
Motorisation 197

286

Index

Museum of English Rural Life, Reading 17

National Agricultural Advisory Service (NAAS) 36, 47, 50, 53, 61–7, 78, 81, 86, 100, 127, 245
National Farm Survey, 1942 60, 184, 199
National Farmers' Union 5, 47, 79, 81, 91, 97, 100–2, 104–5, 160, 217, 245
National Institute of Agricultural Botany (NIAB) 30, 50, 68, 126, 245
National Institute of Agricultural Engineering 30
National Institute for Research in Dairying, Shinfield 50, 66
National Pig Breeders' Association 48
National Union of Agricultural Workers 47
Nickerson Seeds 40, 83
Nix, Professor John 66, 127
Norfolk Agricultural Experimental Station 47
Northfield Committee 168–9
nuclear war 99
Nuffield scholarship 80

Orwin, C.S. 14
Ottawa Conference, 1932 90
owner-occupiers see land, owner-occupied

pesticides 41, 196, 254
pig farming 22, 206–8, 216–23, 231–5, 238–43, 250–1
  disease control 233–4
  performance data 241–2
  pig breeds and breeding 218–20, 232–4
  pig housing 221–3, 238–9
  pig numbers 217, 219–22, 239–41
Pig Improvement Company (PIC) 84, 232–4
Pig Industry Development Authority (PIDA) 67, 235
plant breeding 33
Plant Breeding Institute 30, 33, 83
Plant Virus Research Station 30

Polge, Dr Christopher 33
population growth 2
poultry farming 22, 178, 206, 208, 216, 224–31, 235–8, 242–3, 250–1
  flock size 226–7
  poultry breeds 224, 229
  poultry housing 227–8
  poultry numbers 226–7, 237–8
  poultrymeat production 225–6, 229–30
prices
  agricultural 89, 97–8, 103–4, 108–9
  guaranteed 7, 97, 103–4
  milk 113–14
Prior, James 38
Provincial Advisory Service (pre-World War II) 62–3

radio programmes see broadcasts
Rare Breeds Survival Trust 117, 219
Rayns, Frank 47–8
research, agricultural 8, 26–45, 65–6, 81–6, 161, 244–6
  commercial firms and 40–2
  contraction of 31, 40
  dissemination of see knowledge networks
  expansion of 26–36
  funding/expenditure 26, 31, 42–5, 84–5
  institutes 26–31, 138, 244–5
  purpose of 24, 44–5
  returns to 37–8, 81–5
  staff numbers 33–6
  'triple helix' 25, 39
  units (ARC) 31–3
  universities 34–6
  see also Agricultural Research Act, Agricultural Research Council, MAFF
Rhone-Poulenc 40
Riley, Sir Ralph 33
risk in agriculture 203–5, 250, 259–60
Robbins Report on Higher Education 57–8
Rosenberg, Professor Nathan 10, 253–5
Rothamsted Experimental Station 27, 42, 83–4
Rothschild, Lord 36–9

287

Index

Rothschild report   37–40
Rowson, L.E.   33
Royal Agricultural Society of England   68–9, 139
Royal Commission on Agriculture, 1919   90
Royal Commission on Environmental Pollution   127
Russell, Sir John   44–5

sales and technical representatives   68, 76–7, 80–1
Sanders, Sir Harold   50
science, agricultural   24
Scottish Plant Breeding Station   30, 83
Shaver (poultry)   229
Shell Chemicals   40
silage   9, 41, 50, 66, 82, 138–48, 155–7, 161–2, 254
Slater, Sir William   36, 47
slurry   154–7, 249
Soames, Christopher   48
specialisation in agriculture   22, 111, 185, 199–215, 259
Standard Man Days   190–1, 200–2, 205; *see also* Labour, agricultural
Stapledon, Sir George   42, 62
statistics, agricultural   12–13
Street, A.G.   3, 87
Strutt, Sir Nigel   48
students in agriculture   52–61, 188
Sturrock, F.   48

technical change in agriculture   6–11, 160–1, 182, 198, 246–63

television programmes *see* broadcasts
tenants *see* land, tenanted
The Archers   71, 78
Thornber (poultry)   84, 229
Topley, Professor W.W.C   35
total factor productivity (TFP) in agriculture   6, 93
tractors   83, 194–5, 204, 255
Treasury, H.M., and agricultural policy   36, 104–5, 246
Trend Report (on the organisation of Civil Science)   36–7
tuberculosis, bovine   158–9
Turner, Sir James   47

University Departments of Agriculture   51–5, 58–9, 83

Wain, Professor L.   35, 40
Walker, Peter   109
Waltham, Richard   83, 146
Watson, Sir James Scott   47
Williams, Tom (Baron Williams of Barnburgh)   63, 102
Women's Land Army   52, 183
Woolley, Harold (Baron Woolley)   104
Woolley, Ken   232–4
World War I   4, 89, 165
World War II   2–5, 9, 92–3

Yates, F.   27
Young Farmers' Clubs   72, 78–9, 81, 100